Thoughts From To Heaven

STEVE DIGILIO

I0366610

RedPenguin BOOKS

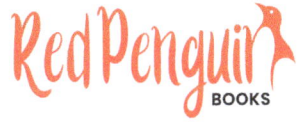

Thoughts From & To Heaven
Copyright © 2025 by Steve DiGiglio
All rights reserved.
Published by Red Penguin Books
Bellerose Village, New York

ISBN
Digital 978-1-63777-710-7
Print 978-1-63777-711-4 | 978-1-63777-712-1

No part of this book may be reproduced in any form or by any electronic or mechanical means, including information storage and retrieval systems, without written permission from the author, except for the use of brief quotations in a book review.

Graphics: Designed by *Freepik*

Epigraph

God morning, branches:

Today's Gospel: Luke 11:29-32

> While still more people gathered in the crowd, Jesus said to them,
> "This generation is an evil generation;
> it seeks a sign, but no sign will be given it,
> except the sign of Jonah.
> Just as Jonah became a sign to the Ninevites,
> so will the Son of Man be to this generation.
> At the judgment
> the queen of the south will rise with the men of this generation
> and she will condemn them,
> because she came from the ends of the earth
> to hear the wisdom of Solomon,
> and there is something greater than Solomon here.
> At the judgment the men of Nineveh will arise with this generation
> and condemn it,
> because at the preaching of Jonah they repented,
> and there is something greater than Jonah here."

Dear friends, the queen of the south was the queen of Sheba in southwestern Arabia, who visited Solomon (1 Kings 10:1-10) and was in awe of the wisdom with which God had endowed the King of Israel. Jesus is the something greater, but recall He is humble. As for signs from God:

GOD, ARE YOU REAL?

> The child whispered, "God, speak to me"
> And a meadowlark sang. The child did not hear.
> So the child yelled, "God, speak to me!"
> And the thunder rolled across the sky but the child did not listen.
> The child looked around and said, "God let me see you"
> and a star shone brightly But the child did not notice and the child shouted,
> "God show me a miracle!" And a life was born but the child did not know.
> So the child cried out in despair,
> "Touch me God, and let me know you are here!"
> Whereupon God reached down and touched the child.
> But the child brushed the butterfly away and walked away.
> ~Author Unknown~

Dear friends, may you take the miracles of which I have been a part as signs.

Blessings

Contents

Epigraph	iii
Introduction	1
Scripture Notes	5
Dearest Anna	579
Love Notes	609
About the Author	793

Introduction

A few years ago, my best friend, Bernie asked if I would talk with Paul, another best friend of his. Paul was very sick. I asked what could or should I do. Bernie said we could talk or write to Paul to help his spirit. Well, one day, I wrote a note to Paul and it began with God morning instead of good morning. After some time, Paul passed away. At a Mass in a beautiful church in Washington, D.C., Paul's hometown, Bernie gave the eulogy, near the end of which he spoke about how *God morning* changed Paul. From being understandably mad at his situation and God, Paul looked forward to meeting God.

After Mass, Paul's family and friends went to a local restaurant to celebrate his life. I sat across from a friend of his, Erin, who asked if she could be part of our prayer group. I said there is no prayer group, it was just three friends talking and helping one another. As I said that, Bernie walked by (God's timing is always perfect). I said to him, "Meet my new friend, Erin, who wants to join our prayer group." Bernie said, "There is no prayer group, it is just three friends talking and helping one another." Then he smiled and said, "Steve, if you would like, the three of us can be a prayer group in honor and memory of Paul." Thus began a wonderful ministry that now has many dozens of participants, including Paul's sister, who later thanked me for comforting her brother and helping him cross over to the other side.

The small undertaking evolved into a ministry to spread the Good News to many. Every day for several years now (no days off), I text, email and post on social media what I call Scripture-based notes that include something from or related to readings in the

Bible and my comment, which varies in length. I loved it when my wife, who went to Heaven four years ago, would ask me what I was thinking about writing and why. I like to say she forgot more about religion than I could ever hope to learn. We were together for several decades and were extremely close. Those discussions brought us even closer to each other and God. If Anna and I did not discuss the note the night before (perhaps she was watching her beloved NY Rangers), she would ask when she awoke the following morning what I wrote and why.

I have been incredibly blessed to have this ministry. I love when a reader writes back that my note inspired them in some way. Some have wondered how I knew they needed to hear that day's message. I am thrilled to know that some readers share my notes with others. Indeed, one morning when I was about to text a gentleman named James, that person texted me asking if I were alright, as he had not received a text and he usually sent it on to others.

By the way, the way I got to be in touch with James is another miracle. Years ago, I sent a birthday card to an old best friend from my youth. Well, the card was returned as undeliverable. My wife was going to put it in the trash and I said, "Don't, I will find out where he is." I jotted down on a piece of paper about a dozen people with the same last name as my old friend and who lived near where I remembered he had lived. Then one afternoon, I called the first name on the list. I introduced myself and the reason for my call. The person was James, my friend's older brother, who said, "I know you." Wow!

Another section of this book includes my love letters to my wife in Heaven. Some are short, others long. I have shared them with family, close friends and the widow(er) groups to which I belong. The letters, which I call Dearest Anna, mean so much to others, besides me. In fact, friends in the widow(er) groups said the letters express how they feel about their spouses who are in Heaven.

The final section I call love notes, which also open with *God morning*. They are simply quotes or sayings about love. They are shared in the same ways as the Scripture notes. I am thrilled that people look forward to these love notes. More than a few have said they are a beautiful way to start the day.

Interestingly, some recipients of the notes thought there was a misspelling in the greeting. Some have responded in similar fashion.

Putting together this book was a labor of love and quite time-consuming. If it inspires one person or provokes a thought or smile, it will have been well worth it. I am so incredibly blessed, this being His latest, and thankful.

Thanks to all who have read my notes over the years, and especially those who said I should write this book.

Thanks to Bernie, my lifelong best friend, who led me to the path that includes this book.

Thanks to Frank, my lifelong friend, big brother and mentor who led me to the path that includes this book.

Thanks to Diane, a fellow traveler in widowhood, who introduced me to Stephanie.

Thanks to Stephanie, the Head Penguin, for believing in me, her thoughtful guidance and enthusiasm.

Thanks and love to Figgy, who rescued me, makes me happy and gives me reason.

Love and thanks to my Anna in Heaven. I am me because of you and I cannot wait to be with you in Paradise.

Above all, thanks be to God.

Scripture Notes

SCRIPTURE NOTES

God morning, disciples,

Today's Gospel
Mark 10:46–52

> As Jesus was leaving Jericho with his disciples and a sizable crowd,
> Bartimaeus, a blind man, the son of Timaeus,
> sat by the roadside begging.
> On hearing that it was Jesus of Nazareth,
> he began to cry out and say,
> "Jesus, son of David, have pity on me."
> And many rebuked him, telling him to be silent.
> But he kept calling out all the more, "Son of David, have pity on me."
> Jesus stopped and said, "Call him."
> So they called the blind man, saying to him,
> "Take courage; get up, Jesus is calling you."
> He threw aside his cloak, sprang up, and came to Jesus.
> Jesus said to him in reply, "What do you want me to do for you?"
> The blind man replied to him, "Master, I want to see."
> Jesus told him, 'Go your way; your faith has saved you."
> Immediately he received his sight
> and followed him on the way.

Dear friends, many of you have heard my story about faith. There are some who are hearing it for the first time. I was once hospitalized with a serious problem and without knowing it was given a medicine that was not normally prescribed for my condition. On my third day in the hospital, my doctor visited me as he said he would. He asked how I was doing. I said, doctor I feel better today than I did yesterday and yesterday better than the day before and by the end of the first day I started feeling better. He smiled and said good it's working. Then he said maybe it's working or perhaps it's your faith. I had an extremely serious problem that I got through a year earlier and told the doctor before he hospitalized me that I would get through this, too. Faith, indeed!

Blessings

God morning, branches,

Today's Gospel
Luke 11:29-32

While still more people gathered in the crowd, Jesus said to them,

> "This generation is an evil generation;
> it seeks a sign, but no sign will be given it,
> except the sign of Jonah.
> Just as Jonah became a sign to the Ninevites,
> so will the Son of Man be to this generation.
> At the judgment
> the queen of the south will rise with the men of this generation
> and she will condemn them,
> because she came from the ends of the earth
> to hear the wisdom of Solomon,
> and there is something greater than Solomon here.
> At the judgment the men of Nineveh will arise with this generation
> and condemn it,
> because at the preaching of Jonah they repented,
> and there is something greater than Jonah here."

Dear friends, the queen of the south was the queen of Sheba in southwestern Arabia, who visited Solomon (1 Kings 10:1-10) and was in awe of the wisdom with which God had endowed the King of Israel. Jesus is the something greater, but recall He is humble. As for signs from God:

GOD ARE YOU REAL

> The child whispered, "God, speak to me"
> And a meadow lark sang. The child did not hear.
> So the child yelled, "God, speak to me!"
> And the thunder rolled across the sky but the child did not listen.
> The child looked around and said, "God let me see you"
> and a star shone brightly But the child did not notice and the child shouted,
> "God show me a miracle!" And a life was born but the child did not know.
> So the child cried out in despair,
> "Touch me God, and let me know you are here!"
> Where upon God reached down and touched the child.
> But the child brushed the butterfly away and walked away.
> ~Author Unknown~

Dear friends, may you take the miracles of which I have been a part as signs.

Blessings

God morning, branches,

Today's Reading I
Wisdom 2:1a, 12-22

> The wicked said among themselves
> thinking not aright:

"Let us beset the just one, because he is obnoxious to us;
he sets himself against our doings,
Reproaches us for transgressions of the law
and charges us with violations of our training.
He professes to have knowledge of God
and styles himself a child of the LORD.
To us he is the censure of our thoughts;
merely to see him is a hardship for us,
Because his life is not like that of others,
and different are his ways.
He judges us debased;
he holds aloof from our paths as from things impure.
He calls blest the destiny of the just
and boasts that God is his Father.
Let us see whether his words be true
let us find out what will happen to him.
For if the just one be the son of God, he will defend him
and deliver him from the hand of his foes.
With revilement and torture let us put him to the test
that we may have proof of his gentleness
and try his patience.
Let us condemn him to a shameful death;
for according to his own words, God will take care of him."
These were their thoughts, but they erred;
for their wickedness blinded them,
and they knew not the hidden counsels of God;
neither did they count on a recompense of holiness
nor discern the innocent souls' reward.

Dear friends, the above was written about two thousand years ago and still holds true today. There are those today who live and think like the wicked in the Reading and persecute Christians. May we persevere in faith not just for ourselves, but also for those who are evil.

Blessings

God morning, disciples,

Today's Reading I
Acts 9:1-20

> Saul, still breathing murderous threats against the disciples of the Lord, went to the high priest and asked him
> for letters to the synagogues in Damascus, that,
> if he should find any men or women who belonged to the Way, he might bring them back to Jerusalem in chains.
> On his journey, as he was nearing Damascus,
> a light from the sky suddenly flashed around him.
> He fell to the ground and heard a voice saying to him, "Saul, Saul, why are you persecuting me?"
> He said, "Who are you, sir?"
> The reply came, "I am Jesus, whom you are persecuting.
> Now get up and go into the city and you will be told what you must do."
> The men who were traveling with him stood speechless,
> for they heard the voice but could see no one. Saul got up from the ground,
> but when he opened his eyes he could see nothing;
> so they led him by the hand and brought him to Damascus.
> For three days he was unable to see, and he neither ate nor drank.

SCRIPTURE NOTES

There was a disciple in Damascus named Ananias, and the Lord said to him in a vision, Ananias."
He answered, "Here I am, Lord."
The Lord said to him, "Get up and go to the street called Straight and ask at the house of Judas for a man from Tarsus named Saul. He is there praying,
and in a vision he has seen a man named Ananias come in and lay his hands on him,
that he may regain his sight." But Ananias replied,
"Lord, I have heard from many sources about this man, what evil things he has done to your holy ones in Jerusalem. And here he has authority from the chief priests
to imprison all who call upon your name." But the Lord said to him,

"Go, for this man is a chosen instrument of mine
to carry my name before Gentiles, kings, and children of Israel, and I will show him what he will have to suffer for my name." So Ananias went and entered the house;
laying his hands on him, he said,
"Saul, my brother, the Lord has sent me,
Jesus who appeared to you on the way by which you came,
that you may regain your sight and be filled with the Holy Spirit."
Immediately things like scales fell from his eyes
and he regained his sight. He got up and was baptized,
and when he had eaten, he recovered his strength.

He stayed some days with the disciples in Damascus,
and he began at once to proclaim Jesus in the synagogues, that he is the Son of God.
All who heard him were astounded and said, "Is not this the man who in Jerusalem ravaged those who call upon this name,

and came here expressly to take them back in chains to the chief priests?"
But Saul grew all the stronger
and confounded the Jews who lived in Damascus, proving that this is the Christ.

Dear friends, I do not like to post and write about something that was done before, but this time is different and there are some readers seeing this for the first time. Think long and hard about the conversion of Saul and then think of what God can do with you. Also, did you notice how many days Saul was blind? For three days he was blind. He regained his sight and was baptized. It can be said he was reborn after three days. It sounds familiar, right?

Blessings

God morning, disciples,

Today's Gospel
John 15:12-17

Jesus said to his disciples:

"This is my commandment: love one another as I love you. No one has greater love than this,
to lay down one's life for one's friends.
You are my friends if you do what I command you. I no longer call you slaves,
because a slave does not know what his master is doing. I have called you friends,
because I have told you everything I have heard from my Father. It was not you who chose me, but I who chose you
and appointed you to go and bear fruit that will remain,

SCRIPTURE NOTES

so that whatever you ask the Father in my name he may give you. This I command you: love one another."

Dear friends, today's Gospel is just thirteen lines or 120 words, yet it is so rich. Jesus no longer calls us slaves, but friends. We did not choose Him, He chose us. Whatever we ask the Father in the name of Jesus may be given to us. All we must do is love one another. Truly, love conquers all and covers a multitude of sins. God is love.

Blessings

God morning, branches,

Today's Gospel
Luke 11:15-26

> When Jesus had driven out a demon, some of the crowd said: "By the power of Beelzebul, the prince of demons,
> he drives out demons."
> Others, to test him, asked him for a sign from heaven. But he knew their thoughts and said to them,
> "Every kingdom divided against itself will be laid waste and house will fall against house.
> And if Satan is divided against himself, how will his kingdom stand? For you say that it is by Beelzebul that I drive out demons.
> If I, then, drive out demons by Beelzebul,
> by whom do your own people drive them out? Therefore they will be your judges.
> But if it is by the finger of God that I drive out demons, then the Kingdom of God has come upon you.

When a strong man fully armed guards his palace, his possessions are safe.
But when one stronger than he attacks and overcomes him, he takes away the armor on which he relied
and distributes the spoils.
Whoever is not with me is against me,
and whoever does not gather with me scatters.

"When an unclean spirit goes out of someone, it roams through arid regions searching for rest but, finding none, it says,
'I shall return to my home from which I came.'
But upon returning, it finds it swept clean and put in order. Then it goes and brings back seven other spirits
more wicked than itself who move in and dwell there, and the last condition of that man is worse than the first."

Origin of A House Divided Cannot Stand
   Many people may recall this expression from one of Abraham Lincoln's famous speeches, the "House Divided Speech," before becoming the 16th American president.
   This expression first appeared in the Bible, specifically *Matthew 12:25*. This Gospel from Luke is similar.
Blessings

God morning, disciples,

Today's Gospel
John 14:1-6

Jesus said to his disciples:
   "Do not let your hearts be troubled.

SCRIPTURE NOTES

> You have faith in God; have faith also in me.
> In my Father's house there are many dwelling places.
> If there were not,
> would I have told you that I am going to prepare a place for you?
> And if I go and prepare a place for you,
> I will come back again and take you to myself,
> so that where I am you also may be.
> Where I am going you know the way."
> Thomas said to him,
> "Master, we do not know where you are going;
> how can we know the way?"
> Jesus said to him, "I am the way and the truth and the life.
> No one comes to the Father except through me."

Dear friends, do not let your hearts be troubled. Jesus is the way and the truth and the life.

Blessings

God morning, disciples,

Today's Gospel
Matthew 12:1-8

> Jesus was going through a field of grain on the sabbath.
> His disciples were hungry
> and began to pick the heads of grain and eat them.
> When the Pharisees saw this, they said to him,
> "See, your disciples are doing what is unlawful to do on the sabbath."
> He said to the them, "Have you not read what David did
> when he and his companions were hungry,

how he went into the house of God and ate the bread of offering,
which neither he nor his companions
but only the priests could lawfully eat?
Or have you not read in the law that on the sabbath
the priests serving in the temple violate the sabbath
and are innocent?
I say to you, something greater than the temple is here.
If you knew what this meant, I desire mercy, not sacrifice,
you would not have condemned these innocent men.
For the Son of Man is Lord of the sabbath."

Dear friends, the Pharisees thought they knew it all. Jesus told that that strict adherence to what they understood to be the law (following Sabbath regulations) was secondary to mercy (allowing the hungry to obtain food). It could also be said the Pharisees were guilty of saying do as we say, not as we do (Jesus did call them hypocrites). I wonder what those, including the disciples, who heard Jesus say "something greater than the temple is here" and "For the Son of Man is Lord of the Sabbath" thought. Imagine the Son of Man telling you "this is what my Father's words mean". May you ponder His words.

Blessings

God morning, branches,

Today's Reading I
1 Timothy 6:2c-12

Beloved:
Teach and urge these things. Whoever teaches something different

and does not agree with the sound words of our Lord Jesus Christ and the religious teaching
is conceited, understanding nothing,
and has a morbid disposition for arguments and verbal disputes. From these come envy, rivalry, insults, evil suspicions,
and mutual friction among people with corrupted minds, who are deprived of the truth,
supposing religion to be a means of gain. Indeed, religion with contentment is a great gain. For we brought nothing into the world,
just as we shall not be able to take anything out of it.
If we have food and clothing, we shall be content with that.
Those who want to be rich are falling into temptation and into a trap and into many foolish and harmful desires,
which plunge them into ruin and destruction. For the love of money is the root of all evils,
and some people in their desire for it have strayed from the faith and have pierced themselves with many pains.

But you, man of God, avoid all this. Instead, pursue righteousness, devotion, faith, love, patience, and gentleness. Compete well for the faith. Lay hold of eternal life,
to which you were called when you made the noble confession in the presence of many witnesses.

Dear friends, may you pursue righteousness, devotion, faith, love, patience, and gentleness. Also, note that money is not the root of all evils as is commonly thought, but the love of money is the root of all evils.

Blessings

SCRIPTURE NOTES

God morning, sisters and brothers,

Today's Reading I
James 2:14-24, 26

What good is it, my brothers and sisters,
if someone says he has faith but does not have works? Can that faith save him?
If a brother or sister has nothing to wear and has no food for the day, and one of you says to them,
"Go in peace, keep warm, and eat well,"
but you do not give them the necessities of the body, what good is it?
So also faith of itself,
if it does not have works, is dead.

Indeed someone might say,
"You have faith and I have works." Demonstrate your faith to me without works,
and I will demonstrate my faith to you from my works. You believe that God is one.
You do well.
Even the demons believe that and tremble. Do you want proof, you ignoramus,
that faith without works is useless?
Was not Abraham our father justified by works when he offered his son Isaac upon the altar?
You see that faith was active along with his works, and faith was completed by the works.
Thus the Scripture was fulfilled that says, Abraham believed God,
and it was credited to him as righteousness, and he was called the friend of God.

See how a person is justified by works and not by faith alone. For just
    as a body without a spirit is dead,
so also faith without works is dead.

Dear friends, may you be justified by your works as faith without works is useless.

This reading has the word "ignoramus", which caught my attention. I could not remember ever hearing or seeing this word in the Bible. When was the last time you used this word?

Blessings

God morning, branches,

Today's Gospel
Matthew 19:3-12

Some Pharisees approached Jesus, and tested him, saying,
"Is it lawful for a man to divorce his wife for any cause whatever?"
He said in reply, "Have you not read that from the beginning
the Creator made them male and female and said,
For this reason a man shall leave his father and mother
and be joined to his wife, and the two shall become one flesh?
So they are no longer two, but one flesh.
Therefore, what God has joined together, man must not separate."
They said to him, "Then why did Moses command
that the man give the woman a bill of divorce and dismiss her?"
He said to them, "Because of the hardness of your hearts
Moses allowed you to divorce your wives,
but from the beginning it was not so.
I say to you, whoever divorces his wife

(unless the marriage is unlawful)
and marries another commits adultery."
His disciples said to him,
"If that is the case of a man with his wife,
it is better not to marry."
He answered, "Not all can accept this word,
but only those to whom that is granted.
Some are incapable of marriage because they were born so;
some, because they were made so by others;
some, because they have renounced marriage
for the sake of the Kingdom of heaven.
Whoever can accept this ought to accept it."

Dear friends, these days many say the Bible and the Constitution are ancient relics. A huge part of their problems is God created them male and female. They also do not accept His idea of marriage. May you not be silent in these troubled times.

Blessings

God morning, brothers and sisters,

Today's Reading I
Rom 7:18-25a

> Brothers and sisters:
> I know that good does not dwell in me, that is, in my flesh. The willing
>   is ready at hand, but doing the good is not.
> For I do not do the good I want, but I do the evil I do not want.
> Now if I do what I do not want, it is no longer I who do it, but sin that
>   dwells in me.

So, then, I discover the principle
that when I want to do right, evil is at hand.
For I take delight in the law of God, in my inner self, but I see in my members another principle
at war with the law of my mind,
taking me captive to the law of sin that dwells in my members. Miserable one that I am!
Who will deliver me from this mortal body? Thanks be to God through Jesus Christ our Lord.

Dear friends, we must constantly use the strength of our Spirit to battle the weakness of our flesh.

Blessings

God morning, branches,

Today's Gospel
Luke 1:57–66

When the time arrived for Elizabeth to have her child
she gave birth to a son.
Her neighbors and relatives heard
that the Lord had shown his great mercy toward her,
and they rejoiced with her.
When they came on the eighth day to circumcise the child,
they were going to call him Zechariah after his father,
but his mother said in reply,
"No. He will be called John."
But they answered her,
"There is no one among your relatives who has this name."

So they made signs, asking his father what he wished him to be called.
He asked for a tablet and wrote, "John is his name,"
and all were amazed.
Immediately his mouth was opened, his tongue freed,
and he spoke blessing God.
Then fear came upon all their neighbors,
and all these matters were discussed
throughout the hill country of Judea.
All who heard these things took them to heart, saying,
"What, then, will this child be?
For surely the hand of the Lord was with him."

Dear friends, "What, then, will this child be? For surely the hand of the Lord was with him." Indeed! I see three miracles in this Gospel. The pregnancy, regaining speech and what the child becomes. It is interesting to think about numbers in the Bible. I also like how the child's name went against the grain.

Blessings

God morning, branches,

Today's Reading 1
ECCL 3:1-11

> There is an appointed time for everything,
> and a time for every thing under the heavens.
> A time to be born, and a time to die;
> a time to plant, and a time to uproot the plant.
> A time to kill, and a time to heal;
> a time to tear down, and a time to build.

A time to weep, and a time to laugh;
a time to mourn, and a time to dance.
A time to scatter stones, and a time to gather them;
a time to embrace, and a time to be far from embraces.
A time to seek, and a time to lose;
a time to keep, and a time to cast away.
A time to rend, and a time to sew;
a time to be silent, and a time to speak.
A time to love, and a time to hate;
a time of war, and a time of peace.
What advantage has the worker from his toil?
I have considered the task that God has appointed
for the sons of men to be busied about.
He has made everything appropriate to its time,
and has put the timeless into their hearts,
without man's ever discovering,
from beginning to end, the work which God has done.

Dear friends,

https://www.bing.com/videos/search?q=byrds+turn+turn+turn&PC=APPL&ru=%2fsearch%3fq%3dbyrds%2b-turn%2bturn%2bturn%26form%3dAPIPH1%26PC%3dAPPL&view=detail&mmscn=vwrc&mid=82391D4353D47A2B922782391D-4353D47A2B9227&FORM=WRVORC

Blessings

God morning, brothers and sisters,

Today's Reading I
1 Thes 4:1-8

SCRIPTURE NOTES

Brothers and sisters,
we earnestly ask and exhort you in the Lord Jesus that,
as you received from us
how you should conduct yourselves to please God–
and as you are conducting yourselves–
you do so even more.
For you know what instructions we gave you through the Lord Jesus.

This is the will of God, your holiness:
that you refrain from immorality,
that each of you know how to acquire a wife for himself
in holiness and honor, not in lustful passion
as do the Gentiles who do not know God;
not to take advantage of or exploit a brother or sister in this matter,
for the Lord is an avenger in all these things,
as we told you before and solemnly affirmed.
For God did not call us to impurity but to holiness.
Therefore, whoever disregards this,
disregards not a human being but God,
who also gives his Holy Spirit to you.

Dear friends, always try to conduct yourselves in a manner to please God. The adversary puts many roadblocks between us and God, which makes that difficult. Remember that God calls us to holiness, but our free will sometimes causes us to disregard God.

    Today's Alleluia reminds us to be vigilant at all times and pray, that we may have the strength to stand before the Son of Man. Remember, we do not know when He will return. Even He does not know when that will be. As I asked yesterday, are you ready to stand before the Son of Man?

Blessings

SCRIPTURE NOTES

Good morning, branches,

Today's Gospel
Exodus 20:1-17

In those days:
God delivered all these commandments:
"I, the LORD, am your God,
who brought you out of the land of Egypt, that place of slavery.
You shall not have other gods besides me.
You shall not carve idols for yourselves
in the shape of anything in the sky above
or on the earth below or in the waters beneath the earth;
you shall not bow down before them or worship them.
For I, the LORD, your God, am a jealous God,
inflicting punishment for their fathers' wickedness
on the children of those who hate me,
down to the third and fourth generation;
but bestowing mercy down to the thousandth generation
on the children of those who love me and keep my commandments.
"You shall not take the name of the LORD, your God, in vain.
For the LORD will not leave unpunished
him who takes his name in vain.
"Remember to keep holy the sabbath day.
Six days you may labor and do all your work,
but the seventh day is the sabbath of the LORD, your God.
No work may be done then either by you, or your son or daughter,
or your male or female slave, or your beast,
or by the alien who lives with you.
In six days the LORD made the heavens and the earth,
the sea and all that is in them;

but on the seventh day he rested.
That is why the LORD has blessed the sabbath day and made it holy.
"Honor your father and your mother,
that you may have a long life in the land
which the LORD, your God, is giving you.
"You shall not kill.
"You shall not commit adultery.
"You shall not steal.
"You shall not bear false witness against your neighbor.
"You shall not covet your neighbor's house.
You shall not covet your neighbor's wife,
nor his male or female slave, nor his ox or ass,
nor anything else that belongs to him."

Dear friends, God's commandments are few and easy to understand. They are not suggestions nor open to interpretation. Yet we have tens of thousands of laws and many are interpreted differently, which leads to more laws and misunderstandings. Think about that for a bit. God gave us a simple gameplan to follow. We do not need to be legal scholars to understand His rules. We allowed the evil one to distract us with seven deadly sins. As for keeping the sabbath day holy, some of us will remember when stores and businesses were closed on Sunday. We even wore our "Sunday best" for church and family dinner. Perhaps we can just try to at least slow down for one day and dedicate some (or more) time to prayer. Life is not about money and acquiring things. May we love others and give thanks more often.

Blessings

SCRIPTURE NOTES

God morning, branches,

Today's Reading I
Acts 5:34–42

> A Pharisee in the Sanhedrin named Gamaliel,
> a teacher of the law, respected by all the people,
> stood up, ordered the Apostles to be put outside for a short time, and
>   said to the Sanhedrin, "Fellow children of Israel,
> be careful what you are about to do to these men.
> Some time ago, Theudas appeared, claiming to be someone important,
>   and about four hundred men joined him, but he was killed,
> and all those who were loyal to him were disbanded and came to nothing.
> After him came Judas the Galilean at the time of the census. He also
>   drew people after him,
> but he too perished and all who were loyal to him were scattered. So
>   now I tell you,
> have nothing to do with these men, and let them go. For if this endeavor
>   or this activity is of human origin, it will destroy itself.
> But if it comes from God, you will not be able to destroy them; you may
>   even find yourselves fighting against God."
> They were persuaded by him.
> After recalling the Apostles, they had them flogged, ordered them to stop
>   speaking in the name of Jesus, and dismissed them.
> So they left the presence of the Sanhedrin, rejoicing that they had been
>   found worthy to suffer dishonor for the sake of the name.
> And all day long, both at the temple and in their homes, they did not
>   stop teaching and proclaiming the Christ, Jesus.

Dear friends, For if this endeavor or this activity is of human origin, it will destroy itself.

But if it comes from God, you will not be able to destroy them; you may even find yourselves fighting against God." Governments, institutions, the media, social networks and individuals have tried to silence Christianity, but have failed because it comes from God. Gamaliel was 100% right.

Blessings

God morning, disciples,

Today's Gospel:
Jn 14:1-6

> Jesus said to his disciples:
> "Do not let your hearts be troubled.
> You have faith in God; have faith also in me.
> In my Father's house there are many dwelling places. If there were not, would I have told you that I am going to prepare a place for you? And
> if I go and prepare a place for you,
> I will come back again and take you to myself, so that where I am you
> also may be.
> Where I am going you know the way." Thomas said to him,
> "Master, we do not know where you are going; how can we know the
> way?"
> Jesus said to him, "I am the way and the truth and the life. No one comes
> to the Father except through me."

Dear friends, Jesus knows his time as one of us is nearing its end and he says "Do not let your hearts be troubled" to comfort His disciples. He reminds His disciples of their faith in God. Similarly, He is reminding us to do likewise. God created us in His Divine Image. Sometimes life seems unfair, but remember God is in full control

When things appear to be bleak, remember His words and do not let your hearts be troubled. After all, you know the Way.

Alleluia

God morning, sisters and brothers,

Today's Reading I
Col 3:12-17

> Brothers and sisters:
> Put on, as God's chosen ones, holy and beloved,
> heartfelt compassion, kindness, humility, gentleness, and patience, bearing with one another and forgiving one another,
> if one has a grievance against another;
> as the Lord has forgiven you, so must you also do. And over all these put on love,
> that is, the bond of perfection.
> And let the peace of Christ control your hearts,
> the peace into which you were also called in one body. And be thankful.
> Let the word of Christ dwell in you richly,
> as in all wisdom you teach and admonish one another, singing psalms, hymns, and spiritual songs
> with gratitude in your hearts to God.
> And whatever you do, in word or in deed, do everything in the name of the Lord Jesus,
> giving thanks to God the Father through him.

Dear sisters and brothers, I think this reading encapsulates how we are to live our lives. Perhaps read it slowly a few times and absorb the words and ideas. There is so much in the Reading, but I love put on love, that is the bond of perfection. Christ is love and He is perfect. We are blessed to be God's chosen ones and as the Reading ends whatever you do, in word or in deed, do everything in the name of the Lord Jesus, giving thanks to God the Father through him. I certainly am so blessed and incredibly thankful to be able to share His words with you. May you live them and pass them on.

Blessings

God morning, branches,

Today's Gospel
Matthew 10:34–11:1

Jesus said to his Apostles:

> "Do not think that I have come to bring peace upon the earth.
> I have come to bring not peace but the sword.
> For I have come to set
> a man against his father,
> a daughter against her mother,
> and a daughter-in-law against her mother-in-law;
> and one's enemies will be those of his household.
>
> "Whoever loves father or mother more than me is not worthy of me,
> and whoever loves son or daughter more than me is not worthy of me;
> and whoever does not take up his cross
> and follow after me is not worthy of me.
> Whoever finds his life will lose it,
> and whoever loses his life for my sake will find it.
>
> "Whoever receives you receives me,
> and whoever receives me receives the one who sent me.

*Whoever receives a prophet because he is a prophet
will receive a prophet's reward,
and whoever receives a righteous man
because he is righteous
will receive a righteous man's reward.
And whoever gives only a cup of cold water
to one of these little ones to drink
because he is a disciple-
amen, I say to you, he will surely not lose his reward."*

When Jesus finished giving these commands to his Twelve disciples, he went away from that place to teach and to preach in their towns.

Dear friends, we might wonder why Jesus said "Do not think that I have come to bring peace upon the earth. I have come to bring not peace but the sword." After all, is He not the Prince of peace and did he not in the Garden of Gethsemane rebuke Peter, who took up a sword to defend Jesus, and tell him to put away his sword, "for all who draw the sword will die by the sword"? Well, the sword of Jesus is the Gospel and those who accept Him and the Gospel may end up divided from those they love. Hebrews 4:12 says For the word of God is living and active, sharper than any two-edged sword, piercing to the division of soul and of spirit, of joints and of marrow, and discerning the thoughts and intentions of the heart. Recall that Jesus says the greatest and first commandment is "You shall love the Lord your God with all your heart, and with all your soul, and with all your mind".

Blessings

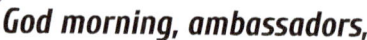

God morning, ambassadors,

In today's readings:
> If you are patient when you suffer for doing what is good, this is a grace before God.
> For to this you have been called, because Christ also suffered for you, leaving you an example that you should follow in his footsteps. He committed no sin, and no deceit was found in his mouth. When he was insulted, he returned no insult;
> when he suffered, he did not threaten;

Jesus certainly set the bar quite high for us. Imagine the horizontal part of the cross to which He was nailed as being that bar. He chose us and, as it says above, for to this we have been called. The cross may be heavy, but the reward is great.

Blessings

God morning, disciples,

Today's Gospel
John 1:35–42

> John was standing with two of his disciples, and as he watched Jesus walk by, he said, "Behold, the Lamb of God." The two disciples heard what he said and followed Jesus. Jesus turned and saw them following him and said to them, "What are you looking for?" They said to him, "Rabbi" (which translated means Teacher), "where are you staying?" He said to them, "Come, and you will see." So they went and saw where he was staying, and they stayed with him that day. It was about four in the afternoon. Andrew, the brother of Simon Peter, was one of the two who heard John and followed Jesus. He first found his own brother Simon and

told him, "We have found the Messiah," which is translated Christ. Then he brought him to Jesus. Jesus looked at him and said, "You are Simon the son of John; you will be called Cephas," which is translated Peter.

Dear friends, imagine you were standing by John when he said, "Behold, the Lamb of God." Also imagine being able to say or hear "We have found the Messiah".

Blessings

God morning, branches,

Today's Gospel
John 5:17-30

> Jesus answered the Jews:
> "My Father is at work until now, so I am at work." For this reason they tried all the more to kill him, because he not only broke the sabbath but he also called God his own father, making himself equal to God.
>
> Jesus answered and said to them,
> "Amen, amen, I say to you, the Son cannot do anything on his own, but only what he sees the Father doing;
> for what he does, the Son will do also. For the Father loves the Son and shows him everything that he himself does, and he will show him greater works than these, so that you may be amazed.
> For just as the Father raises the dead and gives life, so also does the Son give life to whomever he wishes. Nor does the Father judge anyone, but he has given all judgment to the Son,
> so that all may honor the Son just as they honor the Father. Whoever does not honor the Son
> does not honor the Father who sent him.

Amen, amen, I say to you, whoever hears my word and believes in the one who sent me
has eternal life and will not come to condemnation, but has passed from death to life.
Amen, amen, I say to you, the hour is coming and is now here when the dead will hear the voice of the Son of God,
and those who hear will live.
For just as the Father has life in himself,

so also he gave to the Son the possession of life in himself. And he gave him power to exercise judgment,
because he is the Son of Man. Do not be amazed at this,
because the hour is coming in which all who are in the tombs will hear his voice and will come out,
those who have done good deeds to the resurrection of life,
but those who have done wicked deeds to the resurrection of condemnation.

"I cannot do anything on my own;
I judge as I hear, and my judgment is just, because I do not seek my own will
but the will of the one who sent me."

Dear friends, it is not, nor should it ever be, my will. It is and should always be Thy will just as Jesus taught us to pray.
Blessings

God morning, branches,

Today's Reading I
Malachi 3:1-4

SCRIPTURE NOTES

> *Thus says the Lord GOD: Lo, I am sending my messenger*
> *to prepare the way before me;*
> *And suddenly there will come to the temple the Lord whom you seek,*
> *And the messenger of the covenant whom you desire. Yes, he is coming,*
>   *says the Lord of hosts.*
> *But who will endure the day of his coming? And who can stand when*
>   *he appears?*
> *For he is like the refiner's fire, or like the fuller's lye.*
> *He will sit refining and purifying silver, and he will purify the sons of Levi,*
> *Refining them like gold or like silver*
> *that they may offer due sacrifice to the Lord. Then the sacrifice of Judah*
>   *and Jerusalem*
> *will please the Lord,*
> *as in the days of old, as in years gone by.*

Dear friends, is God the center of your life? May you endure the day of His coming and stand when He appears.

Blessings

God morning, disciples,

Today's Gospel
John 6:22-29

> *[After Jesus had fed the five thousand men, his disciples saw him walking on the sea.]*
> *The next day, the crowd that remained across the sea*
> *saw that there had been only one boat there,*
> *and that Jesus had not gone along with his disciples in the boat,*
> *but only his disciples had left.*

Other boats came from Tiberias
near the place where they had eaten the bread
when the Lord gave thanks.
When the crowd saw that neither Jesus nor his disciples were there,
they themselves got into boats
and came to Capernaum looking for Jesus.
And when they found him across the sea they said to him,
"Rabbi, when did you get here?"
Jesus answered them and said,
"Amen, amen, I say to you, you are looking for me
not because you saw sign
but because you ate the loaves and were filled.

Do not work for food that perishes
but for the food that endures for eternal life,
which the Son of Man will give you.
For on him the Father, God, has set his seal."
So they said to him,
"What can we do to accomplish the works of God?"
Jesus answered and said to them,
"This is the work of God, that you believe in the one he sent."

Dear friends, what can we do to accomplish the works of God? Jesus says "This is the work of God, that you believe in the one he sent."

May you not only believe in the One He sent, but also lead others to Him by your words and actions.

Blessings

SCRIPTURE NOTES

God morning, branches,

Today's Gospel
John 10:11-18

Jesus said:

"I am the good shepherd.
A good shepherd lays down his life for the sheep.
A hired man, who is not a shepherd
and whose sheep are not his own,
sees a wolf coming and leaves the sheep and runs away,
and the wolf catches and scatters them.
This is because he works for pay and has no concern for the sheep.
I am the good shepherd,
and I know mine and mine know me,
just as the Father knows me and I know the Father;
and I will lay down my life for the sheep.
I have other sheep that do not belong to this fold.
These also I must lead, and they will hear my voice,
and there will be one flock, one shepherd.
This is why the Father loves me,
because I lay down my life in order to take it up again.
No one takes it from me, but I lay it down on my own.
I have power to lay it down, and power to take it up again.
This command I have received from my Father."

Dear friends, notice Jesus said: "I am the good shepherd. A good shepherd lays down his life for the sheep." The I am points to His unique, divine identity and purpose. He is not just a shepherd, but

a good one. He tells us that He will give His life for His sheep. May we always try to follow the Good Shepherd's examples.

Blessings

God morning, branches,

Today's Reading I
1 John 2:22-28

> Beloved:
> Who is the liar?
> Whoever denies that Jesus is the Christ.
> Whoever denies the Father and the Son, this is the antichrist.
> Anyone who denies the Son does not have the Father,
> but whoever confesses the Son has the Father as well.
> Let what you heard from the beginning remain in you.
> If what you heard from the beginning remains in you,
> then you will remain in the Son and in the Father.
> And this is the promise that he made us: eternal life.
> I write you these things about those who would deceive you.
> As for you,
> the anointing that you received from him remains in you,
> so that you do not need anyone to teach you.
> But his anointing teaches you about everything and is true and not false;
> just as it taught you, remain in him.
>
> And now, children, remain in him,
> so that when he appears we may have confidence
> and not be put to shame by him at his coming.

SCRIPTURE NOTES

Dear friends, there are many liars in the world. May we remain in Him, so that when He appears we may have confidence and not be put to shame by Him at his coming.

Blessings

God morning, branches,

Today's Gospel
John 12:1-11

> Six days before Passover Jesus came to Bethany,
> where Lazarus was, whom Jesus had raised from the dead. They gave a dinner for him there, and Martha served, while Lazarus was one of those reclining at table with him. Mary took a liter of costly perfumed oil
> made from genuine aromatic nard
> and anointed the feet of Jesus and dried them with her hair; the house was filled with the fragrance of the oil.
> Then Judas the Iscariot, one of his disciples, and the one who would betray him, said,
> "Why was this oil not sold for three hundred days' wages and given to the poor?"
> He said this not because he cared about the poor but because he was a thief and held the money bag and used to steal the contributions.
> So Jesus said, "Leave her alone.
> Let her keep this for the day of my burial.
> You always have the poor with you, but you do not always have me."
>
> The large crowd of the Jews found out that he was there and came, not only because of him, but also to see Lazarus,

> whom he had raised from the dead.
> And the chief priests plotted to kill Lazarus too, because many of the Jews were turning away and believing in Jesus because of him.

Dear friends, note that the chief priests plotted to kill Lazarus, too. You would think the chief priests would know about thou shall not kill. Recall what I wrote a few days ago about how power corrupts. Also, I imagine the phrase do as I say, not as I do was applied then as it is today.

Blessings

God morning, branches,

Today's Gospel
Luke 10:25-37

> There was a scholar of the law who stood up to test Jesus and said, "Teacher, what must I do to inherit eternal life?"
> Jesus said to him, "What is written in the law?
> How do you read it?"
> He said in reply,
> "You shall love the Lord, your God,
> with all your heart,
> with all your being,
> with all your strength,
> and with all your mind,
> and your neighbor as yourself."
> He replied to him, "You have answered correctly;
> do this and you will live."
>
> But because he wished to justify himself, he said to Jesus,

SCRIPTURE NOTES

"And who is my neighbor?"
Jesus replied,
"A man fell victim to robbers
as he went down from Jerusalem to Jericho.
They stripped and beat him and went off leaving him half-dead.
A priest happened to be going down that road,
but when he saw him, he passed by on the opposite side.
Likewise a Levite came to the place,
and when he saw him, he passed by on the opposite side.
But a Samaritan traveler who came upon him
was moved with compassion at the sight.
He approached the victim,
poured oil and wine over his wounds and bandaged them.
Then he lifted him up on his own animal,
took him to an inn, and cared for him.
The next day he took out two silver coins
and gave them to the innkeeper with the instruction,
'Take care of him.
If you spend more than what I have given you,
I shall repay you on my way back.'
Which of these three, in your opinion,
was neighbor to the robbers' victim?"
He answered, "The one who treated him with mercy."
Jesus said to him, "Go and do likewise."

Dear friends, may we love the Lord, our God, with all our hearts, with all our beings, with all our strengths, and with all our minds and our neighbor as ourselves. May we also treat others with mercy.

Note this is the story of the Good Samaritan. Samaritans were part Jewish and part Gentile. They were hated by Jews, unfaithful, to be avoided. Yet, Jesus makes a Samaritan one to be followed as he acted correctly and truly kept God's commandments. I imagine the scholar of the law and others who heard this story were shocked. It can be said the Samaritan went above and beyond what is expected. May we do likewise.

Blessings

God morning, branches,

Today's Gospel
Matthew 9:18-26

> While Jesus was speaking, an official came forward,
> knelt down before him, and said,
> ""My daughter has just died.
> But come, lay your hand on her, and she will live.""
> Jesus rose and followed him, and so did his disciples.
> A woman suffering hemorrhages for twelve years came up behind him
> and touched the tassel on his cloak.
> She said to herself, ""If only I can touch his cloak, I shall be cured.""
> Jesus turned around and saw her, and said,
> ""Courage, daughter! Your faith has saved you.""
> And from that hour the woman was cured.
>
> When Jesus arrived at the official's house
> and saw the flute players and the crowd who were making a commotion,
> he said, ""Go away! The girl is not dead but sleeping.""
> And they ridiculed him.
> When the crowd was put out, he came and took her by the hand,
> and the little girl arose.

And news of this spread throughout all that land.

Dear friends, many of you know I have experienced the saving power of my faith. Miracles do happen. Do not be influenced by those who ridicule our faith.

Blessings

God morning, branches,

Today's Gospel
Luke 6:6-11

> On a certain sabbath Jesus went into the synagogue and taught,
> and there was a man there whose right hand was withered.
> The scribes and the Pharisees watched him closely
> to see if he would cure on the sabbath
> so that they might discover a reason to accuse him.
> But he realized their intentions
> and said to the man with the withered hand,
> "Come up and stand before us."
> And he rose and stood there.
> Then Jesus said to them,
> "I ask you, is it lawful to do good on the sabbath
> rather than to do evil,
> to save life rather than to destroy it?"
> Looking around at them all, he then said to him,
> "Stretch out your hand."
> He did so and his hand was restored.
> But they became enraged
> and discussed together what they might do to Jesus.

Dear friends, remember that Jesus knows what is in your mind and He knows it before you even think it. Jesus realized that the Pharisees were watching him, hoping that he would break one rule or another. Thus they would have cause to accuse him of breaking the Sabbath. Yet Jesus shows that love for someone outweighed any other consideration, even the law of not working on the Sabbath. Jesus is love and love is the supreme law.

Blessings

God morning, branches,

> To everything (turn, turn, turn) There is a season (turn, turn, turn) And a time to every purpose, under heaven

> A time to be born, a time to die A time to plant, a time to reap A time to kill, a time to heal A time to laugh, a time to weep

> To everything (turn, turn, turn) There is a season (turn, turn, turn) And a time to every purpose, under heaven

> A time to build up, a time to break down A time to dance, a time to mourn A time to cast away stones, a time to gather stones together

> To everything (turn, turn, turn) There is a season (turn, turn, turn) And a time to every purpose, under heaven

> A time of love, a time of hate A time of war, a time of peace A time you may embrace, a time to refrain from embracing

> To everything (turn, turn, turn) There is a season (turn, turn, turn) And a time to every purpose, under heaven

SCRIPTURE NOTES

A time to gain, a time to lose A time to rend, a time to sew A time for love, a time for hate A time for peace, I swear it's not too late

This song was written by Pete Seeger in the late 1950s and first recorded in 1959. The lyrics – except for the title, which is repeated throughout the song, and the final two lines – consist of the first eight verses of the third chapter of the biblical Book of Ecclesiastes.

The song became an international hit in late 1965 when it was adapted by the American folk rock group the Byrds. Turn! Turn! Turn! (To Everything There Is A Season) The single entered the U.S. chart at number 80 on October 23, 1965, before reaching number one on the Billboard Hot 100 chart on December 4, 1965. In Canada, it reached number 3 on November 29, 1965, and also peaked at number 26 on the UK Singles Chart.

Peace

God morning, branches,

Today's Gospel
Luke 5:17-26

> One day as Jesus was teaching, Pharisees and teachers of the law, who had come from every village of Galilee and Judea and Jerusalem, were sitting there,
> and the power of the Lord was with him for healing.
> And some men brought on a stretcher a man who was paralyzed; they were trying to bring him in and set him in his presence.
> But not finding a way to bring him in because of the crowd, they went up on the roof

and lowered him on the stretcher through the tiles into the middle in front of Jesus.
When Jesus saw their faith, he said, "As for you, your sins are forgiven."

Then the scribes and Pharisees began to ask themselves, "Who is this who speaks blasphemies?
Who but God alone can forgive sins?"
Jesus knew their thoughts and said to them in reply, "What are you thinking in your hearts?
Which is easier, to say, 'Your sins are forgiven,' or to say, 'Rise and walk'?
But that you may know
that the Son of Man has authority on earth to forgive sins"– he said to the one who was paralyzed,
"I say to you, rise, pick up your stretcher, and go home."

He stood up immediately before them, picked up what he had been lying on, and went home, glorifying God.
Then astonishment seized them all and they glorified God, and, struck with awe, they said,
"We have seen incredible things today."

Dear friends, try to imagine what the friends of the paralytic thought and felt about Jesus and their friend. They believed in Jesus and went to extraordinary lengths for their friend. Jesus recognized their faith and healed them spiritually before also physically healing the friend. Might we be paralyzed in some way that prevents us from doing what we know should be done? Might we bring someone to find healing in Jesus? This Gospel concludes with "We have seen incredible things today." I suggest you can cause others to see incredible things everyday. Finally, we can see incredible things on a daily basis by looking at the beauty of His creation.

Blessings

God morning, disciples,

Today's Gospel
Matthew 5:1-12

When Jesus saw the crowds, he went up the mountain, and after he had sat down, his disciples came to him. He began to teach them, saying:

> "Blessed are the poor in spirit,
> for theirs is the Kingdom of heaven.
> Blessed are they who mourn,
> for they will be comforted.
> Blessed are the meek,
> for they will inherit the land.
> Blessed are they who hunger and thirst for righteousness,
> for they will be satisfied.
> Blessed are the merciful,
> for they will be shown mercy.
> Blessed are the clean of heart,
> for they will see God.
> Blessed are the peacemakers,
> for they will be called children of God.
> Blessed are they who are persecuted for the sake of righteousness,
> for theirs is the Kingdom of heaven.
> Blessed are you when they insult you and persecute you

and utter every kind of evil against you falsely because of me.

Rejoice and be glad,
for your reward will be great in heaven.

Thus they persecuted the prophets who were before you."

Dear friends, I imagine the words in today's Gospel are not new to you and you know some of the blessings by heart. I wish to emphasize the last blessing because we are indeed being insulted and persecuted because of our faith. Yes, in 2021. Yes, in America. Keep spreading the Good News, my friends. Rejoice and be glad, for your reward will be great in Heaven.

Blessings

God morning, branches,

Today's Gospel
John 19:25–34

> Standing by the cross of Jesus were his mother
> and his mother's sister, Mary the wife of Clopas, and Mary of Magdala.
> When Jesus saw his mother and the disciple there whom he loved, he
>   said to his mother, "Woman, behold, your son."
> Then he said to the disciple, "Behold, your mother."
> And from that hour the disciple took her into his home. After this, aware
>   that everything was now finished,
> in order that the Scripture might be fulfilled, Jesus said, "I thirst."
> There was a vessel filled with common wine.
> So they put a sponge soaked in wine on a sprig of hyssop and put it up
>   to his mouth.

SCRIPTURE NOTES

When Jesus had taken the wine, he said, "It is finished."
And bowing his head, he handed over the spirit.

Now since it was preparation day,
in order that the bodies might not remain on the cross on the sabbath,
for the sabbath day of that week was a solemn one,
the Jews asked Pilate that their legs be broken and they be taken down.
So the soldiers came and broke the legs of the first
and then of the other one who was crucified with Jesus. But when they came to Jesus and saw that he was already dead,
they did not break his legs,
but one soldier thrust his lance into his side, and immediately Blood and water flowed out.

Dear friends, did you notice that it was not just blood that flowed from His body when the soldier pierced His side, but also water. The blood is for our redemption. The water is for life. Recall that Jesus said He is the living water.

Blessings

God morning, branches,

Today's Gospel
Matthew 28:8-15

Mary Magdalene and the other Mary went away quickly from the tomb,
fearful yet overjoyed,
and ran to announce the news to his disciples.
And behold, Jesus met them on their way and greeted them. They approached, embraced his feet, and did him homage. Then Jesus said to them, "Do not be afraid.

Go tell my brothers to go to Galilee, and there they will see me."

While they were going, some of the guard went into the city and told the chief priests all that had happened.

The chief priests assembled with the elders and took counsel; then they gave a large sum of money to the soldiers,

telling them, "You are to say,

'His disciples came by night and stole him while we were asleep.' And if this gets to the ears of the governor,

we will satisfy him and keep you out of trouble."

The soldiers took the money and did as they were instructed. And this story has circulated among the Jews to the present day.

Dear friends, can you imagine the worry of the chief priests in today's Gospel? To protect their power and positions they bribed the guards and attempted to, as is said nowadays, control the narrative.

Blessings

God morning, branches,

Today's Gospel
Luke 7:1-10

When Jesus had finished all his words to the people, he entered Capernaum.

A centurion there had a slave who was ill and about to die, and he was valuable to him.

When he heard about Jesus, he sent elders of the Jews to him, asking him to come and save the life of his slave.

They approached Jesus and strongly urged him to come, saying, "He deserves to have you do this for him,

SCRIPTURE NOTES

for he loves our nation and he built the synagogue for us." And Jesus went with them,
but when he was only a short distance from the house, the centurion sent friends to tell him,
"Lord, do not trouble yourself,
for I am not worthy to have you enter under my roof. Therefore, I did not consider myself worthy to come to you; but say the word and let my servant be healed.
For I too am a person subject to authority, with soldiers subject to me. And I say to one, 'Go,' and he goes;
and to another, 'Come here,' and he comes; and to my slave, 'Do this,' and he does it." When Jesus heard this he was amazed at him and, turning, said to the crowd following him,
"I tell you, not even in Israel have I found such faith." When the messengers returned to the house,
they found the slave in good health.

Dear friends, may we have the centurion's faith.

For those of the Catholic faith, we imitate the centurion during mass when we say "Lord, I am not worthy that you should enter under my roof, but only say the word and my soul shall be healed."

Blessings

God morning, branches,

Today's Gospel
Luke 7:11-17

Jesus journeyed to a city called Nain,
and his disciples and a large crowd accompanied him.

SCRIPTURE NOTES

As he drew near to the gate of the city,
a man who had died was being carried out,
the only son of his mother, and she was a widow.
A large crowd from the city was with her.
When the Lord saw her,
he was moved with pity for her and said to her,
"Do not weep."
He stepped forward and touched the coffin;
at this the bearers halted,
and he said, "Young man, I tell you, arise!"
The dead man sat up and began to speak,
and Jesus gave him to his mother.
Fear seized them all, and they glorified God, exclaiming,
"A great prophet has arisen in our midst,"
and "God has visited his people."
This report about him spread through the whole of Judea
and in all the surrounding region.

Dear friends, I think there are many in our world who, in a spiritual sense, are like the dead man in the Gospel. May our words and actions cause some to be brought to life in Jesus.

Blessings

God morning, disciples,

Today's Gospel
Luke 8:4-15

When a large crowd gathered, with people from one town after another journeying to Jesus, he spoke in a parable.

SCRIPTURE NOTES

"A sower went out to sow his seed.
And as he sowed, some seed fell on the path and was trampled,
and the birds of the sky ate it up.
Some seed fell on rocky ground, and when it grew,
it withered for lack of moisture.
Some seed fell among thorns,
and the thorns grew with it and choked it.
And some seed fell on good soil, and when it grew,
it produced fruit a hundredfold."
After saying this, he called out,
"Whoever has ears to hear ought to hear."

Then his disciples asked him
what the meaning of this parable might be.
He answered,
"Knowledge of the mysteries of the Kingdom of God
has been granted to you;
but to the rest, they are made known through parables
so that they may look but not see, and hear but not understand.

"This is the meaning of the parable.
The seed is the word of God.
Those on the path are the ones who have heard,
but the Devil comes and takes away the word from their hearts
that they may not believe and be saved.
Those on rocky ground are the ones who, when they hear,
receive the word with joy, but they have no root;
they believe only for a time and fall away in time of temptation.
As for the seed that fell among thorns,
they are the ones who have heard, but as they go along,
they are choked by the anxieties and riches and pleasures of life,

and they fail to produce mature fruit.
But as for the seed that fell on rich soil,
they are the ones who, when they have heard the word,
embrace it with a generous and good heart,
and bear fruit through perseverance."

Dear friends, may you be rich soil.

Blessings

God morning, branches,

Today's Reading 1
Genesis 4:1-15, 25

> The man had relations with his wife Eve, and she conceived and bore Cain, saying,
> "I have produced a man with the help of the LORD." Next she bore his brother Abel.
> Abel became a keeper of flocks, and Cain a tiller of the soil. In the course of time Cain brought an offering to the LORD from the fruit of the soil,
> while Abel, for his part,
> brought one of the best firstlings of his flock.
> The LORD looked with favor on Abel and his offering, but on Cain and his offering he did not.
> Cain greatly resented this and was crestfallen. So the LORD said to Cain:
> "Why are you so resentful and crestfallen. If you do well, you can hold up your head;
> but if not, sin is a demon lurking at the door:
> his urge is toward you, yet you can be his master."

Cain said to his brother Abel, "Let us go out in the field." When they
 were in the field,
Cain attacked his brother Abel and killed him.
Then the LORD asked Cain, "Where is your brother Abel?" He answered,
 "I do not know.
Am I my brother's keeper?"
The LORD then said: "What have you done!
Listen: your brother's blood cries out to me from the soil! Therefore you
 shall be banned from the soil
that opened its mouth to receive
your brother's blood from your hand.
If you till the soil, it shall no longer give you its produce. You shall become
 a restless wanderer on the earth."
Cain said to the LORD: "My punishment is too great to bear. Since you
 have now banished me from the soil,
and I must avoid your presence

and become a restless wanderer on the earth, anyone may kill me at
 sight."
"Not so!" the LORD said to him.
"If anyone kills Cain, Cain shall be avenged sevenfold."
So the LORD put a mark on Cain, lest anyone should kill him at sight.

Adam again had relations with his wife,
and she gave birth to a son whom she called Seth.
"God has granted me more offspring in place of Abel," she said, "because
 Cain slew him."

Dear friends, I imagine you are familiar with today's reading. I wonder if you knew the expression "Am I my brother's keeper" is from it.

Blessings

God morning, branches,

Today's Gospel
Mt 21:23-27

> When Jesus had come into the temple area,
> the chief priests and the elders of the people approached him as he was teaching and said,
> "By what authority are you doing these things? And who gave you this authority?"
> Jesus said to them in reply,
> "I shall ask you one question, and if you answer it for me, then I shall tell you by what authority I do these things. Where was John's baptism from?
> Was it of heavenly or of human origin?"
> They discussed this among themselves and said, "If we say 'Of heavenly origin,' he will say to us, 'Then why did you not believe him?'
> But if we say, 'Of human origin,' we fear the crowd, for they all regard John as a prophet."
> So they said to Jesus in reply, "We do not know." He himself said to them, "Neither shall I tell you by what authority I do these things."

Dear friends, do the chief priests not sound like politicians?
The following is from https://livingspace.sacredspace.ie/A1032G/

Perhaps a word about "authority" may be relevant here. The word comes from the Latin auctoritas, which is itself an abstract noun from the verb augere. Augere means "to increase, make bigger". We find the same verb in the word "author".

A person with 'authority' is not just someone who wields coercive power over others. The exercise of genuine authority is not to control, to keep in line but, on the contrary, to be an agent in releasing the potential that is in people, to be an empowering agent. Jesus did not wield coercive authority. He invited people to follow him. He came to serve not be served. He came to give life, life in its fullness. He came to lead people into the full development of all they could be and were meant to be.

Blessings

God morning, disciples,

Today's Gospel
Luke 6:36–38

> Jesus said to his disciples:
> "Be merciful, just as your Father is merciful.
>
> "Stop judging and you will not be judged.
> Stop condemning and you will not be condemned.
> Forgive and you will be forgiven.
> Give and gifts will be given to you;
> a good measure, packed together, shaken down, and overflowing,
> will be poured into your lap.
> For the measure with which you measure
> will in return be measured out to you."

SCRIPTURE NOTES

Dear friends, Matthew 5:48 says "Be perfect, therefore, as your Heavenly Father is perfect". It might be said that we cannot be perfect, but remember we were created in His Divine Image. I suggest that if we truly follow The Lord's instructions in today's Gospel, we are on the road to perfection.

Blessings

God morning, branches,

Today's Gospel
Luke 18:35-43

> As Jesus approached Jericho
> a blind man was sitting by the roadside begging,
> and hearing a crowd going by, he inquired what was happening.
>
> They told him,
> "Jesus of Nazareth is passing by."
> He shouted, "Jesus, Son of David, have pity on me!" The people walking in front rebuked him,
> telling him to be silent,
> but he kept calling out all the more, "Son of David, have pity on me!"
> Then Jesus stopped and ordered that he be brought to him; and when he came near, Jesus asked him,
> "What do you want me to do for you?" He replied, "Lord, please let me see."
> Jesus told him, "Have sight; your faith has saved you." He immediately received his sight
> and followed him, giving glory to God.
> When they saw this, all the people gave praise to God.

Dear friends, I certainly relate to the blind man in today's Gospel. May your faith be strong enough to save you.

    Praise God!

Blessings

God morning, branches,

Today's Reading I
Acts 2:14, 22-33

> On the day of Pentecost, Peter stood up with the Eleven,
> raised his voice, and proclaimed:
> "You who are Jews, indeed all of you staying in Jerusalem.
> Let this be known to you, and listen to my words.
>
> "You who are children of Israel, hear these words.
> Jesus the Nazorean was a man commended to you by God
> with mighty deeds, wonders, and signs,
> which God worked through him in your midst, as you yourselves know.
> This man, delivered up by the set plan and foreknowledge of God,
> you killed, using lawless men to crucify him.
> But God raised him up, releasing him from the throes of death,
> because it was impossible for him to be held by it.
> For David says of him:
>
> I saw the Lord ever before me,
> with him at my right hand I shall not be disturbed.
> Therefore my heart has been glad and my tongue has exulted;
> my flesh, too, will dwell in hope,
> because you will not abandon my soul to the nether world,
> nor will you suffer your holy one to see corruption.

SCRIPTURE NOTES

You have made known to me the paths of life;
you will fill me with joy in your presence.

My brothers, one can confidently say to you
about the patriarch David that he died and was buried,
and his tomb is in our midst to this day.
But since he was a prophet and knew that God had sworn an oath to him
that he would set one of his descendants upon his throne,
he foresaw and spoke of the resurrection of the Christ,
that neither was he abandoned to the netherworld
nor did his flesh see corruption.
God raised this Jesus;
of this we are all witnesses.
Exalted at the right hand of God,
he poured forth the promise of the Holy Spirit
that he received from the Father, as you both see and hear."

Dear friends, as you know, the Bible is the word of God. Believers might say this when asked why they believe in Easter. I suggest that anyone reading today's reading think in terms of a good courtroom drama. There are witnesses to the life, crucifixion and resurrection of Jesus Christ (God raised this Jesus; of this we are all witnesses.). Now, I understand there are some who say this is hogwash, but, as I have often said, consider who has dominion over this world. Certainly, the evidence of the resurrection goes against everything a particular fallen angel holds dear and his followers will do all they can to get us to doubt the evidence. What then of miracles and the myriad mysteries of the universe? Many say science has the answers, but I like to think as a child does and ask why and how. Perhaps you will recall that yours truly has experienced miracles and I am confident many readers could share their own stories of miracles.

Blessings

God morning, branches,

Today's Reading I
Acts 6:8-15

> Stephen, filled with grace and power,
> was working great wonders and signs among the people.
> Certain members of the so-called Synagogue of Freedmen,
> Cyreneans, and Alexandrians,
> and people from Cilicia and Asia,
> came forward and debated with Stephen,
> but they could not withstand the wisdom and the Spirit with which he spoke.
> Then they instigated some men to say,
> "We have heard him speaking blasphemous words
> against Moses and God."
> They stirred up the people, the elders, and the scribes,
> accosted him, seized him,
> and brought him before the Sanhedrin.
> They presented false witnesses who testified,
> "This man never stops saying things against this holy place and the law.
> For we have heard him claim
> that this Jesus the Nazorean will destroy this place
> and change the customs that Moses handed down to us."
> All those who sat in the Sanhedrin looked intently at him
> and saw that his face was like the face of an angel.

Dear friends, recall that The Lord said "They will persecute and put some of you to death. You will be hated by all because of my name, ...". Perhaps you know that Stephen was stoned to death and became the first Christian martyr. While we do not posses Stephen's grace, power and ability to work great wonders, we are called to proclaim the Good News. There are many government officials around the world who persecute believers and even put some to death. Even in our own country, our faith is under attack. May you have the courage to defend the your beliefs.

Blessings

God morning, branches,

Today's Gospel
Mt 12:38-42

> Some of the scribes and Pharisees said to Jesus,
> "Teacher, we wish to see a sign from you."
> He said to them in reply,
> "An evil and unfaithful generation seeks a sign,
> but no sign will be given it
> except the sign of Jonah the prophet.
> Just as Jonah was in the belly of the whale three days and three nights,
> so will the Son of Man be in the heart of the earth
> three days and three nights.
> At the judgment, the men of Nineveh will arise with this generation
> and condemn it, because they repented at the preaching of Jonah;
> and there is something greater than Jonah here.
> At the judgment the queen of the south will arise with this generation
> and condemn it, because she came from the ends of the earth

to hear the wisdom of Solomon;
and there is something greater than Solomon here."

Dear friends, the queen of the South was the queen of Sheba in southwestern Arabia, who visited Solomon (1 Kings 10:1-10) and was in awe of the wisdom with which God had endowed the King of Israel. Jesus is the something greater, but recall He is humble. As for signs from God:

GOD ARE YOU REAL

The child whispered, "God, speak to me"
And a meadow lark sang. The child did not hear.
So the child yelled, "God, speak to me!"
And the thunder rolled across the sky but the child did not listen.
The child looked around and said, "God let me see you"
and a star shone brightly But the child did not notice and the child shouted,
"God show me a miracle!" And a life was born but the child did not know.
So the child cried out in despair,
"Touch me God, and let me know you are here!"
Where upon God reached down and touched the child.
But the child brushed the butterfly away and walked away.
-Author Unknown-

Blessings

God morning, branches,

Today's Gospel
Luke 1:26-38

In the sixth month,
the angel Gabriel was sent from God
to a town of Galilee called Nazareth,
to a virgin betrothed to a man named Joseph,
of the house of David,
and the virgin's name was Mary.
And coming to her, he said,
"Hail, full of grace! The Lord is with you."
But she was greatly troubled at what was said
and pondered what sort of greeting this might be.
Then the angel said to her,
"Do not be afraid, Mary,
for you have found favor with God.
Behold, you will conceive in your womb and bear a son,
and you shall name him Jesus.
He will be great and will be called Son of the Most High,
and the Lord God will give him the throne of David his father,
and he will rule over the house of Jacob forever,
and of his Kingdom there will be no end."

But Mary said to the angel,
"How can this be,
since I have no relations with a man?"
And the angel said to her in reply,
"The Holy Spirit will come upon you,
and the power of the Most High will overshadow you.
Therefore the child to be born
will be called holy, the Son of God.
And behold, Elizabeth, your relative,
has also conceived a son in her old age,

and this is the sixth month for her who was called barren;
for nothing will be impossible for God."

Mary said, "Behold, I am the handmaid of the Lord.
May it be done to me according to your word."
Then the angel departed from her.

Dear friends, may your faith be as strong as that of our Blessed Mother and remember nothing will be impossible for God. The Lord is with each of us and we have found favor with Him. Each of us has reason for being here and now.

Blessings

God morning, branches,

Today's Reading 1
Sirach 1:1-10

> All wisdom comes from the LORD
> and with him it remains forever, and is before all time
> The sand of the seashore, the drops of rain,
> the days of eternity: who can number these?
> Heaven's height, earth's breadth,
> the depths of the abyss: who can explore these?
> Before all things else wisdom was created;
> and prudent understanding, from eternity.
> The word of God on high is the fountain of wisdom
> and her ways are everlasting.
> To whom has wisdom's root been revealed?
> Who knows her subtleties?
> To whom has the discipline of wisdom been revealed?

And who has understood the multiplicity of her ways?
There is but one, wise and truly awe-inspiring,
seated upon his throne:
There is but one, Most High
all-powerful creator-king and truly awe-inspiring one,
seated upon his throne and he is the God of dominion.
It is the LORD; he created her through the Holy Spirit,
has seen her and taken note of her.
He has poured her forth upon all his works,
upon every living thing according to his bounty;
he has lavished her upon his friends.

Dear friends, wisdom is not a question of knowledge although some knowledge must be a constituent element. Wisdom is the gift to be able to see the whole and to see the inter-relatedness of all the parts. It can only come from experience and applied insight. It is not normally a characteristic of the very young or the very superficial. It is a question of looking into, not just looking at. It's the difference between being dazzlingly knowledgeable, or perhaps very clever, but not wise.

> Ultimately, to grow in Christ is to grow in wisdom. It is to grow into a deeper understanding of the meaning and direction of life. It is a gift God wishes us to have, so let us ask him for it today . *(Source:sacredspace)*

May we grow in wisdom.
Blessings

SCRIPTURE NOTES

God morning, branches,

Today's Gospel
Mark 9:14-29

> As Jesus came down from the mountain with Peter, James, John and approached the other disciples,
> they saw a large crowd around them and scribes arguing with them. Immediately on seeing him,
> the whole crowd was utterly amazed. They ran up to him and greeted him.
> He asked them, "What are you arguing about with them?" Someone from the crowd answered him,
> "Teacher, I have brought to you my son possessed by a mute spirit. Wherever it seizes him, it throws him down;
> he foams at the mouth, grinds his teeth, and becomes rigid.
> I asked your disciples to drive it out, but they were unable to do so." He said to them in reply,
> "O faithless generation, how long will I be with you? How long will I endure you? Bring him to me." They brought the boy to him.
> And when he saw him,
> the spirit immediately threw the boy into convulsions. As he fell to the ground, he began to roll around
> and foam at the mouth.
> Then he questioned his father,
> "How long has this been happening to him?" He replied, "Since childhood. It has often thrown him into fire and into water to kill him.
> But if you can do anything, have compassion on us and help us." Jesus said to him,
> "'If you can!' Everything is possible to one who has faith."

Then the boy's father cried out, "I do believe, help my unbelief!" Jesus, on seeing a crowd rapidly gathering,
rebuked the unclean spirit and said to it, "Mute and deaf spirit, I command you: come out of him and never enter him again!"
Shouting and throwing the boy into convulsions, it came out.
He became like a corpse, which caused many to say, "He is dead!"

But Jesus took him by the hand, raised him, and he stood up. When he entered the house, his disciples asked him in private, "Why could we not drive the spirit out?"
He said to them, "This kind can only come out through prayer."

Dear friends, the Lord said "Everything is possible to one who has faith." Perhaps you will remember my story about my doctor, who after describing an unusual medicine that seemed to be working for me said perhaps it's your faith.

Blessings

God morning, sisters and brothers,

Today's Reading 1
EPH 4:32–5:8

Brothers and sisters:
Be kind to one another, compassionate,
forgiving one another as God has forgiven you in Christ.

Be imitators of God, as beloved children, and live in love,
as Christ loved us and handed himself over for us
as a sacrificial offering to God for a fragrant aroma.

> Immorality or any impurity or greed must not even be mentioned among you,
> as is fitting among holy ones,
> no obscenity or silly or suggestive talk, which is out of place,
> but instead, thanksgiving.
> Be sure of this, that no immoral or impure or greedy person,
> that is, an idolater,
> has any inheritance in the Kingdom of Christ and of God.
>
> Let no one deceive you with empty arguments,
> for because of these things
> the wrath of God is coming upon the disobedient.
> So do not be associated with them.
> For you were once darkness,
> but now you are light in the Lord.
> Live as children of light.

Dear friends, be kind to one another, compassionate, forgiving one another as God has forgiven us in Christ. Be imitators of God, as beloved children, and live in love. For we were once darkness, but now we are light in the Lord. May we live as children of light.

Blessings

God morning, branches,

Today's Gospel
Matthew 19:16-22

> A young man approached Jesus and said,
> "Teacher, what good must I do to gain eternal life?"

He answered him, "Why do you ask me about the good? There is only
    One who is good.
If you wish to enter into life, keep the commandments." He asked him,
    "Which ones?"
And Jesus replied, "You shall not kill; you shall not commit adultery;
you shall not steal;
you shall not bear false witness; honor your father and your mother;
and you shall love your neighbor as yourself." The young man said to him,
"All of these I have observed. What do I still lack?" Jesus said to him, "If
    you wish to be perfect, go, sell what you have and give to the poor,
and you will have treasure in heaven. Then come, follow me."
When the young man heard this statement, he went away sad, for he
    had many possessions.

Dear friends, the young man asked what good must I do to gain eternal life? Remember, it is not so much to pile up good deeds, as to be a loving person. The tougher thing for many (most?) of us to do if we want to be perfect is to sell our possessions and give to the poor. As I have asked, do we own our possessions or do they own us? How many of us define ourselves by our jobs and possessions? If you are asked "Who are you?", why not say "I am a child of God"?

Blessings

God morning, disciples,

Today's Gospel
Matthew 13:47–53

>   Jesus said to the disciples:
>   "The Kingdom of heaven is like a net thrown into the sea,

which collects fish of every kind.
When it is full they haul it ashore
and sit down to put what is good into buckets.
What is bad they throw away.
Thus it will be at the end of the age.
The angels will go out and separate the wicked from the righteous
and throw them into the fiery furnace,
where there will be wailing and grinding of teeth."

"Do you understand all these things?"
They answered, "Yes."
And he replied,
"Then every scribe who has been instructed in the Kingdom of heaven
is like the head of a household who brings from his storeroom
both the new and the old."
When Jesus finished these parables, he went away from there.

Dear friends, may we live a righteous life so as to avoid the fiery furnace.

Blessings

God morning, brothers and sisters,

Today's Reading I
Romans 8:12-17

Brothers and sisters,
we are not debtors to the flesh, to live according to the flesh.
For if you live according to the flesh, you will die,
but if by the spirit you put to death the deeds of the body, you will live.

For those who are led by the Spirit of God are sons of God. For you did not receive a spirit of slavery to fall back into fear, but you received a spirit of adoption,
through which we cry, "Abba, Father!"
The Spirit himself bears witness with our spirit that we are children of God,
and if children, then heirs,
heirs of God and joint heirs with Christ, if only we suffer with him
so that we may also be glorified with him.

Dear friends, may you be led by the Spirit of God and remember we are heirs of God and joint heirs with Jesus Christ if only we suffer with Him. Wow, a heavenly inheritance!

Blessings

God morning, disciples,

Today's Gospel
Matthew 7:1-5

Jesus said to his disciples:
"Stop judging, that you may not be judged. For as you judge, so will you be judged,
and the measure with which you measure will be measured out to you. Why do you notice the splinter in your brother's eye,
but do not perceive the wooden beam in your own eye? How can you say to your brother,
'Let me remove that splinter from your eye,' while the wooden beam is in your eye?

SCRIPTURE NOTES

> You hypocrite, remove the wooden beam from your eye first; then you will see clearly
> to remove the splinter from your brother's eye."

Dear friends, may we remove the wooden beams from our eyes and not judge others.

Blessings

God morning, branches,

Today's Reading I
1 John 1:1-4

> Beloved:
> What was from the beginning,
> what we have heard,
> what we have seen with our eyes,
> what we looked upon
> and touched with our hands
> concerns the Word of life —
> for the life was made visible;
> we have seen it and testify to it
> and proclaim to you the eternal life
> that was with the Father and was made visible to us—
> what we have seen and heard
> we proclaim now to you,
> so that you too may have fellowship with us;
> for our fellowship is with the Father
> and with his Son, Jesus Christ.
> We are writing this so that our joy may be complete.

Dear friends, can you possibly imagine the joy of those who wrote the above reading? They saw the Lord and testify to it! They saw eternal life! How wonderful that they offer us the fellowship they have with the Father and Son!

Blessings

God morning, disciples,

Today's Reading 1
ACTS 6:8-10; 7:54-59

> Stephen, filled with grace and power,
> was working great wonders and signs among the people.
> Certain members of the so-called Synagogue of Freedmen,
> Cyrenians, and Alexandrians,
> and people from Cilicia and Asia,
> came forward and debated with Stephen,
> but they could not withstand the wisdom and the spirit with which he
>   spoke.
>
> When they heard this, they were infuriated,
> and they ground their teeth at him.
> But he, filled with the Holy Spirit,
> looked up intently to heaven
> and saw the glory of God and Jesus standing at the right hand of God,
> and he said,
> "Behold, I see the heavens opened and the Son of Man
> standing at the right hand of God."
> But they cried out in a loud voice, covered their ears,
> and rushed upon him together.

*They threw him out of the city, and began to stone him.
The witnesses laid down their cloaks
at the feet of a young man named Saul.
As they were stoning Stephen, he called out
"Lord Jesus, receive my spirit."*

Dear friends, Saint Stephen, the first martyr, was an ordinary man who realized the value of the Gospel and was willing to risk everything, including his life, to preach it. As Christians, we (ordinary people) are called to spread the good news and we should learn as much as we can about the Word of God in order to do so. Bear in mind we are not ordinary people in the sense we are temples filled with the Holy Spirit and Jesus said His followers would do great works. A great work might be as simple as helping someone in need. We may speak truth, but be hated. Note that Stephen's death was supported by Saul, who later became Paul. May we try to follow Saint Stephen's example. We are far from ordinary, my friends.

Blessings

God morning, branches,

Today's Reading 1
1 Peter 1:3-9

> Blessed be the God and Father of our Lord Jesus Christ, who in his great mercy gave us a new birth to a living hope through the resurrection of Jesus Christ from the dead,
> to an inheritance that is imperishable, undefiled, and unfading, kept in heaven for you

who by the power of God are safeguarded through faith, to a salvation
that is ready to be revealed in the final time. In this you rejoice, although now for a little while
you may have to suffer through various trials, so that the genuineness of your faith,
more precious than gold that is perishable even though tested by fire, may prove to be for praise, glory, and honor
at the revelation of Jesus Christ.
Although you have not seen him you love him;
even though you do not see him now yet you believe in him, you rejoice with an indescribable and glorious joy,
as you attain the goal of faith, the salvation of your souls.

Dear friends, I imagine most of us will agree we have suffered or are suffering through various trials. Take heart and have faith that we will prevail with God's help.

Blessings

God morning, branches,

Today's Reading I
Isaiah 65:17-21

Thus says the LORD:
Lo, I am about to create new heavens and a new earth;
The things of the past shall not be remembered or come to mind.
Instead, there shall always be rejoicing and happiness in what I create;
For I create Jerusalem to be a joy and its people to be a delight;
I will rejoice in Jerusalem
and exult in my people.

> No longer shall the sound of weeping be heard there, or the sound of crying;
> No longer shall there be in it
> an infant who lives but a few days,
> or an old man who does not round out his full lifetime; He dies a mere youth who reaches but a hundred years,
> and he who fails of a hundred shall be thought accursed. They shall live in the houses they build,
> and eat the fruit of the vineyards they plant.

Dear friends, the new heavens and earth sound wonderful, but some of this reading might raise questions about time. I call to your attention 2 Peter 3:8, which says one day is like a thousand years. Big difference, right? I humbly suggest that was written for us to understand our idea of time is nothing like God's idea. I further humbly suggest that as God is infinite or eternal that there is neither a beginning nor an end. Einstein said time is an illusion. Some might want to point to what we call months, years, minutes and so on, but those ideas are based on what humans can see and comprehend. In any event, life in His Kingdom will be Heavenly.

Blessings

God morning, branches,

Today's Gospel
Mt 8:5-11

> When Jesus entered Capernaum,
> a centurion approached him and appealed to him, saying,

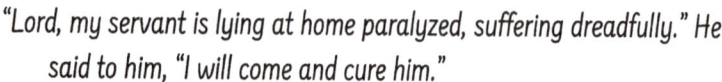

"Lord, my servant is lying at home paralyzed, suffering dreadfully." He said to him, "I will come and cure him."
The centurion said in reply,
"Lord, I am not worthy to have you enter under my roof; only say the word and my servant will be healed.
For I too am a man subject to authority, with soldiers subject to me.
And I say to one, 'Go,' and he goes;
and to another, 'Come here,' and he comes; and to my slave, 'Do this,' and he does it."
When Jesus heard this, he was amazed and said to those following him, "Amen, I say to you, in no one in Israel have I found such faith.
I say to you, many will come from the east and the west, and will recline with Abraham, Isaac, and Jacob
at the banquet in the Kingdom of heaven."

Dear friends, may you have the centurion's faith.
For those of the Catholic faith, we imitate the centurion during mass when we say "Lord, I am not worthy that you should enter under my roof, but only say the word and my soul shall be healed."
Blessings

God morning, disciples,

Today's Gospel
John 16:29-33

The disciples said to Jesus,
"Now you are talking plainly, and not in any figure of speech. Now we realize that you know everything

and that you do not need to have anyone question you. Because of this
we believe that you came from God." Jesus answered them, "Do
you believe now?
Behold, the hour is coming and has arrived
when each of you will be scattered to his own home and you will leave
me alone.
But I am not alone, because the Father is with me.
I have told you this so that you might have peace in me. In the world
you will have trouble,
but take courage, I have conquered the world."

Dear friends, Jesus says "In the world you will have trouble, but take courage, I have conquered the world." Notice there is no mention of a rose garden. We are instructed elsewhere to rejoice in our sufferings.

Blessings

God morning, branches,

Today's Gospel
Mt 4:18-22

As Jesus was walking by the Sea of Galilee, he saw two brothers,
Simon who is called Peter, and his brother Andrew,
casting a net into the sea; they were fishermen.
He said to them,
"Come after me, and I will make you fishers of men."
At once they left their nets and followed him.
He walked along from there and saw two other brothers,
James, the son of Zebedee, and his brother John.

They were in a boat, with their father Zebedee, mending their nets. He called them, and immediately they left their boat and their father and followed him.

Dear friends, Jesus calls each of us to be fishers of men. Will you accept His invitation to follow Him? I imagine you will say "of course", but you should know the adversary will try to distract you. We can be fishers of men through our words and actions in our daily lives.

Blessings

God morning, branches,

Today's Gospel
John 7:40-53

> Some in the crowd who heard these words of Jesus said,
> "This is truly the Prophet."
> Others said, "This is the Christ."
> But others said, "The Christ will not come from Galilee, will he?
> Does not Scripture say that the Christ will be of David's family
> and come from Bethlehem, the village where David lived?"
> So a division occurred in the crowd because of him.
> Some of them even wanted to arrest him,
> but no one laid hands on him.
>
> So the guards went to the chief priests and Pharisees,
> who asked them, "Why did you not bring him?"
> The guards answered, "Never before has anyone spoken like this man."
> So the Pharisees answered them, "Have you also been deceived?
> Have any of the authorities or the Pharisees believed in him?

SCRIPTURE NOTES

But this crowd, which does not know the law, is accursed."
Nicodemus, one of their members who had come to him earlier, said to them,
"Does our law condemn a man before it first hears him
and finds out what he is doing?"
They answered and said to him,
"You are not from Galilee also, are you?
Look and see that no prophet arises from Galilee."

Then each went to his own house.

Dear friends, the guards answered, "Never before has anyone spoken like this man." I imagine the guards had come across all different kinds of people, from the highest leaders, intellectuals, common folk on down. Yet, they said "Never before has anyone spoken like this man." I wonder how their lives might have changed after hearing Him. I will venture to say no one has spoken like Him since the guards heard Him. When reading His words, I wonder if we might think of what the guards said.

Blessings

God morning, disciples,

Today's Gospel:
MT 9:35-10:1, 5A, 6-8

> Jesus went around to all the towns and villages, teaching in their synagogues,
> proclaiming the Gospel of the Kingdom, and curing every disease and illness.

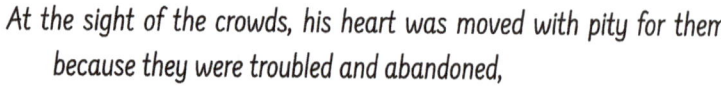

SCRIPTURE NOTES

> At the sight of the crowds, his heart was moved with pity for them
>   because they were troubled and abandoned,
> like sheep without a shepherd. Then he said to his disciples,
> "The harvest is abundant but the laborers are few; so ask the master of the harvest
> to send out laborers for his harvest." Then he summoned his Twelve disciples
> and gave them authority over unclean spirits to drive them out and to cure every disease and every illness.
> Jesus sent out these Twelve after instructing them thus, "Go to the lost sheep of the house of Israel.
> As you go, make this proclamation: 'The Kingdom of heaven is at hand.' Cure the sick, raise the dead,
> cleanse lepers, drive out demons.
> Without cost you have received; without cost you are to give."

Dear friends, we are called to be laborers for Jesus. We may not have the authority over unclean spirits or to cure anyone, at least directly. Our work may lead the afflicted to the One who does cure. Without cost we have received (consider your blessings including His grace), without cost we are to give.

Alleluia

God morning, disciples,

Today's Gospel
Luke 5:27–32

> Jesus saw a tax collector named Levi sitting at the customs post. He said to him, "Follow me."

SCRIPTURE NOTES

And leaving everything behind, he got up and followed him.
Then Levi gave a great banquet for him in his house,
and a large crowd of tax collectors
and others were at table with them.
The Pharisees and their scribes complained to his disciples, saying,
"Why do you eat and drink with tax collectors and sinners?"
Jesus said to them in reply,
"Those who are healthy do not need a physician, but the sick do.
I have not come to call the righteous to repentance but sinners."

Dear friends, I wonder if there is anyone among us who does not need the Great Physician.

Blessings

God morning, branches,

Today's Reading II
2 Peter 1:16-19

Beloved:
We did not follow cleverly devised myths
when we made known to you
the power and coming of our Lord Jesus Christ,
but we had been eyewitnesses of his majesty.
For he received honor and glory from God the Father
when that unique declaration came to him from the majestic glory,
"This is my Son, my beloved, with whom I am well pleased."
We ourselves heard this voice come from heaven
while we were with him on the holy mountain.
Moreover, we possess the prophetic message that is altogether reliable.

> You will do well to be attentive to it,
> as to a lamp shining in a dark place,
> until day dawns and the morning star rises in your hearts.

Dear friends, I guess it can be said that this reading comes right from the horse's mouth; the writers were eyewitnesses to His majesty. They did not follow some cleverly devised myths. There are some who have attempted to show our faith is based on a cleverly devised myth only to be converted! His messages are altogether reliable. The Bible is the undisputed best-selling book of all time with an estimated 5 billion copies sold and distributed. Not bad for a myth, eh. I remind you, though you may be the only Bible some people read...you may be the only Jesus some people see. Indeed, we will do well to be attentive to His messages.

Blessings

God morning, disciples,

Today's Gospel
John 6:60–69

> Many of the disciples of Jesus who were listening said, "This saying is hard; who can accept it?"
> Since Jesus knew that his disciples were murmuring about this, he said to them, "Does this shock you?
> What if you were to see the Son of Man ascending to where he was before? It is the Spirit that gives life, while the flesh is of no avail. The words I have spoken to you are Spirit and life. But there are some of you who do not believe."

Jesus knew from the beginning the ones who would not believe and the one who would betray him.
And he said, "For this reason I have told you that no one can come to me unless it is granted him by my Father."

As a result of this,
many of his disciples returned to their former way of life and no longer walked with him.
Jesus then said to the Twelve, "Do you also want to leave?" Simon Peter answered him, "Master, to whom shall we go? You have the words of eternal life.
We have come to believe
and are convinced that you are the Holy One of God."

Dear friends, the disciples who returned to their former ways of life said "This saying is hard; who can accept it?"

Following Jesus is hard. May you have the discipline to follow Him. Indeed, if not Jesus, to whom shall we go?

Blessings

God morning, branches,

Today's Reading I
1 Jn 5:14-21

Beloved:
We have this confidence in him
that if we ask anything according to his will, he hears us.
And if we know that he hears us in regard to whatever we ask, we know that what we have asked him for is ours.

If anyone sees his brother sinning, if the sin is not deadly, he should pray to God and he will give him life.
This is only for those whose sin is not deadly. There is such a thing as deadly sin,
about which I do not say that you should pray.
All wrongdoing is sin, but there is sin that is not deadly.

We know that anyone begotten by God does not sin; but the one begotten by God he protects,
and the Evil One cannot touch him. We know that we belong to God,
and the whole world is under the power of the Evil One. We also know that the Son of God has come
and has given us discernment to know the one who is true. And we are in the one who is true,
in his Son Jesus Christ.
He is the true God and eternal life. Children, be on your guard against idols.

Dear friends, the whole world is under the power of the Evil One. He knows our weaknesses better than we do. Unfortunately, there are far too many who do not know this. Be on your guard against idols.
Blessings

God morning, disciples,

Today's Gospel
Jn 15:18-21

Jesus said to his disciples:
"If the world hates you, realize that it hated me first.

SCRIPTURE NOTES

*If you belonged to the world, the world would love its own; but because you do not belong to the world,
and I have chosen you out of the world, the world hates you.
Remember the word I spoke to you, 'No slave is greater than his master.'
If they persecuted me, they will also persecute you. If they kept my word, they will also keep yours.
And they will do all these things to you on account of my name, because they do not know the one who sent me."*

Dear friends, they persecuted Him and as He said we will be persecuted because we are His chosen ones. We have not been handed over by our enemies to face trial. We have not been physically beaten.

Persecution takes many forms. A dictionary defines persecute thusly: to harass or punish in a manner designed to injure, grieve, or afflict specifically.

Consider that May 6 was our National Day of Prayer and a man who professes to be a devout Catholic failed to mention God even once in his proclamation. He also failed to mention Jesus Christ in an Easter video. Also consider that freedom of religion is part of the First Amendment, which is under attack, as is freedom of speech. Pay attention, speak up and take action.

Blessings

God morning, ambassadors,

Today's Reading I
2 *Cor* 5:14-21

Brothers and sisters:

The love of Christ impels us,
once we have come to the conviction that one died for all;
therefore, all have died.
He indeed died for all,
so that those who live might no longer live for themselves
but for him who for their sake died and was raised.

Consequently, from now on we regard no one according to the flesh;
even if we once knew Christ according to the flesh,
yet now we know him so no longer.
So whoever is in Christ is a new creation:
the old things have passed away;
behold, new things have come.
And all this is from God,
who has reconciled us to himself through Christ
and given us the ministry of reconciliation,
namely, God was reconciling the world to himself in Christ,
not counting their trespasses against them
and entrusting to us the message of reconciliation.
So we are ambassadors for Christ,
as if God were appealing through us.
We implore you on behalf of Christ,
be reconciled to God.
For our sake he made him to be sin who did not know sin,
so that we might become the righteousness of God in him.

Dear friends, we are ambassadors for Christ, as if God were appealing through us. May your words and actions show Christ to others and lead those who do not know Him to The Lord. It is a huge job, but remember nothing is impossible when you are guided by the Spirit and realize who is in control.

Blessings

God morning, disciples,

Today's Gospel
Matthew 17:14-20

> A man came up to Jesus, knelt down before him, and said,
> "Lord, have pity on my son, who is a lunatic and suffers severely;
> often he falls into fire, and often into water.
> I brought him to your disciples, but they could not cure him."
> Jesus said in reply,
> "O faithless and perverse generation, how long will I be with you?
> How long will I endure you?
> Bring the boy here to me."
> Jesus rebuked him and the demon came out of him,
> and from that hour the boy was cured.
> Then the disciples approached Jesus in private and said,
> "Why could we not drive it out?"
> He said to them, "Because of your little faith.
> Amen, I say to you, if you have faith the size of a mustard seed,
> you will say to this mountain,
> 'Move from here to there,' and it will move.
> Nothing will be impossible for you."

Dear friends, if Jesus thought that generation was faithless and perverse, I wonder what He thinks of the current time. It took a

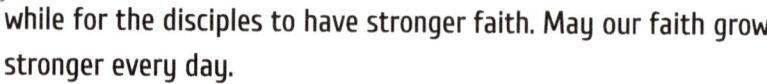

while for the disciples to have stronger faith. May our faith grow stronger every day.

Blessings

God morning, branches,

Today's Gospel
Mt 19:13-15

> Children were brought to Jesus
> that he might lay his hands on them and pray.
> The disciples rebuked them, but Jesus said,
> "Let the children come to me, and do not prevent them;
> for the Kingdom of heaven belongs to such as these."
> After he placed his hands on them, he went away.

Dear friends, this is one of my favorite Gospels. Jesus welcomes the children and blesses them and proclaims that the kingdom of heaven belongs to them and to those who are childlike. Children are trusting, innocent, teachable, and unassuming. Some may say they are weak, humble and unimportant. May you be like a child.

Today is the Memorial of Saint Maximilian Kolbe, Priest and Martyr. Saint Kolbe gave his life to save that of a stranger at the Nazi concentration camp at Auschwitz. Greater love than this no man hath, that a man lay down his life for his friends. *John 15:13*

Blessings

SCRIPTURE NOTES

God morning, disciples,

Today's Gospel
John 15:9-17

> Jesus said to his disciples:
> "As the Father loves me, so I also love you.
> Remain in my love.
> If you keep my commandments, you will remain in my love,
> just as I have kept my Father's commandments
> and remain in his love.
>
> "I have told you this so that my joy might be in you
> and your joy might be complete.
> This is my commandment: love one another as I love you.
> No one has greater love than this,
> to lay down one's life for one's friends.
> You are my friends if you do what I command you.
> I no longer call you slaves,
> because a slave does not know what his master is doing.
> I have called you friends,
> because I have told you everything I have heard from my Father.
> It was not you who chose me, but I who chose you
> and appointed you to go and bear fruit that will remain,
> so that whatever you ask the Father in my name he may give you.
> This I command you: love one another."

Dear friends, Jesus chose us, calls us friends and loves us. All we need to do to remain in His love is love one another. Why would anyone not abide by His commandment to love one another?

Love

God morning, disciples,

Today's Gospel
Matthew 6:24–34

> Jesus said to his disciples:
> "No one can serve two masters.
> He will either hate one and love the other, or be devoted to one and despise the other. You cannot serve God and mammon.
>
> "Therefore I tell you, do not worry about your life, what you will eat or drink,
> or about your body, what you will wear.
> Is not life more than food and the body more than clothing? Look at the birds in the sky;
> they do not sow or reap, they gather nothing into barns, yet your heavenly Father feeds them.
> Are not you more important than they?
> Can any of you by worrying add a single moment to your life-span? Why are you anxious about clothes?
> Learn from the way the wild flowers grow. They do not work or spin.
> But I tell you that not even Solomon in all his splendor was clothed like one of them.
> If God so clothes the grass of the field,
> which grows today and is thrown into the oven tomorrow, will he not much more provide for you, O you of little faith? So do not worry and say, 'What are we to eat?'
> or 'What are we to drink?' or 'What are we to wear?' All these things the pagans seek.
> Your heavenly Father knows that you need them all.

> But seek first the Kingdom of God and his righteousness, and all these things will be given you besides.
> Do not worry about tomorrow; tomorrow will take care of itself. Sufficient for a day is its own evil."

Dear friends, there is so much to consider in today's Gospel, but I want to focus on "Can any of you by worrying add a single moment to your life-span?" because I believe we all worry to some degree. Some worries are small, others large. While we have free will, God is in control. Rather than adding a single moment to our lives, worrying can subtract moments. Watch the birds and look at the wild flowers, then smile, say a prayer of thanks to our heavenly Father and seek His Kingdom.

Blessings

God morning, branches,

Today's Gospel
Luke 20:27–40

> Some Sadducees, those who deny that there is a resurrection,
> came forward and put this question to Jesus, saying,
> "Teacher, Moses wrote for us,
> If someone's brother dies leaving a wife but no child,
> his brother must take the wife
> and raise up descendants for his brother.
> Now there were seven brothers;
> the first married a woman but died childless.
> Then the second and the third married her,
> and likewise all the seven died childless.

SCRIPTURE NOTES

Finally the woman also died.
Now at the resurrection whose wife will that woman be?
For all seven had been married to her."
Jesus said to them,
"The children of this age marry and remarry;
but those who are deemed worthy to attain to the coming age
and to the resurrection of the dead
neither marry nor are given in marriage.
They can no longer die,
for they are like angels;
and they are the children of God
because they are the ones who will rise.
That the dead will rise
even Moses made known in the passage about the bush,
when he called 'Lord'
the God of Abraham, the God of Isaac, and the God of Jacob;
and he is not God of the dead, but of the living,
for to him all are alive."
Some of the scribes said in reply,
"Teacher, you have answered well."
And they no longer dared to ask him anything.

Dear friends, Jesus knew the trick question he would be asked before it was even thought of by the Sadducees. Jesus answers in a way that describes how we think in this life, "The children of this age marry and remarry;". Then He gives the Sadducees, and us, things to consider about our lives in Heaven. I imagine the Sadducees were frustrated and wonder if any then followed Christ. May we expand our minds to think at a higher level.

Blessings

God morning, disciples,

Today's Gospel
John 15:18-21

> Jesus said to his disciples:
> "If the world hates you, realize that it hated me first.
> If you belonged to the world, the world would love its own;
> but because you do not belong to the world,
> and I have chosen you out of the world,
> the world hates you.
> Remember the word I spoke to you,
> 'No slave is greater than his master.'
> If they persecuted me, they will also persecute you.
> If they kept my word, they will also keep yours.
> And they will do all these things to you on account of my name,
> because they do not know the one who sent me."

Dear friends, if the world hates you because of your faith, remember you are in the best company. May you belong to the Word, not the world.

Blessings

God morning, branches,

Today's Gospel
Matthew 13:24-30

> Jesus proposed a parable to the crowds.
> "The Kingdom of heaven may be likened to a man who sowed good seed in his field.

SCRIPTURE NOTES

> While everyone was asleep his enemy came
> and sowed weeds all through the wheat, and then went off. When the crop grew and bore fruit, the weeds appeared as well. The slaves of the householder came to him and said,
> 'Master, did you not sow good seed in your field? Where have the weeds come from?'
> He answered, 'An enemy has done this.'
> His slaves said to him, 'Do you want us to go and pull them up?' He replied, 'No, if you pull up the weeds
> you might uproot the wheat along with them. Let them grow together until harvest;
> then at harvest time I will say to the harvesters,
> "First collect the weeds and tie them in bundles for burning; but gather the wheat into my barn."'"

Dear friends, I imagine many of us wonder why God allows evil (the weeds) to grow with good (the wheat). God permits evil and good to co-exist until the end and it is up to us to be and do good. We should be like the wheat, not the weeds. If we choose to be indifferent, guess what happens.

Blessings

God morning, branches,

Today's Gospel
Mark 10:13-16

> People were bringing children to Jesus that he might touch them, but the disciples rebuked them.
> When Jesus saw this he became indignant and said to them,

"Let the children come to me; do not prevent them,
for the Kingdom of God belongs to such as these.
Amen, I say to you,
whoever does not accept the Kingdom of God like a child
will not enter it."
Then he embraced the children and blessed them,
placing his hands on them.

Dear friends, we are God's children, but perhaps some of us have been corrupted or hardened. Perhaps we are not as trusting or accepting as a child. Come to Jesus, as we are helpless without Him. May you depend on Jesus for His blessings, especially for salvation. May you accept the Kingdom of God as does a child.

Blessings

God morning, branches,

Today's Gospel
Luke 18:9-14

Jesus addressed this parable
to those who were convinced of their own righteousness
and despised everyone else.
"Two people went up to the temple area to pray;
one was a Pharisee and the other was a tax collector.
The Pharisee took up his position and spoke this prayer to himself,
'O God, I thank you that I am not like the rest of humanity —
greedy, dishonest, adulterous — or even like this tax collector.
I fast twice a week,
and I pay tithes on my whole income.'

But the tax collector stood off at a distance
and would not even raise his eyes to heaven
but beat his breast and prayed,
'O God, be merciful to me a sinner.'
I tell you, the latter went home justified, not the former;
for everyone who exalts himself will be humbled,
and the one who humbles himself will be exalted."

Dear friends, I noticed this Gospel appeared several times since I started this ministry. God must have a reason for this circumstance. Recall that we are called to follow in the footsteps of Jesus, who is the epitome of humility. Satan, on the other hand, is the exact opposite and rules the world, which seems to be more prideful by the day.

May we humble ourselves and may God be merciful to me, a sinner.

Blessings

God morning, disciples,

Today's Gospel
Luke 21:34-36

Jesus said to his disciples:

"Beware that your hearts do not become drowsy from carousing and
    drunkenness
and the anxieties of daily life,
and that day catch you by surprise like a trap. For that day will assault
    everyone
who lives on the face of the earth. Be vigilant at all times

and pray that you have the strength
to escape the tribulations that are imminent and to stand before the Son of Man."

Dear friends, in today's Gospel, Jesus is advising us to live as fully as we can in His presence. In so doing, we will not be caught unaware if we are called to stand before Him. Be vigilant at all times and do not let temptations overpower you.

Blessings

God morning, disciples,

Today's Gospel
Matthew 25:14-30

Jesus told his disciples this parable:

"A man going on a journey
called in his servants and entrusted his possessions to them.
To one he gave five talents; to another, two; to a third, one—
to each according to his ability.
Then he went away.
Immediately the one who received five talents went and traded with them,
and made another five.
Likewise, the one who received two made another two.
But the man who received one went off and dug a hole in the ground
and buried his master's money.
After a long time
the master of those servants came back and settled accounts with them.
The one who had received five talents

came forward bringing the additional five.
He said, 'Master, you gave me five talents.
See, I have made five more.'
His master said to him, 'Well done, my good and faithful servant.
Since you were faithful in small matters,
I will give you great responsibilities.
Come, share your master's joy.'
Then the one who had received two talents also came forward and said,
'Master, you gave me two talents.
See, I have made two more.'
His master said to him, 'Well done, my good and faithful servant.
Since you were faithful in small matters,
I will give you great responsibilities.
Come, share your master's joy.'
Then the one who had received the one talent came forward and said,
'Master, I knew you were a demanding person,
harvesting where you did not plant
and gathering where you did not scatter;
so out of fear I went off and buried your talent in the ground.
Here it is back.'
His master said to him in reply, 'You wicked, lazy servant!
So you knew that I harvest where I did not plant
and gather where I did not scatter?
Should you not then have put my money in the bank
so that I could have got it back with interest on my return?
Now then! Take the talent from him and give it to the one with ten.
For to everyone who has,
more will be given and he will grow rich;
but from the one who has not,
even what he has will be taken away.

And throw this useless servant into the darkness outside,
where there will be wailing and grinding of teeth.'"

Dear friends, in today's Gospel, Jesus is the one going on a trip. We are the servants who have been given certain talents to use to the best of our abilities to spread the Word before His Second Coming. May you be successful with your talents and share in His joy in Paradise.

Blessings

God morning, branches,

Today's Gospel
Luke14:1, 7–11

On a sabbath Jesus went to dine
at the home of one of the leading Pharisees,
and the people there were observing him carefully.

He told a parable to those who had been invited,
noticing how they were choosing the places of honor at the table. "When
    you are invited by someone to a wedding banquet,
do not recline at table in the place of honor.
A more distinguished guest than you may have been invited by him, and
    the host who invited both of you may approach you and say, 'Give
    your place to this man,'
and then you would proceed with embarrassment to take the lowest
    place.
Rather, when you are invited, go and take the lowest place
so that when the host comes to you he may say, 'My friend, move up
    to a higher position.'

Then you will enjoy the esteem of your companions at the table. For everyone who exalts himself will be humbled,
but the one who humbles himself will be exalted."

Dear friends, may you be humble. If ego gets in the way, remember the humility of our Savior.

Blessings

God morning, branches,

Today's Reading I
1 John 2:18-21

> Children, it is the last hour;
> and just as you heard that the antichrist was coming, so now many antichrists have appeared.
> Thus we know this is the last hour.
> They went out from us, but they were not really of our number; if they had been, they would have remained with us.
> Their desertion shows that none of them was of our number. But you have the anointing that comes from the Holy One, and you all have knowledge.
> I write to you not because you do not know the truth
> but because you do, and because every lie is alien to the truth.

Dear friends, there certainly are many antichrists (simply anyone against Christ) in the world and among us. As far as John saying it is the last hour, consider the passage elsewhere about a thousand years and one day.

Blessings

SCRIPTURE NOTES

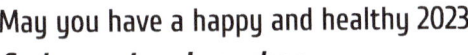

May you have a happy and healthy 2023.
God morning, branches,

Today's Reading 2
1 Corinthians 1:26-31

> Consider your own calling, brothers and sisters. Not many of you were wise by human standards, not many were powerful,
> not many were of noble birth.
> Rather, God chose the foolish of the world to shame the wise, and God chose the weak of the world to shame the strong, and God chose the lowly and despised of the world,
> those who count for nothing,
> to reduce to nothing those who are something, so that no human being might boast before God. It is due to him that you are in Christ Jesus, who became for us wisdom from God,
> as well as righteousness, sanctification, and redemption, so that, as it is written,
> "Whoever boasts, should boast in the Lord."

Dear friends, I imagine some (many? most?) of us have wondered about the reason we are here. Well, we were created to be examples of and to glorify God. As the above reading says, not many of us are wise, powerful or of noble birth, yet we are here. Some of us will shame the wise or the strong. Remember, we were chosen by God for a purpose. It is suggested that a calling could be as simple as living life according to the teachings of Jesus, thereby boasting in the Lord.

Blessings

God morning, branches,

I am sure you are familiar with the Gospels for Palm Sunday, which commemorate the triumphal entry of Jesus Christ into Jerusalem as a king.

Perhaps you are not as familiar with some of the symbols in the Palm Sunday Gospels.

Zechariah chapter 9, verse 9 foretells: "The coming of Zion's King–see, your King comes to you, righteous and victorious, lowly and riding on a donkey, on a colt, the foal of a donkey", which is quoted in the Gospels.

Every Jew would know Zechariah's messianic prophecy. That's why the crowds hailed Jesus as their king shouting, "Hosanna! Blessed is he who comes in the name of the Lord!"

The symbolism of the donkey may refer to the Eastern tradition that it is an animal of peace, unlike the horse, which is the animal of war. Donkeys and references to peace are mentioned a few times in the Old Testament. Jesus is known as the Prince of Peace.

In the Greco-Roman culture of the Roman Empire, which strongly influenced Christian tradition, the palm branch was a symbol of triumph and victory. In ancient times, palm branches symbolized goodness and victory. They were often depicted on coins and important buildings.

As I was preparing this note, I realized that I often start my notes with "God morning, branches", which is in reference to the Scripture reading Jesus is the vine, we are the branches. I connected the meaning of the palm branches to that greeting and the greeting became more profound.

May the peace of the Lord, which passes all human understanding be with you.

Happy & Blessed Palm Sunday

God morning, branches,

Today's Reading 2
2 Timothy 1:6-8, 13-14

> Beloved:
> I remind you, to stir into flame
> the gift of God that you have through the imposition of my hands. For
>   God did not give us a spirit of cowardice
> but rather of power and love and self-control.
> So do not be ashamed of your testimony to our Lord, nor of me, a prisoner for his sake;
> but bear your share of hardship for the gospel with the strength that
>   comes from God.
>
> Take as your norm the sound words that you heard from me, in the faith
>   and love that are in Christ Jesus.
> Guard this rich trust with the help of the Holy Spirit that dwells within us.

Dear friends, God did not give us a spirit of cowardice but rather of power and love and self-control. May we use our powers to the best of our abilities and thereby proclaim His Word.

Blessings

SCRIPTURE NOTES

God morning, branches,

Today's Gospel
John 8:1-11

> Jesus went to the Mount of Olives.
> But early in the morning he arrived again in the temple area,
> and all the people started coming to him,
> and he sat down and taught them.
> Then the scribes and the Pharisees brought a woman
> who had been caught in adultery
> and made her stand in the middle.
> They said to him,
> "Teacher, this woman was caught
> in the very act of committing adultery.
> Now in the law, Moses commanded us to stone such women.
> So what do you say?"
> They said this to test him,
> so that they could have some charge to bring against him.
> Jesus bent down and began to write on the ground with his finger.
> But when they continued asking him,
> he straightened up and said to them,
> "Let the one among you who is without sin
> be the first to throw a stone at her."
> Again he bent down and wrote on the ground.
> And in response, they went away one by one,
> beginning with the elders.
> So he was left alone with the woman before him.
> Then Jesus straightened up and said to her,
> "Woman, where are they?
> Has no one condemned you?"

> She replied, "No one, sir."
> Then Jesus said, "Neither do I condemn you.
> Go, and from now on do not sin any more."

Dear friends, I am sure you have heard and said "let him who is without sin cast the first stone". If the world took this to heart, fewer stones would be cast. Remember, when you point your finger at someone you have three fingers pointing back at yourself! The Pharisees tried to trap Jesus and discovered they had trapped themselves (their fingers were pointing back at themselves).

If and when I get to Heaven I hope to learn what Jesus wrote in the dirt.

Blessings

God morning, branches,

Today's Gospel
Luke 10:1-12, 17-20

> At that time the Lord appointed seventy-two others
> whom he sent ahead of him in pairs
> to every town and place he intended to visit.
> He said to them,
> "The harvest is abundant but the laborers are few;
> so ask the master of the harvest
> to send out laborers for his harvest.
> Go on your way;
> behold, I am sending you like lambs among wolves.
> Carry no money bag, no sack, no sandals;
> and greet no one along the way.

Into whatever house you enter, first say,
'Peace to this household.'
If a peaceful person lives there,
your peace will rest on him;
but if not, it will return to you.
Stay in the same house and eat and drink what is offered to you,
for the laborer deserves his payment.
Do not move about from one house to another.
Whatever town you enter and they welcome you,
eat what is set before you,
cure the sick in it and say to them,
'The kingdom of God is at hand for you.'
Whatever town you enter and they do not receive you,
go out into the streets and say,
'The dust of your town that clings to our feet,
even that we shake off against you.'
Yet know this: the kingdom of God is at hand.
I tell you,
it will be more tolerable for Sodom on that day than for that town."

The seventy-two returned rejoicing, and said,
"Lord, even the demons are subject to us because of your name."
Jesus said, "I have observed Satan fall like lightning from the sky.
Behold, I have given you the power to 'tread upon serpents' and scorpions
and upon the full force of the enemy and nothing will harm you.
Nevertheless, do not rejoice because the spirits are subject to you,
but rejoice because your names are written in heaven."

Dear friends, can you imagine what the seventy-two felt when they were chosen by Jesus to spread the Good News? They were given extraordinary powers, including those to drive out demons. Can you imagine their lives after having done so. We know nothing about them, except that their names were written in Heaven.

The harvest is greater today. We are called to go out as sheep among the wolves. The extraordinary powers we have are the power of His word and the fact that He is with us. Sometimes a kind word may bring comfort and peace to a family member, friend, neighbor, colleague, acquaintance or stranger. Rejoice for your names are written in Heaven.

Blessings

God morning, brothers and sisters,

Today's Reading II
James 2:1-5

> My brothers and sisters, show no partiality
> as you adhere to the faith in our glorious Lord Jesus Christ.
> For if a man with gold rings and fine clothes
> comes into your assembly,
> and a poor person in shabby clothes also comes in,
> and you pay attention to the one wearing the fine clothes
> and say, "Sit here, please,"
> while you say to the poor one, "Stand there," or "Sit at my feet,"
> have you not made distinctions among yourselves
> and become judges with evil designs?
>
> Listen, my beloved brothers and sisters.
> Did not God choose those who are poor in the world
> to be rich in faith and heirs of the kingdom
> that he promised to those who love him?

Dear friends, I imagine many of us have been guilty of showing favoritism at one time or another despite having heard many times throughout our lives to not judge a book by its cover.

Blessings

God morning, branches,

I wondered about the symbols associated with Pentecost.

The name of the day itself is derived from the Greek word "pentecoste," meaning 50th.

Wind
Representing God's first breath of love (Ruah) into all of creation. A "driving wind" surrounded the apostles on that first Pentecost to strengthen them in their faith. The breath of the Holy Spirit – and sometimes a gusting wind – strengthens and challenges God's people on their faith journey.

Fire
Representing the Holy Spirit, who filled the apostles with enthusiasm, replacing their fear with the courage to go forth and share Christ's story. "Tongues of fire ... came to rest on each one of them."

Red
The color of liturgical vestments on Pentecost, representing the dynamism of the Holy Spirit and the zeal of those who open their hearts to the Spirit.

Water
Representing new life and the commitment first made at the time of our baptism and renewed throughout our faith lives.

SCRIPTURE NOTES

Dove
Representing the Holy Spirit that descended "like a dove" and hovered over Jesus when he was baptized. Symbol of peace.

Blessings

God morning, brothers and sisters,

Today's Gospel
Luke 3:1-6

> In the fifteenth year of the reign of Tiberius Caesar,
> when Pontius Pilate was governor of Judea,
> and Herod was tetrarch of Galilee,
> and his brother Philip tetrarch of the region
> of Ituraea and Trachonitis,
> and Lysanias was tetrarch of Abilene,
> during the high priesthood of Annas and Caiaphas,
> the word of God came to John the son of Zechariah in the desert.
> John went throughout the whole region of the Jordan,
> proclaiming a baptism of repentance for the forgiveness of sins,
> as it is written in the book of the words of the prophet Isaiah:
>
> A voice of one crying out in the desert:
> "Prepare the way of the Lord,
> make straight his paths.
> Every valley shall be filled
> and every mountain and hill shall be made low.
> The winding roads shall be made straight,
> and the rough ways made smooth,
> and all flesh shall see the salvation of God."

Dear friends, are you prepared for the Lord's arrival? Have you cleared all the obstacles that may prevent Jesus from having a straight path to you?

Blessings

God morning, sisters and brothers,

Today's Reading II
Rom 10:8-13

> Brothers and sisters: What does Scripture say?
> The word is near you,
> in your mouth and in your heart —that is, the word of faith that we preach—,
> for, if you confess with your mouth that Jesus is Lord
> and believe in your heart that God raised him from the dead, you will be saved.
> For one believes with the heart and so is justified, and one confesses with the mouth and so is saved. For the Scripture says,
> No one who believes in him will be put to shame. For there is no distinction between Jew and Greek;
> the same Lord is Lord of all, enriching all who call upon him.
> For "everyone who calls on the name of the Lord will be saved."

Dear sisters and brothers, I imagine each of you believes in your heart and confesses with your mouth and therefore will be saved. That is awesome (the only time I use this word is when speaking about God or anything related to Him). May you conduct yourselves in such a way so as to get others to be saved.

Blessings

SCRIPTURE NOTES

God morning, sisters and brothers,

Today's Reading 2
2 Thes 2:16-3:5

> Brothers and sisters:
> May our Lord Jesus Christ himself and God our Father, who has loved us and given us everlasting encouragement and good hope through his grace,
> encourage your hearts and strengthen them in every good deed and word.
>
> Finally, brothers and sisters, pray for us,
> so that the word of the Lord may speed forward and be glorified, as it did among you,
> and that we may be delivered from perverse and wicked people, for not all have faith.
> But the Lord is faithful;
> he will strengthen you and guard you from the evil one.
> We are confident of you in the Lord that what we instruct you, you are doing and will continue to do.
> May the Lord direct your hearts to the love of God and to the endurance of Christ.

Dear friends, may our hearts be encouraged and strengthened in every good deed and word. May we be delivered from perverse and wicked people.

Blessings

God morning, branches,

Today's Reading II
1 Peter 2:4-9

> Beloved:
> Come to him, a living stone, rejected by human beings but chosen and
>   precious in the sight of God,
> and, like living stones,
> let yourselves be built into a spiritual house
> to be a holy priesthood to offer spiritual sacrifices acceptable to God
>   through Jesus Christ.
> For it says in Scripture:
> Behold, I am laying a stone in Zion, a cornerstone, chosen and precious,
> and whoever believes in it shall not be put to shame.
> Therefore, its value is for you who have faith, but for those without faith:
>   The stone that the builders rejected
> has become the cornerstone, and
> A stone that will make people stumble, and a rock that will make them
>   fall.
> They stumble by disobeying the word, as is their destiny.
>
> You are "a chosen race, a royal priesthood, a holy nation, a people of
>   his own,
> so that you may announce the praises" of him
> who called you out of darkness into his wonderful light.

Dear friends, like living stones, let yourselves be built into a spiritual house. You are far more precious than diamonds, sapphires, rubies and emeralds.

Blessings

SCRIPTURE NOTES

God morning, branches,

Today's Gospel
John 10:27-30

> Jesus said:
> "My sheep hear my voice;
> I know them, and they follow me.
> I give them eternal life, and they shall never perish.
> No one can take them out of my hand.
> My Father, who has given them to me, is greater than all,
> and no one can take them out of the Father's hand.
> The Father and I are one."

Dear friends, in a world where the noise and distractions seem to increase daily, it can sometimes require great effort to hear the Lord's voice and follow Him. We might not take or make the time to go to our private room to pray or reflect. I suggest that we might take a moment or three to hear the birds chirping early in the morning, listen to the rain, smell the roses or coffee, watch the clouds go by, listen to a child laugh, do a good deed or anything that keeps you in touch with Him. After all, He always protects us and has given us eternal life.

Blessings

God morning, branches,

Today's Reading II
John 4:7-10

> Beloved, let us love one another, because love is of God;

everyone who loves is begotten by God and knows God. Whoever is without love does not know God, for God is love. In this way the love of God was revealed to us:

God sent his only Son into the world so that we might have life through him. In this is love:

not that we have loved God, but that he loved us and sent his Son as expiation for our sins.

Dear friends, whoever is without love does not know God, for God is love. God has been removed from schools, work, public places and so on. Is it any wonder, then, why there are so many problems in the world? The evil one loves the increasingly loveless world.

Blessings

God morning, sisters and brothers,

Today's Reading 2
Romans 8:9, 11-13

Brothers and sisters: You are not in the flesh;
on the contrary, you are in the spirit,
if only the Spirit of God dwells in you.
Whoever does not have the Spirit of Christ does not belong to him. If the Spirit of the one who raised Jesus from the dead dwells in you, the one who raised Christ from the dead
will give life to your mortal bodies also, through his Spirit that dwells in you. Consequently, brothers and sisters,
we are not debtors to the flesh, to live according to the flesh.
For if you live according to the flesh, you will die,
but if by the Spirit you put to death the deeds of the body, you will live.

Dear friends, may we not be debtors to the flesh and live by the Spirit.

Blessings

God morning, branches,

Today's Reading 1
Deuteronomy 30:10-14

> Moses said to the people:
> "If only you would heed the voice of the LORD, your God,
> and keep his commandments and statutes
> that are written in this book of the law,
> when you return to the LORD, your God,
> with all your heart and all your soul.
>
> "For this command that I enjoin on you today
> is not too mysterious and remote for you.
> It is not up in the sky, that you should say,
> 'Who will go up in the sky to get it for us
> and tell us of it, that we may carry it out?'
> Nor is it across the sea, that you should say,
> 'Who will cross the sea to get it for us
> and tell us of it, that we may carry it out?'
> No, it is something very near to you,
> already in your mouths and in your hearts;
> you have only to carry it out."

Dear friends, God's commandments are not mysterious and remote. Indeed, they are quite clear and already in our mouths and hearts.

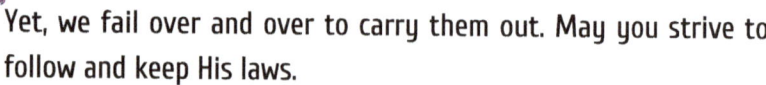

Yet, we fail over and over to carry them out. May you strive to follow and keep His laws.

Blessings

God morning, sisters and brothers,

Today's Reading 2
James 5:7-10

> Be patient, brothers and sisters,
> until the coming of the Lord.
> See how the farmer waits for the precious fruit of the earth,
> being patient with it
> until it receives the early and the late rains.
> You too must be patient.
> Make your hearts firm,
> because the coming of the Lord is at hand.
> Do not complain, brothers and sisters, about one another,
> that you may not be judged.
> Behold, the Judge is standing before the gates.
> Take as an example of hardship and patience, brothers and sisters,
> the prophets who spoke in the name of the Lord.

Dear friends, the world is quite hectic, especially around the holidays, and causes our patience to wear thin. May we have the patience of a farmer. I imagine you have heard of the patience of a saint.

Blessings

SCRIPTURE NOTES

God morning, branches,

Today's Alleluia
Ephesians 1:17-18

> R. Alleluia, alleluia.
> May the Father of our Lord Jesus Christ
> enlighten the eyes of our hearts,
> that we may know what is the hope that
> belongs to our call.
> R. Alleluia, alleluia.

Dear friends, may you pray for God to grant you the spirit of wisdom and revelation into a deeper and more intimate knowledge of Him so that you will have a continual revelation of Him and His ways, which will transform your lives. God wants us to know Him intimately, and because His ways are so unfathomable, He has given us the Holy Spirit to enable us to come into that continual revelation, or the communication of the knowledge of God to the soul.

Alleluia

God morning, branches,

Today's Reading 1
Sirach 15:15-20

> If you choose you can keep the commandments, they will save you; if
>   you trust in God, you too shall live;
> he has set before you fire and water

to whichever you choose, stretch forth your hand. Before man are life
and death, good and evil, whichever he chooses shall be given him.
Immense is the wisdom of the Lord;
he is mighty in power, and all-seeing.
The eyes of God are on those who fear him; he understands man's
every deed.
No one does he command to act unjustly, to none does he give license
to sin.

Dear friends, If you choose you can keep the commandments, they will save you. God does not force you to do anything. He rewards those who keep his commandments. Choose wisely.

Blessings

God morning, branches,

Today's Reading II
2 Cor 5:6-10

Brothers and sisters:
We are always courageous,
although we know that while we are at home in the body
we are away from the Lord,
for we walk by faith, not by sight.
Yet we are courageous,
and we would rather leave the body and go home to the Lord.
Therefore, we aspire to please him,
whether we are at home or away.
For we must all appear before the judgment seat of Christ,
so that each may receive recompense

according to what he did in the body, whether good or evil.

Dear friends, be mindful of your actions and words for we must all appear before the judgment seat of Christ, so that each may receive recompense, according to what he did in the body, whether good or evil. If you have done wrong, confess and seek forgiveness for you do not know the time of your judgment.

I imagine you have heard or used the phrase "we walk by faith, not by sight". Now you know its origin. Our lives should be guided by our faith in God's promise and guidance, not what we can physically see or understand. This is not easy, but He never said life would be so.

Blessings

God morning, sisters and brothers,

Today's Reading II
Phil 3:17-4:1

> Join with others in being imitators of me, brothers and sisters,
> and observe those who thus conduct themselves
> according to the model you have in us.
> For many, as I have often told you
> and now tell you even in tears,
> conduct themselves as enemies of the cross of Christ.
> Their end is destruction.
> Their God is their stomach;
> their glory is in their "shame."
> Their minds are occupied with earthly things.
> But our citizenship is in heaven,

and from it we also await a savior, the Lord Jesus Christ.
He will change our lowly body
to conform with his glorified body
by the power that enables him also
to bring all things into subjection to himself.

Therefore, my brothers and sisters,
whom I love and long for, my joy and crown,
in this way stand firm in the Lord.

Dear sisters and brothers, may our minds not be occupied with earthly things as our citizenship is in Heaven. Pass on the things and riches of this life for a heavenly future.

Blessings

God morning, branches,

Today's Reading 1
1 Kings 19:9a, 11-13a

At the mountain of God, Horeb,
Elijah came to a cave where he took shelter.
Then the LORD said to him,
"Go outside and stand on the mountain before the LORD;
the LORD will be passing by."
A strong and heavy wind was rending the mountains
and crushing rocks before the LORD—
but the LORD was not in the wind.
After the wind there was an earthquake—
but the LORD was not in the earthquake.
After the earthquake there was fire—

> but the LORD was not in the fire.
> After the fire there was a tiny whispering sound.
> When he heard this,
> Elijah hid his face in his cloak
> and went and stood at the entrance of the cave.

Dear friends, God is everywhere, but in this reading He did not speak to Elijah in the wind, earthquake or fire. He was a tiny whispering sound. Our world is busy and noisy; certainly He can make Himself heard above the din. Perhaps He wants to speak to us in a whisper to get us away from all the distractions the evil one places in our lives. May we make some time to be surrounded by quiet so that we may hear God whisper to us.

Blessings

God morning, branches,

Today's Gospel
Luke 21:5-19

> While some people were speaking about
> how the temple was adorned with costly stones and votive offerings,
> Jesus said, "All that you see here--
> the days will come when there will not be left
> a stone upon another stone that will not be thrown down."
>
> Then they asked him,
> "Teacher, when will this happen?
> And what sign will there be when all these things are about to happen?"
> He answered,
> "See that you not be deceived,

for many will come in my name, saying,
'I am he,' and 'The time has come.'
Do not follow them!
When you hear of wars and insurrections,
do not be terrified; for such things must happen first,
but it will not immediately be the end."

Then he said to them,
"Nation will rise against nation, and kingdom against kingdom.
There will be powerful earthquakes, famines, and plagues
from place to place;
and awesome sights and mighty signs will come from the sky.

"Before all this happens, however,
they will seize and persecute you,
they will hand you over to the synagogues and to prisons,
and they will have you led before kings and governors
because of my name.
It will lead to your giving testimony.
Remember, you are not to prepare your defense beforehand,
for I myself shall give you a wisdom in speaking
that all your adversaries will be powerless to resist or refute.
You will even be handed over by parents, brothers, relatives, and friends,
and they will put some of you to death.
You will be hated by all because of my name,
but not a hair on your head will be destroyed.
By your perseverance you will secure your lives."

Dear friends, consider that we are temples and we might at times be too prideful, which can distract us from God. Perhaps the temples could be our possessions. Jesus tells us not to put them ahead of

God as some day they will be gone. Jesus also tells us to beware of false prophets, who are everywhere on the internet and elsewhere. Finally, Jesus tells us we will be persecuted, even by our loved ones, because of His name. The Lord says do not worry because our faith and perseverance will secure our lives.

Blessings

God morning, sisters and brothers,

Today's Reading 2
Hebrews 12:1-4

> Brothers and sisters:
> Since we are surrounded by so great a cloud of witnesses, let us rid ourselves of every burden and sin that clings to us and persevere in running the race that lies before us
> while keeping our eyes fixed on Jesus, the leader and perfecter of faith. For the sake of the joy that lay before him he endured the cross, despising its shame,
> and has taken his seat at the right of the throne of God. Consider how he endured such opposition from sinners, in order that you may not grow weary and lose heart.
> In your struggle against sin
> you have not yet resisted to the point of shedding blood.

Dear friends, may we persevere in running the race that lies before us while keeping our eyes fixed on Jesus, the leader and perfecter of faith.

Blessings

SCRIPTURE NOTES

God morning, branches,

Today's Gospel
John 1:29-34

> John the Baptist saw Jesus coming toward him and said, "Behold, the Lamb of God, who takes away the sin of the world. He is the one of whom I said,
> 'A man is coming after me who ranks ahead of me because he existed before me.'
> I did not know him,
> but the reason why I came baptizing with water was that he might be made known to Israel." John testified further, saying,
> "I saw the Spirit come down like a dove from heaven and remain upon him.
> I did not know him,
> but the one who sent me to baptize with water told me, 'On whomever you see the Spirit come down and remain, he is the one who will baptize with the Holy Spirit.'
> Now I have seen and testified that he is the Son of God."

Dear friends, can you imagine how those who were there with John felt when John said, "Behold, the Lamb of God, who takes away the sin of the world and Now I have seen and testified that he is the Son of God."

I imagine we usually read the words in the Bible. I challenge you to try to experience them.

Blessings

SCRIPTURE NOTES

God morning, disciples,

Today's Gospel
John 2:1-11

There was a wedding at Cana in Galilee,
and the mother of Jesus was there.
Jesus and his disciples were also invited to the wedding.
When the wine ran short,
the mother of Jesus said to him,
"They have no wine."
And Jesus said to her,
"Woman, how does your concern affect me?
My hour has not yet come."
His mother said to the servers,
"Do whatever he tells you."
Now there were six stone water jars there for Jewish ceremonial washings,
each holding twenty to thirty gallons.
Jesus told them,
"Fill the jars with water."
So they filled them to the brim.
Then he told them,
"Draw some out now and take it to the headwaiter."
So they took it.
And when the headwaiter tasted the water that had become wine,
without knowing where it came from
– although the servers who had drawn the water knew –,
the headwaiter called the bridegroom and said to him,
"Everyone serves good wine first,
and then when people have drunk freely, an inferior one;
but you have kept the good wine until now."

*Jesus did this as the beginning of his signs at Cana in Galilee
and so revealed his glory,
and his disciples began to believe in him.*

Dear friends, many recall the story about Jesus changing water to wine (His first miracle in public). There are quite a few things to ponder in this Gospel. His mother sets the stage for the miracle. He says "My hour has not yet come." His mother knows a miracle is about to take place and tells the servers to "Do whatever he tells you." Imagine being a server seeing the water become wine. Imagine being the headwaiter who tastes the good wine. Imagine being the disciples watching all this taking place.

Yes, Jesus changed the water to wine. We "take this as gospel". We believe it to be true. Remember, the words in the Gospel are His words. I submit that when we ponder, reflect and question His words (or anything else) we may get closer to knowing and understanding. Consider we were created in His Divine Image and His Spirit dwells within us.

Blessings

God morning, disciples,

Today's Gospel
John 20:19-31

> On the evening of that first day of the week,
> when the doors were locked, where the disciples were, for fear of the Jews,
> Jesus came and stood in their midst and said to them, "Peace be with you."

When he had said this, he showed them his hands and his side. The
    disciples rejoiced when they saw the Lord.
Jesus said to them again, "Peace be with you. As the Father has sent
    me, so I send you."
And when he had said this, he breathed on them and said to them,
    "Receive the Holy Spirit.
Whose sins you forgive are forgiven them, and whose sins you retain
    are retained."

Thomas, called Didymus, one of the Twelve, was not with them when
    Jesus came.
So the other disciples said to him, "We have seen the Lord." But he said
    to them,
"Unless I see the mark of the nails in his hands and put my finger into
    the nailmarks
and put my hand into his side, I will not believe."

Now a week later his disciples were again inside and Thomas was with
    them.
Jesus came, although the doors were locked,
and stood in their midst and said, "Peace be with you."
Then he said to Thomas, "Put your finger here and see my hands, and
    bring your hand and put it into my side,
and do not be unbelieving, but believe."
Thomas answered and said to him, "My Lord and my God!"
Jesus said to him, "Have you come to believe because you have seen me?

Blessed are those who have not seen and have believed."

Now Jesus did many other signs in the presence of his disciples that are
    not written in this book.

But these are written that you may come to believe that Jesus is the
   Christ, the Son of God,
and that through this belief you may have life in his name.

Dear friends, we are blessed as we believe despite not having seen. We are not like doubting Thomas.
   Peace be with you.
Blessings

God morning, disciples,

Today's Gospel
Luke 18:1-8

Jesus told his disciples a parable
about the necessity for them to pray always without becoming weary.
He said, "There was a judge in a certain town
who neither feared God nor respected any human being.
And a widow in that town used to come to him and say,
'Render a just decision for me against my adversary.'
For a long time the judge was unwilling, but eventually he thought,
'While it is true that I neither fear God nor respect any human being,
because this widow keeps bothering me
I shall deliver a just decision for her
lest she finally come and strike me.'"
The Lord said, "Pay attention to what the dishonest judge says.
Will not God then secure the rights of his chosen ones
who call out to him day and night?
Will he be slow to answer them?
I tell you, he will see to it that justice is done for them speedily.

But when the Son of Man comes, will he find faith on earth?"

Dear friends, may we pray always without becoming weary.

Blessings

God morning, branches,

Today's Gospel
Luke 10:38-42

> Jesus entered a village
> where a woman whose name was Martha welcomed him.
> She had a sister named Mary
> who sat beside the Lord at his feet listening to him speak.
> Martha, burdened with much serving, came to him and said,
> "Lord, do you not care
> that my sister has left me by myself to do the serving?
> Tell her to help me."
> The Lord said to her in reply,
> "Martha, Martha, you are anxious and worried about many things.
> There is need of only one thing.
> Mary has chosen the better part
> and it will not be taken from her."

Dear friends, Martha was doing the things we are taught to do: be hospitable and serve the Lord. Jesus says say was doing good things, except that we are also taught to not be anxious or worry. Mary chose the better thing, which was to listen to and learn from the Lord.

In the past two days, I wrote that we should ponder and try to understand His words. May you choose the better thing.

Blessings

God morning, branches,

Today's Reading 2
Romans 1:1-7

> Paul, a slave of Christ Jesus,
> called to be an apostle and set apart for the gospel of God,
> which he promised previously through his prophets in the holy Scriptures,
> the gospel about his Son, descended from David according to the flesh,
> but established as Son of God in power
> according to the Spirit of holiness
> through resurrection from the dead, Jesus Christ our Lord.
> Through him we have received the grace of apostleship,
> to bring about the obedience of faith,
> for the sake of his name, among all the Gentiles,
> among whom are you also, who are called to belong to Jesus Christ;
> to all the beloved of God in Rome, called to be holy.
> Grace to you and peace from God our Father
> and the Lord Jesus Christ.

Dear friends, like Paul, we are servants of Christ Jesus and are called to bring the Good News to those we meet. Remember, actions speak louder than words. Grace to you and peace from God our Father and the Lord Jesus Christ.

Blessings

God morning, sisters and brothers,

Today's Reading 2
Ephesians 5:8-14

> Brothers and sisters:
> You were once darkness,
> but now you are light in the Lord.
> Live as children of light,
> for light produces every kind of goodness
> and righteousness and truth.
> Try to learn what is pleasing to the Lord.
> Take no part in the fruitless works of darkness;
> rather expose them, for it is shameful even to mention
> the things done by them in secret;
> but everything exposed by the light becomes visible,
> for everything that becomes visible is light.
> Therefore, it says:
> "Awake, O sleeper,
> and arise from the dead,
> and Christ will give you light."

Dear friends, may we take no part in the fruitless works of darkness, who is the evil one. May we show others the way to the light by our actions.

Blessings

God morning, branches,

Today's Reading 1
Isaiah 56:1, 6-7

SCRIPTURE NOTES

Thus says the LORD:
Observe what is right, do what is just;
for my salvation is about to come,
my justice, about to be revealed.

The foreigners who join themselves to the LORD,
ministering to him,
loving the name of the LORD,
and becoming his servants—
all who keep the sabbath free from profanation
and hold to my covenant,
them I will bring to my holy mountain
and make joyful in my house of prayer;
their burnt offerings and sacrifices
will be acceptable on my altar,
for my house shall be called
a house of prayer for all peoples.

Dear friends, may we observe what is right, do what is just.
Blessings

God morning, branches,

Today's Gospel
Luke 13:22-30

Jesus passed through towns and villages,
teaching as he went and making his way to Jerusalem.
Someone asked him,
"Lord, will only a few people be saved?"
He answered them,

SCRIPTURE NOTES

"Strive to enter through the narrow gate,
for many, I tell you, will attempt to enter
but will not be strong enough.
After the master of the house has arisen and locked the door,
then will you stand outside knocking and saying,
'Lord, open the door for us.'
He will say to you in reply,
'I do not know where you are from.
And you will say,
'We ate and drank in your company and you taught in our streets.'
Then he will say to you,
'I do not know where you are from.
Depart from me, all you evildoers!'
And there will be wailing and grinding of teeth
when you see Abraham, Isaac, and Jacob
and all the prophets in the kingdom of God
and you yourselves cast out.
And people will come from the east and the west
and from the north and the south
and will recline at table in the kingdom of God.
For behold, some are last who will be first,
and some are first who will be last."

Dear friends, may you strive to enter through the narrow gate. Notice there is another mention of the last and first.

Blessings

SCRIPTURE NOTES

God morning, branches,

Today's Reading 1
Genesis 11:1-9

> The whole world spoke the same language, using the same words. While the people were migrating in the east,
> they came upon a valley in the land of Shinar and settled there. They said to one another,
> "Come, let us mold bricks and harden them with fire." They used bricks for stone, and bitumen for mortar. Then they said, "Come, let us build ourselves a city and a tower with its top in the sky,
> and so make a name for ourselves;
> otherwise we shall be scattered all over the earth."
>
> The LORD came down to see the city and the tower that the people had built.
> Then the LORD said: "If now, while they are one people, all speaking the same language,
> they have started to do this,
> nothing will later stop them from doing whatever they presume to do. Let us then go down there and confuse their language,
> so that one will not understand what another says."
> Thus the LORD scattered them from there all over the earth, and they stopped building the city.
> That is why it was called Babel,
> because there the LORD confused the speech of all the world. It was from that place that he scattered them all over the earth.

Dear friends, apparently being scattered all over the earth and speaking different tongues has not stopped people from doing whatever they presume to do. The above reading might bring to mind an expression from a Proverb, "Pride goeth before the fall." Today, many are prideful and do whatever they presume to do. The enemy is having a field day with the prideful. Be careful not to set yourselves up for a calamitous fall.

Blessings

God morning, brothers and sisters,

Today's Reading II
1 John 3:1-2

> Beloved:
> See what love the Father has bestowed on us that we may be called the children of God. Yet so we are.
> The reason the world does not know us
> is that it did not know him.
> Beloved, we are God's children now;
> what we shall be has not yet been revealed.
> We do know that when it is revealed we shall be like him, for we shall see him as he is.

My dear brothers and sisters, we often describe ourselves in many ways. Have you ever described yourself as a child of God? First and foremost, you are and always will be a child of God. Think about The Lord's Prayer, which begins with Our Father. We are members of a divine family and should treat one another accordingly. If we did, perhaps "Thy will be done on earth as it is in heaven" would become a reality.

Blessings

God morning, brothers and sisters,

Today's Reading 1I
Eph 4:1-6

> Brothers and sisters:
> I, a prisoner for the Lord,
> urge you to live in a manner worthy of the call you have received, with
>   all humility and gentleness, with patience,
> bearing with one another through love,
> striving to preserve the unity of the spirit through the bond of peace:
>   one body and one Spirit,
> as you were also called to the one hope of your call; one Lord, one faith,
>   one baptism;
> one God and Father of all,
> who is over all and through all and in all.

May you always live this Reading.
Blessings

God morning, branches,

Today's Reading 2
1 Timothy 6:11-16

> But you, man of God, pursue righteousness,
> devotion, faith, love, patience, and gentleness.
> Compete well for the faith.
> Lay hold of eternal life, to which you were called
> when you made the noble confession in the presence of many witnesses. I
> charge you before God, who gives life to all things,

SCRIPTURE NOTES

and before Christ Jesus,
who gave testimony under Pontius Pilate for the noble confession,
to keep the commandment without stain or reproach
until the appearance of our Lord Jesus Christ
that the blessed and only ruler
will make manifest at the proper time,
the King of kings and Lord of lords,
who alone has immortality, who dwells in unapproachable light,
and whom no human being has seen or can see.
To him be honor and eternal power. Amen.

Dear friends, may we pursue righteousness, devotion, faith, love, patience, gentleness and compete well for the faith.

Blessings

God morning, ambassadors,

Today's Reading II
2 Corinthians 5:17-21

> Brothers and sisters:
> Whoever is in Christ is a new creation:
> the old things have passed away;
> behold, new things have come.
> And all this is from God,
> who has reconciled us to himself through Christ
> and given us the ministry of reconciliation,
> namely, God was reconciling the world to himself in Christ,
> not counting their trespasses against them
> and entrusting to us the message of reconciliation.

So we are ambassadors for Christ,
as if God were appealing through us.
We implore you on behalf of Christ,
be reconciled to God.
For our sake he made him to be sin who did not know sin,
so that we might become the righteousness of God in him.

Dear friends, we are ambassadors for Christ. May we act accordingly.

Blessings

God morning, brothers and sisters,

Today's Reading II
1 Thes 3:12—4:2

Brothers and sisters:
May the Lord make you increase and abound in love
for one another and for all,
just as we have for you,
so as to strengthen your hearts,
to be blameless in holiness before our God and Father
at the coming of our Lord Jesus with all his holy ones. Amen.

Finally, brothers and sisters,
we earnestly ask and exhort you in the Lord Jesus that,
as you received from us
how you should conduct yourselves to please God
and as you are conducting yourselves
you do so even more.
For you know what instructions we gave you through the Lord Jesus.

Dear friends, may you abound in love and conduct yourselves in ways that please our heavenly Father.

Blessings

God morning, brothers and sisters,

Today's Reading II
1 *Corinthians* 12:31–13:13

> Brothers and sisters:
> Strive eagerly for the greatest spiritual gifts. But I shall show you a still more excellent way.

If I speak in human and angelic tongues, but do not have love,
I am a resounding gong or a clashing cymbal. And if I have the gift of prophecy,
and comprehend all mysteries and all knowledge; if I have all faith so as to move mountains,
but do not have love, I am nothing. If I give away everything I own,
and if I hand my body over so that I may boast, but do not have love, I gain nothing.

Love is patient, love is kind.
It is not jealous, it is not pompous, It is not inflated, it is not rude,
it does not seek its own interests,
it is not quick-tempered, it does not brood over injury, it does not rejoice over wrongdoing
but rejoices with the truth.
It bears all things, believes all things, hopes all things, endures all things.

Love never fails.

If there are prophecies, they will be brought to nothing; if tongues, they
    will cease;
if knowledge, it will be brought to nothing.
For we know partially and we prophesy partially,
but when the perfect comes, the partial will pass away. When I was a
    child, I used to talk as a child,
think as a child, reason as a child;

when I became a man, I put aside childish things.
At present we see indistinctly, as in a mirror,
but then face to face.
At present I know partially;
then I shall know fully, as I am fully known.
So faith, hope, love remain, these three;
but the greatest of these is love.

Dear friends, love is the excellent way. God is love and we were created in His Divine Image.

Love

God morning, disciples,

Today's Gospel
Mt 28:16-20

    The eleven disciples went to Galilee,
    to the mountain to which Jesus had ordered them.
    When they all saw him, they worshiped, but they doubted.
    Then Jesus approached and said to them,
    "All power in heaven and on earth has been given to me.
    Go, therefore, and make disciples of all nations,

baptizing them in the name of the Father,
and of the Son, and of the Holy Spirit,
teaching them to observe all that I have commanded you.
And behold, I am with you always, until the end of the age."

Dear friends, like the eleven, we are called to spread the Good News. Remember actions speak louder than words. May you follow the Spirit's guidance. If and when you are doubtful, as were the eleven, know that Jesus is with you always.

Alleluia

God morning, sisters and brothers,

Today's Reading 2
2 Thes 1:11-2:2

> Brothers and sisters:
> We always pray for you,
> that our God may make you worthy of his calling
> and powerfully bring to fulfillment every good purpose and every effort
>   of faith,
> that the name of our Lord Jesus may be glorified in you, and you in him,
> in accord with the grace of our God and Lord Jesus Christ.
>
> We ask you, brothers and sisters,
> with regard to the coming of our Lord Jesus Christ
> and our assembling with him,
> not to be shaken out of your minds suddenly, or to be alarmed
> either by a "spirit," or by an oral statement,
> or by a letter allegedly from us
> to the effect that the day of the Lord is at hand.

SCRIPTURE NOTES

Dear friends, may God make us worthy of His calling and powerfully bring to fulfillment every good purpose and every effort of faith.

Blessings

God morning, branches,

Today's Gospel
Luke 12:13-21

> Someone in the crowd said to Jesus,
> "Teacher, tell my brother to share the inheritance with me."
> He replied to him,
> "Friend, who appointed me as your judge and arbitrator?"
> Then he said to the crowd,
> "Take care to guard against all greed,
> for though one may be rich,
> one's life does not consist of possessions."
>
> Then he told them a parable.
> "There was a rich man whose land produced a bountiful harvest.
> He asked himself, 'What shall I do,
> for I do not have space to store my harvest?'
> And he said, 'This is what I shall do:
> I shall tear down my barns and build larger ones.
> There I shall store all my grain and other goods
> and I shall say to myself, "Now as for you,
> you have so many good things stored up for many years,
> rest, eat, drink, be merry!"'
> But God said to him,
> 'You fool, this night your life will be demanded of you;

and the things you have prepared, to whom will they belong?'
Thus will it be for all who store up treasure for themselves but
are not rich in what matters to God."

Dear friends, may we take care to guard against all greed as one's life does not consist of possessions. There is no Brink's truck behind the hearse. May we not store up riches for ourselves and be rich in what matters to God.

Blessings

God morning, branches,

Today's Gospel
Luke 15:1–10

> The tax collectors and sinners were all drawing near to listen to Jesus,
> but the Pharisees and scribes began to complain, saying,
> "This man welcomes sinners and eats with them."
> So Jesus addressed this parable to them.
> "What man among you having a hundred sheep and losing one of them
> would not leave the ninety-nine in the desert
> and go after the lost one until he finds it?
> And when he does find it,
> he sets it on his shoulders with great joy
> and, upon his arrival home,
> he calls together his friends and neighbors and says to them,
> 'Rejoice with me because I have found my lost sheep.'
> I tell you, in just the same way
> there will be more joy in heaven over one sinner who repents
> than over ninety-nine righteous people

who have no need of repentance.
"Or what woman having ten coins and losing one
would not light a lamp and sweep the house,
searching carefully until she finds it?
And when she does find it,
she calls together her friends and neighbors
and says to them,
'Rejoice with me because I have found the coin that I lost.'
In just the same way, I tell you,
there will be rejoicing among the angels of God
over one sinner who repents."

Dear friends, may your words and actions lead a sinner to repent and cause the angels to rejoice.

Blessings

God morning, disciples,

Today's Gospel
Matthew 16:13-23

Jesus went into the region of Caesarea Philippi
and he asked his disciples,
"Who do people say that the Son of Man is?"
They replied, "Some say John the Baptist, others Elijah,
still others Jeremiah or one of the prophets."
He said to them, "But who do you say that I am?"
Simon Peter said in reply,
"You are the Christ, the Son of the living God."
Jesus said to him in reply, "Blessed are you, Simon son of Jonah.

For flesh and blood has not revealed this to you, but my heavenly Father.
And so I say to you, you are Peter,
and upon this rock I will build my Church,
and the gates of the netherworld shall not prevail against it.
I will give you the keys to the Kingdom of heaven.
Whatever you bind on earth shall be bound in heaven;
and whatever you loose on earth shall be loosed in heaven."
Then he strictly ordered his disciples
to tell no one that he was the Christ.

From that time on, Jesus began to show his disciples
that he must go to Jerusalem and suffer greatly
from the elders, the chief priests, and the scribes,
and be killed and on the third day be raised.
Then Peter took Jesus aside and began to rebuke him,
"God forbid, Lord! No such thing shall ever happen to you."
He turned and said to Peter,
"Get behind me, Satan! You are an obstacle to me.
You are thinking not as God does, but as human beings do."

Dear friends, who do you say the Son of Man is? You might be quick to respond. Perhaps the response is like a reflex action. Maybe a word or phrase said by rote. Some may answer with a question. Others may answer what they hope He is. Some may answer what they want Him to be. Peter replied "You are the Christ, the Son of the living God." I submit those are not just words, but truth. Do you, think, believe or know?

Blessings

God morning, branches,

Today's Reading 1
1 John 3:11-21

Beloved:
This is the message you have heard from the beginning: we should love one another,
unlike Cain who belonged to the Evil One and slaughtered his brother.
Why did he slaughter him? Because his own works were evil, and those of his brother righteous.
Do not be amazed, then, brothers and sisters, if the world hates you. We know that we have passed from death to life
because we love our brothers.
Whoever does not love remains in death. Everyone who hates his brother is a murderer,
and you know that no murderer has eternal life remaining in him. The way we came to know love
was that he laid down his life for us;
so we ought to lay down our lives for our brothers. If someone who has worldly means
sees a brother in need and refuses him compassion, how can the love of God remain in him?
Children, let us love not in word or speech but in deed and truth.

Now this is how we shall know that we belong to the truth and reassure our hearts before him
in whatever our hearts condemn,
for God is greater than our hearts and knows everything. Beloved, if our hearts do not condemn us,
we have confidence in God.

SCRIPTURE NOTES

Dear friends, we know there is so much evil in our world. We also know bad news is good for the print and electronic media. I imagine you have heard of Damar Hamlin, the young football player who went into cardiac arrest while playing football on Monday night. The outpouring of prayers, love and financial assistance is quite heartwarming. Truly, many have expressed love through their actions. Let us pray for Damar and that we continue to love one another.

Blessings

God morning, disciples,

Today's Gospel
Luke 11:5-13

Jesus said to his disciples:

> "Suppose one of you has a friend
> to whom he goes at midnight and says,
> 'Friend, lend me three loaves of bread,
> for a friend of mine has arrived at my house from a journey
> and I have nothing to offer him,'
> and he says in reply from within,
> 'Do not bother me; the door has already been locked
> and my children and I are already in bed.
> I cannot get up to give you anything.'
> I tell you, if he does not get up to give him the loaves
> because of their friendship,
> he will get up to give him whatever he needs
> because of his persistence.
> "And I tell you, ask and you will receive;

seek and you will find;
knock and the door will be opened to you.
For everyone who asks, receives;
and the one who seeks, finds;
and to the one who knocks, the door will be opened.
What father among you would hand his son a snake
when he asks for a fish?
Or hand him a scorpion when he asks for an egg?
If you then, who are wicked,
know how to give good gifts to your children,
how much more will the Father in heaven give the Holy Spirit
to those who ask him?"

Dear friends, I imagine many (most?) of us have struggled with the problem of unanswered prayer. I think God answers our prayers in His time and he knows what is best for us. We may ask for the wrong thing, but we will receive what we need, rather than what we want. May we be persistent in asking, seeking and knocking.

Blessings

God morning, branches,

Today's Gospel
Matthew 10:7-15

Jesus said to his Apostles:

> "As you go, make this proclamation: 'The Kingdom of heaven is at hand.'
> Cure the sick, raise the dead,
> cleanse the lepers, drive out demons.

> *Without cost you have received; without cost you are to give. Do not take gold or silver or copper for your belts;*
> *no sack for the journey, or a second tunic, or sandals, or walking stick. The laborer deserves his keep.*
> *Whatever town or village you enter, look for a worthy person in it, and stay there until you leave.*
> *As you enter a house, wish it peace. If the house is worthy,*
> *let your peace come upon it;*
> *if not, let your peace return to you.*
> *Whoever will not receive you or listen to your words--*
> *go outside that house or town and shake the dust from your feet. Amen, I say to you, it will be more tolerable*
> *for the land of Sodom and Gomorrah on the day of judgment than for that town."*

Dear friends, without cost you have received; without cost you are to give. God gives His word, love, mercy, grace and forgiveness to us freely and abundantly. Jesus says what we have received without cost, we are to give likewise. Do not let the adversary keep you from doing so. Sounds simple, right?

Blessings

God morning, branches,

Today's Gospel
John 12:24-26

> Jesus said to his disciples: "Amen, amen, I say to you,
> unless a grain of wheat falls to the ground and dies, it remains just a grain of wheat;

but if it dies, it produces much fruit. Whoever loves his life loses it,
and whoever hates his life in this world will preserve it for eternal life.
Whoever serves me must follow me,
and where I am, there also will my servant be. The Father will honor whoever serves me."

Dear friends, it is said that life is a precious gift. Yes, this life is precious and I think the next one is far beyond our understanding. It must be beyond wonderful. I also think the evil one makes sure we get enough things in this life to try to distract us from the next life. I wonder if we own our possessions or if they own us. May we focus on our next life in Heaven with Jesus and our Father.

Blessings

God morning, branches,

Today's Gospel
Mark 7:24-30

Jesus went to the district of Tyre.
He entered a house and wanted no one to know about it,
but he could not escape notice.
Soon a woman whose daughter had an unclean spirit heard about him.
She came and fell at his feet.
The woman was a Greek, a Syrophoenician by birth,
and she begged him to drive the demon out of her daughter.
He said to her, "Let the children be fed first.
For it is not right to take the food of the children
and throw it to the dogs."
She replied and said to him,

"Lord, even the dogs under the table eat the children's scraps."
Then he said to her, "For saying this, you may go.
The demon has gone out of your daughter."
When the woman went home, she found the child lying in bed and the demon gone.

Dear friends, what a wonderful story about the power of faith and prayer. The prayers of a woman who was not part of the tribe of Jesus were answered. Can you imagine what she was thinking on her way home and when she saw her daughter cured of the demon. May this story increase your power of faith and prayer. May it also be a reminder of how to treat those who are different from us.

Blessings

God morning, brothers and sisters,

Today's Gospel
Matthew 7:7-12

> Jesus said to his disciples:
> "Ask and it will be given to you; seek and you will find;
> knock and the door will be opened to you.
> For everyone who asks, receives; and the one who seeks, finds; and to
>   the one who knocks, the door will be opened.
> Which one of you would hand his son a stone when he asked for a loaf
>   of bread,
> or a snake when he asked for a fish? If you then, who are wicked,
> know how to give good gifts to your children,
> how much more will your heavenly Father give good things to those
>   who ask him.

> "Do to others whatever you would have them do to you. This is the law and the prophets."

Dear friends, may you do as the Lord says and follow the golden rule. Wouldn't it be wonderful if many did so?

Blessings

God morning, branches,

Today's Reading I
Wisdom 7:22b–8:1

> In Wisdom is a spirit intelligent, holy, unique,
> Manifold, subtle, agile, clear, unstained, certain,
> Not baneful, loving the good, keen, unhampered, beneficent, kindly,
> Firm, secure, tranquil,
> all-powerful, all-seeing, And pervading all spirits,
> though they be intelligent, pure and very subtle. For Wisdom is mobile beyond all motion,
> and she penetrates and pervades all things by reason of her purity. For she is an aura of the might of God
> and a pure effusion of the glory of the Almighty; therefore nought that is sullied enters into her.
> For she is the refulgence of eternal light, the spotless mirror of the power of God, the image of his goodness.
> And she, who is one, can do all things,
> and renews everything while herself perduring; And passing into holy souls from age to age,
> she produces friends of God and prophets.

> For there is nought God loves, be it not one who dwells with Wisdom.
>> For she is fairer than the sun
> and surpasses every constellation of the stars. Compared to light, she takes precedence;
> for that, indeed, night supplants,
> but wickedness prevails not over Wisdom.
>
> Indeed, she reaches from end to end mightily and governs all things well.

Dear friends, the spirit of Wisdom is intelligent and holy. It is of one nature but reveals itself in many ways. It is not made of any material substance, and it moves about freely. It is clear, clean, and confident; it cannot be harmed. It loves what is good. It is sharp and unconquerable, kind, and a friend of humanity. It is dependable and sure, and has no worries. It has power over everything, and sees everything. It penetrates every spirit that is intelligent and pure, no matter how delicate its substance may be. (Source: Biblegateway)

May your spirit be intelligent and pure.

Blessings

God morning, branches,

Today's Reading II
Revelation 1:5-8

> Jesus Christ is the faithful witness,
> the firstborn of the dead and ruler of the kings of the earth.
> To him who loves us and has freed us from our sins by his blood,
> who has made us into a kingdom, priests for his God and Father,
> to him be glory and power forever and ever. Amen.
> Behold, he is coming amid the clouds,

and every eye will see him,
even those who pierced him.
All the peoples of the earth will lament him.
Yes. Amen.

"I am the Alpha and the Omega, " says the Lord God,
"the one who is and who was and who is to come, the almighty."

Dear friends, I imagine some of us have thought we are the Alpha and Omega. Jesus is the beginning and the end. We fit in the middle and must look to Him for the reason we exist. All that we do should be for His glory.

Blessings

God morning, branches,

Today, we celebrate Memorial of Our Lady of Sorrows. *Stabat Mater*

At the cross her station keeping, Stood the mournful Mother weeping, Close to Jesus to the last.

Through her heart, his sorrow sharing, All his bitter anguish bearing, Now at length the sword had passed.

Oh, how sad and sore distressed Was that Mother highly blessed Of the sole begotten One!

Christ above in torment hangs, She beneath beholds the pangs Of her dying, glorious Son.

Is there one who would not weep, 'Whelmed in miseries so deep, Christ's dear Mother to behold?

Can the human heart refrain From partaking in her pain, In that mother's pain untold?

Bruised, derided, cursed, defiled, She beheld her tender Child,
All with bloody scourges rent.

For the sins of his own nation Saw him hang in desolation Till his spirit forth he sent.

O sweet Mother! font of love,
Touch my spirit from above, Make my heart with yours accord.

Make me feel as you have felt; Make my soul to glow and melt With the love of Christ, my Lord.

Holy Mother, pierce me through, In my heart each wound renew Of my Savior crucified.

Let me share with you his pain, Who for all our sins was slain, Who for me in torments died.

Let me mingle tears with you, Mourning him who mourned for me, All the days that I may live.

By the cross with you to stay, There with you to weep and pray, Is all I ask of you to give.

Virgin of all virgins blest! Listen to my fond request:
Let me share your grief divine.

Let me to my latest breath, In my body bear the death Of that dying Son of yours.

Wounded with his every wound, Steep my soul till it has swooned In his very Blood away.

SCRIPTURE NOTES

Be to me, O Virgin, nigh, Lest in flames I burn and die, In his awful judgment day.

Christ, when you shall call me hence, Be your Mother my defense, Be your cross my victory.

While my body here decays,
May my soul your goodness praise, Safe in heaven eternally.

Amen. (Alleluia)

Blessings

God morning, branches,

Today's Gospel
Matthew 18:21–19:1

Peter approached Jesus and asked him, "Lord, if my brother sins against me, how often must I forgive him?
As many as seven times?"
Jesus answered, "I say to you, not seven times but seventy-seven times. That is why the Kingdom of heaven may be likened to a king
who decided to settle accounts with his servants. When he began the accounting,
a debtor was brought before him who owed him a huge amount. Since he had no way of paying it back,
his master ordered him to be sold,
along with his wife, his children, and all his property, in payment of the debt.
At that, the servant fell down, did him homage, and said, 'Be patient with me, and I will pay you back in full.' Moved with compassion the master of that servant

let him go and forgave him the loan.

When that servant had left, he found one of his fellow servants who owed him a much smaller amount.

He seized him and started to choke him, demanding, 'Pay back what you owe.'

Falling to his knees, his fellow servant begged him, 'Be patient with me, and I will pay you back.'

But he refused.

Instead, he had the fellow servant put in prison until he paid back the debt.

Now when his fellow servants saw what had happened, they were deeply disturbed,

and went to their master and reported the whole affair.

His master summoned him and said to him, 'You wicked servant! I forgave you your entire debt because you begged me to.

Should you not have had pity on your fellow servant, as I had pity on you?'

Then in anger his master handed him over to the torturers until he should pay back the whole debt.

So will my heavenly Father do to you,

unless each of you forgives his brother from his heart."

When Jesus finished these words, he left Galilee and went to the district of Judea across the Jordan.

Dear friends, God is all merciful and forgiving to us, should we not be likewise to others?

Blessings

SCRIPTURE NOTES

God morning, branches,

Today's Gospel
Luke 7:36–50

A certain Pharisee invited Jesus to dine with him,
and he entered the Pharisee's house and reclined at table. Now there was a sinful woman in the city
who learned that he was at table in the house of the Pharisee. Bringing an alabaster flask of ointment,
she stood behind him at his feet weeping and began to bathe his feet with her tears. Then she wiped them with her hair,
kissed them, and anointed them with the ointment.
When the Pharisee who had invited him saw this he said to himself, "If this man were a prophet,
he would know who and what sort of woman this is who is touching him, that she is a sinner."
Jesus said to him in reply,
"Simon, I have something to say to you." "Tell me, teacher," he said.
"Two people were in debt to a certain creditor;
one owed five hundred days' wages and the other owed fifty. Since they were unable to repay the debt, he forgave it for both. Which of them will love him more?"
Simon said in reply,
"The one, I suppose, whose larger debt was forgiven." He said to him, "You have judged rightly."
Then he turned to the woman and said to Simon, "Do you see this woman?
When I entered your house, you did not give me water for my feet, but she has bathed them with her tears
and wiped them with her hair. You did not give me a kiss,

but she has not ceased kissing my feet since the time I entered. You did not anoint my head with oil,
but she anointed my feet with ointment.
So I tell you, her many sins have been forgiven; hence, she has shown great love.
But the one to whom little is forgiven, loves little."

He said to her, "Your sins are forgiven." The others at table said to themselves, "Who is this who even forgives sins?" But he said to the woman,
"Your faith has saved you; go in peace."

May your faith be as strong as that of the woman in the above Gospel.

Peace

God morning, brothers and sisters,

Today's Reading I
James 2:1-9

> My brothers and sisters, show no partiality
> as you adhere to the faith in our glorious Lord Jesus Christ. For if a man with gold rings and fine clothes
> comes into your assembly,
> and a poor person with shabby clothes also comes in, and you pay attention to the one wearing the fine clothes and say, "Sit here, please,"
> while you say to the poor one, "Stand there," or "Sit at my feet," have you not made distinctions among yourselves
> and become judges with evil designs?

SCRIPTURE NOTES

> Listen, my beloved brothers and sisters.
> Did not God choose those who are poor in the world to be rich in faith
> and heirs of the Kingdom
> that he promised to those who love him? But you dishonored the poor.
> Are not the rich oppressing you?
> And do they themselves not haul you off to court?
> Is it not they who blaspheme the noble name that was invoked over
> you? However, if you fulfill the royal law according to the Scripture,
> You shall love your neighbor as yourself, you are doing well. But if you
> show partiality, you commit sin,
> and are convicted by the law as transgressors.

Dear friends, may you not show partiality and judge others. May you love your neighbor as yourself.

Blessings

God morning, branches,

Today's Gospel
Luke 16:19–31

> Jesus said to the Pharisees:
> "There was a rich man who dressed in purple garments and fine linen
> and dined sumptuously each day.
> And lying at his door was a poor man named Lazarus, covered with sores,
> who would gladly have eaten his fill of the scraps
> that fell from the rich man's table.
> Dogs even used to come and lick his sores.
> When the poor man died,
> he was carried away by angels to the bosom of Abraham.

*The rich man also died and was buried,
and from the netherworld, where he was in torment,
he raised his eyes and saw Abraham far off
and Lazarus at his side.
And he cried out, 'Father Abraham, have pity on me.
Send Lazarus to dip the tip of his finger in water and cool my tongue,
for I am suffering torment in these flames.'
Abraham replied, 'My child,
remember that you received what was good during your lifetime
while Lazarus likewise received what was bad;
but now he is comforted here, whereas you are tormented.
Moreover, between us and you a great chasm is established
to prevent anyone from crossing
who might wish to go from our side to yours
or from your side to ours.'
He said, 'Then I beg you, father, send him
to my father's house,
for I have five brothers, so that he may warn them,
lest they too come to this place of torment.'
But Abraham replied, 'They have Moses and the prophets.
Let them listen to them.'
He said, 'Oh no, father Abraham,
but if someone from the dead goes to them, they will repent.'
Then Abraham said,
'If they will not listen to Moses and the prophets,
neither will they be persuaded
if someone should rise from the dead.'"*

Dear friends, The Bible is full of great stories, many of which could be called mysteries. A rich man dies and is tormented in the netherworld. He pleads for a dead man, who is on the other side, to be sent to warn his brothers so that they may repent to avoid the place of torment. Abraham responds they did not listen to Moses and the prophets, neither will they be persuaded if someone should rise from the dead. To whom was Abraham referring when he said someone rising from the dead?

Blessings

God morning, branches,

> Yet you do not know what tomorrow will bring. What is your life? For you are a mist that appears for a little time and then vanishes.
> *James 4:14*

Dear friends,

The Dash Poem by Linda Ellis

I read of a man who stood to speak
At the funeral of a friend
He referred to the dates on the tombstone
From the beginning...to the end

He noted that first came the date of birth
And spoke the following date with tears,
But he said what mattered most of all
Was the dash between those years

For that dash represents all the time
That they spent alive on earth.
And now only those who loved them
Know what that little line is worth

For it matters not, how much we own,
The cars...the house...the cash.
What matters is how we live and love
And how we spend our dash.

So, think about this long and hard.
Are there things you'd like to change?
For you never know how much time is left
That can still be rearranged.

If we could just slow down enough
To consider what's true and real
And always try to understand
The way other people feel.

And be less quick to anger

And show appreciation more
And love the people in our lives
Like we've never loved before.

If we treat each other with respect
And more often wear a smile,
Remembering this special dash
Might only last a little while

So, when your eulogy is being read
With your life's actions to rehash...
Would you be proud of the things they say
About how you spent YOUR dash?

Blessings

God morning, disciples,

Today's Gospel
Luke 24:35–48

> The disciples of Jesus recounted what had taken place along the way, and how they had come to recognize him in the breaking of bread.
>
> While they were still speaking about this, he stood in their midst and said to them, "Peace be with you."
> But they were startled and terrified
> and thought that they were seeing a ghost. Then he said to them, "Why are you troubled? And why do questions arise in your hearts?
> Look at my hands and my feet, that it is I myself.
> Touch me and see, because a ghost does not have flesh and bones as you can see I have."
> And as he said this,
> he showed them his hands and his feet.
> While they were still incredulous for joy and were amazed, he asked them, "Have you anything here to eat?"
> They gave him a piece of baked fish; he took it and ate it in front of them.
>
> He said to them,
> "These are my words that I spoke to you while I was still with you, that everything written about me in the law of Moses
> and in the prophets and psalms must be fulfilled."
> Then he opened their minds to understand the Scriptures. And he said to them,
> "Thus it is written that the Christ would suffer and rise from the dead on the third day
> and that repentance, for the forgiveness of sins, would be preached in his name

to all the nations, beginning from Jerusalem. You are witnesses of these things."

Dear friends, I struggle quite often with trying to understand Scripture and I imagine I am not alone with this struggle. Jesus appeared to His disciples and they were startled and terrified despite having spent years at His side learning and witnessing. Imagine learning from Him and still not understanding. This reminded me of the saying "For my thoughts are not your thoughts, neither are your ways my ways," (Isaiah 55:8). Now think about the line "Then he opened their minds to understand the Scriptures."

May we ponder His words and pray He opens our minds to understand the Scriptures.

Blessings

God morning, branches.

Today's Reading 1
Ecclesiastes 1:2-11

> Vanity of vanities, says Qoheleth,
> vanity of vanities! All things are vanity!
> What profit has man from all the labor
> which he toils at under the sun?
> One generation passes and another comes,
> but the world forever stays.
> The sun rises and the sun goes down;
> then it presses on to the place where it rises.
> Blowing now toward the south, then toward the north,
> the wind turns again and again, resuming its rounds.

SCRIPTURE NOTES

*All rivers go to the sea,
yet never does the sea become full.
To the place where they go,
the rivers keep on going.
All speech is labored;
there is nothing one can say.
The eye is not satisfied with seeing
nor is the ear satisfied with hearing.*

*What has been, that will be;
what has been done, that will be done.
Nothing is new under the sun.
Even the thing of which we say, "See, this is new!"
has already existed in the ages that preceded us.
There is no remembrance of the men of old;
nor of those to come will there be any remembrance
among those who come after them.*

Dear friends, the word "Ecclesiastes" is a Greek translation of the original Hebrew title of the book, Qoheleth (ko-HEHL-ehth), a word which means "Teacher", one who conducts an assembly or a school. The Greek word for 'assembly' is 'ekklesia'. This reading teaches wisdom by highlighting the emptiness of most human pursuits, all is vanity. The theme of the whole book is expressed in the opening words of today's reading: "All is vanity." The original meaning of the Hebrew word translated 'vanity' was 'mist' or 'breath'. It is one of the traditional group of images (water, shadow, smoke, etc.) used in Hebrew poetry to describe the transitory nature of human life. The basic thrust of Ecclesiastes is that all of life is meaningless, useless, hollow, futile and vain if it is not rightly related to God. Only when based on God and His Word is life worthwhile.

SCRIPTURE NOTES

May our lives be based on God and His Word.

By the way, some of Shakespeare's works draw from the Bible, including Ecclesiastes.

Blessings

God morning, branches,

Today's Gospel
Luke 11:14-23

> Jesus was driving out a demon that was mute,
> and when the demon had gone out,
> the mute man spoke and the crowds were amazed.
> Some of them said, "By the power of Beelzebul, the prince of demons,
> he drives out demons."
> Others, to test him, asked him for a sign from heaven.
> But he knew their thoughts and said to them,
> "Every kingdom divided against itself will be laid waste
> and house will fall against house.
> And if Satan is divided against himself,
> how will his kingdom stand?
> For you say that it is by Beelzebul that I drive out demons.
> If I, then, drive out demons by Beelzebul,
> by whom do your own people drive them out?
> Therefore they will be your judges.
> But if it is by the finger of God that I drive out demons,
> then the Kingdom of God has come upon you.
> When a strong man fully armed guards his palace,
> his possessions are safe.
> But when one stronger than he attacks and overcomes him,

he takes away the armor on which he relied
and distributes the spoils.
Whoever is not with me is against me,
and whoever does not gather with me scatters."

Dear friends, may you be with Jesus and gather others to be with Him.

President Abraham Lincoln's famous House Divided speech begins with "A house divided against itself cannot stand."

Blessings

God morning, brothers and sisters,

Today's Reading I
Romans 6:19-23

Brothers and sisters:
I am speaking in human terms because of the weakness of your nature.
For just as you presented the parts of your bodies as slaves to impurity and to lawlessness for lawlessness,
so now present them as slaves to righteousness for sanctification.
For when you were slaves of sin, you were free from righteousness.
But what profit did you get then
from the things of which you are now ashamed?
For the end of those things is death.
But now that you have been freed from sin and have become slaves of God,
the benefit that you have leads to sanctification,
and its end is eternal life.
For the wages of sin is death,

but the gift of God is eternal life in Christ Jesus our Lord.

Dear friends, while Jesus freed us from sin, our human condition can cause us to be weak. I imagine many of us struggle with impurities more than we would like. The evil one preys on our weaknesses. I pray that we succeed in becoming slaves to righteousness and God.

Blessings

God morning, disciples,

Today's Gospel
Matthew 24:42-51

> Jesus said to his disciples:
> "Stay awake!
> For you do not know on which day your Lord will come.
> Be sure of this: if the master of the house
> had known the hour of night when the thief was coming,
> he would have stayed awake
> and not let his house be broken into.
> So too, you also must be prepared,
> for at an hour you do not expect, the Son of Man will come.
>
> "Who, then, is the faithful and prudent servant,
> whom the master has put in charge of his household
> to distribute to them their food at the proper time?
> Blessed is that servant whom his master on his arrival finds doing so.
> Amen, I say to you, he will put him in charge of all his property.
> But if that wicked servant says to himself, 'My master is long delayed,'
> and begins to beat his fellow servants,
> and eat and drink with drunkards,

the servant's master will come on an unexpected day
and at an unknown hour and will punish him severely
and assign him a place with the hypocrites,
where there will be wailing and grinding of teeth."

Dear friends, are you prepared to meet Jesus? Remember, He may come at any time.

Blessings

God morning, branches,

Today's Reading II
Acts 13:22-26

> In those days, Paul said:
> "God raised up David as king;
> of him God testified,
> I have found David, son of Jesse, a man after my own heart;
> he will carry out my every wish.
> From this man's descendants God, according to his promise,
> has brought to Israel a savior, Jesus.
> John heralded his coming by proclaiming a baptism of repentance
> to all the people of Israel;
> and as John was completing his course, he would say,
> 'What do you suppose that I am? I am not he.
> Behold, one is coming after me;
> I am not worthy to unfasten the sandals of his feet.'
>
> "My brothers, sons of the family of Abraham,
> and those others among you who are God-fearing,
> to us this word of salvation has been sent."

SCRIPTURE NOTES

Dear friends, I am sure you have heard and maybe used the expression "a man after my own heart".

Blessings

God morning, branches,

Today's Gospel
John 1:45-51

> Philip found Nathanael and told him,
> "We have found the one about whom Moses wrote in the law, and also the prophets, Jesus son of Joseph, from Nazareth." But Nathanael said to him,
> "Can anything good come from Nazareth?" Philip said to him, "Come and see."
> Jesus saw Nathanael coming toward him and said of him, "Here is a true child of Israel.
> There is no duplicity in him."
> Nathanael said to him, "How do you know me?" Jesus answered and said to him,
> "Before Philip called you, I saw you under the fig tree." Nathanael answered him,
> "Rabbi, you are the Son of God; you are the King of Israel." Jesus answered and said to him,
> "Do you believe
> because I told you that I saw you under the fig tree? You will see greater things than this."
> And he said to him, "Amen, amen, I say to you, you will see heaven opened and the angels of God ascending and descending on the Son of Man."

Dear friends, can you imagine how you would feel if Philip said to you "We have found the one about whom Moses wrote in the law, and also the prophets, Jesus son of Joseph, from Nazareth." What if you are here when He returns? May your actions introduce others to Jesus.

Blessings

God morning, disciples,

Today's Gospel
Mt 24:42-51

> Jesus said to his disciples: "Stay awake!
> For you do not know on which day your Lord will come. Be sure of this:
>> if the master of the house
> had known the hour of night when the thief was coming, he would have
>> stayed awake
> and not let his house be broken into. So too, you also must be prepared, for at an hour you do not expect, the Son of Man will come.
>
> "Who, then, is the faithful and prudent servant, whom the master has
>> put in charge of his household to distribute to them their food at the proper time?
> Blessed is that servant whom his master on his arrival finds doing so.
>> Amen, I say to you, he will put him in charge of all his property.
> But if that wicked servant says to himself, 'My master is long delayed,'
>> and begins to beat his fellow servants,
> and eat and drink with drunkards,

> the servant's master will come on an unexpected day and at an unknown hour and will punish him severely and assign him a place with the hypocrites,
> where there will be wailing and grinding of teeth."

Dear friends, are you ready? Stay awake!

Blessings

God morning, disciples,

Today's Gospel
Matthew 23:1-12

> Jesus spoke to the crowds and to his disciples, saying,
> "The scribes and the Pharisees
> have taken their seat on the chair of Moses.
> Therefore, do and observe all things whatsoever they tell you,
> but do not follow their example.
> For they preach but they do not practice.
> They tie up heavy burdens hard to carry
> and lay them on people's shoulders,
> but they will not lift a finger to move them.
> All their works are performed to be seen.
> They widen their phylacteries and lengthen their tassels.
> They love places of honor at banquets, seats of honor in synagogues,
> greetings in marketplaces, and the salutation 'Rabbi.'
> As for you, do not be called 'Rabbi.'
> You have but one teacher, and you are all brothers.
> Call no one on earth your father;
> you have but one Father in heaven.

Do not be called 'Master';
you have but one master, the Christ.
The greatest among you must be your servant.
Whoever exalts himself will be humbled;
but whoever humbles himself will be exalted."

Dear friends, may we practice what we preach and be humble.

Good morning, sisters and brothers,

Today's Reading I
Ephesians 6:10-20

Draw your strength from the Lord and from his mighty power.
Put on the armor of God so that you may be able to stand firm
against the tactics of the Devil.
For our struggle is not with flesh and blood
but with the principalities, with the powers,
with the world rulers of this present darkness,
with the evil spirits in the heavens.
Therefore, put on the armor of God,
that you may be able to resist on the evil day
and, having done everything, to hold your ground.
So stand fast with your loins girded in truth,
clothed with righteousness as a breastplate,
and your feet shod in readiness for the Gospel of peace.
In all circumstances, hold faith as a shield,
to quench all the flaming arrows of the Evil One.
And take the helmet of salvation and the sword of the Spirit,
which is the word of God.

With all prayer and supplication,
pray at every opportunity in the Spirit.
To that end, be watchful with all perseverance and supplication
for all the holy ones and also for me,
that speech may be given me to open my mouth,
to make known with boldness the mystery of the Gospel
for which I am an ambassador in chains,
so that I may have the courage to speak as I must.

Dear friends, we are no match for the evil one on our own. Do not let your foolish pride tell you otherwise. Only with God's help will we achieve victory over the adversary.

Blessings

God morning, branches,

Today's Reading I
Acts 5:27-33

> When the court officers had brought the Apostles in
> and made them stand before the Sanhedrin,
> the high priest questioned them,
> "We gave you strict orders did we not,
> to stop teaching in that name.
> Yet you have filled Jerusalem with your teaching
> and want to bring this man's blood upon us."
> But Peter and the Apostles said in reply,
> "We must obey God rather than men.
> The God of our ancestors raised Jesus,
> though you had him killed by hanging him on a tree.

SCRIPTURE NOTES

God exalted him at his right hand as leader and savior
to grant Israel repentance and forgiveness of sins.
We are witnesses of these things,
as is the Holy Spirit whom God has given to those who obey him."

When they heard this,
they became infuriated and wanted to put them to death.

Dear friends, we must obey God rather than men. Some of the laws written by man might not coincide with God's laws.

Blessings

God morning, branches,

Today's Gospel
John 1:47–51

Jesus saw Nathanael coming toward him and said of him,
"Here is a true child of Israel.
There is no duplicity in him."
Nathanael said to him, "How do you know me?"
Jesus answered and said to him,
"Before Philip called you, I saw you under the fig tree."
Nathanael answered him,
"Rabbi, you are the Son of God; you are the King of Israel."
Jesus answered and said to him,
"Do you believe
because I told you that I saw you under the fig tree?
You will see greater things than this."
And he said to him, "Amen, amen, I say to you,
you will see heaven opened

and the angels of God ascending and descending on the Son of Man."

Dear friends, Nathaniel wondered how Jesus knew him. In John 1:45-46, Nathaniel says to Philip "Can there any good thing come out of Nazareth?" Nathaniel was called to follow Jesus and was told he would see great things. We know that Jesus knows us better than we know ourselves. As followers of Jesus, we see great things perhaps through our prayers.

Blessings

God morning, branches,

Today's Reading I
1 John 2:3-11

> Beloved:
> The way we may be sure that we know Jesus
> is to keep his commandments.
> Whoever says, "I know him," but does not keep his commandments
> is a liar, and the truth is not in him.
> But whoever keeps his word,
> the love of God is truly perfected in him.
> This is the way we may know that we are in union with him:
> whoever claims to abide in him ought to walk just as he walked.
>
> Beloved, I am writing no new commandment to you
> but an old commandment that you had from the beginning.
> The old commandment is the word that you have heard.
> And yet I do write a new commandment to you,
> which holds true in him and among you,
> for the darkness is passing away,

and the true light is already shining.

Whoever says he is in the light,
yet hates his brother, is still in the darkness.
Whoever loves his brother remains in the light,
and there is nothing in him to cause a fall.
Whoever hates his brother is in darkness;
he walks in darkness
and does not know where he is going
because the darkness has blinded his eyes.

Dear friends, it is very simple, there are ten commandments to follow. You likely know them by heart. As I have written, God is love and if we love one another it is unlikely that we break a commandment. May we walk just as He walked.

Blessings

God morning, disciples,

Today' Reading I
Acts 14:19-28

In those days, some Jews from Antioch and Iconium
arrived and won over the crowds.
They stoned Paul and dragged him out of the city,
supposing that he was dead.
But when the disciples gathered around him,
he got up and entered the city.
On the following day he left with Barnabas for Derbe.
After they had proclaimed the good news to that city
and made a considerable number of disciples,

they returned to Lystra and to Iconium and to Antioch.
They strengthened the spirits of the disciples
and exhorted them to persevere in the faith, saying,
"It is necessary for us to undergo many hardships
to enter the Kingdom of God."
They appointed presbyters for them in eachChurch and,
with prayer and fasting, commended them to the Lord
in whom they had put their faith.
Then they traveled through Pisidia and reached Pamphylia.
After proclaiming the word at Perga they went down to Attalia.
From there they sailed to Antioch,
where they had been commended to the grace of God
for the work they had now accomplished.
And when they arrived, they called the Church together
and reported what God had done with them
and how he had opened the door of faith to the Gentiles.
Then they spent no little time with the disciples.

Dear friends, "It is necessary for us to undergo many hardships to enter the Kingdom of God." Whenever a hardship befalls you recall 2 Corinthians 4:17-18, which says "For our present troubles are small and won't last very long. Yet they produce for us a glory that vastly outweighs them and will last forever! So we don't look at the troubles we can see now; rather, we fix our gaze on things that cannot be seen. For the things we see now will soon be gone, but the things we cannot see will last forever." Also, do not forget, The Lord is right there with you!

Blessings

God morning, sisters and brothers,

Today's Reading 1
Galatians 1:13-24

Brothers and sisters:
You heard of my former way of life in Judaism,
how I persecuted the Church of God beyond measure
and tried to destroy it,
and progressed in Judaism
beyond many of my contemporaries among my race,
since I was even more a zealot for my ancestral traditions.
But when he, who from my mother's womb had set me apart
and called me through his grace,
was pleased to reveal his Son to me,
so that I might proclaim him to the Gentiles,
I did not immediately consult flesh and blood,
nor did I go up to Jerusalem
to those who were Apostles before me;
rather, I went into Arabia and then returned to Damascus.

Then after three years I went up to Jerusalem to confer with Cephas
and remained with him for fifteen days.
But I did not see any other of the Apostles,
only James the brother of the Lord.
(As to what I am writing to you, behold,
before God, I am not lying.)
Then I went into the regions of Syria and Cilicia.
And I was unknown personally to the churches of Judea
that are in Christ;
they only kept hearing that "the one who once was persecuting us

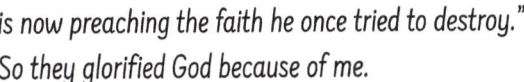

is now preaching the faith he once tried to destroy."
So they glorified God because of me.

Dear friends, Paul persecuted the Church of God beyond measure and tried to destroy it. God, through His grace, called Paul to a job for which he never applied, nor was he looking to make a substantial change in his life's direction. If God could save Paul, then He can save anyone. May we be open to His call. May we focus on Christ, not traditions.

Blessings

God morning, brothers and sisters,

Today's Reading 1
1 Jn 4:19-5:4

> Beloved, we love God because he first loved us.
> If anyone says, "I love God," but hates his brother, he is a liar;
> for whoever does not love a brother whom he has seen cannot love God whom he has not seen.
> This is the commandment we have from him: Whoever loves God must also love his brother.
>
> Everyone who believes that Jesus is the Christ is begotten by God, and everyone who loves the Father
> loves also the one begotten by him.
> In this way we know that we love the children of God when we love God and obey his commandments.
> For the love of God is this,
> that we keep his commandments.
> And his commandments are not burdensome,

for whoever is begotten by God conquers the world.
And the victory that conquers the world is our faith.

Dear friends, I submit loving our brothers and sisters is easier to do than not doing so.

It is easier to smile as it requires fewer muscles than it takes to frown. Smiling needs no language and is understood by all.

It is easier to tell the truth than to remember a lie.

Love and kindness need no language and are understood by all.

God is love and we were created in His image. Love comes easily. To not love takes work. Take the easy way and love.

Love

God morning, disciples,

Today's Gospel
Mt 9:32-38

> A demoniac who could not speak was brought to Jesus, and when the demon was driven out the mute man spoke. The crowds were amazed and said,
> "Nothing like this has ever been seen in Israel." But the Pharisees said, "He drives out demons by the prince of demons." Jesus went around to all the towns and villages, teaching in their synagogues,
> proclaiming the Gospel of the Kingdom, and curing every disease and illness.
> At the sight of the crowds, his heart was moved with pity for them because they were troubled and abandoned,
> like sheep without a shepherd. Then he said to his disciples,

"The harvest is abundant but the laborers are few; so ask the master of the harvest
to send out laborers for his harvest."

Dear friends, the harvest is abundant but the laborers are few. We are called to be laborers for the Lord. Spread the Good News by your words and actions. The reward for doing so is heavenly and infinite.

Blessings

God morning, brothers and sisters,

Today's Reading I
Colossians 2:6-15

> Brothers and sisters:
> As you received Christ Jesus the Lord, walk in him,
> rooted in him and built upon him
> and established in the faith as you were taught,
> abounding in thanksgiving.
> See to it that no one captivate you with an empty, seductive philosophy
> according to the tradition of men,
> according to the elemental powers of the world
> and not according to Christ.
>
> For in him dwells the whole fullness of the deity bodily,
> and you share in this fullness in him,
> who is the head of every principality and power.
> In him you were also circumcised
> with a circumcision not administered by hand,
> by stripping off the carnal body, with the circumcision of Christ.
> You were buried with him in baptism,

in which you were also raised with him
through faith in the power of God,
who raised him from the dead.
And even when you were dead in transgressions
and the uncircumcision of your flesh,
he brought you to life along with him,
having forgiven us all our transgressions;
obliterating the bond against us, with its legal claims,
which was opposed to us,
he also removed it from our midst, nailing it to the cross;
despoiling the principalities and the powers,
he made a public spectacle of them,
leading them away in triumph by it.

Dear friends, see to it that no one captivates you with an empty, seductive philosophy
    according to the tradition of men, according to the elemental powers of the world and not according to Christ. The world has been trying to ban our Lord and His teachings for ages. Now we have social media and companies that cancel what they do not like. Funny, though, they do not realize God cannot be canceled. Hold your ground and resist empty and seductive teachings.

Blessings

God morning, disciples,
Today's Gospel
Luke 6:12-19

> Jesus departed to the mountain to pray, and he spent the night in prayer to God.
> When day came, he called his disciples to himself,
> and from them he chose Twelve, whom he also named Apostles: Simon, whom he named Peter, and his brother Andrew,
> James, John, Philip, Bartholomew,
> Matthew, Thomas, James the son of Alphaeus, Simon who was called a Zealot,
> and Judas the son of James,
> and Judas Iscariot, who became a traitor.
>
> And he came down with them and stood on a stretch of level ground. A great crowd of his disciples and a large number of the people
> from all Judea and Jerusalem
> and the coastal region of Tyre and Sidon
> came to hear him and to be healed of their diseases;
> and even those who were tormented by unclean spirits were cured. Everyone in the crowd sought to touch him
> because power came forth from him and healed them all.

Dear friends, did you notice Jesus departed to the mountain to pray, and he spent the night in prayer to God. Think about going to a private room to pray for whatever amount of time, but certainly not all night. Everyone in the crowd sought to touch him because power came forth from him and healed them all. Now we might not be able to touch Him or His garments to feel His power, but He can touch us through our prayers.

Blessings

SCRIPTURE NOTES

God morning, disciples,

Today's Gospel
Mark 7:1-13

When the Pharisees with some scribes who had come from Jerusalem gathered around Jesus,
they observed that some of his disciples ate their meals with unclean, that is, unwashed, hands.
(For the Pharisees and, in fact, all Jews,
do not eat without carefully washing their hands, keeping the tradition of the elders.
And on coming from the marketplace
they do not eat without purifying themselves.
And there are many other things that they have traditionally observed, the purification of cups and jugs and kettles and beds.)
So the Pharisees and scribes questioned him,
"Why do your disciples not follow the tradition of the elders but instead eat a meal with unclean hands?"
He responded,
"Well did Isaiah prophesy about you hypocrites, as it is written:

This people honors me with their lips,
    but their hearts are far from me;
In vain do they worship me,
    teaching as doctrines human precepts.

You disregard God's commandment but cling to human tradition." He went on to say,
"How well you have set aside the commandment of God in order to uphold your tradition!
For Moses said,

Honor your father and your mother,
and Whoever curses father or mother shall die. Yet you say,
'If someone says to father or mother,
"Any support you might have had from me is qorban"' (meaning, dedicated to God),
you allow him to do nothing more for his father or mother. You nullify the word of God
in favor of your tradition that you have handed on. And you do many such things."

Dear friends, may you not nullify the word of God.

Blessings

God morning, branches,

Today's Reading I
Isaiah 55:10-11

> Thus says the LORD:
> Just as from the heaven
> the rain and snow come down
> And do not return there
> till they have watered the earth,
> making it fertile and fruitful,
> Giving seed to the one who sows
> and bread to the one who eats,
> So shall my word be
> that goes forth from my mouth;
> It shall not return to me void,
> but shall do my will,

achieving the end for which I sent it.

Dear friends, may God's word water your being and make it fertile and fruitful. God's word is pure rain for your soul and life. Without His word we are dust. May you spread His word.

Blessings

God morning, disciples,

Today's Gospel
Mt 5:13-16

> Jesus said to his disciples: "You are the salt of the earth.
> But if salt loses its taste, with what can it be seasoned? It is no longer good for anything
> but to be thrown out and trampled underfoot. You are the light of the world.
> A city set on a mountain cannot be hidden.
> Nor do they light a lamp and then put it under a bushel basket; it is set on a lampstand,
> where it gives light to all in the house.
> Just so, your light must shine before others, that they may see your good deeds
> and glorify your heavenly Father."

Dear friends, did you know salt was a very valuable commodity. The Greeks thought it contained something almost divine. The Romans, at times, paid their soldiers with salt. So you are valuable and can preserve what is good and bring flavor to life. Shine on, my brothers and sisters.

Blessings

SCRIPTURE NOTES

God morning, disciples,

Today's Gospel
Matthew 14:22-36

Jesus made the disciples get into a boat
and precede him to the other side of the sea, while he dismissed the crowds.
After doing so, he went up on the mountain by himself to pray. When it was evening he was there alone.
Meanwhile the boat, already a few miles offshore,
was being tossed about by the waves, for the wind was against it. During the fourth watch of the night,
he came toward them, walking on the sea.
When the disciples saw him walking on the sea they were terrified. "It is a ghost," they said, and they cried out in fear.
At once Jesus spoke to them, "Take courage, it is I; do not be afraid." Peter said to him in reply,
"Lord, if it is you, command me to come to you on the water." He said, "Come."
Peter got out of the boat and began to walk on the water toward Jesus. But when he saw how strong the wind was he became frightened; and, beginning to sink, he cried out, "Lord, save me!"
Immediately Jesus stretched out his hand and caught him, and said to him, "O you of little faith, why did you doubt?" After they got into the boat, the wind died down.
Those who were in the boat did him homage, saying, "Truly, you are the Son of God."

After making the crossing, they came to land at Gennesaret. When the men of that place recognized him,

they sent word to all the surrounding country. People brought to him
all those who were sick
and begged him that they might touch only the tassel on his cloak, and
as many as touched it were healed.

Dear friends, Peter, a human, walked on water. Well, at least until he took his focus off of Jesus. As Jesus rescued Peter, He said "O you of little faith, why did you doubt?" I imagine you have used or heard this expression many times. Now you know its origin. In Gennesaret, the sick needed only to touch a tassel on His cloak to be healed. What faith! You might recall my stories of how faith healed my serious medical problems. May we keep our focus Jesus.

Blessings

God morning, disciples,

Today's Gospel
Matthew 18:1-5, 10, 12-14

The disciples approached Jesus and said,
"Who is the greatest in the Kingdom of heaven?"
He called a child over, placed it in their midst, and said,
"Amen, I say to you, unless you turn and become like children,
you will not enter the Kingdom of heaven.
Whoever becomes humble like this child
is the greatest in the Kingdom of heaven.
And whoever receives one child such as this in my name receives me.

"See that you do not despise one of these little ones,
for I say to you that their angels in heaven
always look upon the face of my heavenly Father.

What is your opinion?
If a man has a hundred sheep and one of them goes astray,
will he not leave the ninety-nine in the hills
and go in search of the stray?
And if he finds it, amen, I say to you, he rejoices more over it
than over the ninety-nine that did not stray.
In just the same way, it is not the will of your heavenly Father
that one of these little ones be lost."

Dear friends, may you be as humble as a child. May you also look at God's magnificent creation with the eyes and mind of a child.

Blessings

God morning, brothers and sisters,

Today's Reading II
1 Cor 3:9c-11, 16-17

> Brothers and sisters:
> You are God's building.
> According to the grace of God given to me, like a wise master builder I laid a foundation, and another is building upon it.
> But each one must be careful how he builds upon it,
> for no one can lay a foundation other than the one that is there, namely, Jesus Christ.
> Do you not know that you are the temple of God, and that the Spirit of God dwells in you?
> If anyone destroys God's temple, God will destroy that person;
> for the temple of God, which you are, is holy.

Dear friends, read this Reading again slowly and let it sink in. Do not ever think that you are average. We have an obligation to maintain ourselves in such a way as to glorify God, the master builder.

Blessings

God morning,

Today's Gospel
Lk 16:9-15

Jesus said to his disciples:

> "I tell you, make friends for yourselves with dishonest wealth,
> so that when it fails, you will be welcomed into eternal dwellings.
> The person who is trustworthy in very small matters
> is also trustworthy in great ones;
> and the person who is dishonest in very small matters
> is also dishonest in great ones.
> If, therefore, you are not trustworthy with dishonest wealth,
> who will trust you with true wealth?
> If you are not trustworthy with what belongs to another,
> who will give you what is yours?
> No servant can serve two masters.
> He will either hate one and love the other,
> or be devoted to one and despise the other.
> You cannot serve God and mammon."

> The Pharisees, who loved money,
> heard all these things and sneered at him.
> And he said to them,
> "You justify yourselves in the sight of others,

but God knows your hearts;
for what is of human esteem is an abomination in the sight of God."

Dear friends, may we be trustworthy and not put money before God, who knows our hearts.

Blessings

God morning, branches,

Today's First Reading:
WIS 6:12-16

> Resplendent and unfading is wisdom,
> and she is readily perceived by those who love her,
> and found by those who seek her.
> She hastens to make herself known in anticipation of their desire;
> Whoever watches for her at dawn shall not be disappointed,
> for he shall find her sitting by his gate.
> For taking thought of wisdom is the perfection of prudence,
> and whoever for her sake keeps vigil
> shall quickly be free from care;
> because she makes her own rounds, seeking those worthy of her,
> and graciously appears to them in the ways,
> and meets them with all solicitude.

Dear friends, may you be worthy of her and be free from care.

Blessings

SCRIPTURE NOTES

God morning, disciples,

Today's Reading I
Acts 11:19-26

> Those who had been scattered by the persecution
> that arose because of Stephen
> went as far as Phoenicia, Cyprus, and Antioch,
> preaching the word to no one but Jews.
> There were some Cypriots and Cyrenians among them, however,
> who came to Antioch and began to speak to the Greeks as well,
> proclaiming the Lord Jesus.
> The hand of the Lord was with them
> and a great number who believed turned to the Lord.
> The news about them reached the ears of the Church in Jerusalem,
> and they sent Barnabas to go to Antioch.
> When he arrived and saw the grace of God,
> he rejoiced and encouraged them all
> to remain faithful to the Lord in firmness of heart,
> for he was a good man, filled with the Holy Spirit and faith.
> And a large number of people was added to the Lord.
> Then he went to Tarsus to look for Saul,
> and when he had found him he brought him to Antioch.
> For a whole year they met with the Church
> and taught a large number of people,
> and it was in Antioch that the disciples
> were first called Christians.

Dear friends, I imagine you have called yourselves Christians for a long time. Now you know about when and where the term originated.

SCRIPTURE NOTES

Some years ago, a friend and I were talking about politics. My friend, who happens to be Jewish, said Steve, sometimes you have very liberal beliefs and other times very conservative. He then asked me what I was. I thought for a moment and looked heavenward. I looked at my friend, smiled and said I am a Christian and try to do the right things.

Blessings

God morning, branches,

Today's Reading 1
Acts 2:36–41

> On the day of Pentecost, Peter said to the Jewish people, "Let the whole house of Israel know for certain
> that God has made him both Lord and Christ, this Jesus whom you crucified."
>
> Now when they heard this, they were cut to the heart, and they asked Peter and the other Apostles,
> "What are we to do, my brothers?" Peter said to them,
> "Repent and be baptized, every one of you,
> in the name of Jesus Christ, for the forgiveness of your sins; and you will receive the gift of the Holy Spirit.
> For the promise is made to you and to your children and to all those far off,
> whomever the Lord our God will call."
> He testified with many other arguments, and was exhorting them, "Save yourselves from this corrupt generation."
> Those who accepted his message were baptized,

and about three thousand persons were added that day.

Dear friends, save yourselves from this corrupt generation, indeed.

Blessings

God morning, sisters and brothers,

Today's Reading 1
1 Cor 12:12-14, 27-31a

> Brothers and sisters:
> As a body is one though it has many parts,
> and all the parts of the body, though many, are one body, so also Christ.
> For in one Spirit we were all baptized into one Body, whether Jews or Greeks, slaves or free persons,
> and we were all given to drink of one Spirit.
>
> Now the body is not a single part, but many.
>
> Now you are Christ's Body, and individually parts of it. Some people God has designated in the Church
> to be, first, Apostles; second, prophets; third, teachers; then, mighty deeds;
> then gifts of healing, assistance, administration, and varieties of tongues.
> Are all Apostles? Are all prophets? Are all teachers? Do all work mighty deeds? Do all have gifts of healing? Do all speak in tongues? Do all interpret?
> Strive eagerly for the greatest spiritual gifts.

Dear friends, we are Christ's body!

Remarkable. May we strive eagerly for the greatest spiritual gifts.

Blessings

God morning, disciples,

Today's Gospel
Matthew 5:43-48

> Jesus said to his disciples:
> "You have heard that it was said,
> You shall love your neighbor and hate your enemy. But I say to you, love your enemies
> and pray for those who persecute you,
> that you may be children of your heavenly Father, for he makes his sun rise on the bad and the good, and causes rain to fall on the just and the unjust.
> For if you love those who love you, what recompense will you have? Do not the tax collectors do the same?
> And if you greet your brothers only, what is unusual about that?
> Do not the pagans do the same?
> So be perfect, just as your heavenly Father is perfect."

Dear friends, the Lord says be unusual and perfect, just as your heavenly Father is perfect. Well, we cannot be perfect, but it is worth trying to be so. Would you rather be average, mediocre or the like?

Aim high!

Aim for Heaven!

Blessings

SCRIPTURE NOTES

God morning, brothers and sisters,

Today's Reading I
James 1:12-18

> Blessed is he who perseveres in temptation,
> for when he has been proven he will receive the crown of life that he promised to those who love him.
> No one experiencing temptation should say, "I am being tempted by God";
> for God is not subject to temptation to evil, and he himself tempts no one.
> Rather, each person is tempted when lured and enticed by his desire.
> Then desire conceives and brings forth sin,
> and when sin reaches maturity it gives birth to death.
>
> Do not be deceived, my beloved brothers and sisters: all good giving and every perfect gift is from above, coming down from the Father of lights,
> with whom there is no alteration or shadow caused by change. He willed to give us birth by the word of truth
> that we may be a kind of firstfruits of his creatures.

Dear friends, I imagine some (many?) of us have said "I am being tempted by God" without realizing He is not subject to temptation to evil and He tempts no one. God made us human and gave us free will. The adversary knows our weaknesses better than we do and uses that understanding to tempt us to do evil things. We have free will, choose wisely. May you persevere in temptation and be blessed.

One of Henry Ford's famous quotes about the Model T was, "Any customer can have a car painted any color that he wants, so long as it is black." Aren't you glad God gave us a choice?

Blessings

SCRIPTURE NOTES

God morning, disciples,

Today's Gospel
John 14:27-31a

> Jesus said to his disciples:
> "Peace I leave with you; my peace I give to you.
> Not as the world gives do I give it to you.
> Do not let your hearts be troubled or afraid.
> You heard me tell you,
> 'I am going away and I will come back to you.'
> If you loved me,
> you would rejoice that I am going to the Father;
> for the Father is greater than I.
> And now I have told you this before it happens,
> so that when it happens you may believe.
> I will no longer speak much with you,
> for the ruler of the world is coming.
> He has no power over me,
> but the world must know that I love the Father
> and that I do just as the Father has commanded me."

Dear friends, Jesus said the ruler of the world is coming. It is interesting that a recent study of American Christians found four out of ten Christians (40%) strongly agreed that Satan "is not a living being but is a symbol of evil." An additional two out of ten Christians (19%) said they "agree somewhat" with that perspective. Is it any wonder why the world is so troubled?

Blessings

SCRIPTURE NOTES

God morning, disciples,

Today's Gospel
Luke 10:1–9

> The Lord Jesus appointed seventy-two disciples
> whom he sent ahead of him in pairs
> to every town and place he intended to visit.
> He said to them,
> "The harvest is abundant but the laborers are few;
> so ask the master of the harvest
> to send out laborers for his harvest.
> Go on your way;
> behold, I am sending you like lambs among wolves.
> Carry no money bag, no sack, no sandals;
> and greet no one along the way.
> Into whatever house you enter,
> first say, 'Peace to this household.'
> If a peaceful person lives there,
> your peace will rest on him;
> but if not, it will return to you.
> Stay in the same house and eat and drink what is offered to you,
> for the laborer deserves payment.
> Do not move about from one house to another.
> Whatever town you enter and they welcome you,
> eat what is set before you,
> cure the sick in it and say to them,
> 'The Kingdom of God is at hand for you.'"

Dear friends, the harvest is greater today. We are called to go out as sheep among the wolves. The extraordinary powers we have are

SCRIPTURE NOTES

the power of His word and the fact that He is with us. Sometimes a kind word may bring comfort and peace to a family member, friend, neighbor, colleague, acquaintance or stranger. Rejoice for your names are written in Heaven.

Blessings

God morning, branches,

Today's Reading I
Acts 7:51—8:1a

> Stephen said to the people, the elders, and the scribes: "You stiff-necked people, uncircumcised in heart and ears, you always oppose the Holy Spirit;
> you are just like your ancestors.
> Which of the prophets did your ancestors not persecute?
> They put to death those who foretold the coming of the righteous one, whose betrayers and murderers you have now become.
> You received the law as transmitted by angels, but you did not observe it."
>
> When they heard this, they were infuriated, and they ground their teeth at him.
> But Stephen, filled with the Holy Spirit,
> looked up intently to heaven and saw the glory of God and Jesus standing at the right hand of God,
> and Stephen said, "Behold, I see the heavens opened and the Son of Man standing at the right hand of God." But they cried out in a loud voice,
> covered their ears, and rushed upon him together.
> They threw him out of the city, and began to stone him. The witnesses laid down their cloaks

at the feet of a young man named Saul.
As they were stoning Stephen, he called out, "Lord Jesus, receive my spirit."
Then he fell to his knees and cried out in a loud voice, "Lord, do not hold this sin against them";
and when he said this, he fell asleep.

Now Saul was consenting to his execution.

Dear friends, in many ways, the deeds, persecution and death of Stephen should sound familiar to you as Stephen followed in the Lord's footsteps to the end. The story of Stephen ends with Saul consenting to the execution. Perhaps this is the beginning of Saul's conversion. Consider that God was going to use a tragic loss to create something exceptional. Think of what God could do in your life.

Blessings

God morning, branches,

Today's Gospel
Matthew 19:23-30

Jesus said to his disciples:
"Amen, I say to you, it will be hard for one who is rich to enter the Kingdom of heaven.
Again I say to you,
it is easier for a camel to pass through the eye of a needle than for one who is rich to enter the Kingdom of God."
When the disciples heard this, they were greatly astonished and said, "Who then can be saved?"

SCRIPTURE NOTES

Jesus looked at them and said, "For men this is impossible,
but for God all things are possible." Then Peter said to him in reply,
"We have given up everything and followed you. What will there be for us?"
Jesus said to them, "Amen, I say to you
that you who have followed me, in the new age, when the Son of Man is seated on his throne of glory, will yourselves sit on twelve thrones,
judging the twelve tribes of Israel.
And everyone who has given up houses or brothers or sisters or father or mother or children or lands
for the sake of my name will receive a hundred times more, and will inherit eternal life.
But many who are first will be last, and the last will be first."

Dear friends, did you notice Jesus said it would be hard for one who is rich to enter the Kingdom of God? He did not say it was impossible. I think He means do not focus your attention on earthly possessions. Indeed, it is written elsewhere to store up treasures in Heaven. Remember to trust His promises, help the less fortunate and be thankful.

Blessings

God morning, sisters and brothers,

Today's Reading 1
2 THES 2:1-3A, 14-17

We ask you, brothers and sisters,
with regard to the coming of our Lord Jesus Christ
and our assembling with him,

not to be shaken out of your minds suddenly,
or to be alarmed either by a "spirit," or by an oral statement,
or by a letter allegedly from us
to the effect that the day of the Lord is at hand.
Let no one deceive you in any way.

To this end he has also called you through our Gospel
to possess the glory of our Lord Jesus Christ.
Therefore, brothers and sisters, stand firm
and hold fast to the traditions that you were taught,
either by an oral statement or by a letter of ours.

May our Lord Jesus Christ himself and God our Father,
who has loved us and given us everlasting encouragement
and good hope through his grace,
encourage your hearts and strengthen them
in every good deed and word.

Dear friends, may you stand firm and hold fast to the traditions that you were taught, either by an oral statement or by a letter of ours. There are some who say our traditions, indeed even the Bible itself, are irrelevant in today's world. Let no one deceive you in any way.

Blessings

God morning, disciples,

Today's Gospel
John 16:5-11

Jesus said to his disciples:

"Now I am going to the one who sent me,
and not one of you asks me, 'Where are you going?'
But because I told you this, grief has filled your hearts.
But I tell you the truth, it is better for you that I go.
For if I do not go, the Advocate will not come to you.
But if I go, I will send him to you.
And when he comes he will convict the world
in regard to sin and righteousness and condemnation:
sin, because they do not believe in me;
righteousness, because I am going to the Father
and you will no longer see me;
condemnation, because the ruler of this world has been condemned."

Dear friends, recently I wrote that a sizeable percentage of Christians did not believe in the adversary. The last line in today's Gospel is another reminder he is real, among us and in control. Beware, for he is cunning and a master of deception.

Blessings

God morning, disciples,

Today's Reading I
Acts 9:1-22

> Saul, still breathing murderous threats against the disciples of the Lord,
> went to the high priest and asked him
> for letters to the synagogues in Damascus, that,
> if he should find any men or women who belonged to the Way, he might
> bring them back to Jerusalem in chains.
> On his journey, as he was nearing Damascus,

a light from the sky suddenly flashed around him.
He fell to the ground and heard a voice saying to him, "Saul, Saul, why are you persecuting me?"
He said, "Who are you, sir?"
The reply came, "I am Jesus, whom you are persecuting.
Now get up and go into the city and you will be told what you must do." The men who were traveling with him stood speechless,
for they heard the voice but could see no one. Saul got up from the ground,
but when he opened his eyes he could see nothing;
so they led him by the hand and brought him to Damascus.
For three days he was unable to see, and he neither ate nor drank.
There was a disciple in Damascus named Ananias, and the Lord said to him in a vision, AAnanias." He answered, "Here I am, Lord."
The Lord said to him, "Get up and go to the street called Straight and ask at the house of Judas for a man from Tarsus named Saul. He is there praying,
and in a vision he has seen a man named Ananias come in and lay his hands on him,
that he may regain his sight." But Ananias replied,
"Lord, I have heard from many sources about this man, what evil things he has done to your holy ones in Jerusalem.
And here he has authority from the chief priests to imprison all who call upon your name."
But the Lord said to him,
"Go, for this man is a chosen instrument of mine
to carry my name before Gentiles, kings, and children of Israel, and I will show him what he will have to suffer for my name." So Ananias went and entered the house;

SCRIPTURE NOTES

laying his hands on him, he said,
"Saul, my brother, the Lord has sent me,
Jesus who appeared to you on the way by which you came,
that you may regain your sight and be filled with the Holy Spirit."
Immediately things like scales fell from his eyes
and he regained his sight. He got up and was baptized,
and when he had eaten, he recovered his strength.

He stayed some days with the disciples in Damascus,
and he began at once to proclaim Jesus in the synagogues, that he is
the Son of God.
All who heard him were astounded and said, "Is not this the man who
in Jerusalem ravaged those who call upon this name,
and came here expressly to take them back in chains to the chief priests?"
But Saul grew all the stronger
and confounded the Jews who lived in Damascus, proving that this is
the Christ.

Dear friends, think long and hard about the conversion of Saul and then think of what God can do with you. Also, did you notice how many days Saul was blind?

Blessings

God morning, branches,

Today's Reading 1
1 Peter 5:5b–14

Beloved:
Clothe yourselves with humility
in your dealings with one another, for:

*God opposes the proud
but bestows favor on the humble.*

*So humble yourselves under the mighty hand of God, that he may exalt you in due time.
Cast all your worries upon him because he cares for you.*

*Be sober and vigilant.
Your opponent the Devil is prowling around like a roaring lion looking for someone to devour.
Resist him, steadfast in faith,
knowing that your brothers and sisters throughout the world undergo the same sufferings.
The God of all grace
who called you to his eternal glory through Christ Jesus will himself restore, confirm, strengthen, and establish you after you have suffered a little.
To him be dominion forever. Amen.*

*I write you this briefly through Silvanus, whom I consider a faithful brother,
exhorting you and testifying that this is the true grace of God. Remain firm in it.
The chosen one at Babylon sends you greeting, as does Mark, my son.
Greet one another with a loving kiss.
Peace to all of you who are in Christ.*

Dear friends, we might find it difficult to be humble in this me, me, me world. Consider who Jesus is and how He is the perfect example of humility and we are called to follow His examples.

Blessings

SCRIPTURE NOTES

God morning, disciples,

Today's Gospel
Matthew 13:36–43

> Jesus dismissed the crowds and went into the house.
> His disciples approached him and said,
> "Explain to us the parable of the weeds in the field."
> He said in reply, "He who sows good seed is the Son of Man,
> the field is the world, the good seed the children of the Kingdom.
> The weeds are the children of the Evil One,
> and the enemy who sows them is the Devil.
> The harvest is the end of the age, and the harvesters are angels.
> Just as weeds are collected and burned up with fire,
> so will it be at the end of the age.
> The Son of Man will send his angels,
> and they will collect out of his Kingdom
> all who cause others to sin and all evildoers.
> They will throw them into the fiery furnace,
> where there will be wailing and grinding of teeth.
> Then the righteous will shine like the sun
> in the Kingdom of their Father.
> Whoever has ears ought to hear."

Dear friends, may you be good seeds and not weeds; the choice is yours. God gave you two ears. Listen, learn and live. May you shine like the sun, here and then in His Kingdom.

Blessings

SCRIPTURE NOTES

God morning, disciples,

Today's Gospel
Matthew 6:7-15

> Jesus said to his disciples:
> "In praying, do not babble like the pagans,
> who think that they will be heard because of their many words.
> Do not be like them.
> Your Father knows what you need before you ask him.
>
> "This is how you are to pray:
>
> Our Father who art in heaven,
> hallowed be thy name,
> thy Kingdom come,
> thy will be done,
> on earth as it is in heaven.
> Give us this day our daily bread;
> and forgive us our trespasses,
> as we forgive those who trespass against us;
> and lead us not into temptation,
> but deliver us from evil.
>
> "If you forgive men their transgressions,
> your heavenly Father will forgive you.
> But if you do not forgive men,
> neither will your Father forgive your transgressions."

Dear friends, Jesus gave us this prayer. I am pretty sure we all say it. May we live it and follow in His footsteps.

Blessings

SCRIPTURE NOTES

God morning, disciples,

Today's Gospel
Matthew 8:23-27

> As Jesus got into a boat, his disciples followed him. Suddenly a violent storm came up on the sea,
> so that the boat was being swamped by waves; but he was asleep.
> They came and woke him, saying, "Lord, save us! We are perishing!"
> He said to them, "Why are you terrified, O you of little faith?" Then he got up, rebuked the winds and the sea,
> and there was great calm.
> The men were amazed and said, "What sort of man is this, whom even the winds and the sea obey?"

Dear friends, Jesus can calm any storm we face. After all, He created everything. May your faith never be little. I think you will find the following parts of three Psalms interesting.

> You silence the roaring of the seas, the roaring of their waves, the tumult of the peoples. Psalm 65:7
> You rule the raging of the sea; when its waves rise, you still them. Psalm 89:9

> Then they cried to the Lord in their trouble, and he brought them out from their distress; he made the storm be still, and the waves of the sea were hushed. Psalm 107:28-29

Blessings

God morning, branches,

Today's Gospel
Mathew 4:18-22

> As Jesus was walking by the Sea of Galilee, he saw two brothers,
> Simon who is called Peter, and his brother Andrew,
> casting a net into the sea; they were fishermen.
> He said to them,
> "Come after me, and I will make you fishers of men."
> At once they left their nets and followed him.
> He walked along from there and saw two other brothers,
> James, the son of Zebedee, and his brother John.
> They were in a boat, with their father Zebedee, mending their nets.
> He called them, and immediately they left their boat and their father
> and followed him.

Dear friends, Jesus calls each of us to be fishers of men. Will you accept His invitation to follow Him? I imagine you will say "of course", but you should know the adversary will try to distract you. We can be fishers of men through our words and actions in our daily lives.

Blessings

God morning, branches,

Today's Reading 1
Romans 12:9-16

> Brothers and sisters:
> Let love be sincere;

hate what is evil,
hold on to what is good;
love one another with mutual affection;
anticipate one another in showing honor.
Do not grow slack in zeal,
be fervent in spirit,
serve the Lord.
Rejoice in hope,
endure in affliction,
persevere in prayer.
Contribute to the needs of the holy ones,
exercise hospitality.
Bless those who persecute you,
bless and do not curse them.
Rejoice with those who rejoice,
weep with those who weep.
Have the same regard for one another;
do not be haughty but associate with the lowly;
do not be wise in your own estimation.

Dear friends, there are many exhortations in this Reading. There are the Ten Commandments. I believe if we love one another as Jesus tells us, following these exhortations and Commandments should be easy. If only …

May you make every effort to live today's Reading.

Blessings

SCRIPTURE NOTES

God morning, branches,

Today's Gospel
Luke 4:38–44

> After Jesus left the synagogue, he entered the house of Simon.
> Simon's mother-in-law was afflicted with a severe fever,
> and they interceded with him about her.
> He stood over her, rebuked the fever, and it left her.
> She got up immediately and waited on them.
>
> At sunset, all who had people sick with various diseases brought them to him.
> He laid his hands on each of them and cured them.
> And demons also came out from many, shouting, "You are the Son of God."
> But he rebuked them and did not allow them to speak
> because they knew that he was the Christ.
>
> At daybreak, Jesus left and went to a deserted place.
> The crowds went looking for him, and when they came to him,
> they tried to prevent him from leaving them.
> But he said to them, "To the other towns also
> I must proclaim the good news of the Kingdom of God,
> because for this purpose I have been sent."
> And he was preaching in the synagogues of Judea.

Dear friends, even demons know who Jesus is. Jesus knew what His mission was here; to proclaim the good news. Many in our world do not know Jesus or the good news. We are called to proclaim the good news by our words and actions.

Blessings

SCRIPTURE NOTES

God morning, brothers and sisters.

Today's Reading 1
Romans 13:8-10

> Brothers and sisters:
>
> Owe nothing to anyone, except to love one another;
> for the one who loves another has fulfilled the law.
> The commandments, You shall not commit adultery;
> you shall not kill;
> you shall not steal;
> you shall not covet,
> and whatever other commandment there may be,
> are summed up in this saying, namely,
> You shall love your neighbor as yourself.
> Love does no evil to the neighbor;
> hence, love is the fulfillment of the law.

Dear friends, many parts of the Bible talk about love. I think 1 John 4:8 says it best: But anyone who does not love does not know God, for God is love.

> "Amor vincit omnia, et nos cedamus amori.
> Love conquers all things, so we too shall yield to love." - *Virgil, Eclogues*

> The phrase "love conquers all" became popular in the 14th century, with a character from Chaucer's 'Canterbury Tales' wearing a brooch with the phrase in Latin (*Amor vincit omnia*).

Love

SCRIPTURE NOTES

God morning, branches,

Today's Gospel
John 14:6-14

> Jesus said to Thomas, "I am the way and the truth and the life. No one comes to the Father except through me.
> If you know me, then you will also know my Father. From now on you do know him and have seen him." Philip said to him,
> "Master, show us the Father, and that will be enough for us." Jesus said to him, "Have I been with you for so long a time and you still do not know me, Philip?
> Whoever has seen me has seen the Father. How can you say, 'Show us the Father'?
> Do you not believe that I am in the Father and the Father is in me? The words that I speak to you I do not speak on my own.
> The Father who dwells in me is doing his works.
> Believe me that I am in the Father and the Father is in me, or else, believe because of the works themselves.
> Amen, amen, I say to you,
> whoever believes in me will do the works that I do, and will do greater ones than these,
> because I am going to the Father.
> And whatever you ask in my name, I will do, so that the Father may be glorified in the Son.
> If you ask anything of me in my name, I will do it."

Dear friends, may we do some of the works He did.
Blessings

SCRIPTURE NOTES

God morning, branches,

Today's Reading 1
Is 40:25–31

> To whom can you liken me as an equal?
> says the Holy One.
> Lift up your eyes on high
> and see who has created these things:
> He leads out their army and numbers them,
> calling them all by name.
> By his great might and the strength of his power
> not one of them is missing!
> Why, O Jacob, do you say,
> and declare, O Israel,
> "My way is hidden from the LORD,
> and my right is disregarded by my God"?
> Do you not know
> or have you not heard?
> The LORD is the eternal God,
> creator of the ends of the earth.
> He does not faint nor grow weary,
> and his knowledge is beyond scrutiny.
> He gives strength to the fainting;
> for the weak he makes vigor abound.
> Though young men faint and grow weary,
> and youths stagger and fall,
> They that hope in the LORD will renew their strength,
> they will soar as with eagles' wings;
> They will run and not grow weary,
> walk and not grow faint.

SCRIPTURE NOTES

Dear friends, may we hope in the LORD so as to renew our strength, soar as with eagles' wings, run and not grow weary, walk and not grow faint.

Blessings

God morning, disciples,

Today's Gospel
Matthew 5:17-19

> Jesus said to his disciples:
> "Do not think that I have come to abolish the law or the prophets. I have come not to abolish but to fulfill.
> Amen, I say to you, until heaven and earth pass away, not the smallest letter or the smallest part of a letter will pass from the law,
> until all things have taken place.
> Therefore, whoever breaks one of the least of these commandments and teaches others to do so
> will be called least in the Kingdom of heaven.
> But whoever obeys and teaches these commandments will be called greatest in the Kingdom of heaven."

Dear friends, Jesus said he came to fulfill the law. There are many instances in Scripture where He teaches that all the law and the prophets are comprehended in these two precepts: Thou shalt love the Lord thy God with all thy heart, and thou shalt love thy neighbour as thyself. As I have said, if you love you will not break any law or Commandment. May you be called among the greatest in the Kingdom of Heaven.

Love,

SCRIPTURE NOTES

God morning, disciples,

Today's Gospel
Mark 7:14–23

> Jesus summoned the crowd again and said to them,
> "Hear me, all of you, and understand.
> Nothing that enters one from outside can defile that person;
> but the things that come out from within are what defile."
>
> When he got home away from the crowd
> his disciples questioned him about the parable.
> He said to them,
> "Are even you likewise without understanding?
> Do you not realize that everything
> that goes into a person from outside cannot defile,
> since it enters not the heart but the stomach
> and passes out into the latrine?"
> (Thus he declared all foods clean.)
> "But what comes out of the man, that is what defiles him.
> From within the man, from his heart,
> come evil thoughts, unchastity, theft, murder,
> adultery, greed, malice, deceit,
> licentiousness, envy, blasphemy, arrogance, folly.
> All these evils come from within and they defile."

Dear friends, the Lord knows what is in our hearts.

> He said "Blessed are the pure of heart" *(Matthew 5:8)*.

May you pray this prayer: A pure heart create for me, O God, put a steadfast spirit within me. Do not cast me away from your presence nor deprive me of your Holy Spirit. *Psalm 51*

Love

God morning, disciples,

Today's Gospel
Matthew 15:21-28

> At that time Jesus withdrew to the region of Tyre and Sidon.
> And behold, a Canaanite woman of that district came and called out,
> "Have pity on me, Lord, Son of David!
> My daughter is tormented by a demon." But he did not say a word in answer to her. His disciples came and asked him,
> "Send her away, for she keeps calling out after us." He said in reply,
> "I was sent only to the lost sheep of the house of Israel."
> But the woman came and did him homage, saying, "Lord, help me." He said in reply,
> "It is not right to take the food of the children and throw it to the dogs."
> She said, "Please, Lord, for even the dogs eat the scraps that fall from the table of their masters."
> Then Jesus said to her in reply, "O woman, great is your faith!
> Let it be done for you as you wish."
> And her daughter was healed from that hour.

Dear friends, the Canaanite woman certainly not of the house of Israel, but somehow recognized the importance of Jesus. She was able to convince Jesus of her sincerity and concern for her daughter, not herself. Jesus then proclaims "O woman, great is your faith!

Let it be done as you wish." What a wonderful lesson of faith and compassion for those who differ from us. We can only wonder if this woman became a Christian and helped others to do likewise. My guess is yes to both. You know that I relate to the faith part of this Gospel. Miracles do happen.

Blessings

God morning, sisters and brothers,

Today's Reading 1
2 COR 9:6-10

> Brothers and sisters:
> Whoever sows sparingly will also reap sparingly,
> and whoever sows bountifully will also reap bountifully.
> Each must do as already determined, without sadness or compulsion,
> for God loves a cheerful giver.
> Moreover, God is able to make every grace abundant for you,
> so that in all things, always having all you need,
> you may have an abundance for every good work.
> As it is written:
> > He scatters abroad, he gives to the poor;
> > > his righteousness endures forever.
>
> The one who supplies seed to the sower and bread for food
> will supply and multiply your seed
> and increase the harvest of your righteousness.

Dear friends, may you sow bountifully.

Blessings

SCRIPTURE NOTES

God morning, branches,

Today's Gospel
Luke 17:11-19

> As Jesus continued his journey to Jerusalem, he traveled through Samaria and Galilee.
> As he was entering a village, ten lepers met him.
> They stood at a distance from him and raised their voice, saying, "Jesus, Master! Have pity on us!"
> And when he saw them, he said, "Go show yourselves to the priests."
> As they were going they were cleansed.
> And one of them, realizing he had been healed, returned, glorifying God in a loud voice;
> and he fell at the feet of Jesus and thanked him. He was a Samaritan.
> Jesus said in reply,
> "Ten were cleansed, were they not? Where are the other nine?
> Has none but this foreigner returned to give thanks to God?" Then he said to him, "Stand up and go;
> your faith has saved you."

Dear friends, many of you have heard my story about faith. There are some who may be hearing it for the first time. I was once hospitalized with a serious problem and without knowing it was given a medicine that was not normally prescribed for my condition. On my third day in the hospital, my doctor visited me as he said he would. He asked how I was doing. I said, doctor I feel better today than I did yesterday and yesterday better than the day before and by the end of the first day I started feeling better. He smiled and said good it's working. Then he said maybe it's working or perhaps it's your faith. I had an extremely serious problem that I got through (with lots of prayers) a year earlier and told the doctor before he hospitalized me that I would get through this, too. Faith, indeed!

Blessings

God morning, branches,

Today's Reading 2
1 Corinthians 9:16-19, 22-23

> Brothers and sisters:
> If I preach the gospel, this is no reason for me to boast,
> for an obligation has been imposed on me,
> and woe to me if I do not preach it!
> If I do so willingly, I have a recompense,
> but if unwillingly, then I have been entrusted with a stewardship.
> What then is my recompense?
> That, when I preach,
> I offer the gospel free of charge
> so as not to make full use of my right in the gospel.
>
> Although I am free in regard to all,
> I have made myself a slave to all
> so as to win over as many as possible.
> To the weak I became weak, to win over the weak.
> I have become all things to all, to save at least some.
> All this I do for the sake of the gospel,
> so that I too may have a share in it.

Dear friends, may we offer the Gospel free of charge to others by our words and actions. The reward is and will be Heavenly.

Blessings

God morning, branches,

Today's Reading I:
Acts 3:1-10

> Peter and John were going up to the temple area for the three o'clock hour of prayer.
> And a man crippled from birth was carried
> and placed at the gate of the temple called "the Beautiful Gate" every day to beg for alms from the people who entered the temple.
> When he saw Peter and John about to go into the temple, he asked for alms.
> But Peter looked intently at him, as did John, and said, "Look at us."
> He paid attention to them, expecting to receive something from them. Peter said, "I have neither silver nor gold,
> but what I do have I give you:
> in the name of Jesus Christ the Nazorean, rise and walk." Then Peter took him by the right hand and raised him up, and immediately his feet and ankles grew strong.
> He leaped up, stood, and walked around, and went into the temple with them, walking and jumping and praising God.
> When all the people saw him walking and praising God, they recognized him as the one
> who used to sit begging at the Beautiful Gate of the temple, and they were filled with amazement and astonishment
> at what had happened to him.

Dear friends, like Peter, you may not have silver or gold. May you be amazed and astonished at the infinite amount of love, mercy and blessings available to you from Jesus Christ. May you be thankful for everything and freely share them with others and maybe lead others to the Light.

Blessings

God morning, sisters and brothers,

Reading 1
Galatians 5:18-25

> Brothers and sisters:
> If you are guided by the Spirit, you are not under the law. Now the works
> of the flesh are obvious:
> immorality, impurity, licentiousness, idolatry, sorcery, hatreds, rivalry,
> jealousy,
> outbursts of fury, acts of selfishness, dissensions, factions, occasions of
> envy, drinking bouts, orgies, and the like.
> I warn you, as I warned you before,
> that those who do such things will not inherit the Kingdom of God. In
> contrast, the fruit of the Spirit is love, joy, peace,
> patience, kindness, generosity, faithfulness, gentleness, self-control.
> Against such there is no law.
> Now those who belong to Christ Jesus have crucified their flesh with its
> passions and desires.
> If we live in the Spirit, let us also follow the Spirit.

Dear friends, may we live in and follow the Spirit.

Blessings

SCRIPTURE NOTES

God morning, branches,

Today's First Reading
Romans 2:1-11

> You, O man, are without excuse, every one of you who passes judgment.
> For by the standard by which you judge another you condemn yourself, since you, the judge, do the very same things.
> We know that the judgment of God on those who do such things is true. Do you suppose, then, you who judge those who engage in such things and yet do them yourself,
> that you will escape the judgment of God?
> Or do you hold his priceless kindness, forbearance, and patience in low esteem, unaware that the kindness of God
> would lead you to repentance?
> By your stubbornness and impenitent heart, you are storing up wrath for yourself
> for the day of wrath and revelation of the just judgment of God,
> who will repay everyone according to his works,
> eternal life to those who seek glory, honor, and immortality through perseverance in good works,
> but wrath and fury to those who selfishly disobey the truth and obey wickedness.
> Yes, affliction and distress will come upon everyone who does evil, Jew first and then Greek.
> But there will be glory, honor, and peace for everyone who does good, Jew first and then Greek.
> There is no partiality with God.

Dear friends, I imagine you have been admonished numerous times about being judgmental. Unfortunately, there are many around the world who are willing to cast the first (second, third, etc) stone despite not being sinless. Beware, some may even set traps to make you cast a stone. May you seek glory, honor, and immortality through perseverance in good works and gain eternal life.

Blessings

God morning, branches,

Today's Gospel
Mt 11:25-27

> At that time Jesus exclaimed:
> "I give praise to you, Father, Lord of heaven and earth, for although you have hidden these things
> from the wise and the learned
> you have revealed them to the childlike.
> Yes, Father, such has been your gracious will.
> All things have been handed over to me by my Father. No one knows the Son except the Father,
> and no one knows the Father except the Son
> and anyone to whom the Son wishes to reveal him."

Dear friends, it is interesting that the wise and learned do not understand like those who are childlike, which is not to be confused with childish. Someone who is wise or learned might be proud or immodest. Someone who is childlike might be humble, innocent or trusting.

The Venerable Bishop Fulton Sheen once told this story of a boy who just came home from a catechism class.

His father, who was an atheist, always prodded him and asked this little boy often to defend his faith, one that his mother had instilled deeply in him. On this day, the father asked his son, "So what did you learn today in catechism?" The boy answered, "Well, I learned that God is our Father, Son and Holy Spirit. And that the Father, Son and Holy Spirit are all equal to each other." "No, that is not possible," the father said. "A father and a son cannot be equal to each other because a father is greater than his son. I have lived much longer than you, haven't I?" And his son said, "But you didn't become a father until I became a son."

Blessings

God morning, sisters and brothers,

Today's Reading II
Phil 2:6-11

> Brothers and sisters:
> Christ Jesus, though he was in the form of God,
> did not regard equality with God something to be grasped.
> Rather, he emptied himself,
> taking the form of a slave,
> coming in human likeness;
> and found human in appearance,
> he humbled himself,
> becoming obedient to death,
> even death on a cross.
> Because of this, God greatly exalted him
> and bestowed on him the name
> that is above every name,

that at the name of Jesus
every knee should bend,
of those in heaven and on earth and under the earth,
and every tongue confess that
Jesus Christ is Lord,
to the glory of God the Father.

Dear friends, Christ Jesus, though he was in the form of God took on human form and, among other things, humbled himself. May we remember this when we feel proud.

Blessings

God morning, brothers and sisters,

Today's Reading I
2 *Corinthians* 9:6-11

> Brothers and sisters, consider this:
> whoever sows sparingly will also reap sparingly,
> and whoever sows bountifully will also reap bountifully.
> Each must do as already determined, without sadness or compulsion,
> for God loves a cheerful giver.
> Moreover, God is able to make every grace abundant for you,
> so that in all things, always having all you need,
> you may have an abundance for every good work.
> As it is written:
> He scatters abroad, he gives to the poor;
> his righteousness endures forever.
> The one who supplies seed to the sower and bread for food
> will supply and multiply your seed

and increase the harvest of your righteousness.
You are being enriched in every way for all generosity,
which through us produces thanksgiving to God.

May you be a cheerful giver and sow bountifully.

Blessings

God morning, disciples,

Today's Gospel
John 15:1-8

Jesus said to his disciples:
"I am the true vine, and my Father is the vine grower.
He takes away every branch in me that does not bear fruit,
and everyone that does he prunes so that it bears more fruit.
You are already pruned because of the word that I spoke to you.
Remain in me, as I remain in you.
Just as a branch cannot bear fruit on its own
unless it remains on the vine,
so neither can you unless you remain in me.
I am the vine, you are the branches.
Whoever remains in me and I in him will bear much fruit,
because without me you can do nothing.
Anyone who does not remain in me
will be thrown out like a branch and wither;
people will gather them and throw them into a fire
and they will be burned.
If you remain in me and my words remain in you,
ask for whatever you want and it will be done for you.

By this is my Father glorified,
that you bear much fruit and become my disciples."

Dear friends, may you remain in the Lord, bear much fruit, become one of His disciples and, thereby, glorify God. Remember, without Jesus you can do nothing.

Blessings

God morning, branches,

Today's Gospel
John 3:16-21

> God so loved the world that he gave his only-begotten Son,
> so that everyone who believes in him might not perish
> but might have eternal life.
> For God did not send his Son into the world to condemn the world,
> but that the world might be saved through him.
> Whoever believes in him will not be condemned,
> but whoever does not believe has already been condemned,
> because he has not believed in the name of the only-begotten Son of God.
> And this is the verdict,
> that the light came into the world,
> but people preferred darkness to light,
> because their works were evil.
> For everyone who does wicked things hates the light
> and does not come toward the light,
> so that his works might not be exposed.
> But whoever lives the truth comes to the light,
> so that his works may be clearly seen as done in God.

Dear friends, John 3:16 is the world's most popular Bible verse, according to a source. You might recall a famous college football player had John 3:16 for his eye black during his college times. A lay minister said: "As I have reflected on these words over the years, I've moved into an understanding not just about God's love for the world and everyone in it (including me) but what it meant for the first person who heard those words: Nicodemus. I wonder how many passwords include John 3:16. I imagine some who were in the dark and others who were on the fence came to the light because of this Gospel reading. May we lead others to Jesus by our words and actions.

Blessings

God morning, branches,

Today's Gospel
Jn 17:11b–19

> Lifting up his eyes to heaven, Jesus prayed, saying:
> "Holy Father, keep them in your name
> that you have given me,
> so that they may be one just as we are one.
> When I was with them I protected them in your name that you gave me,
> and I guarded them, and none of them was lost
> except the son of destruction,
> in order that the Scripture might be fulfilled.
> But now I am coming to you.
> I speak this in the world
> so that they may share my joy completely.
> I gave them your word, and the world hated them,

because they do not belong to the world
any more than I belong to the world.
I do not ask that you take them out of the world
but that you keep them from the Evil One.
They do not belong to the world
any more than I belong to the world.
Consecrate them in the truth.
Your word is truth.
As you sent me into the world,
so I sent them into the world.
And I consecrate myself for them,
so that they also may be consecrated in truth."

Dear friends, Jesus asks his Holy Father to keep us from the Evil One. Remember, though, we have free will and God does not force Himself on His creation. If we ask for His help, He will give it freely and abundantly. Recall 1 Peter 5:8, which says Be sober-minded; be watchful. Your adversary the devil prowls around like a roaring lion, seeking someone to devour. Be sober-minded and watchful.

Blessings

God morning, disciples,

Today's Gospel
Mt 6:1-6, 16-18

> Jesus said to his disciples:
> "Take care not to perform righteous deeds in order that people may see them;

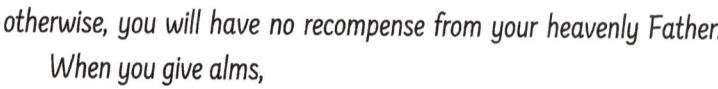

otherwise, you will have no recompense from your heavenly Father.
　　When you give alms,
do not blow a trumpet before you,
as the hypocrites do in the synagogues and in the streets to win the
　　praise of others.
Amen, I say to you,
they have received their reward. But when you give alms,
do not let your left hand know what your right is doing, so that your
　　almsgiving may be secret.
And your Father who sees in secret will repay you.

"When you pray,
do not be like the hypocrites,
who love to stand and pray in the synagogues and on street corners so
　　that others may see them.
Amen, I say to you,
they have received their reward.
But when you pray, go to your inner room, close the door, and pray to
　　your Father in secret.
And your Father who sees in secret will repay you.

"When you fast,
do not look gloomy like the hypocrites. They neglect their appearance,
so that they may appear to others to be fasting. Amen, I say to you,
　　they have received their reward. But when you fast,
anoint your head and wash your face,
so that you may not appear to be fasting, except to your Father who
　　is hidden.
And your Father who sees what is hidden will repay you."

Dear friends, may we not be hypocrites.

Blessings

God morning, branches,

Today's Reading I
Ephesians 4:1-7, 11-13

> Brothers and sisters:
> I, a prisoner for the Lord,
> urge you to live in a manner worthy of the call you have received,
> with all humility and gentleness, with patience,
> bearing with one another through love,
> striving to preserve the unity of the Spirit
> through the bond of peace:
> one Body and one Spirit,
> as you were also called to the one hope of your call;
> one Lord, one faith, one baptism;
> one God and Father of all,
> who is over all and through all and in all.
>
> But grace was given to each of us
> according to the measure of Christ's gift.
>
> And he gave some as Apostles, others as prophets,
> others as evangelists, others as pastors and teachers,
> to equip the holy ones for the work of ministry,
> for building up the Body of Christ,
> until we all attain to the unity of faith
> and knowledge of the Son of God, to mature manhood,
> to the extent of the full stature of Christ.

SCRIPTURE NOTES

Dear friends, may we live in a manner worthy of the call we have received, with all humility and gentleness, with patience, bearing with one another through love.

Blessings

God morning, disciples,

Today's Gospel
Matthew 7:15-20

> Jesus said to his disciples:
> "Beware of false prophets, who come to you in sheep's clothing, but underneath are ravenous wolves.
> By their fruits you will know them.
> Do people pick grapes from thornbushes, or figs from thistles? Just so, every good tree bears good fruit,
> and a rotten tree bears bad fruit. A good tree cannot bear bad fruit, nor can a rotten tree bear good fruit.
> Every tree that does not bear good fruit will be cut down and thrown into the fire.
> So by their fruits you will know them."

Dear friends, the internet and social media are fertile grounds for false prophets, who are wolves in sheep's clothing. They are not easy to spot as the evil one is the master of deception. They can be detected by their works. Do their actions match their words? Saint Paul wrote of the 'fruit of the Spirit' (Galatians 5:22–23) when he lists love, joy, peace, patience, kindness, generosity, faithfulness, gentleness and self-control as evidence of God's work.

By the way, does the phrase wolves in sheep's clothing sound familiar? You probably have heard or used it. Now you know its origin.

Blessings

God morning, disciples,

Today's Gospel
Mark 6:53-56

> After making the crossing to the other side of the sea,
> Jesus and his disciples came to land at Gennesaret
> and tied up there.
> As they were leaving the boat, people immediately recognized him.
> They scurried about the surrounding country
> and began to bring in the sick on mats
> to wherever they heard he was.
> Whatever villages or towns or countryside he entered,
> they laid the sick in the marketplaces
> and begged him that they might touch only the tassel on his cloak;
> and as many as touched it were healed.

Dear friends, imagine that all the sick had to do to be healed was touch the tassel of His cloak. May we have the faith of the sick and their family and friends in this Gospel.

Blessings

God morning, disciples,

Today's Gospel
Mk 7:1–13

> When the Pharisees with some scribes who had come from Jerusalem
> gathered around Jesus,
> they observed that some of his disciples ate their meals
> with unclean, that is, unwashed, hands.
> (For the Pharisees and, in fact, all Jews,
> do not eat without carefully washing their hands,
> keeping the tradition of the elders.
> And on coming from the marketplace
> they do not eat without purifying themselves.
> And there are many other things that they have traditionally observed,
> the purification of cups and jugs and kettles and beds.)
> So the Pharisees and scribes questioned him,
> "Why do your disciples not follow the tradition of the elders
> but instead eat a meal with unclean hands?"
> He responded,
> "Well did Isaiah prophesy about you hypocrites,
> as it is written:
>
> This people honors me with their lips,
> but their hearts are far from me;
> In vain do they worship me,
> teaching as doctrines human precepts.
>
> You disregard God's commandment but cling to human tradition."
> He went on to say,
> "How well you have set aside the commandment of God
> in order to uphold your tradition!

> For Moses said,
> Honor your father and your mother,
> and Whoever curses father or mother shall die.
> Yet you say,
> 'If someone says to father or mother,
> "Any support you might have had from me is qorban"'
> (meaning, dedicated to God),
> you allow him to do nothing more for his father or mother.
> You nullify the word of God
> in favor of your tradition that you have handed on.
> And you do many such things."

Dear friends, may we not nullify the word of God in favor of traditions.

Blessings

God morning, branches,

Today's Reading I
James 4:13–17

> Beloved:
> Come now, you who say,
> "Today or tomorrow we shall go into such and such a town, spend a year there doing business, and make a profit"–
> you have no idea what your life will be like tomorrow.
> You are a puff of smoke that appears briefly and then disappears.
> Instead you should say,
> "If the Lord wills it, we shall live to do this or that." But now you are boasting in your arrogance.

All such boasting is evil.
So for one who knows the right thing to do and does not do it, it is a sin.

Dear friends, we are but puffs of smoke. May we not be arrogant and do the right thing. Remember, we are not in control; God is in control. When we make plans, we should think God willing. May you have a long, happy, healthy and blessed life, God willing.

Blessings

God morning, branches,

Tuesday's Gospel
Matthew 23:23-26

> Jesus said:
> "Woe to you, scribes and Pharisees, you hypocrites.
> You pay tithes of mint and dill and cummin,
> and have neglected the weightier things of the law:
> judgment and mercy and fidelity.
> But these you should have done, without neglecting the others.
> Blind guides, who strain out the gnat and swallow the camel!"Woe to
>   you, scribes and Pharisees, you hypocrites.
> You cleanse the outside of cup and dish,
> but inside they are full of plunder and self-indulgence.
> Blind Pharisee, cleanse first the inside of the cup,
> so that the outside also may be clean."

Dear friends, may we not be hypocrites like the scribes and Pharisees. May we not just give the outward appearance of our

faith, but actually live it. May we have the true gospel spirit, which is one of love, integrity, compassion and a sense of justice for all.

Blessings

God morning, disciples,

Today's Gospel
Matthew 20:1-16

> Jesus told his disciples this parable:
> "The Kingdom of heaven is like a landowner
> who went out at dawn to hire laborers for his vineyard. After agreeing with them for the usual daily wage,
> he sent them into his vineyard. Going out about nine o'clock,
> he saw others standing idle in the marketplace, and he said to them, 'You too go into my vineyard, and I will give you what is just.'
> So they went off.
> And he went out again around noon,
> and around three o'clock, and did likewise. Going out about five o'clock,
> he found others standing around, and said to them, 'Why do you stand here idle all day?'
> They answered, 'Because no one has hired us.' He said to them, 'You too go into my vineyard.'
> When it was evening the owner of the vineyard said to his foreman, 'Summon the laborers and give them their pay,
> beginning with the last and ending with the first.' When those who had started about five o'clock came, each received the usual daily wage.
> So when the first came, they thought that they would receive more, but each of them also got the usual wage.

And on receiving it they grumbled against the landowner, saying, 'These
  last ones worked only one hour,
and you have made them equal to us, who bore the day's burden and
  the heat.' He said to one of them in reply,
'My friend, I am not cheating you.
Did you not agree with me for the usual daily wage? Take what is yours
  and go.
What if I wish to give this last one the same as you? Or am I not free
  to do as I wish with my own money? Are you envious because I
  am generous?'
Thus, the last will be first, and the first will be last."

Dear friends, the first workers were paid what they bargained for and deserved. They should have been happy. Instead, they were jealous and angry despite the fact the landowner did nothing wrong. We all have received gifts from God and should not be envious of others. We are here by His grace. What we have is His gift to us. It is not our choice, but His. This is not the first time you have heard about being first or last. May we be content with the gifts God has given to us.

Blessings

God morning, branches,

Today's Gospel
Luke 21:12-19

Jesus said to the crowd:
"They will seize and persecute you,

> they will hand you over to the synagogues and to prisons, and they
> will have you led before kings and governors because of my name.
> It will lead to your giving testimony.
> Remember, you are not to prepare your defense beforehand, for I myself
> shall give you a wisdom in speaking
> that all your adversaries will be powerless to resist or refute. You will
> even be handed over by parents,
> brothers, relatives, and friends,
> and they will put some of you to death.
> You will be hated by all because of my name, but not a hair on your
> head will be destroyed.
> By your perseverance you will secure your lives."

Dear friends, you might think what Jesus says in today's Gospel could not happen today. I submit to you that there are some who are being persecuted because of His name. Remember, it has happened many times in the past and evil is prevalent in our world.

Blessings

God morning, branches,

Today's Reading I
Acts 22:3-16

> Paul addressed the people in these words: "I am a Jew, born in Tarsus in Cilicia, but brought up in this city.
> At the feet of Gamaliel I was educated strictly in our ancestral law and was zealous for God, just as all of you are today.
> I persecuted this Way to death,

binding both men and women and delivering them to prison. Even the high priest and the whole council of elders
can testify on my behalf.
For from them I even received letters to the brothers and set out for Damascus to bring back to Jerusalem in chains for punishment those there as well.

"On that journey as I drew near to Damascus,
about noon a great light from the sky suddenly shone around me. I fell to the ground and heard a voice saying to me,
'Saul, Saul, why are you persecuting me?' I replied, 'Who are you, sir?' And he said to me,
'I am Jesus the Nazorean whom you are persecuting.' My companions saw the light
but did not hear the voice of the one who spoke to me. I asked, 'What shall I do, sir?'
The Lord answered me, 'Get up and go into Damascus, and there you will be told about everything
appointed for you to do.'
Since I could see nothing because of the brightness of that light, I was led by hand by my companions and entered Damascus.

"A certain Ananias, a devout observer of the law, and highly spoken of by all the Jews who lived there, came to me and stood there and said,
'Saul, my brother, regain your sight.'
And at that very moment I regained my sight and saw him. Then he said,
'The God of our ancestors designated you to know his will, to see the Righteous One, and to hear the sound of his voice; for you will be his witness before all
to what you have seen and heard. Now, why delay?

SCRIPTURE NOTES

Get up and have yourself baptized and your sins washed away, calling upon his name.'"

Dear friends, think about what God did for Saint Paul and imagine what He could do for you.

Alleluia

God morning, disciples,

Today's Gospel
Mark 10:32-45

> The disciples were on the way, going up to Jerusalem,
> and Jesus went ahead of them.
> They were amazed, and those who followed were afraid.
> Taking the Twelve aside again, he began to tell them
> what was going to happen to him.
> "Behold, we are going up to Jerusalem, and the Son of Man
> will be handed over to the chief priests and the scribes,
> and they will condemn him to death
> and hand him over to the Gentiles who will mock him,
> spit upon him, scourge him, and put him to death,
> but after three days he will rise."
> Then James and John, the sons of Zebedee,
> came to Jesus and said to him,
> 'Teacher, we want you to do for us whatever we ask of you."
> He replied, 'What do you wish me to do for you?"
> They answered him,
> "Grant that in your glory
> we may sit one at your right and the other at your left."

Jesus said to them, "You do not know what you are asking.
Can you drink the chalice that I drink
or be baptized with the baptism with which I am baptized?"
They said to him, 'We can."
Jesus said to them, "The chalice that I drink, you will drink,
and with the baptism with which I am baptized, you will be baptized;
but to sit at my right or at my left is not mine to give
but is for those for whom it has been prepared."
When the ten heard this, they became indignant at James and John.
Jesus summoned them and said to them,
"You know that those who are recognized as rulers over the Gentiles
lord it over them,
and their great ones make their authority over them felt.
But it shall not be so among you.
Rather, whoever wishes to be great among you will be your servant;
whoever wishes to be first among you will be the slave of all.
For the Son of Man did not come to be served but to serve
and to give his life as a ransom for many."

Dear friends, as we are called to follow Jesus, we should remember that we are called to serve. It is that simple, but not easy. We must deny ourselves. We must serve even in difficult times. We must not choose those we serve.

Blessings

God morning, brothers and sisters,

Today's Reading I
1 Thes 2:9-13

> You recall, brothers and sisters, our toil and drudgery. Working night and day in order not to burden any of you, we proclaimed to you the Gospel of God.
> You are witnesses, and so is God,
> how devoutly and justly and blamelessly we behaved toward you believers.
> As you know, we treated each one of you as a father treats his children, exhorting and encouraging you and insisting
> that you walk in a manner worthy of the God who calls you into his Kingdom and glory.
>
> And for this reason we too give thanks to God unceasingly, that, in receiving the word of God from hearing us,
> you received it not as the word of men, but as it truly is, the word of God, which is now at work in you who believe.

Dear friends, I pray that my daily notes encourage you to walk in a manner worthy of God, who calls you into His Kingdom and glory. I, too, thank God for using me to deliver His words to you and pray they work in you.

Blessings

God morning, branches,

Today's Reading I
1 John 1:5–2:2

> Beloved:
> This is the message that we have heard from Jesus Christ and proclaim to you:

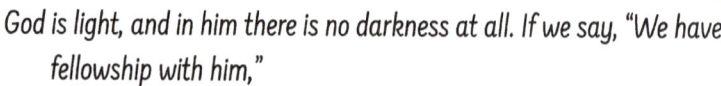

SCRIPTURE NOTES

God is light, and in him there is no darkness at all. If we say, "We have fellowship with him,"
while we continue to walk in darkness, we lie and do not act in truth.
But if we walk in the light as he is in the light, then we have fellowship with one another,
and the Blood of his Son Jesus cleanses us from all sin. If we say, "We are without sin,"
we deceive ourselves, and the truth is not in us.
If we acknowledge our sins, he is faithful and just
and will forgive our sins and cleanse us from every wrongdoing. If we say, "We have not sinned," we make him a liar,
and his word is not in us.

My children, I am writing this to you so that you may not commit sin. But if anyone does sin, we have an Advocate with the Father, Jesus Christ the righteous one.
He is expiation for our sins,
and not for our sins only but for those of the whole world.

Dear friends, may we walk in His light, acknowledge our sins and try to not sin.

Blessings

God morning, sisters and brothers,

Today's Reading I
Romans 10:9-18

Brothers and sisters:
If you confess with your mouth that Jesus is Lord
and believe in your heart that God raised him from the dead,

you will be saved.
For one believes with the heart and so is justified,
and one confesses with the mouth and so is saved.
The Scripture says,
No one who believes in him will be put to shame.
There is no distinction between Jew and Greek;
the same Lord is Lord of all,
enriching all who call upon him.
For everyone who calls on the name of the Lord will be saved.

But how can they call on him in whom they have not believed?
And how can they believe in him of whom they have not heard?
And how can they hear without someone to preach?
And how can people preach unless they are sent?
As it is written,
How beautiful are the feet of those who bring the good news!
But not everyone has heeded the good news;
for Isaiah says, Lord, who has believed what was heard from us?
Thus faith comes from what is heard,
and what is heard comes through the word of Christ.
But I ask, did they not hear?
Certainly they did; for

Their voice has gone forth to all the earth,
and their words to the ends of the world.

Dear friends, we are called to proclaim the Good News. May we do so by our words and actions. May our feet be beautiful.

Blessings

SCRIPTURE NOTES

God morning, sisters and brothers,

Today's Reading 1
James 1:1-11

> James, a servant of God and of the Lord Jesus Christ,
> to the twelve tribes in the dispersion, greetings.
>
> Consider it all joy, my brothers and sisters,
> when you encounter various trials,
> for you know that the testing of your faith produces perseverance.
> And let perseverance be perfect,
> so that you may be perfect and complete, lacking in nothing.
> But if any of you lacks wisdom,
> he should ask God who gives to all generously and ungrudgingly,
> and he will be given it.
> But he should ask in faith, not doubting,
> for the one who doubts is like a wave of the sea
> that is driven and tossed about by the wind.
> For that person must not suppose that he will receive anything from the Lord,
> since he is a man of two minds, unstable in all his ways.
>
> The brother in lowly circumstances
> should take pride in high standing,
> and the rich one in his lowliness,
> for he will pass away "like the flower of the field."
> For the sun comes up with its scorching heat and dries up the grass,
> its flower droops, and the beauty of its appearance vanishes.
> So will the rich person fade away in the midst of his pursuits.

Dear friends, I imagine we have trouble considering our various trials to be all joy, but remember God can get us through anything if we truly believe. May we persevere in our faith and not doubt that He will help us. May we take pride in our lowly circumstances.

Blessings

God morning, disciples,

Today's Gospel
Matthew 21:33–43, 45–46

> Jesus said to the chief priests and the elders of the people:
> "Hear another parable.
> There was a landowner who planted a vineyard,
> put a hedge around it,
> dug a wine press in it, and built a tower.
> Then he leased it to tenants and went on a journey.
> When vintage time drew near,
> he sent his servants to the tenants to obtain his produce.
> But the tenants seized the servants and one they beat,
> another they killed, and a third they stoned.
> Again he sent other servants, more numerous than the first ones,
> but they treated them in the same way.
> Finally, he sent his son to them,
> thinking, 'They will respect my son.'
> But when the tenants saw the son, they said to one another,
> 'This is the heir.
> Come, let us kill him and acquire his inheritance.'
> They seized him, threw him out of the vineyard, and killed him.
> What will the owner of the vineyard do to those tenants when he comes?"

They answered him,
"He will put those wretched men to a wretched death
and lease his vineyard to other tenants
who will give him the produce at the proper times."
Jesus said to them, "Did you never read in the Scriptures:

The stone that the builders rejected
has become the cornerstone;
by the Lord has this been done,
and it is wonderful in our eyes?

Therefore, I say to you,
the Kingdom of God will be taken away from you
and given to a people that will produce its fruit."
When the chief priests and the Pharisees heard his parables,
they knew that he was speaking about them.
And although they were attempting to arrest him,
they feared the crowds, for they regarded him as a prophet.

Dear friends, Jesus was regarded as a prophet, when in fact He is the cornerstone! May He be the cornerstone of our lives. When we see a building, which is probably often, may we look to the cornerstone and recall the cornerstone of our lives. I consider that to be a form of prayer. May we produce fruit that allows us to receive the Kingdom.

Blessings

God morning, branches,

Today's Reading 1
Jer 17:5-10

SCRIPTURE NOTES

Thus says the LORD:
Cursed is the man who trusts in human beings,
who seeks his strength in flesh,
whose heart turns away from the LORD.
He is like a barren bush in the desert
that enjoys no change of season,
But stands in a lava waste,
a salt and empty earth.
Blessed is the man who trusts in the LORD,
whose hope is the LORD.
He is like a tree planted beside the waters
that stretches out its roots to the stream:
It fears not the heat when it comes,
its leaves stay green;
In the year of drought it shows no distress,
but still bears fruit.
More tortuous than all else is the human heart,
beyond remedy; who can understand it?
I, the LORD, alone probe the mind
and test the heart,
To reward everyone according to his ways,
according to the merit of his deeds.

Dear friends, may you trust in the Lord and not man. That should be an easy decision.

Blessings

SCRIPTURE NOTES

God morning, disciples,

Today's Gospel
Matthew 20:17-28

> As Jesus was going up to Jerusalem,
> he took the Twelve disciples aside by themselves,
> and said to them on the way,
> "Behold, we are going up to Jerusalem,
> and the Son of Man will be handed over to the chief priests
> and the scribes,
> and they will condemn him to death,
> and hand him over to the Gentiles
> to be mocked and scourged and crucified,
> and he will be raised on the third day."
> Then the mother of the sons of Zebedee approached Jesus with her sons
> and did him homage, wishing to ask him for something.
> He said to her, "What do you wish?"
> She answered him,
> "Command that these two sons of mine sit,
> one at your right and the other at your left, in your kingdom."
> Jesus said in reply,
> "You do not know what you are asking.
> Can you drink the chalice that I am going to drink?"
> They said to him, "We can."
> He replied,
> "My chalice you will indeed drink,
> but to sit at my right and at my left,
> this is not mine to give
> but is for those for whom it has been prepared by my Father."
> When the ten heard this,

they became indignant at the two brothers.
But Jesus summoned them and said,
"You know that the rulers of the Gentiles lord it over them,
and the great ones make their authority over them felt.
But it shall not be so among you.
Rather, whoever wishes to be great among you shall be your servant;
whoever wishes to be first among you shall be your slave.
Just so, the Son of Man did not come to be served but to serve
and to give his life as a ransom for many."

Dear friends, whenever we start thinking of how important we think we are, we would do well to consider that the Son of Man did not come to be served, but to serve. Like Jesus, we came here not to be served, but to serve.

Blessings

God morning, branches,

Today's Gospel
Luke 4:24–30

> Jesus said to the people in the synagogue at Nazareth:
> "Amen, I say to you,
> no prophet is accepted in his own native place.
> Indeed, I tell you, there were many widows in Israel
> in the days of Elijah
> when the sky was closed for three and a half years
> and a severe famine spread over the entire land.
> It was to none of these that Elijah was sent,
> but only to a widow in Zarephath in the land of Sidon.

> Again, there were many lepers in Israel
> during the time of Elisha the prophet;
> yet not one of them was cleansed, but only Naaman the Syrian."
> When the people in the synagogue heard this,
> they were all filled with fury.
> They rose up, drove him out of the town,
> and led him to the brow of the hill
> on which their town had been built,
> to hurl him down headlong.
> But he passed through the midst of them and went away.

Dear friends, the people in the synagogue were furious with Jesus because He spoke of other prophets of the people's faith who rescued nonbelievers or people unlike them. Remember, Jesus came to rescue those who believe in Him. Recall the Great Physician story. Apparently, the people in the synagogue were quite prejudiced. May we not be like them. We are all God's children.

Blessings

God morning, branches,

Today's Reading 1
Hebrews 13:1-8

> Let brotherly love continue.
> Do not neglect hospitality,
> for through it some have unknowingly entertained angels.
> Be mindful of prisoners as if sharing their imprisonment,
> and of the ill-treated as of yourselves,
> for you also are in the body.

> Let marriage be honored among all
> and the marriage bed be kept undefiled,
> for God will judge the immoral and adulterers.
> Let your life be free from love of money
> but be content with what you have,
> for he has said, I will never forsake you or abandon you.
> Thus we may say with confidence:
> The Lord is my helper,
> and I will not be afraid.
> What can anyone do to me?
>
> Remember your leaders who spoke the word of God to you.
> Consider the outcome of their way of life and imitate their faith.
> Jesus Christ is the same yesterday, today, and forever.

Dear friends, always let love continue. Jesus is always the same because He is perfect. Hopefully, we are better today than yesterday and will be even better every day as we work towards being perfect.

Blessings

God morning, branches,

Today's Gospel
Matthew 13:54–58

> Jesus came to his native place and taught the people in their synagogue. They were astonished and said,
> "Where did this man get such wisdom and mighty deeds? Is he not the carpenter's son?
> Is not his mother named Mary

and his brothers James, Joseph, Simon, and Judas? Are not his sisters all with us?
Where did this man get all this?" And they took offense at him. But Jesus said to them,
"A prophet is not without honor except in his native place and in his own house."
And he did not work many mighty deeds there because of their lack of faith.

Dear friends, Jesus left his home to begin the work that was His reason for being. Instead of receiving joyous accolades for all His wonderful accomplishments, He was met with derision. Imagine a small town boy goes out and performs miracles. Perhaps those in His hometown were jealous and prejudiced. I wonder if at some time we may have acted like those in Jesus' hometown.

Blessings

God morning, branches,

Today's Reading I
2 John 1:4-9

[Chosen Lady:]
I rejoiced greatly to find some of your children walking in the truth
just as we were commanded by the Father.
But now, Lady, I ask you,
not as though I were writing a new commandment
but the one we have had from the beginning:
let us love one another.
For this is love, that we walk according to his commandments;

> this is the commandment, as you heard from the beginning,
> in which you should walk.
> Many deceivers have gone out into the world,
> those who do not acknowledge Jesus Christ as coming in the flesh;
> such is the deceitful one and the antichrist.
> Look to yourselves that you do not lose what we worked for
> but may receive a full recompense.
> Anyone who is so "progressive"
> as not to remain in the teaching of the Christ does not have God;
> whoever remains in the teaching has the Father and the Son.

Dear friends, let us love one another. For this is love, that we walk according to His commandments. Beware the many deceivers and those who do not remain in the teaching of the Christ.

Blessings,

God morning, branches,

Today's Gospel
Matthew 9:27-31

> As Jesus passed by, two blind men followed him, crying out,
> "Son of David, have pity on us!"
> When he entered the house,
> the blind men approached him and Jesus said to them,
> "Do you believe that I can do this?"
> "Yes, Lord," they said to him.
> Then he touched their eyes and said,
> "Let it be done for you according to your faith."
> And their eyes were opened.

Jesus warned them sternly,
"See that no one knows about this."
But they went out and spread word of him through all that land.

Dear friends, as we see here and have seen in other readings, faith can work miracles (and I know this from my experiences). Perhaps you have cried out to the Lord for help with something and feel He has not heard you. He hears everything spoken and unspoken. He knows your thoughts better than you do and before you even think them. Remember, His ways are not our ways and His time is not our time. It is often said that God works in mysterious ways. Well, they are not mysterious to Him.

By the way, if you were blind and given sight by the Lord, would you shout for joy and openly praise Him despite His admonition to be silent?

Blessings

God morning, disciples,

Today's Gospel
Luke 6:43–49

> Jesus said to his disciples:
> "A good tree does not bear rotten fruit,
> nor does a rotten tree bear good fruit.
> For every tree is known by its own fruit.
> For people do not pick figs from thornbushes,
> nor do they gather grapes from brambles.
> A good person out of the store of goodness in his heart produces good,
> but an evil person out of a store of evil produces evil;

for from the fullness of the heart the mouth speaks.

"Why do you call me, 'Lord, Lord,' but not do what I command?
I will show you what someone is like who comes to me,
listens to my words, and acts on them.
That one is like a man building a house,
who dug deeply and laid the foundation on rock;
when the flood came, the river burst against that house
but could not shake it because it had been well built.
But the one who listens and does not act
is like a person who built a house on the ground
without a foundation.
When the river burst against it,
it collapsed at once and was completely destroyed."

Dear friends, may we go to Jesus, listen to His words and act on them. He is the foundation of our existence.

Blessings

God morning, disciples,

Today's Gospel
Matthew 13:10-17

> The disciples approached Jesus and said,
> "Why do you speak to the crowd in parables?"
> He said to them in reply,
> "Because knowledge of the mysteries of the Kingdom of heaven
> has been granted to you, but to them it has not been granted.
> To anyone who has, more will be given and he will grow rich;
> from anyone who has not, even what he has will be taken away.

This is why I speak to them in parables, because
they look but do not see and hear but do not listen or understand.
Isaiah's prophecy is fulfilled in them, which says:

You shall indeed hear but not understand,
you shall indeed look but never see.
Gross is the heart of this people,
they will hardly hear with their ears,
they have closed their eyes,
lest they see with their eyes
and hear with their ears
and understand with their hearts and be converted
and I heal them.

"But blessed are your eyes, because they see,
and your ears, because they hear.
Amen, I say to you, many prophets and righteous people
longed to see what you see but did not see it,
and to hear what you hear but did not hear it."

Dear friends, may your eyes and ears be blessed.
Blessings

God morning, disciples,

Today's Gospel
Matthew 16:24-28

> Jesus said to his disciples,
> "Whoever wishes to come after me must deny himself,
> take up his cross, and follow me.

SCRIPTURE NOTES

*For whoever wishes to save his life will lose it,
but whoever loses his life for my sake will find it.
What profit would there be for one to gain the whole world
and forfeit his life?
Or what can one give in exchange for his life?
For the Son of Man will come with his angels in his Father's glory,
and then he will repay each according to his conduct.
Amen, I say to you, there are some standing here
who will not taste death
until they see the Son of Man coming in his Kingdom."*

Dear friends, have you denied yourself anything lately?
Have you walked in His footsteps recently?
Following the Lord is not easy, but the rewards are heavenly.

Blessings

God morning, branches,

*Today's Gospel
Matthew 22:34-40*

*When the Pharisees heard that Jesus had silenced the Sadducees,
they gathered together, and one of them,
a scholar of the law, tested him by asking,
"Teacher, which commandment in the law is the greatest?"
He said to him,
"You shall love the Lord, your God, with all your heart,
with all your soul, and with all your mind.
This is the greatest and the first commandment.
The second is like it:*

You shall love your neighbor as yourself.
The whole law and the prophets depend on these two commandments."

Dear friends, I believe that if we keep these commandments, all the others could never be violated. If everyone loved one another, would it not be heavenly?

Blessings

God morning, disciples,

Today's Gospel
Matthew 16:13-20

Jesus went into the region of Caesarea Philippi and
he asked his disciples,
"Who do people say that the Son of Man is?"
They replied, "Some say John the Baptist, others Elijah,
still others Jeremiah or one of the prophets."
He said to them, "But who do you say that I am?"
Simon Peter said in reply,
"You are the Christ, the Son of the living God."
Jesus said to him in reply,
"Blessed are you, Simon son of Jonah.
For flesh and blood has not revealed this to you, but my heavenly Father.
And so I say to you, you are Peter,
and upon this rock I will build my church,
and the gates of the netherworld shall not prevail against it.
I will give you the keys to the kingdom of heaven.
Whatever you bind on earth shall be bound in heaven;
and whatever you loose on earth shall be loosed in heaven."

> *Then he strictly ordered his disciples*
> *to tell no one that he was the Christ,*

Dear friends, Peter identified Jesus as "You are the Christ, the Son of the living God."

Jesus said to him in reply, "Blessed are you, Simon son of Jonah. For flesh and blood

has not revealed this to you, but my heavenly Father. Peter was chosen by Jesus to follow Him. Peter saw Jesus perform many miracles and heard His teachings. Think of that: despite all Peter had seen and heard, his understanding was a gift from God. What an amazing gift! May we take some time to consider and be thankful for our gifts. I dare say we have not opened all our gifts and more are in our future.

Blessings

God morning, branches,

Todays' Gospel
Mark 6:17-29

> Herod was the one who had John the Baptist arrested and bound in prison
> on account of Herodias,
> the wife of his brother Philip, whom he had married.
> John had said to Herod,
> "It is not lawful for you to have your brother's wife."
> Herodias harbored a grudge against him
> and wanted to kill him but was unable to do so.
> Herod feared John, knowing him to be a righteous and holy man,
> and kept him in custody.

SCRIPTURE NOTES

When he heard him speak he was very much perplexed,
yet he liked to listen to him.
She had an opportunity one day when Herod, on his birthday,
gave a banquet for his courtiers,
his military officers, and the leading men of Galilee.
Herodias' own daughter came in
and performed a dance that delighted Herod and his guests.
The king said to the girl,
"Ask of me whatever you wish and I will grant it to you."
He even swore many things to her,
"I will grant you whatever you ask of me,
even to half of my kingdom."
She went out and said to her mother,
"What shall I ask for?"
She replied, "The head of John the Baptist."
The girl hurried back to the king's presence and made her request,
"I want you to give me at once
on a platter the head of John the Baptist."
The king was deeply distressed,
but because of his oaths and the guests
he did not wish to break his word to her.
So he promptly dispatched an executioner with orders
to bring back his head.
He went off and beheaded him in the prison.
He brought in the head on a platter and gave it to the girl.
The girl in turn gave it to her mother.
When his disciples heard about it,
they came and took his body and laid it in a tomb.

Dear friends, John the Baptist was beheaded because he spoke truth to power. Herod enjoyed listening to John, but was more worried about losing face in front of his guests. Now, while Herod was clearly wrong so were his wife and her daughter. It is interesting that John set the stage for Jesus in life and death.

Blessings

God morning, branches,

Today's Gospel
Matthew 23:27-32

> Jesus said,
> "Woe to you, scribes and Pharisees, you hypocrites.
> You are like whitewashed tombs, which appear beautiful on the outside,
> but inside are full of dead men's bones and every kind of filth.
> Even so, on the outside you appear righteous,
> but inside you are filled with hypocrisy and evildoing.
>
> "Woe to you, scribes and Pharisees, you hypocrites.
> You build the tombs of the prophets
> and adorn the memorials of the righteous,
> and you say, 'If we had lived in the days of our ancestors,
> we would not have joined them in shedding the prophets' blood.'
> Thus you bear witness against yourselves
> that you are the children of those who murdered the prophets;
> now fill up what your ancestors measured out!"

Dear friends, be careful to not be like whitewashed tombs.

Blessings

God morning, disciples,

Today's Gospel
Luke 4:31-37

> Jesus went down to Capernaum, a town of Galilee.
> He taught them on the sabbath,
> and they were astonished at his teaching
> because he spoke with authority.
> In the synagogue there was a man with the spirit of an unclean demon,
> and he cried out in a loud voice,
> "What have you to do with us, Jesus of Nazareth?
> Have you come to destroy us?
> I know who you are–the Holy One of God!"
> Jesus rebuked him and said, "Be quiet! Come out of him!"
> Then the demon threw the man down in front of them
> and came out of him without doing him any harm.
> They were all amazed and said to one another,
> "What is there about his word?
> For with authority and power he commands the unclean spirits,
> and they come out."
> And news of him spread everywhere in the surrounding region.

Dear friends, they were astonished at his teaching because he spoke with authority. May we read God's words with authority as if Jesus is reading them to us.

Blessings

SCRIPTURE NOTES

God morning, branches,

Today's Gospel
Luke 5:1-11

While the crowd was pressing in on Jesus and listening to the word of God,
he was standing by the Lake of Gennesaret.
He saw two boats there alongside the lake;
the fishermen had disembarked and were washing their nets.
Getting into one of the boats, the one belonging to Simon,
he asked him to put out a short distance from the shore.
Then he sat down and taught the crowds from the boat.
After he had finished speaking, he said to Simon,
"Put out into deep water and lower your nets for a catch."
Simon said in reply,
"Master, we have worked hard all night and have caught nothing,
but at your command I will lower the nets."
When they had done this, they caught a great number of fish
and their nets were tearing.
They signaled to their partners in the other boat
to come to help them.
They came and filled both boats
so that the boats were in danger of sinking.
When Simon Peter saw this, he fell at the knees of Jesus and said,
"Depart from me, Lord, for I am a sinful man."
For astonishment at the catch of fish they had made seized him
and all those with him,
and likewise James and John, the sons of Zebedee,
who were partners of Simon.
Jesus said to Simon, "Do not be afraid;
from now on you will be catching men."

When they brought their boats to the shore,
they left everything and followed him.

Dear friends, I imagine we all have worked hard all night and caught nothing. Remember, if God asks you to do something, he will give you the tools to accomplish your mission. May we be fishers of men through our words and actions.

Blessings

God morning, branches,

Today's Reading I
Romans 8:28-30

> Brothers and sisters:
> We know that all things work for good for those who love God,
> who are called according to his purpose.
> For those he foreknew he also predestined
> to be conformed to the image of his Son,
> so that he might be the firstborn
> among many brothers.
> And those he predestined he also called;
> and those he called he also justified;
> and those he justified he also glorified.

Dear friends, I am pretty sure you love God, but perhaps you have wondered at times whether something was working for good. I know I have struggled with this far more than a few times. Perhaps we were distracted (by you know who) from the good that happened. Maybe we were not in tune with what God was saying so we might need to pray more for guidance. I imagine you have had an a ha moment where you finally figured out or saw the good of something. God takes everything that happens in our lives to mold us into the image of His Son. Keep in mind that many things in Jesus' life did not appear to be good or understandable, but He ended up at the right hand of His Father.

Blessings

God morning, branches,

Today's Reading 1
Colossians 3:1-11

> Brothers and sisters:
> If you were raised with Christ, seek what is above,
> where Christ is seated at the right hand of God.
> Think of what is above, not of what is on earth.
> For you have died, and your life is hidden with Christ in God.
> When Christ your life appears,
> then you too will appear with him in glory.
>
> Because of these the wrath of God is coming upon the disobedient.
> By these you too once conducted yourselves, when you lived in that way.
> But now you must put them all away:
> anger, fury, malice, slander,
> and obscene language out of your mouths.
> Stop lying to one another,
> since you have taken off the old self with its practices
> and have put on the new self,
> which is being renewed, for knowledge,
> in the image of its creator.

> Here there is not Greek and Jew,
> circumcision and uncircumcision,
> barbarian, Scythian, slave, free;
> but Christ is all and in all.

Dear friends, may we think of what is above, not of what is on earth. May we also put to death, then, the parts of you that are earthly: immorality, impurity, passion, evil desire, and the greed that is idolatry, as well as the others noted above. All these are tools of the evil one and we are called to be like Christ.

Blessings

God morning, sisters and brothers,

Today's Reading 2
Phil 1:20c-24, 27a

> Brothers and sisters:
> Christ will be magnified in my body, whether by life or by death.
> For to me life is Christ, and death is gain.
> If I go on living in the flesh,
> that means fruitful labor for me.
> And I do not know which I shall choose.
> I am caught between the two.
> I long to depart this life and be with Christ,
> for that is far better.
> Yet that I remain in the flesh
> is more necessary for your benefit.
>
> Only, conduct yourselves in a way worthy of the gospel of Christ.

SCRIPTURE NOTES

Dear friends, this is a very interesting reading in that life is precious, but Paul longs to depart this life and be with Christ. Think about that; which would you choose?

May we conduct ourselves in a way worthy of the gospel of Christ.

Blessings

God morning, branches,

Today's Gospel
Luke 9:1-6

> Jesus summoned the Twelve and gave them power and authority
> over all demons and to cure diseases,
> and he sent them to proclaim the Kingdom of God
> and to heal the sick.
> He said to them, "Take nothing for the journey,
> neither walking stick, nor sack, nor food, nor money,
> and let no one take a second tunic.
> Whatever house you enter, stay there and leave from there.
> And as for those who do not welcome you,
> when you leave that town,
> shake the dust from your feet in testimony against them."
> Then they set out and went from village to village
> proclaiming the good news and curing diseases everywhere.

Dear friends, we do not have power and authority over demons or to cure diseases. We do have the power, through our words and actions, to lead those who are sick or troubled to the Great Physician.

Blessings

God morning, branches,

Today's Reading 2
Philippians 2:1-5

> Brothers and sisters:
> If there is any encouragement in Christ,
> any solace in love,
> any participation in the Spirit,
> any compassion and mercy,
> complete my joy by being of the same mind, with the same love,
> united in heart, thinking one thing.
> Do nothing out of selfishness or out of vainglory;
> rather, humbly regard others as more important than yourselves,
> each looking out not for his own interests,
> but also for those of others.
>
> Have in you the same attitude
> that is also in Christ Jesus.

Dear friends, today's message is the exact opposite of the me, me, me world. May we do nothing out of selfishness or out of vainglory; rather, humbly regard others as more important than ourselves, each looking out not for his own interests, but also for those of others. As we profess to be Christians, we should have His attitude.

Blessings

God morning, disciples,

Today's Gospel
Luke 10:17-24

SCRIPTURE NOTES

*The seventy-two disciples returned rejoicing and said to Jesus,
"Lord, even the demons are subject to us because of your name."
Jesus said, "I have observed Satan fall like lightning from the sky.
Behold, I have given you the power
'to tread upon serpents' and scorpions
and upon the full force of the enemy
and nothing will harm you.
Nevertheless, do not rejoice because the spirits are subject to you,
but rejoice because your names are written in heaven."*

*At that very moment he rejoiced in the Holy Spirit and said,
"I give you praise, Father, Lord of heaven and earth,
for although you have hidden these things
from the wise and the learned
you have revealed them to the childlike.
Yes, Father, such has been your gracious will.
All things have been handed over to me by my Father.
No one knows who the Son is except the Father,
and who the Father is except the Son
and anyone to whom the Son wishes to reveal him."*

*Turning to the disciples in private he said,
"Blessed are the eyes that see what you see.
For I say to you,
many prophets and kings desired to see what you see,
but did not see it,
and to hear what you hear, but did not hear it."*

Dear friends, the name of Jesus is quite powerful. We know that at the name of Jesus every knee should bow, in heaven and on earth and under the earth and everyone who calls on the name of the Lord will be saved. Who could blame the seventy-two for rejoicing? The Lord, however, offers another lesson in humility in today's Gospel.

Blessings

God morning, sisters and brothers,

Today's Reading 2
Philippians 4:6-9

> Brothers and sisters:
> Have no anxiety at all, but in everything,
> by prayer and petition, with thanksgiving,
> make your requests known to God.
> Then the peace of God that surpasses all understanding
> will guard your hearts and minds in Christ Jesus.
>
> Finally, brothers and sisters,
> whatever is true, whatever is honorable,
> whatever is just, whatever is pure,
> whatever is lovely, whatever is gracious,
> if there is any excellence
> and if there is anything worthy of praise,
> think about these things.
> Keep on doing what you have learned and received
> and heard and seen in me.
> Then the God of peace will be with you.

Dear friends, we were created in the image of God, whose peace surpasses all understanding. As we are human we are subject to anxiety, doubt, uneasiness, fear and the like. The evil one knows our weaknesses and is always seeking to exploit them. Jesus told his disciples to not be anxious about anything. Give everything up to God. Remember, Jesus is known as the Prince of Peace. The name "Prince of Peace" is the Hebrew Sar Shalom, which means "the one who removes all peace-disturbing factors and secures the peace."

Peace

God morning, branches,

Today's Gospel
Luke 11:37-41

> After Jesus had spoken,
> a Pharisee invited him to dine at his home.
> He entered and reclined at table to eat.
> The Pharisee was amazed to see
> that he did not observe the prescribed washing before the meal.
> The Lord said to him, "Oh you Pharisees!
> Although you cleanse the outside of the cup and the dish,
> inside you are filled with plunder and evil.
> You fools!
> Did not the maker of the outside also make the inside?
> But as to what is within, give alms,
> and behold, everything will be clean for you."

Dear friends, Jesus knew the traditions, but wanted to prove a point: the Pharisee's hypocrisy. On the surface he appeared to be clean, not so within. May we take a look inside ourselves to see if we are clean.

Blessings

SCRIPTURE NOTES

God morning, branches,

Today's Gospel
Luke 11:47–54

> The Lord said:
> "Woe to you who build the memorials of the prophets
> whom your fathers killed.
> Consequently, you bear witness and give consent
> to the deeds of your ancestors,
> for they killed them and you do the building.
> Therefore, the wisdom of God said,
> 'I will send to them prophets and Apostles;
> some of them they will kill and persecute'
> in order that this generation might be charged
> with the blood of all the prophets
> shed since the foundation of the world,
> from the blood of Abel to the blood of Zechariah
> who died between the altar and the temple building.
> Yes, I tell you, this generation will be charged with their blood!
> Woe to you, scholars of the law!
> You have taken away the key of knowledge.
> You yourselves did not enter and you stopped those trying to enter."
> When Jesus left, the scribes and Pharisees
> began to act with hostility toward him
> and to interrogate him about many things,
> for they were plotting to catch him at something he might say.

Dear friends, Jesus pointed out the hypocrisy of the religious leaders. When they realized he was aware of their misdeeds and hypocrisy, they plotted against him so as to maintain their status.

Remember the phrase power corrupts? May we not be hypocrites or proud.

Blessings

God morning, disciples,

Today's Gospel
Luke 12:1-7

> At that time:
> So many people were crowding together
> that they were trampling one another underfoot.
> Jesus began to speak, first to his disciples,
> "Beware of the leaven-that is, the hypocrisy-of the Pharisees.
>
> "There is nothing concealed that will not be revealed,
> nor secret that will not be known.
> Therefore whatever you have said in the darkness
> will be heard in the light,
> and what you have whispered behind closed doors
> will be proclaimed on the housetops.
> I tell you, my friends,
> do not be afraid of those who kill the body
> but after that can do no more.
> I shall show you whom to fear.
> Be afraid of the one who after killing
> has the power to cast into Gehenna;
> yes, I tell you, be afraid of that one.
> Are not five sparrows sold for two small coins?
> Yet not one of them has escaped the notice of God.

> Even the hairs of your head have all been counted.
> Do not be afraid.
> You are worth more than many sparrows."

Dear friends, Jesus offers another warning about hypocrisy. He also tells us that God knows everything about us, to not be afraid and that we are precious to Him and our Father. May we praise them and make them proud of us.

The line "Even the hairs of your head have all been counted" has very special meaning to me as one of my oldest and dearest friends recited it to me a long time ago. Interesting that he cut my hair for decades. My big brother and teacher. He is a big reason that I write these morning notes.

Blessings

God morning, disciples,

Today's Gospel
Luke 12:8-12

> Jesus said to his disciples:
> "I tell you,
> everyone who acknowledges me before others
> the Son of Man will acknowledge before the angels of God.
> But whoever denies me before others
> will be denied before the angels of God.
>
> "Everyone who speaks a word against the Son of Man will be forgiven,
> but the one who blasphemes against the Holy Spirit
> will not be forgiven.
> When they take you before synagogues and before rulers and authorities,

> do not worry about how or what your defense will be
> or about what you are to say.
> For the Holy Spirit will teach you at that moment what you should say."

Dear friends, Jesus is very clear that whoever denies Him before other will be denied before the angels of God. He is also clear about anyone who blasphemes against the Holy Spirit. This is unforgivable as it is a deliberate and persistent rejection of God's offer of salvation through the gospel. It is an attitude of heart that does not want God's forgiveness or acknowledge His work. May we acknowledge Jesus before others and always ask the Holy Spirit to guide us.

Blessings

God morning, disciples,

Today's Gospel
Matthew 22:15-21

> The Pharisees went off
> and plotted how they might entrap Jesus in speech.
> They sent their disciples to him, with the Herodians, saying,
> "Teacher, we know that you are a truthful man
> and that you teach the way of God in accordance with the truth.
> And you are not concerned with anyone's opinion,
> for you do not regard a person's status.
> Tell us, then, what is your opinion:
> Is it lawful to pay the census tax to Caesar or not?"
> Knowing their malice, Jesus said,
> "Why are you testing me, you hypocrites?
> Show me the coin that pays the census tax."

> Then they handed him the Roman coin.
> He said to them, "Whose image is this and whose inscription?"
> They replied, "Caesar's."
> At that he said to them,
> "Then repay to Caesar what belongs to Caesar
> and to God what belongs to God."

Dear friends, another story about so-called religious leaders trying to trap Jesus with the hope of making Him unpopular. As always, Jesus knows what is going on and responds in such a way as to confound them. Remember, nothing really belongs to Caesar or us; everything is a gift from and belongs to God.

Blessings

God morning, disciples,

Today's Gospel
Luke 12:35-38

> Jesus said to his disciples:
> "Gird your loins and light your lamps
> and be like servants who await their master's return from a wedding,
> ready to open immediately when he comes and knocks.
> Blessed are those servants
> whom the master finds vigilant on his arrival.
> Amen, I say to you, he will gird himself,
> have them recline at table, and proceed to wait on them.
> And should he come in the second or third watch
> and find them prepared in this way,
> blessed are those servants."

Dear friends, may we be like servants who await their master's return from a wedding, ready to open immediately when he comes and knocks. Keep in my mind, we must be ever vigilant as the time of His return is unknown.

Blessings

God morning, sisters and brothers,

Today's Reading 1
Romans 6:12-18

> Brothers and sisters:
> Sin must not reign over your mortal bodies
> so that you obey their desires.
> And do not present the parts of your bodies to sin
> as weapons for wickedness,
> but present yourselves to God as raised from the dead to life
> and the parts of your bodies to God
> as weapons for righteousness.
> For sin is not to have any power over you,
> since you are not under the law but under grace.
>
> What then? Shall we sin because we are not under the law
> but under grace?
> Of course not!
> Do you not know that if you present yourselves
> to someone as obedient slaves,
> you are slaves of the one you obey,
> either of sin, which leads to death,
> or of obedience, which leads to righteousness?

> But thanks be to God that, although you were once slaves of sin,
> you have become obedient from the heart
> to the pattern of teaching to which you were entrusted.
> Freed from sin, you have become slaves of righteousness.

Dear friends, we were created in the divine image of God and are bodies are temples. We are human and the evil one works tirelessly to get us to sin in any way possible. May we have the strength to reject sin in all its forms.

Blessings

God morning, disciples,

Today's Gospel
Luke 9:51-56

> When the days for Jesus to be taken up were fulfilled,
> he resolutely determined to journey to Jerusalem,
> and he sent messengers ahead of him.
> On the way they entered a Samaritan village
> to prepare for his reception there,
> but they would not welcome him
> because the destination of his journey was Jerusalem.
> When the disciples James and John saw this they asked,
> "Lord, do you want us to call down fire from heaven
> to consume them?"
> Jesus turned and rebuked them,
> and they journeyed to another village.

Dear friends, the disciples were clearly angry the Samaritans would not welcome Jesus and wanted to call down fire from heaven to consume them. Jesus rebuked them. The message is not only are we to love those who are like us, but also those who are different. Also consider the story of Jesus and the Samaritan woman.

Blessings

God morning, branches,

Today's Reading 2
1 John 3:1-3

> Beloved:
> See what love the Father has bestowed on us
> that we may be called the children of God.
> Yet so we are.
> The reason the world does not know us
> is that it did not know him.
> Beloved, we are God's children now;
> what we shall be has not yet been revealed.
> We do know that when it is revealed we shall be like him,
> for we shall see him as he is.
> Everyone who has this hope based on him makes himself pure,
> as he is pure.

Dear friends, we are God's children. Think of it: Our Father is the Creator of the universe. Our Father is the King.

Blessings

God morning, branches,

Today's Gospel
Luke 14:1-6

> On a sabbath Jesus went to dine
> at the home of one of the leading Pharisees,
> and the people there were observing him carefully.
> In front of him there was a man suffering from dropsy.
> Jesus spoke to the scholars of the law and Pharisees in reply, asking,
> "Is it lawful to cure on the sabbath or not?"
> But they kept silent; so he took the man and,
> after he had healed him, dismissed him.
> Then he said to them
> "Who among you, if your son or ox falls into a cistern,
> would not immediately pull him out on the sabbath day?"
> But they were unable to answer his question.

Dear friends, God rested on the seventh day and commands us to keep the Sabbath holy. In this Gospel, Jesus shows that we can honor the Sabbath by loving others and being compassionate. We may go to church and recite prayers, but, as Jesus shows us, actions speak louder than words when honoring God.

Blessings

God morning, branches,

Today's Gospel
Luke 14:12-14

> On a sabbath Jesus went to dine

at the home of one of the leading Pharisees.
He said to the host who invited him,
"When you hold a lunch or a dinner,
do not invite your friends or your brothers or sisters
or your relatives or your wealthy neighbors,
in case they may invite you back and you have repayment.
Rather, when you hold a banquet,
invite the poor, the crippled, the lame, the blind;
blessed indeed will you be because of their inability to repay you.
For you will be repaid at the resurrection of the righteous."

Dear friends, the holidays are approaching and I imagine many are making plans for family dinners and events. I wonder if we could be kind enough to remember the poor, the crippled, the lame, the blind and so on through charitable contributions.

Blessings

God morning, branches,

Today's Reading I
Acts 4:13-21

> *Observing the boldness of Peter and John*
> *and perceiving them to be uneducated, ordinary men,*
> *the leaders, elders, and scribes were amazed,*
> *and they recognized them as the companions of Jesus.*
> *Then when they saw the man who had been cured standing there with them,*
> *they could say nothing in reply.*
> *So they ordered them to leave the Sanhedrin,*

and conferred with one another, saying,
"What are we to do with these men?
Everyone living in Jerusalem knows that a remarkable sign
was done through them, and we cannot deny it.
But so that it may not be spread any further among the people,
let us give them a stern warning
never again to speak to anyone in this name."
So they called them back
and ordered them not to speak or teach at all in the name of Jesus.
Peter and John, however, said to them in reply,
"Whether it is right in the sight of God
for us to obey you rather than God, you be the judges.
It is impossible for us not to speak about what we have seen and heard."
After threatening them further,
they released them,
finding no way to punish them,
on account of the people who were all praising God
for what had happened.

Dear friends, whether to obey God or man should be an easy decision. It should not be impossible for us to speak about what we have seen and heard. The leaders in this story tried to censor Peter and John. Today, some two thousand years later, leaders continue to try to censor Christians. May we obey God and speak about what we have seen and heard.

Blessings

SCRIPTURE NOTES

Good morning, disciples,

Today's Reading 1
Acts 6:1-7

> As the number of disciples continued to grow,
> the Hellenists complained against the Hebrews
> because their widows
> were being neglected in the daily distribution.
> So the Twelve called together the community of the disciples and said,
> "It is not right for us to neglect the word of God to serve at table.
> Brothers, select from among you seven reputable men,
> filled with the Spirit and wisdom,
> whom we shall appoint to this task,
> whereas we shall devote ourselves to prayer
> and to the ministry of the word."
> The proposal was acceptable to the whole community,
> so they chose Stephen, a man filled with faith and the Holy Spirit,
> also Philip, Prochorus, Nicanor, Timon, Parmenas,
> and Nicholas of Antioch, a convert to Judaism.
> They presented these men to the Apostles
> who prayed and laid hands on them.
> The word of God continued to spread,
> and the number of the disciples in Jerusalem increased greatly;
> even a large group of priests were becoming obedient to the faith.

Dear friends, may we never neglect widows, orphans or anyone in need. May we continue to spread the word of God through our words and actions.

Blessings

God morning, sisters and brothers,

Today's Reading 1
Romans 12:5-16ab

> Brothers and sisters:
> We, though many, are one Body in Christ
> and individually parts of one another.
> Since we have gifts that differ according to the grace given to us,
> let us exercise them:
> if prophecy, in proportion to the faith;
> if ministry, in ministering;
> if one is a teacher, in teaching;
> if one exhorts, in exhortation;
> if one contributes, in generosity;
> if one is over others, with diligence;
> if one does acts of mercy, with cheerfulness.
>
> Let love be sincere;
> hate what is evil,
> hold on to what is good;
> love one another with mutual affection;
> anticipate one another in showing honor.
> Do not grow slack in zeal,
> be fervent in spirit,
> serve the Lord.
> Rejoice in hope,
> endure in affliction,
> persevere in prayer.
> Contribute to the needs of the holy ones,
> exercise hospitality.

Bless those who persecute you,
bless and do not curse them.
Rejoice with those who rejoice,
weep with those who weep.
Have the same regard for one another;
do not be haughty but associate with the lowly.

Dear friends, read the first few lines slowly a couple of times. We are all part of the one Body in Christ. We all have gifts and they are meant to be shared. The second part of the Reading instructs us how to act as true Christians. May we share our gifts and act as true Christians.

Blessings

God morning, disciples,

Today's Gospel
Luke 17:1-6

> Jesus said to his disciples,
> "Things that cause sin will inevitably occur,
> but woe to the one through whom they occur.
> It would be better for him if a millstone were put around his neck
> and he be thrown into the sea
> than for him to cause one of these little ones to sin.
> Be on your guard!
> If your brother sins, rebuke him;
> and if he repents, forgive him.
> And if he wrongs you seven times in one day
> and returns to you seven times saying, 'I am sorry,'

you should forgive him."

And the Apostles said to the Lord, "Increase our faith."
The Lord replied, "If you have faith the size of a mustard seed,
you would say to this mulberry tree,
'Be uprooted and planted in the sea,' and it would obey you."

Dear friends, I imagine we all have heard the parables of the mustard seed many times. Have you ever thought of Jesus as a mustard seed? A person of very humble beginnings becomes the focus of a major worldwide religion. A person performs miracles that are not captured by cameras or phones. There was no technology to capture His life for instant broadcast. There were those whose status was threatened by a simple man and His followers and they sought to keep the seed from taking root. The religion is the tree grown from the tiny seed and we are like the birds nesting in the tree. Perhaps you will think of Jesus when you use mustard.

Blessings

God morning, branches,

Today's Gospel
Luke 17:7-10

Jesus said to the Apostles:
"Who among you would say to your servant
who has just come in from plowing or tending sheep in the field,
'Come here immediately and take your place at table'?
Would he not rather say to him,
'Prepare something for me to eat.
Put on your apron and wait on me while I eat and drink.

You may eat and drink when I am finished'?
Is he grateful to that servant because he did what was commanded?
So should it be with you.
When you have done all you have been commanded, say,
'We are unprofitable servants;
we have done what we were obliged to do.'"

Dear friends, we might think the master in this reading is cruel to his servant. The master probably believes he is doing what he should because of his position. Here Jesus teaches that serving others is a privilege. We are slaves to Him and our duty never ends. Recall that Jesus said He came not to be served, but to serve.

Blessings

God morning, branches,

Today's Reading 1
Acts 8:1b-8

> There broke out a severe persecution of the Church in Jerusalem,
> and all were scattered
> throughout the countryside of Judea and Samaria,
> except the Apostles.
> Devout men buried Stephen and made a loud lament over him.
> Saul, meanwhile, was trying to destroy the Church;
> entering house after house and dragging out men and women,
> he handed them over for imprisonment.
>
> Now those who had been scattered went about preaching the word.
> Thus Philip went down to the city of Samaria
> and proclaimed the Christ to them.

> With one accord, the crowds paid attention to what was said by Philip
> when they heard it and saw the signs he was doing.
> For unclean spirits, crying out in a loud voice,
> came out of many possessed people,
> and many paralyzed and crippled people were cured.
> There was great joy in that city.

Dear friends, this reading is about events some 2,000 years ago and part of it applies today. There are those who seek to persecute and destroy the Church. Now consider the Church is not a building; we are the Church. Despite efforts to silence us, may we proclaim the Good News by our words and actions.

Blessings

God morning, branches,

Today's Gospel
John 10:1-10

> Jesus said:
> "Amen, amen, I say to you,
> whoever does not enter a sheepfold through the gate
> but climbs over elsewhere is a thief and a robber.
> But whoever enters through the gate is the shepherd of the sheep.
> The gatekeeper opens it for him, and the sheep hear his voice,
> as he calls his own sheep by name and leads them out.
> When he has driven out all his own,
> he walks ahead of them, and the sheep follow him,
> because they recognize his voice.
> But they will not follow a stranger;

they will run away from him,
because they do not recognize the voice of strangers."
Although Jesus used this figure of speech,
they did not realize what he was trying to tell them.

So Jesus said again, "Amen, amen, I say to you,
I am the gate for the sheep.
All who came before me are thieves and robbers,
but the sheep did not listen to them.
I am the gate.
Whoever enters through me will be saved,
and will come in and go out and find pasture.
A thief comes only to steal and slaughter and destroy;
I came so that they might have life and have it more abundantly."

Dear friends, may we follow the Good Shepherd and not fall prey to thieves, which can take many forms. The evil one is the liar extraordinaire who has endless ways to try to steal, slaughter and destroy us. He will go to great lengths to keep us from recognizing the voice of Jesus. May we enter the one true gate and be saved.

Blessings

God morning, branches,

Today's Reading 1
Acts 12:24–13:5a

> The word of God continued to spread and grow.
>
> After Barnabas and Saul completed their relief mission,
> they returned to Jerusalem,

taking with them John, who is called Mark.

Now there were in the Church at Antioch prophets and teachers:
Barnabas, Symeon who was called Niger, Lucius of Cyrene,
Manaen who was a close friend of Herod the tetrarch, and Saul.
While they were worshiping the Lord and fasting, the Holy Spirit said,
"Set apart for me Barnabas and Saul
for the work to which I have called them."
Then, completing their fasting and prayer,
they laid hands on them and sent them off.

So they, sent forth by the Holy Spirit,
went down to Seleucia
and from there sailed to Cyprus.
When they arrived in Salamis,
they proclaimed the word of God in the Jewish synagogues.

Dear friends, May the word of God continue to spread and grow through our words and actions.
Blessings

God morning, branches,

Today's Reading I
Acts 13:26-33

When Paul came to Antioch in Pisidia, he said in the synagogue:
"My brothers, children of the family of Abraham,
and those others among you who are God-fearing,
to us this word of salvation has been sent.
The inhabitants of Jerusalem and their leaders failed to recognize him,

> and by condemning him they fulfilled the oracles of the prophets
> that are read sabbath after sabbath.
> For even though they found no grounds for a death sentence,
> they asked Pilate to have him put to death,
> and when they had accomplished all that was written about him,
> they took him down from the tree and placed him in a tomb.
> But God raised him from the dead,
> and for many days he appeared to those
> who had come up with him from Galilee to Jerusalem.
> These are now his witnesses before the people.
> We ourselves are proclaiming this good news to you
> that what God promised our fathers
> he has brought to fulfillment for us, their children, by raising up Jesus,
> as it is written in the second psalm,
> You are my Son; this day I have begotten you."

Dear friends, can you possibly imagine what it was like to be among those to whom Jesus appeared after his Resurrection? Imagine being a witness and then proclaiming the Good News! We can certainly be witnesses. I have shared a few of the miracles I have experienced and I am sure many of you have also experienced miracles. Should you not recall miracles of your own, you can rejoice and proclaim the Good News knowing that you are among some who have experienced them. By the way, do we not experience miracles on a daily basis as part of His creation?

Blessings

God morning, branches,

Today's Gospel
Jn 14:7-14

> Jesus said to his disciples:
> "If you know me, then you will also know my Father.
> From now on you do know him and have seen him."
> Philip said to Jesus,
> "Master, show us the Father, and that will be enough for us."
> Jesus said to him, "Have I been with you for so long a time
> and you still do not know me, Philip?
> Whoever has seen me has seen the Father.
> How can you say, 'Show us the Father'?
> Do you not believe that I am in the Father and the Father is in me?
> The words that I speak to you I do not speak on my own.
> The Father who dwells in me is doing his works.
> Believe me that I am in the Father and the Father is in me,
> or else, believe because of the works themselves.
> Amen, amen, I say to you,
> whoever believes in me will do the works that I do,
> and will do greater ones than these,
> because I am going to the Father.
> And whatever you ask in my name, I will do,
> so that the Father may be glorified in the Son.
> If you ask anything of me in my name, I will do it."

Dear friends, I have struggled often with thoughts about Jesus, God the Father and other things. This Gospel provides some level of comfort where Jesus says "Have I been with you for so long a

SCRIPTURE NOTES

time and you still do not know me, Philip? If Philip and the others were not sure about Jesus and what He said, I am in good company.

As for asking anything in His name, consider that God answers our prayers in His time and way, not ours. I think this passage refers to our needs, not wants.

May we continue to ponder our relationships with the Lord.

Blessings

God morning, branches,

Today's Reading 1
Acts 14:5-18

> There was an attempt in Iconium
> by both the Gentiles and the Jews,
> together with their leaders,
> to attack and stone Paul and Barnabas.
> They realized it,
> and fled to the Lycaonian cities of Lystra and Derbe
> and to the surrounding countryside,
> where they continued to proclaim the Good News.
>
> At Lystra there was a crippled man, lame from birth,
> who had never walked.
> He listened to Paul speaking, who looked intently at him,
> saw that he had the faith to be healed,
> and called out in a loud voice, "Stand up straight on your feet."
> He jumped up and began to walk about.
> When the crowds saw what Paul had done,
> they cried out in Lycaonian,

"The gods have come down to us in human form."
They called Barnabas "Zeus" and Paul "Hermes,"
because he was the chief speaker.
And the priest of Zeus, whose temple was at the entrance to the city,
brought oxen and garlands to the gates,
for he together with the people intended to offer sacrifice.

The Apostles Barnabas and Paul tore their garments
when they heard this and rushed out into the crowd, shouting,
"Men, why are you doing this?
We are of the same nature as you, human beings.
We proclaim to you good news
that you should turn from these idols to the living God,
who made heaven and earth and sea and all that is in them.
In past generations he allowed all Gentiles to go their own ways;
yet, in bestowing his goodness,
he did not leave himself without witness,
for he gave you rains from heaven and fruitful seasons,
and filled you with nourishment and gladness for your hearts."
Even with these words, they scarcely restrained the crowds
from offering sacrifice to them.

Dear friends, I imagine we think of idolatry as an ancient way of worshiping gods and we tend to miss the idols in our own life. Idolatry is alive and well today, and all human beings are prone to have idols in our lives. Idolatry isn't confined to worshipping a golden statue or praying to trinkets. It's much broader than that. Idolatry can take many forms, the evil one is at work here. An idol is when something or someone becomes more important to us than God. The list could include identity, money, material things, job or

status, sex, phones and technology. May God be first in our lives and may we have the faith of the crippled man.

Blessings

God morning, branches,

Today's Reading 1
Acts 16:22-34

> The crowd in Philippi joined in the attack on Paul and Silas,
> and the magistrates had them stripped
> and ordered them to be beaten with rods.
> After inflicting many blows on them,
> they threw them into prison
> and instructed the jailer to guard them securely.
> When he received these instructions, he put them in the innermost cell
> and secured their feet to a stake.
>
> About midnight, while Paul and Silas were praying
> and singing hymns to God as the prisoners listened,
> there was suddenly such a severe earthquake
> that the foundations of the jail shook;
> all the doors flew open, and the chains of all were pulled loose.
> When the jailer woke up and saw the prison doors wide open,
> he drew his sword and was about to kill himself,
> thinking that the prisoners had escaped.
> But Paul shouted out in a loud voice,
> "Do no harm to yourself; we are all here."
> He asked for a light and rushed in and,
> trembling with fear, he fell down before Paul and Silas.

> Then he brought them out and said,
> "Sirs, what must I do to be saved?"
> And they said, "Believe in the Lord Jesus
> and you and your household will be saved."
> So they spoke the word of the Lord to him and to everyone in his house.
> He took them in at that hour of the night and bathed their wounds;
> then he and all his family were baptized at once.
> He brought them up into his house and provided a meal
> and with his household rejoiced at having come to faith in God.

Dear friends, this Reading is a wonderful story (are not most?). Crowds attacked Paul and Silas (are we not under attack?). They are beaten, thrown in prison and secured, to boot (pun unintended). Still, Paul and Silas pray and sing hymns (could we under such circumstances?), likely to the amazement of those who listened to them. God provides a way to freedom, but Paul, rather than escape, prevents the guard from killing himself. The guard trembling with fear fell down before Paul and Silas and asked how he could be saved. He bathed their wounds, brought them home and provided a meal. I imagine the guard and his family shared their story and spread the Good News to others.

Blessings

God morning, branches,

The word "awesome" appears dozens of times in the Bible. For example, God is called the "great and awesome God" in Deuteronomy 7:21 and Nehemiah 1:5. He is awesome in His majesty (Job 37:22), His holiness (Psalm 99:3), and His glory (Exodus 15:11). God is awesome in His sanctuary (Psalm 68:35). He comes to us in awesome majesty (Job 37:22). God is "more awesome than all who surround him" (Psalm 89:7).

His name is to be honored and respected.

It is commonplace to describe people, events, surprises, and even dessert as "awesome." But God is also described as awesome, and nothing and no one comes anywhere close to His awesomeness. Perhaps the evil one causes us to use the word "awesome" to describe people, places and things to denigrate God.

Words matter, my friends. After all, as it is written "In the beginning was the Word, and the Word was with God, and the Word was God." and "And the Word became flesh and dwelt among us."

I suggest things of nature, His creation, can be described as awesome. A sunrise and sunset, for example. A chocolate cake might be delicious, not awesome.

Blessings

God morning, branches,

Today's Reading 1
Wisdom 13:1-9

> All men were by nature foolish who were in ignorance of God,
> and who from the good things seen did not succeed in knowing him who is,
> and from studying the works did not discern the artisan;
> But either fire, or wind, or the swift air,
> or the circuit of the stars, or the mighty water,
> or the luminaries of heaven, the governors of the world, they considered gods.
> Now if out of joy in their beauty they thought them gods,

let them know how far more excellent is the Lord than these;
for the original source of beauty fashioned them.
Or if they were struck by their might and energy,
let them from these things realize how much more powerful is he who made them.
For from the greatness and the beauty of created things
their original author, by analogy, is seen.
But yet, for these the blame is less;
For they indeed have gone astray perhaps,
though they seek God and wish to find him.
For they search busily among his works,
but are distracted by what they see, because the things seen are fair.
But again, not even these are pardonable.
For if they so far succeeded in knowledge
that they could speculate about the world,
how did they not more quickly find its Lord?

Dear friends, I imagine we all look for beautiful sunrises, sunsets, rainbows and other things in nature. While we admire the beauty that is all around us, may we take a moment to give thanks to the Creator of it all.

Blessings

God morning, branches,

Today's Gospel
John 4:5-42

> Jesus came to a town of Samaria called Sychar,
> near the plot of land that Jacob had given to his son Joseph.

SCRIPTURE NOTES

Jacob's well was there.
Jesus, tired from his journey, sat down there at the well.
It was about noon.
A woman of Samaria came to draw water.
Jesus said to her,
"Give me a drink."
His disciples had gone into the town to buy food.
The Samaritan woman said to him,
"How can you, a Jew, ask me, a Samaritan woman, for a drink?"
—For Jews use nothing in common with Samaritans.—
Jesus answered and said to her,
"If you knew the gift of God
and who is saying to you, 'Give me a drink, '
you would have asked him
and he would have given you living water."
The woman said to him,
"Sir, you do not even have a bucket and the cistern is deep;
where then can you get this living water?
Are you greater than our father Jacob,
who gave us this cistern and drank from it himself
with his children and his flocks?"
Jesus answered and said to her,
"Everyone who drinks this water will be thirsty again;
but whoever drinks the water I shall give will never thirst;
the water I shall give will become in him
a spring of water welling up to eternal life."
The woman said to him,
"Sir, give me this water, so that I may not be thirsty
or have to keep coming here to draw water."
Jesus said to her,

"Go call your husband and come back."
The woman answered and said to him,
"I do not have a husband."
Jesus answered her,
"You are right in saying, 'I do not have a husband.'
For you have had five husbands,
and the one you have now is not your husband.
What you have said is true."
The woman said to him,
"Sir, I can see that you are a prophet.
Our ancestors worshiped on this mountain;
but you people say that the place to worship is in Jerusalem."
Jesus said to her,
"Believe me, woman, the hour is coming
when you will worship the Father
neither on this mountain nor in Jerusalem.
You people worship what you do not understand;
we worship what we understand,
because salvation is from the Jews.
But the hour is coming, and is now here,
when true worshipers will worship the Father in Spirit and truth;
and indeed the Father seeks such people to worship him.
God is Spirit, and those who worship him
must worship in Spirit and truth."
The woman said to him,
"I know that the Messiah is coming, the one called the Christ;
when he comes, he will tell us everything."
Jesus said to her,
"I am he, the one speaking with you."
At that moment his disciples returned,

and were amazed that he was talking with a woman,
but still no one said, "What are you looking for?"
or "Why are you talking with her?"
The woman left her water jar
and went into the town and said to the people,
"Come see a man who told me everything I have done.
Could he possibly be the Christ?"
They went out of the town and came to him.
Meanwhile, the disciples urged him, "Rabbi, eat."
But he said to them,
"I have food to eat of which you do not know."
So the disciples said to one another,
"Could someone have brought him something to eat?"
Jesus said to them,
"My food is to do the will of the one who sent me
and to finish his work.
Do you not say, 'In four months the harvest will be here'?
I tell you, look up and see the fields ripe for the harvest.
The reaper is already receiving payment
and gathering crops for eternal life,
so that the sower and reaper can rejoice together.
For here the saying is verified that 'One sows and another reaps.'
I sent you to reap what you have not worked for;
others have done the work,
and you are sharing the fruits of their work."
Many of the Samaritans of that town began to believe in him
because of the word of the woman who testified,
"He told me everything I have done."
When the Samaritans came to him,
they invited him to stay with them;

SCRIPTURE NOTES

and he stayed there two days.
Many more began to believe in him because of his word,
and they said to the woman,
"We no longer believe because of your word;
for we have heard for ourselves,
and we know that this is truly the savior of the world."

Dear friends, the Samaritan woman said to him, "How can you, a Jew, ask me, a Samaritan woman, for a drink?" —For Jews use nothing in common with Samaritans.

Afterwards there was acceptance between the two different groups of people. Imagine if that would happen today. May our actions bring about such change.

Blessings

God morning, branches,

Today's Reading 1
Acts 22:30; 23:6-11

Wishing to determine the truth
about why Paul was being accused by the Jews,
the commander freed him
and ordered the chief priests and the whole Sanhedrin to convene.
Then he brought Paul down and made him stand before them.

Paul was aware that some were Sadducees and some Pharisees,
so he called out before the Sanhedrin,
"My brothers, I am a Pharisee, the son of Pharisees;
I am on trial for hope in the resurrection of the dead."
When he said this,

> a dispute broke out between the Pharisees and Sadducees,
> and the group became divided.
> For the Sadducees say that there is no resurrection
> or angels or spirits,
> while the Pharisees acknowledge all three.
> A great uproar occurred,
> and some scribes belonging to the Pharisee party
> stood up and sharply argued,
> "We find nothing wrong with this man.
> Suppose a spirit or an angel has spoken to him?"
> The dispute was so serious that the commander,
> afraid that Paul would be torn to pieces by them,
> ordered his troops to go down and rescue Paul from their midst
> and take him into the compound.
> The following night the Lord stood by him and said, "Take courage.
> For just as you have borne witness to my cause in Jerusalem,
> so you must also bear witness in Rome."

Dear friends, Paul suffered for preaching the Good News and the Lord stood by him and said, "Take courage. For just as you have borne witness to my cause in Jerusalem, so you must also bear witness in Rome." A case can be made that anyone preaching the Good News today might be treated harshly. Take courage, the Lord is by your side as you bear witness to His cause.

Blessings

God morning, branches,

Today's Reading 1
Acts 28:16-20, 30-31

SCRIPTURE NOTES

When he entered Rome, Paul was allowed to live by himself, with the soldier who was guarding him.

Three days later he called together the leaders of the Jews. When they had gathered he said to them, "My brothers, although I had done nothing against our people or our ancestral customs, I was handed over to the Romans as a prisoner from Jerusalem. After trying my case the Romans wanted to release me, because they found nothing against me deserving the death penalty. But when the Jews objected, I was obliged to appeal to Caesar, even though I had no accusation to make against my own nation. This is the reason, then, I have requested to see you and to speak with you, for it is on account of the hope of Israel that I wear these chains."

He remained for two full years in his lodgings. He received all who came to him, and with complete assurance and without hindrance he proclaimed the Kingdom of God and taught about the Lord Jesus Christ.

Dear friends, Paul preached the Good News and was handed over to the authorities. He was tried and released because they found nothing against him deserving the death penalty. The leading Jews were not happy. Recall that Pilate found nothing wrong with Jesus and the Jews were not happy. Now, some two thousand years later, Jesus has done nothing wrong and many are unhappy with Him. They try to remove God from wherever they can. They ignore God's commandments and Jesus' teachings. They claim Father and Son are ancient relics and irrelevant. I do not think God will laugh when all is said and done, but I think you get my point. May we receive all who come to us and with complete assurance and without hindrance proclaim the Good News.

Blessings

God morning, disciples,

Today's Gospel
John 21:15-19

> After Jesus had revealed himself to his disciples and eaten breakfast with them,
> he said to Simon Peter,
> "Simon, son of John, do you love me more than these?"
> Simon Peter answered him, "Yes, Lord, you know that I love you."
> Jesus said to him, "Feed my lambs."
> He then said to Simon Peter a second time,
> "Simon, son of John, do you love me?"
> Simon Peter answered him, "Yes, Lord, you know that I love you."
> He said to him, "Tend my sheep."
> He said to him the third time,
> "Simon, son of John, do you love me?"
> Peter was distressed that he had said to him a third time,
> "Do you love me?" and he said to him,
> "Lord, you know everything; you know that I love you."
> Jesus said to him, "Feed my sheep.
> Amen, amen, I say to you, when you were younger,
> you used to dress yourself and go where you wanted;
> but when you grow old, you will stretch out your hands,
> and someone else will dress you
> and lead you where you do not want to go."

He said this signifying by what kind of death he would glorify God. And when he had said this, he said to him, "Follow me."

Dear friends, I imagine we all say we believe in Jesus. I wonder how many actually follow Him. You see, we can say we try to live according to His teachings and call ourselves Christians, but Jesus is clear in what it means to follow Him. In Luke 14, He says "If you come to me but will not leave your family, you cannot be my follower. You must love me more than your father, mother, wife, children, brothers, and sisters—even more than your own life! Whoever will not carry the cross that is given to them when they follow me cannot be my follower." Also know that some of His early followers gave up lucrative positions and their worldly possessions. Following His teachings and ways is one thing, following Him is another, and tougher.

Blessings

God morning, branches,

Reading I
Jer 7:23-28

> Thus says the LORD:
> This is what I commanded my people:
> Listen to my voice;
> then I will be your God and you shall be my people.
> Walk in all the ways that I command you,
> so that you may prosper.
>
> But they obeyed not, nor did they pay heed.
> They walked in the hardness of their evil hearts

and turned their backs, not their faces, to me.
From the day that your fathers left the land of Egypt even to this day,
I have sent you untiringly all my servants the prophets.
Yet they have not obeyed me nor paid heed;
they have stiffened their necks and done worse than their fathers.
When you speak all these words to them,
they will not listen to you either;
when you call to them, they will not answer you.
Say to them:
This is the nation that does not listen
to the voice of the LORD, its God,
or take correction.
Faithfulness has disappeared;
the word itself is banished from their speech.

Dear friends, I believe the above rings so true today. Far too many have lost faith and the Word is certainly banished by big tech and media censors. We have much to do in our battle for the Lord.

Blessings

God morning, branches,

Today's Gospel
John 9:1-41

> As Jesus passed by he saw a man blind from birth.
> His disciples asked him,
> "Rabbi, who sinned, this man or his parents,
> that he was born blind?"
> Jesus answered,

"Neither he nor his parents sinned;
it is so that the works of God might be made visible through him.
We have to do the works of the one who sent me while it is day.
Night is coming when no one can work.
While I am in the world, I am the light of the world."
When he had said this, he spat on the ground
and made clay with the saliva,
and smeared the clay on his eyes,
and said to him,
"Go wash in the Pool of Siloam" —which means Sent—.
So he went and washed, and came back able to see.
His neighbors and those who had seen him earlier as a beggar said,
"Isn't this the one who used to sit and beg?"
Some said, "It is, "
but others said, "No, he just looks like him."
He said, "I am."
So they said to him, "How were your eyes opened?"
He replied,
"The man called Jesus made clay and anointed my eyes
and told me, 'Go to Siloam and wash.'
So I went there and washed and was able to see."
And they said to him, "Where is he?"
He said, "I don't know."
They brought the one who was once blind to the Pharisees.
Now Jesus had made clay and opened his eyes on a sabbath.
So then the Pharisees also asked him how he was able to see.
He said to them,
"He put clay on my eyes, and I washed, and now I can see."
So some of the Pharisees said,
"This man is not from God,

because he does not keep the sabbath."
But others said,
"How can a sinful man do such signs?"
And there was a division among them.
So they said to the blind man again,
"What do you have to say about him,
since he opened your eyes?"
He said, "He is a prophet."
Now the Jews did not believe
that he had been blind and gained his sight
until they summoned the parents of the one who had gained his sight.
They asked them,
"Is this your son, who you say was born blind?
How does he now see?"
His parents answered and said,
"We know that this is our son and that he was born blind.
We do not know how he sees now,
nor do we know who opened his eyes.
Ask him, he is of age;
he can speak for himself."
His parents said this because they were afraid
of the Jews, for the Jews had already agreed
that if anyone acknowledged him as the Christ,
he would be expelled from the synagogue.
For this reason his parents said,
"He is of age; question him."
So a second time they called the man who had been blind
and said to him, "Give God the praise!
We know that this man is a sinner."
He replied,

"If he is a sinner, I do not know.
One thing I do know is that I was blind and now I see."
So they said to him,
"What did he do to you?
How did he open your eyes?"
He answered them,
"I told you already and you did not listen.
Why do you want to hear it again?
Do you want to become his disciples, too?"
They ridiculed him and said,
"You are that man's disciple;
we are disciples of Moses!
We know that God spoke to Moses,
but we do not know where this one is from."
The man answered and said to them,
"This is what is so amazing,
that you do not know where he is from, yet he opened my eyes.
We know that God does not listen to sinners,
but if one is devout and does his will, he listens to him.
It is unheard of that anyone ever opened the eyes of a person born blind.
If this man were not from God,
he would not be able to do anything."
They answered and said to him,
"You were born totally in sin,
and are you trying to teach us?"
Then they threw him out.
When Jesus heard that they had thrown him out,
he found him and said, Do you believe in the Son of Man?"
He answered and said,
"Who is he, sir, that I may believe in him?"

Jesus said to him,
"You have seen him,
the one speaking with you is he."
He said,
"I do believe, Lord," and he worshiped him.
Then Jesus said,
"I came into this world for judgment,
so that those who do not see might see,
and those who do see might become blind."
Some of the Pharisees who were with him heard this
and said to him, "Surely we are not also blind, are we?"
Jesus said to them,
"If you were blind, you would have no sin;
but now you are saying, 'We see,' so your sin remains.

Dear friends, I think today's Gospel has a couple of things to discuss. I will choose "Rabbi, who sinned, this man or his parents, that he was born blind?"

Jesus answered,
"Neither he nor his parents sinned;
it is so that the works of God might be made visible through him.
We have to do the works of the one who sent me while it is day.

I imagine many of us have wondered why bad things happen in our world, especially as God is in control of everything. Well, as Jesus said "Neither he nor his parents sinned; it is so that the works of God might be made visible through him. I have told my stories of miracles in my life. As Jesus also said "We have to do the works of the one who sent me

while it is day." We do not have the power to give physical sight, but we can, and are called to, help others. Love has no boundaries.

Blessings

God morning, branches,

Today's Gospel
John 4:43-54

> At that time Jesus left [Samaria] for Galilee.
> For Jesus himself testified
> that a prophet has no honor in his native place.
> When he came into Galilee, the Galileans welcomed him,
> since they had seen all he had done in Jerusalem at the feast;
> for they themselves had gone to the feast.
>
> Then he returned to Cana in Galilee,
> where he had made the water wine.
> Now there was a royal official whose son was ill in Capernaum.
> When he heard that Jesus had arrived in Galilee from Judea,
> he went to him and asked him to come down
> and heal his son, who was near death.
> Jesus said to him,
> "Unless you people see signs and wonders, you will not believe."
> The royal official said to him,
> "Sir, come down before my child dies."
> Jesus said to him, "You may go; your son will live."
> The man believed what Jesus said to him and left.
> While the man was on his way back,
> his slaves met him and told him that his boy would live.

He asked them when he began to recover.
They told him,
"The fever left him yesterday, about one in the afternoon."
The father realized that just at that time Jesus had said to him,
"Your son will live,"
and he and his whole household came to believe.
Now this was the second sign Jesus did
when he came to Galilee from Judea.

Dear friends, I wonder how many others came to believe in Jesus through the father and his household. I also wonder how many others come to believe through us. May our words and deeds lead others to Jesus.

Blessings

God morning, branches,

Today's Gospel
John 5:31-47

Jesus said to the Jews:
"If I testify on my own behalf, my testimony is not true.
But there is another who testifies on my behalf,
and I know that the testimony he gives on my behalf is true.
You sent emissaries to John, and he testified to the truth.
I do not accept human testimony,
but I say this so that you may be saved.
He was a burning and shining lamp,
and for a while you were content to rejoice in his light.
But I have testimony greater than John's.

The works that the Father gave me to accomplish,
these works that I perform testify on my behalf
that the Father has sent me.
Moreover, the Father who sent me has testified on my behalf.
But you have never heard his voice nor seen his form,
and you do not have his word remaining in you,
because you do not believe in the one whom he has sent.
You search the Scriptures,
because you think you have eternal life through them;
even they testify on my behalf.
But you do not want to come to me to have life.

"I do not accept human praise;
moreover, I know that you do not have the love of God in you.
I came in the name of my Father,
but you do not accept me;
yet if another comes in his own name,
you will accept him.
How can you believe, when you accept praise from one another
and do not seek the praise that comes from the only God?
Do not think that I will accuse you before the Father:
the one who will accuse you is Moses,
in whom you have placed your hope.
For if you had believed Moses,
you would have believed me,
because he wrote about me.
But if you do not believe his writings,
how will you believe my words?"

Dear friends, may we be mindful about who to trust and believe. May we also provide testimony about Jesus to others by our words and actions.

Blessings

God morning, branches,

Today's Reading 1
Jas 4:1-10

> Beloved:
> Where do the wars and where do the conflicts among you come from?
> Is it not from your passions that make war within your members?
> You covet but do not possess.
> You kill and envy but you cannot obtain;
> you fight and wage war.
> You do not possess because you do not ask.
> You ask but do not receive, because you ask wrongly,
> to spend it on your passions.
> Adulterers!
> Do you not know that to be a lover of the world means enmity with God?
> Therefore, whoever wants to be a lover of the world
> makes himself an enemy of God.
> Or do you suppose that the Scripture speaks without meaning when
>   it says,
> The spirit that he has made to dwell in us tends toward jealousy?
> But he bestows a greater grace; therefore, it says:
> God resists the proud,
> but gives grace to the humble.
> So submit yourselves to God.

> Resist the Devil, and he will flee from you.
> Draw near to God, and he will draw near to you.
> Cleanse your hands, you sinners,
> and purify your hearts, you of two minds.
> Begin to lament, to mourn, to weep.
> Let your laughter be turned into mourning
> and your joy into dejection.
> Humble yourselves before the Lord
> and he will exalt you.

Dear friends, if we are lovers of the world, we are enemies of God. The evil one has many ways to try to get us to be lovers of the world, but remember, bad things happen to lovers of the world. May we humble ourselves and draw near to God.

Blessings

God morning, branches,

Today's Reading 1
Isaiah 52:13—53:12

> See, my servant shall prosper,
>   he shall be raised high and greatly exalted.
> Even as many were amazed at him--
>   so marred was his look beyond human semblance
>   and his appearance beyond that of the sons of man--
> so shall he startle many nations,
>   because of him kings shall stand speechless;
> for those who have not been told shall see,
>   those who have not heard shall ponder it.

SCRIPTURE NOTES

Who would believe what we have heard?
    To whom has the arm of the LORD been revealed?
He grew up like a sapling before him,
    like a shoot from the parched earth;
there was in him no stately bearing to make us look at him,
    nor appearance that would attract us to him.
He was spurned and avoided by people,
    a man of suffering, accustomed to infirmity,
one of those from whom people hide their faces,
    spurned, and we held him in no esteem.

Yet it was our infirmities that he bore,
    our sufferings that he endured,
while we thought of him as stricken,
    as one smitten by God and afflicted.
But he was pierced for our offenses,
    crushed for our sins;
upon him was the chastisement that makes us whole,
    by his stripes we were healed.
We had all gone astray like sheep,
    each following his own way;
but the LORD laid upon him
    the guilt of us all.

Though he was harshly treated, he submitted
    and opened not his mouth;
like a lamb led to the slaughter
    or a sheep before the shearers,
    he was silent and opened not his mouth.
Oppressed and condemned, he was taken away,
    and who would have thought any more of his destiny?

When he was cut off from the land of the living,
    and smitten for the sin of his people,
a grave was assigned him among the wicked
    and a burial place with evildoers,
though he had done no wrong
    nor spoken any falsehood.
But the LORD was pleased
    to crush him in infirmity.

If he gives his life as an offering for sin,
    he shall see his descendants in a long life,
    and the will of the LORD shall be accomplished through him.

Because of his affliction
    he shall see the light in fullness of days;
through his suffering, my servant shall justify many,
    and their guilt he shall bear.
Therefore I will give him his portion among the great,
    and he shall divide the spoils with the mighty,
because he surrendered himself to death
    and was counted among the wicked;
and he shall take away the sins of many,
    and win pardon for their offenses.

Dear friends,
    No one has greater love than this, to lay down one's life for one's friends.
    John 15:13
Blessings

God morning, branches,

Luke 22:19-20

> Then he took the bread, said the blessing, broke it, and gave it to them, saying, "This is my body, which will be given for you; do this in memory of me."
>
> And likewise the cup after they had eaten, saying, "This cup is the new covenant in my blood, which will be shed for you.

Dear friends, The Passover solemnity was usually concluded with eating a little bread and drinking a cup of wine. Jesus, therefore, when he instituted the Lord's supper, did not appoint any new rite, but appropriated an old one to a new purpose. Hence the propriety of the expression, This do in remembrance of me.

Blessings

God morning, branches,

Today's Gospel
John 11:45-56

> Many of the Jews who had come to Mary
> and seen what Jesus had done began to believe in him.
> But some of them went to the Pharisees
> and told them what Jesus had done.
> So the chief priests and the Pharisees
> convened the Sanhedrin and said,
> "What are we going to do?
> This man is performing many signs.
> If we leave him alone, all will believe in him,

and the Romans will come
and take away both our land and our nation."
But one of them, Caiaphas,
who was high priest that year, said to them,
"You know nothing,
nor do you consider that it is better for you
that one man should die instead of the people,
so that the whole nation may not perish."
He did not say this on his own,
but since he was high priest for that year,
he prophesied that Jesus was going to die for the nation,
and not only for the nation,
but also to gather into one the dispersed children of God.
So from that day on they planned to kill him.

So Jesus no longer walked about in public among the Jews,
but he left for the region near the desert,
to a town called Ephraim,
and there he remained with his disciples.

Now the Passover of the Jews was near,
and many went up from the country to Jerusalem
before Passover to purify themselves.
They looked for Jesus and said to one another
as they were in the temple area, "What do you think?
That he will not come to the feast?"

Dear friends, the religious leaders worried that Jesus was a threat to their power and planned to go to great lengths to maintain their power. Keep in mind that this happened about 2,000 years ago and think if that were an isolated incident. Certainly not. I am sure you have heard the expression power corrupts. May we be careful to not fall into the power trap, and care more for others and less about ourselves.

Blessings

God morning, branches,

Today's Gospel:
Jn 10:31-42

> The Jews picked up rocks to stone Jesus.
> Jesus answered them, "I have shown you many good works from my
>   Father.
> For which of these are you trying to stone me?"
> The Jews answered him,
> "We are not stoning you for a good work but for blasphemy.
> You, a man, are making yourself God."
> Jesus answered them,
> "Is it not written in your law, 'I said, 'You are gods'"?
> If it calls them gods to whom the word of God came,
> and Scripture cannot be set aside,
> can you say that the one
> whom the Father has consecrated and sent into the world
> blasphemes because I said, 'I am the Son of God'?
> If I do not perform my Father's works, do not believe me;
> but if I perform them, even if you do not believe me,
> believe the works, so that you may realize and understand
> that the Father is in me and I am in the Father."
> Then they tried again to arrest him;
> but he escaped from their power.

> *He went back across the Jordan*
> *to the place where John first baptized, and there he remained.*
> *Many came to him and said,*
> *"John performed no sign,*
> *but everything John said about this man was true."*
> *And many there began to believe in him.*

Dear friends, Jesus performed many miracles and quoted from Scripture that He is the Christ but the Jewish leaders willfully refused to believe. Did they refuse to believe because Jesus is the extremely humble son of a carpenter and from Nazareth (what good can come from there?). Surely they expected God and His Son to be something grand and glorious. Does the expression about judging a book by its cover come to mind? Perhaps they thought they knew so much better than everyone and wanted to keep their power. Consider yourselves blessed, Dear friends, as John 20:29 proclaims Blessed are those who have not seen yet believe.

Blessings

God morning, branches,

Today's Gospel
John 8:51-59

> *Jesus said to the Jews:*
> *"Amen, amen, I say to you,*
> *whoever keeps my word will never see death."*
> *So the Jews said to him,*
> *"Now we are sure that you are possessed.*
> *Abraham died, as did the prophets, yet you say,*

'Whoever keeps my word will never taste death.'
Are you greater than our father Abraham, who died?
Or the prophets, who died?
Who do you make yourself out to be?"
Jesus answered, "If I glorify myself, my glory is worth nothing;
but it is my Father who glorifies me,
of whom you say, 'He is our God.'
You do not know him, but I know him.
And if I should say that I do not know him,
I would be like you a liar.
But I do know him and I keep his word.
Abraham your father rejoiced to see my day;
he saw it and was glad."
So the Jews said to him,
"You are not yet fifty years old and you have seen Abraham?"
Jesus said to them, "Amen, amen, I say to you,
before Abraham came to be, I AM."
So they picked up stones to throw at him;
but Jesus hid and went out of the temple area.

Dear friends, I love readings which contain "I AM", one of God's names. I think we could consider it a form of prayer when we use that phrase in any conversation if it causes us to think about God. Think how simple that could be. We might say "I am going to the store, park, beach or whatever" and for a moment reflect on Him.

Blessings

God morning, disciples,

Today's Gospel
John 8:31–42

> Jesus said to those Jews who believed in him,
> "If you remain in my word, you will truly be my disciples,
> and you will know the truth, and the truth will set you free."
> They answered him, "We are descendants of Abraham
> and have never been enslaved to anyone.
> How can you say, 'You will become free'?"
> Jesus answered them, "Amen, amen, I say to you,
> everyone who commits sin is a slave of sin.
> A slave does not remain in a household forever,
> but a son always remains.
> So if the Son frees you, then you will truly be free.
> I know that you are descendants of Abraham.
> But you are trying to kill me,
> because my word has no room among you.
> I tell you what I have seen in the Father's presence;
> then do what you have heard from the Father."
>
> They answered and said to him, "Our father is Abraham."
> Jesus said to them, "If you were Abraham's children,
> you would be doing the works of Abraham.
> But now you are trying to kill me,
> a man who has told you the truth that I heard from God;
> Abraham did not do this.
> You are doing the works of your father!"
> So they said to him, "We were not born of fornication.
> We have one Father, God."

> Jesus said to them, "If God were your Father, you would love me,
> for I came from God and am here;
> I did not come on my own, but he sent me."

Dear friends, any wonder why God is banned? Some do not want us free. They have more lies than Carter has pills. They want their way, not His. May we remain in His word, be His disciples, and set free by the truth.

Blessings

God morning, branches,

Today's Gospel
Matthew 1:16, 18-21, 24a

> Jacob was the father of Joseph, the husband of Mary.
> Of her was born Jesus who is called the Christ.
> Now this is how the birth of Jesus Christ came about.
> When his mother Mary was betrothed to Joseph,
> but before they lived together,
> she was found with child through the Holy Spirit.
> Joseph her husband, since he was a righteous man,
> yet unwilling to expose her to shame,
> decided to divorce her quietly.
> Such was his intention when, behold,
> the angel of the Lord appeared to him in a dream and said,
> "Joseph, son of David,
> do not be afraid to take Mary your wife into your home.
> For it is through the Holy Spirit
> that this child has been conceived in her.

> She will bear a son and you are to name him Jesus,
> because he will save his people from their sins."
> When Joseph awoke,
> he did as the angel of the Lord had commanded him
> and took his wife into his home.

Dear friends, virtually nothing is known about Saint Joseph, but we know he was a righteous man. You might consider that he was extremely humble, obedient to God and look where that got him. A good example to follow, no?

Blessings

God morning, branches,

Today's Reading I
Isaiah 1:10, 16–20

> Hear the word of the LORD,
> princes of Sodom!
> Listen to the instruction of our God,
> people of Gomorrah!
>
> Wash yourselves clean!
> Put away your misdeeds from before my eyes;
> cease doing evil; learn to do good.
> Make justice your aim: redress the wronged,
> hear the orphan's plea, defend the widow.
>
> Come now, let us set things right,
> says the LORD:
> Though your sins be like scarlet,

they may become white as snow;
Though they be crimson red,
they may become white as wool.
If you are willing, and obey,
you shall eat the good things of the land;
But if you refuse and resist,
the sword shall consume you:
for the mouth of the LORD has spoken!

Dear friends, may we hear the word of the Lord and listen to His instructions. After all, they are for our own good. May we put away our misdeeds, cease doing evil and learn to do good. Let us set things right.

Blessings

God morning, branches,

Today's Reading 1
Dn 9:4b–10

"Lord, great and awesome God,
you who keep your merciful covenant toward those who love you
and observe your commandments!
We have sinned, been wicked and done evil;
we have rebelled and departed from your commandments and your laws.
We have not obeyed your servants the prophets,
who spoke in your name to our kings, our princes,
our fathers, and all the people of the land.
Justice, O Lord, is on your side;
we are shamefaced even to this day:

we, the men of Judah, the residents of Jerusalem,
and all Israel, near and far,
in all the countries to which you have scattered them
because of their treachery toward you.
O LORD, we are shamefaced, like our kings, our princes, and our fathers,
for having sinned against you.
But yours, O Lord, our God, are compassion and forgiveness!
Yet we rebelled against you
and paid no heed to your command, O LORD, our God,
to live by the law you gave us through your servants the prophets."

Dear friends, I believe today's Reading fits our time. We should be shamefaced, seek forgiveness and try harder to do right.

Blessings

God morning, disciples,

Today's Gospel
Matthew 25:31-46

Jesus said to his disciples:
"When the Son of Man comes in his glory,
and all the angels with him,
he will sit upon his glorious throne,
and all the nations will be assembled before him.
And he will separate them one from another,
as a shepherd separates the sheep from the goats.
He will place the sheep on his right and the goats on his left.
Then the king will say to those on his right,
'Come, you who are blessed by my Father.

Inherit the kingdom prepared for you from the foundation of the world.
For I was hungry and you gave me food,
I was thirsty and you gave me drink,
a stranger and you welcomed me,
naked and you clothed me,
ill and you cared for me,
in prison and you visited me.'
Then the righteous will answer him and say,
'Lord, when did we see you hungry and feed you,
or thirsty and give you drink?
When did we see you a stranger and welcome you,
or naked and clothe you?
When did we see you ill or in prison, and visit you?'
And the king will say to them in reply,
'Amen, I say to you, whatever you did
for one of these least brothers of mine, you did for me.'
Then he will say to those on his left,
'Depart from me, you accursed,
into the eternal fire prepared for the Devil and his angels.
For I was hungry and you gave me no food,
I was thirsty and you gave me no drink,
a stranger and you gave me no welcome,
naked and you gave me no clothing,
ill and in prison, and you did not care for me.'
Then they will answer and say,
'Lord, when did we see you hungry or thirsty
or a stranger or naked or ill or in prison,
and not minister to your needs?'
He will answer them, 'Amen, I say to you,
what you did not do for one of these least ones,

you did not do for me.'
And these will go off to eternal punishment,
but the righteous to eternal life."

Dear friends, may we help the least among us.
Blessings

God morning, branches,

This weekend, the Church celebrates one of the great solemnities in our calendar: the feast of the Most Holy Body and Blood of Christ (more popularly known by its Latin name, Corpus Christi). Established in the 13th century and born out of popular devotion to Jesus Christ in the Eucharist, this feast is an opportunity to honour and give thanks for the great gift of the Blessed Sacrament beyond the daily sacrifice of the Mass.

To help you celebrate this great feast and meditate on the mystery of the Eucharist, here are a few quotes from some of our saints.

St. Irenaeus (c. 130 – c. 202)
"Then, again, how can they say that the flesh, which is nourished with the body of the Lord and with His blood, goes to corruption, and does not partake of life? ... For as the bread, which is produced from the earth, when it receives the invocation of God, is no longer common bread, but the Eucharist, consisting of two realities, earthly and heavenly; so also our bodies, when they receive the Eucharist, are no longer corruptible, having the hope of the resurrection to eternity." – Against Heresies

St. Catherine of Siena (1347 – 1380)

"'For as the sun cannot be divided into light, heat, and colour, the whole of God and the whole of man cannot be separated under the white mantle of the host; for even if the host should be divided into a million particles (if it were possible) in each particle should I be present, whole God and whole Man. When you break a mirror the reflection to be seen in it is not broken; similarly, when the host is divided God and man are not divided, but remain in each particle.'" – The Dialogue

St. Thérèse of Lisieux (1873 – 1897)
"Oh, my darling, think, then, that Jesus is there in the Tabernacle expressly for you, for you alone-, He is burning with the desire to enter your heart." – Letter to Marie Guérin

St. John Paul II (1920 – 2005)
"The Eucharist is truly a glimpse of heaven appearing on earth. It is a glorious ray of the heavenly Jerusalem which pierces the clouds of our history and lights up our journey." – Ecclesia de Eucharistia

Blessings

God morning, disciples,

Today's Gospel
Mk 11:27-33

> Jesus and his disciples returned once more to Jerusalem.
> As he was walking in the temple area,
> the chief priests, the scribes, and the elders
> approached him and said to him,
> "By what authority are you doing these things?
> Or who gave you this authority to do them?"

SCRIPTURE NOTES

> Jesus said to them, "I shall ask you one question.
> Answer me, and I will tell you by what authority I do these things.
> Was John's baptism of heavenly or of human origin? Answer me."
> They discussed this among themselves and said,
> "If we say, 'Of heavenly origin,' he will say,
> 'Then why did you not believe him?'
> But shall we say, 'Of human origin'?"-
> they feared the crowd,
> for they all thought John really was a prophet.
> So they said to Jesus in reply, "We do not know."
> Then Jesus said to them,
> "Neither shall I tell you by what authority I do these things."

Dear friends, the Jewish authorities were clearly disturbed with Jesus and their potential loss of power. They had heard of or witnessed his Miracles and teachings. It is likely they knew of John's witness of the dove and its meaning. Jesus certainly knew what was in their hearts and minds. He knows likewise about us. May we be careful to not be like those who questioned Him.

Blessings

God morning, disciples,

Today's Gospel
Luke 9:22-25

> Jesus said to his disciples:
> "The Son of Man must suffer greatly and be rejected
> by the elders, the chief priests, and the scribes,
> and be killed and on the third day be raised."

*Then he said to all,
"If anyone wishes to come after me, he must deny himself
and take up his cross daily and follow me.
For whoever wishes to save his life will lose it,
but whoever loses his life for my sake will save it.
What profit is there for one to gain the whole world
yet lose or forfeit himself?"*

Dear friends, indeed, what profit is there for one to gain the whole world yet lose or forfeit himself. This world is temporary and controlled by the evil one. Be careful and choose wisely.

Blessings

God morning, ambassadors,

*Today's Second Reading:
2 Cor 5:20—6:2*

> *Brothers and sisters:
> We are ambassadors for Christ,
> as if God were appealing through us.
> We implore you on behalf of Christ,
> be reconciled to God.
> For our sake he made him to be sin who did not know sin,
> so that we might become the righteousness of God in him.*
>
> *Working together, then,
> we appeal to you not to receive the grace of God in vain.
> For he says:*
>
> *In an acceptable time I heard you,*

and on the day of salvation I helped you.

Behold, now is a very acceptable time;
behold, now is the day of salvation.

Dear friends, we are ambassadors for Christ. What an awesome responsibility and privilege.

Blessings

God morning, branches,

Today's Gospel
Mk 1:40–45

> A leper came to Jesus and kneeling down begged him and said,
> "If you wish, you can make me clean."
> Moved with pity, he stretched out his hand,
> touched him, and said to him,
> "I do will it. Be made clean."
> The leprosy left him immediately, and he was made clean.
> Then, warning him sternly, he dismissed him at once.
> He said to him, "See that you tell no one anything,
> but go, show yourself to the priest
> and offer for your cleansing what Moses prescribed;
> that will be proof for them."
> The man went away and began to publicize the whole matter.
> He spread the report abroad
> so that it was impossible for Jesus to enter a town openly.
> He remained outside in deserted places,
> and people kept coming to him from everywhere.

SCRIPTURE NOTES

Dear friends, Jesus cured the leper and warned him to tell no one. Apparently the leper was overwhelmed to be cured and who can blame him for sharing his good news. Unlike the leper, we are called to share the Good News through our words and actions. May we lead others to the Light.

Blessings

God morning, branches,

Today's Gospel
Mark 7:31-37

> Jesus left the district of Tyre
> and went by way of Sidon to the Sea of Galilee,
> into the district of the Decapolis.
> And people brought to him a deaf man who had a speech impediment
> and begged him to lay his hand on him.
> He took him off by himself away from the crowd.
> He put his finger into the man's ears
> and, spitting, touched his tongue;
> then he looked up to heaven and groaned, and said to him,
> "Ephphatha!" (that is, "Be opened!")
> And immediately the man's ears were opened,
> his speech impediment was removed,
> and he spoke plainly.
> He ordered them not to tell anyone.
> But the more he ordered them not to,
> the more they proclaimed it.
> They were exceedingly astonished and they said,
> "He has done all things well.

He makes the deaf hear and the mute speak."

Dear friends, may God improve our ability to hear His word more clearly and to better speak His word to others.

Blessings

God morning, branches,

Today's Reading 1
2 Pt 1:2-7

> Beloved:
> May grace and peace be yours in abundance
> through knowledge of God and of Jesus our Lord.
>
> His divine power has bestowed on us
> everything that makes for life and devotion,
> through the knowledge of him
> who called us by his own glory and power.
> Through these, he has bestowed on us
> the precious and very great promises,
> so that through them you may come to share in the divine nature,
> after escaping from the corruption that is in the world
> because of evil desire.
> For this very reason,
> make every effort to supplement your faith with virtue,
> virtue with knowledge, knowledge with self-control,
> self-control with endurance, endurance with devotion,
> devotion with mutual affection, mutual affection with love.

SCRIPTURE NOTES

Dear friends, may we have grace and peace in abundance in this world. The evil one does all he can to keep this from happening. I learned that each of the qualities mentioned in the last four lines hold deep significance across cultures and philosophies. I find it interesting that they end in love as God is love. Our faith instructs us to love everyone, not just those we choose. Love can never lose.

Love

God morning, disciples,

Today's Gospel
Mk 12:13-17

> Some Pharisees and Herodians were sent
> to Jesus to ensnare him in his speech.
> They came and said to him,
> "Teacher, we know that you are a truthful man
> and that you are not concerned with anyone's opinion.
> You do not regard a person's status
> but teach the way of God in accordance with the truth.
> Is it lawful to pay the census tax to Caesar or not?
> Should we pay or should we not pay?"
> Knowing their hypocrisy he said to them,
> "Why are you testing me?
> Bring me a denarius to look at."
> They brought one to him and he said to them,
> "Whose image and inscription is this?"
> They replied to him, "Caesar's."
> So Jesus said to them,
> "Repay to Caesar what belongs to Caesar

and to God what belongs to God."
They were utterly amazed at him.

Dear friends, another story about so-called religious leaders trying to trap Jesus with the hope of making Him unpopular. As always, Jesus knows what is going on and responds in such a way as to confound them. Remember, nothing really belongs to Caesar or us; everything is a gift from and belongs to God.

Blessings

God morning, branches,

Today's Gospel:
Mk 12:28-34

> One of the scribes came to Jesus and asked him,
> "Which is the first of all the commandments?"
> Jesus replied, "The first is this:
> Hear, O Israel!
> The Lord our God is Lord alone!
> You shall love the Lord your God with all your heart,
> with all your soul, with all your mind,
> and with all your strength.
> The second is this:
> You shall love your neighbor as yourself.
> There is no other commandment greater than these."
> The scribe said to him, "Well said, teacher.
> You are right in saying,
> He is One and there is no other than he.
> And to love him with all your heart,

with all your understanding,
with all your strength,
and to love your neighbor as yourself
is worth more than all burnt offerings and sacrifices."
And when Jesus saw that he answered with understanding,
he said to him, "You are not far from the Kingdom of God."
And no one dared to ask him any more questions.

Dear friends, love is worth more than all burnt offerings and sacrifices. Remember, God is love and we were created in His image. If we believe and understand as the scribe did, we are not far from the Kingdom of God. May you think about this a few times as you go through your days.

This Gospel has appeared a few times since I began this ministry. Do you know there are six hundred and thirteen commandments in the Pentateuch, the first five books of The Bible? The term "Pentateuch" comes from the Greek term pentáteuchos meaning "five-volumed (book) after the Jewish designation, "the five-fifths of the law". These five books form the theological foundation of the Bible.

As I have written about other readings like this one, if we love, it is unlikely that we would break other commandments. Love is the greatest law.

Love

God morning, branches,

A Reading
2 Tm 2:8-15

Beloved:
Remember Jesus Christ, raised from the dead, a descendant of David:
such is my Gospel, for which I am suffering,
even to the point of chains, like a criminal.
But the word of God is not chained.
Therefore, I bear with everything for the sake of those who are chosen,
so that they too may obtain the salvation that is in Christ Jesus,
together with eternal glory.
This saying is trustworthy:

If we have died with him
we shall also live with him;
if we persevere
we shall also reign with him.
But if we deny him
he will deny us.
If we are unfaithful
he remains faithful,
for he cannot deny himself.

Remind people of these things
and charge them before God to stop disputing about words.
This serves no useful purpose since it harms those who listen.
Be eager to present yourself as acceptable to God,
a workman who causes no disgrace,
imparting the word of truth without deviation.

Dear friends, may we impart the word of truth without deviation. The word of God is not chained despite the efforts of some to cause it to be so.

Blessings

SCRIPTURE NOTES

God morning, branches,

Today's Reading 1
2 Tm 4:1-8

> Beloved:
> I charge you in the presence of God and of Christ Jesus,
> who will judge the living and the dead,
> and by his appearing and his kingly power:
> proclaim the word;
> be persistent whether it is convenient or inconvenient;
> convince, reprimand, encourage through all patience and teaching.
> For the time will come when people will not tolerate sound doctrine
> but, following their own desires and insatiable curiosity,
> will accumulate teachers and will stop listening to the truth
> and will be diverted to myths.
> But you, be self-possessed in all circumstances;
> put up with hardship;
> perform the work of an evangelist;
> fulfill your ministry.
>
> For I am already being poured out like a libation,
> and the time of my departure is at hand.
> I have competed well;
> I have finished the race; I have kept the faith.
> From now on the crown of righteousness awaits me,
> which the Lord, the just judge,
> will award to me on that day, and not only to me,
> but to all who have longed for his appearance.

Dear friends, the time when people will not tolerate sound doctrine but, following their own desires and insatiable curiosity, will accumulate teachers and will stop listening to the truth and will be diverted to myths came a long time ago. May our words and deeds lead others to Jesus.

Blessings

God morning, branches,

Today's Gospel
Mark 6:30-34

> The Apostles gathered together with Jesus
> and reported all they had done and taught.
> He said to them,
> "Come away by yourselves to a deserted place and rest a while."
> People were coming and going in great numbers,
> and they had no opportunity even to eat.
> So they went off in the boat by themselves to a deserted place.
> People saw them leaving and many came to know about it.
> They hastened there on foot from all the towns
> and arrived at the place before them.
>
> When Jesus disembarked and saw the vast crowd,
> his heart was moved with pity for them,
> for they were like sheep without a shepherd;
> and he began to teach them many things.

Dear friends, the news about the works and miracles performed by Jesus and the Apostles spread far and wide just by word of mouth. People were coming and going in great numbers. Think if Jesus should return today how overwhelming the crowds would be. I think His heart would be moved with pity for us because even with all our creature comforts, we are still like lost sheep. Until He returns may we try to live as we should by helping and loving one another.

Blessings

God morning, sisters and brothers,

Today's Reading 2
2 Cor 4:13—5:1

> Brothers and sisters:
> Since we have the same spirit of faith,
> according to what is written, I believed, therefore I spoke,
> we too believe and therefore we speak,
> knowing that the one who raised the Lord Jesus
> will raise us also with Jesus
> and place us with you in his presence.
> Everything indeed is for you,
> so that the grace bestowed in abundance on more and more people
> may cause the thanksgiving to overflow for the glory of God.
> Therefore, we are not discouraged;
> rather, although our outer self is wasting away,
> our inner self is being renewed day by day.
> For this momentary light affliction
> is producing for us an eternal weight of glory
> beyond all comparison,
> as we look not to what is seen but to what is unseen;
> for what is seen is transitory, but what is unseen is eternal.
> For we know that if our earthly dwelling, a tent,
> should be destroyed,
> we have a building from God,

a dwelling not made with hands, eternal in heaven.

Dear friends, may we look not to what is seen but to what is unseen; for what is seen is transitory, but what is unseen is eternal.

Blessings

God morning, disciples,

Today's Gospel
Mt 5:20-26

> Jesus said to his disciples:
> "I tell you, unless your righteousness surpasses that
> of the scribes and Pharisees,
> you will not enter into the Kingdom of heaven.
>
> "You have heard that it was said to your ancestors,
> You shall not kill; and whoever kills will be liable to judgment.
> But I say to you, whoever is angry with his brother
> will be liable to judgment,
> and whoever says to his brother, Raqa,
> will be answerable to the Sanhedrin,
> and whoever says, 'You fool,' will be liable to fiery Gehenna.
> Therefore, if you bring your gift to the altar,
> and there recall that your brother
> has anything against you,
> leave your gift there at the altar,
> go first and be reconciled with your brother,
> and then come and offer your gift.
> Settle with your opponent quickly while on the way to court with him.
> Otherwise your opponent will hand you over to the judge,

and the judge will hand you over to the guard,
and you will be thrown into prison.
Amen, I say to you,
you will not be released until you have paid the last penny."

Dear friends, Scribes and Pharisees were righteous and people of the law. Jesus asks for more – for the compassion that sees beyond the law and people's weaknesses to the glory and love of God in each and all. May we live according to Jesus' wishes for us. Yes, it is very difficult, but nothing is impossible with God. Remember, the reward is the Kingdom of Heaven.

Blessings

God morning, branches,

Today's Reading 1
1 Kgs 21:1-16

Naboth the Jezreelite had a vineyard in Jezreel
next to the palace of Ahab, king of Samaria.
Ahab said to Naboth, "Give me your vineyard to be my vegetable garden,
since it is close by, next to my house.
I will give you a better vineyard in exchange, or,
if you prefer, I will give you its value in money."
Naboth answered him, "The LORD forbid
that I should give you my ancestral heritage."
Ahab went home disturbed and angry at the answer
Naboth the Jezreelite had made to him:
"I will not give you my ancestral heritage."
Lying down on his bed, he turned away from food and would not eat.

SCRIPTURE NOTES

His wife Jezebel came to him and said to him,
"Why are you so angry that you will not eat?"
He answered her, "Because I spoke to Naboth the Jezreelite
and said to him, 'Sell me your vineyard, or,
if you prefer, I will give you a vineyard in exchange.'
But he refused to let me have his vineyard."
His wife Jezebel said to him,
"A fine ruler over Israel you are indeed!
Get up.
Eat and be cheerful.
I will obtain the vineyard of Naboth the Jezreelite for you."

So she wrote letters in Ahab's name and,
having sealed them with his seal,
sent them to the elders and to the nobles
who lived in the same city with Naboth.
This is what she wrote in the letters:
"Proclaim a fast and set Naboth at the head of the people.
Next, get two scoundrels to face him
and accuse him of having cursed God and king.
Then take him out and stone him to death."
His fellow citizens—the elders and nobles who dwelt in his city—
did as Jezebel had ordered them in writing,
through the letters she had sent them.
They proclaimed a fast and placed Naboth at the head of the people.
Two scoundrels came in and confronted him with the accusation,
"Naboth has cursed God and king."
And they led him out of the city and stoned him to death.
Then they sent the information to Jezebel
that Naboth had been stoned to death.

When Jezebel learned that Naboth had been stoned to death,
she said to Ahab,
"Go on, take possession of the vineyard
of Naboth the Jezreelite that he refused to sell you,
because Naboth is not alive, but dead."
On hearing that Naboth was dead, Ahab started off on his way
down to the vineyard of Naboth the Jezreelite,
to take possession of it.

Dear friends, I imagine you know that Jezebel was an evil woman. What about the scoundrels and others who participated in her plan? Be careful, my friends, there is evil all around and it takes many forms.

Blessings

God morning, disciples,

Today's Gospel
Mark 6:1-6

Jesus departed from there and came to his native place, accompanied
by his disciples.
When the sabbath came he began to teach in the synagogue,
and many who heard him were astonished.
They said, "Where did this man get all this?
What kind of wisdom has been given him?
What mighty deeds are wrought by his hands!
Is he not the carpenter, the son of Mary,
and the brother of James and Joseph and Judas and Simon?
And are not his sisters here with us?"

SCRIPTURE NOTES

And they took offense at him.
Jesus said to them,
"A prophet is not without honor except in his native place
and among his own kin and in his own house."
So he was not able to perform any mighty deed there,
apart from curing a few sick people by laying his hands on them.
He was amazed at their lack of faith.

May we never be perfidious or obstinate like the Nazarenes in this Gospel.

Blessings

God morning, branches,

Today's Gospel
Mark 5:21-43

When Jesus had crossed again in the boat
to the other side,
a large crowd gathered around him, and he stayed close to the sea.
One of the synagogue officials, named Jairus, came forward.
Seeing him he fell at his feet and pleaded earnestly with him, saying,
"My daughter is at the point of death.
Please, come lay your hands on her
that she may get well and live."
He went off with him
and a large crowd followed him.

There was a woman afflicted with hemorrhages for twelve years.
She had suffered greatly at the hands of many doctors
and had spent all that she had.
Yet she was not helped but only grew worse.

SCRIPTURE NOTES

She had heard about Jesus and came up behind him in the crowd
and touched his cloak.
She said, "If I but touch his clothes, I shall be cured."
Immediately her flow of blood dried up.
She felt in her body that she was healed of her affliction.
Jesus, aware at once that power had gone out from him,
turned around in the crowd and asked, "Who has touched my clothes?"
But his disciples said to him,
"You see how the crowd is pressing upon you,
and yet you ask, Who touched me?"
And he looked around to see who had done it.
The woman, realizing what had happened to her,
approached in fear and trembling.
She fell down before Jesus and told him the whole truth.
He said to her, "Daughter, your faith has saved you.
Go in peace and be cured of your affliction."

While he was still speaking,
people from the synagogue official's house arrived and said,
"Your daughter has died; why trouble the teacher any longer?"
Disregarding the message that was reported,
Jesus said to the synagogue official,
"Do not be afraid; just have faith."
He did not allow anyone to accompany him inside
except Peter, James, and John, the brother of James.
When they arrived at the house of the synagogue official,
he caught sight of a commotion,
people weeping and wailing loudly.
So he went in and said to them,
"Why this commotion and weeping?

> The child is not dead but asleep."
> And they ridiculed him.
> Then he put them all out.
> He took along the child's father and mother
> and those who were with him
> and entered the room where the child was.
> He took the child by the hand and said to her, "Talitha koum,"
> which means, "Little girl, I say to you, arise!"
> The girl, a child of twelve, arose immediately and walked around.
> At that they were utterly astounded.
> He gave strict orders that no one should know this
> and said that she should be given something to eat.

Dear friends, may our faith be as strong as that of the woman afflicted with hemorrhages for twelve years. Many of you know my stories about serious medical problems and how one of my doctors, when informed of my good progress said maybe it's the medicine (experimental), perhaps it is your faith. Faith, indeed!

Blessings

God morning, disciples,

Today's Gospel
Mark 5:1-20

> Jesus and his disciples came to the other side of the sea,
> to the territory of the Gerasenes.
> When he got out of the boat,
> at once a man from the tombs who had an unclean spirit met him.
> The man had been dwelling among the tombs,

and no one could restrain him any longer, even with a chain.
In fact, he had frequently been bound with shackles and chains,
but the chains had been pulled apart by him and the shackles smashed,
and no one was strong enough to subdue him.
Night and day among the tombs and on the hillsides
he was always crying out and bruising himself with stones.
Catching sight of Jesus from a distance,
he ran up and prostrated himself before him,
crying out in a loud voice,
"What have you to do with me, Jesus, Son of the Most High God?
I adjure you by God, do not torment me!"
(He had been saying to him, "Unclean spirit, come out of the man!")
He asked him, "What is your name?"
He replied, "Legion is my name. There are many of us."
And he pleaded earnestly with him
not to drive them away from that territory.

Now a large herd of swine was feeding there on the hillside.
And they pleaded with him,
"Send us into the swine. Let us enter them."
And he let them, and the unclean spirits came out and entered the swine.
The herd of about two thousand rushed down a steep bank into the sea,
where they were drowned.
The swineherds ran away and reported the incident in the town
and throughout the countryside.
And people came out to see what had happened.
As they approached Jesus,
they caught sight of the man who had been possessed by Legion,
sitting there clothed and in his right mind.
And they were seized with fear.

Those who witnessed the incident explained to them what had happened
to the possessed man and to the swine.
Then they began to beg him to leave their district.
As he was getting into the boat,
the man who had been possessed pleaded to remain with him.
But Jesus would not permit him but told him instead,
"Go home to your family and announce to them
all that the Lord in his pity has done for you."
Then the man went off and began to proclaim in the Decapolis
what Jesus had done for him; and all were amazed.

Dear friends, as they approached Jesus, they caught sight of the man who had been possessed by Legion, sitting there clothed and in his right mind. Jesus brought a man possessed by Legion to his right mind. Imagine what Jesus could do for us.

Blessings

God morning, disciples,

Today's Gospel:
Mark 4:35-41

> On that day, as evening drew on, Jesus said to his disciples:
> "Let us cross to the other side."
> Leaving the crowd, they took Jesus with them in the boat just as he was.
> And other boats were with him.
> A violent squall came up and waves were breaking over the boat,
> so that it was already filling up.
> Jesus was in the stern, asleep on a cushion.
> They woke him and said to him,

> "Teacher, do you not care that we are perishing?"
> He woke up,
> rebuked the wind, and said to the sea, "Quiet! Be still!"
> The wind ceased and there was great calm.
> Then he asked them, "Why are you terrified?
> Do you not yet have faith?"
> They were filled with great awe and said to one another,
> "Who then is this whom even wind and sea obey?"

Dear friends, who then is this whom even wind and sea obey, indeed? Have you ever been terrified by something? Even Jesus' closest disciples, who had witnessed numerous miracles, were terrified in this Gospel reading. When your faith seems to fail you, recall Jeremiah 29:11, which says "For I know the plans I have for you," declares the LORD, "plans to prosper you and not to harm you, plans to give you hope and a future." Always be hopeful.

Blessings

God morning, branches,

Today's Reading I
2 Tm 1:1–8

> Paul, an Apostle of Christ Jesus by the will of God
> for the promise of life in Christ Jesus,
> to Timothy, my dear child:
> grace, mercy, and peace from God the Father
> and Christ Jesus our Lord.
>
> I am grateful to God,
> whom I worship with a clear conscience as my ancestors did,

as I remember you constantly in my prayers, night and day.
I yearn to see you again, recalling your tears,
so that I may be filled with joy,
as I recall your sincere faith
that first lived in your grandmother Lois
and in your mother Eunice
and that I am confident lives also in you.

For this reason, I remind you to stir into flame
the gift of God that you have through the imposition of my hands.
For God did not give us a spirit of cowardice
but rather of power and love and self-control.
So do not be ashamed of your testimony to our Lord,
nor of me, a prisoner for his sake;
but bear your share of hardship for the Gospel
with the strength that comes from God.

Dear friends, God did not give us a spirit of cowardice, but rather of power and love and self-control. May we not be ashamed of our testimony to our Lord. Many in the world are against us and God. May we bear our share of hardship for the Gospel with the strength that comes from God.

Blessings

God morning, branches,

Today's Gospel
Mark 4:1-20

On another occasion, Jesus began to teach by the sea.
A very large crowd gathered around him

so that he got into a boat on the sea and sat down.
And the whole crowd was beside the sea on land.
And he taught them at length in parables,
and in the course of his instruction he said to them,
"Hear this! A sower went out to sow.
And as he sowed, some seed fell on the path,
and the birds came and ate it up.
Other seed fell on rocky ground where it had little soil.
It sprang up at once because the soil was not deep.
And when the sun rose, it was scorched and it withered for lack of roots.
Some seed fell among thorns, and the thorns grew up and choked it
and it produced no grain.
And some seed fell on rich soil and produced fruit.
It came up and grew and yielded thirty, sixty, and a hundredfold."
He added, "Whoever has ears to hear ought to hear."

And when he was alone,
those present along with the Twelve
questioned him about the parables.
He answered them,
"The mystery of the Kingdom of God has been granted to you.
But to those outside everything comes in parables, so that
they may look and see but not perceive,
and hear and listen but not understand,
in order that they may not be converted and be forgiven."

Jesus said to them, "Do you not understand this parable?
Then how will you understand any of the parables?
The sower sows the word.
These are the ones on the path where the word is sown.
As soon as they hear, Satan comes at once

and takes away the word sown in them.
And these are the ones sown on rocky ground who,
when they hear the word, receive it at once with joy.
But they have no roots; they last only for a time.
Then when tribulation or persecution comes because of the word,
they quickly fall away.
Those sown among thorns are another sort.
They are the people who hear the word,
but worldly anxiety, the lure of riches,
and the craving for other things intrude and choke the word,
and it bears no fruit.
But those sown on rich soil are the ones who hear the word and accept it
and bear fruit thirty and sixty and a hundredfold."

Dear friends, may we be like rich soil and hear the word and accept it and bear fruit thirty and sixty and a hundredfold.

Blessings

God morning, branches,

Today's Gospel
Mark 3:22-30

The scribes who had come from Jerusalem said of Jesus,
"He is possessed by Beelzebul," and
"By the prince of demons he drives out demons."

Summoning them, he began to speak to them in parables,
"How can Satan drive out Satan?
If a kingdom is divided against itself, that kingdom cannot stand.
And if a house is divided against itself,

that house will not be able to stand.
And if Satan has risen up against himself and is divided,
he cannot stand;
that is the end of him.
But no one can enter a strong man's house to plunder his property
unless he first ties up the strong man.
Then he can plunder his house.
Amen, I say to you, all sins and all blasphemies
that people utter will be forgiven them.
But whoever blasphemes against the Holy Spirit
will never have forgiveness,
but is guilty of an everlasting sin."
For they had said, "He has an unclean spirit."

Dear friends, the scribes heard of and witnessed Jesus' works yet refused to accept His divinity and ministry, which came to Him by the Spirit when He was baptized. The sin that cannot be forgiven is the sin of rejecting Jesus Christ and His work.

Blessings

God morning, disciples,

Today's Gospel
Mark 1:14-20

> After John had been arrested,
> Jesus came to Galilee proclaiming the gospel of God:
> "This is the time of fulfillment.
> The kingdom of God is at hand.
> Repent, and believe in the gospel."

As he passed by the Sea of Galilee,
he saw Simon and his brother Andrew casting their nets into the sea;
they were fishermen.
Jesus said to them,
"Come after me, and I will make you fishers of men."
Then they abandoned their nets and followed him.
He walked along a little farther
and saw James, the son of Zebedee, and his brother John.
They too were in a boat mending their nets.
Then he called them.
So they left their father Zebedee in the boat
along with the hired men and followed him.

Dear friends, may our words and actions make us fishers of men.
Blessings

God morning, disciples,

Today's Gospel
Mark 3:7–12

Jesus withdrew toward the sea with his disciples.
A large number of people followed from Galilee and from Judea.
Hearing what he was doing,
a large number of people came to him also from Jerusalem,
from Idumea, from beyond the Jordan,
and from the neighborhood of Tyre and Sidon.
He told his disciples to have a boat ready for him because of the crowd,
so that they would not crush him.
He had cured many and, as a result, those who had diseases

> *were pressing upon him to touch him.*
> *And whenever unclean spirits saw him they would fall down before him and shout, "You are the Son of God."*
> *He warned them sternly not to make him known.*

Dear friends, a large number of people followed Jesus because they heard of his miraculous healing power. They just wanted to touch Him. What great faith they had. I imagine there were many more who wanted to follow Him, but could not. News of the miracles spread by word of mouth. Two thousand years on, we have the internet to spread word of His miraculous deeds and the Good News, yet much of the world chooses to live in darkness. May we live our lives in such a way so as to give others hope and lead them to Jesus, who continues to perform miracles. I have been blessed to have experienced and witnessed miracles.

Blessings

God morning, branches,

Today's Gospel:
Mark 3:1-6

> *Jesus entered the synagogue.*
> *There was a man there who had a withered hand.*
> *They watched Jesus closely*
> *to see if he would cure him on the sabbath*
> *so that they might accuse him.*
> *He said to the man with the withered hand,*
> *"Come up here before us."*
> *Then he said to the Pharisees,*

"Is it lawful to do good on the sabbath rather than to do evil,
to save life rather than to destroy it?"
But they remained silent.
Looking around at them with anger
and grieved at their hardness of heart,
Jesus said to the man, "Stretch out your hand."
He stretched it out and his hand was restored.
The Pharisees went out and immediately took counsel
with the Herodians against him to put him to death.

Dear friends, approximately two thousand years since the above story and nothing much has changed for the better. Bad tries to drive out good. The world is full of hypocrites. The hearts of too many people are hard. It is up to us to fight these evils, either in word or deed.

Blessings

God morning, sisters and brothers,

Today's Reading II
1 Cor 6:13c-15a, 17-20

Brothers and sisters:
The body is not for immorality, but for the Lord,
and the Lord is for the body;
God raised the Lord and will also raise us by his power.

Do you not know that your bodies are members of Christ?
But whoever is joined to the Lord becomes one Spirit with him.
Avoid immorality.
Every other sin a person commits is outside the body,

SCRIPTURE NOTES

but the immoral person sins against his own body.
Do you not know that your body
is a temple of the Holy Spirit within you,
whom you have from God, and that you are not your own?
For you have been purchased at a price.
Therefore glorify God in your body.

Dear friends, may we glorify God in our bodies.

Blessings

God morning, branches,

Today's Gospel
Mark 2:13-17

Jesus went out along the sea.
All the crowd came to him and he taught them.
As he passed by, he saw Levi, son of Alphaeus,
sitting at the customs post.
Jesus said to him, "Follow me."
And he got up and followed Jesus.
While he was at table in his house,
many tax collectors and sinners sat with Jesus and his disciples;
for there were many who followed him.
Some scribes who were Pharisees saw that Jesus was eating with sinners
and tax collectors and said to his disciples,
"Why does he eat with tax collectors and sinners?"
Jesus heard this and said to them,
"Those who are well do not need a physician, but the sick do.
I did not come to call the righteous but sinners."

Dear friends, I wonder who among us does not need the Great Physician? He is on call every moment of our lives and will me us wherever we find ourselves. Why not at least make an appointment for a check-up? There is no wait required. Perhaps recommend His services to someone.

Blessings

God morning, branches,

Today's Gospel
Mark 2:1-12

> When Jesus returned to Capernaum after some days,
> it became known that he was at home.
> Many gathered together so that there was no longer room for them,
> not even around the door,
> and he preached the word to them.
> They came bringing to him a paralytic carried by four men.
> Unable to get near Jesus because of the crowd,
> they opened up the roof above him.
> After they had broken through,
> they let down the mat on which the paralytic was lying.
> When Jesus saw their faith, he said to him,
> "Child, your sins are forgiven."
> Now some of the scribes were sitting there asking themselves,
> "Why does this man speak that way? He is blaspheming.
> Who but God alone can forgive sins?"
> Jesus immediately knew in his mind what
> they were thinking to themselves,
> so he said, "Why are you thinking such things in your hearts?

Which is easier, to say to the paralytic,
'Your sins are forgiven,'
or to say, 'Rise, pick up your mat and walk'?
But that you may know
that the Son of Man has authority to forgive sins on earth"
-he said to the paralytic,
"I say to you, rise, pick up your mat, and go home."
He rose, picked up his mat at once,
and went away in the sight of everyone.
They were all astounded
and glorified God, saying, "We have never seen anything like this."

Dear friends, try to imagine what the friends of the paralytic thought and felt about Jesus and their friend. They believed in Jesus and went to extraordinary lengths for their friend. Jesus recognized their faith and healed them spiritually before also physically healing the friend. Might we be paralyzed in some way that prevents us from doing what we know should be done? Might we bring someone to find healing in Jesus? This Gospel concludes with "We have seen incredible things today." I suggest you can cause others to see incredible things everyday. Finally, we can see incredible things on a daily basis by looking at the beauty of His creation.

Blessings

God morning, branches,

Today's Reading I
1 Samuel 3:1-10, 19-20

During the time young Samuel was minister to the LORD under Eli,

a revelation of the LORD was uncommon and vision infrequent.
One day Eli was asleep in his usual place.
His eyes had lately grown so weak that he could not see.
The lamp of God was not yet extinguished,
and Samuel was sleeping in the temple of the LORD
where the ark of God was.
The LORD called to Samuel, who answered, "Here I am."

Samuel ran to Eli and said, "Here I am. You called me."
"I did not call you," Eli said. "Go back to sleep."
So he went back to sleep.
Again the LORD called Samuel, who rose and went to Eli.
"Here I am," he said. "You called me."
But Eli answered, "I did not call you, my son. Go back to sleep."
At that time Samuel was not familiar with the LORD,
because the LORD had not revealed anything to him as yet.
The LORD called Samuel again, for the third time.
Getting up and going to Eli, he said, "Here I am.
You called me."
Then Eli understood that the LORD was calling the youth.
So Eli said to Samuel, "Go to sleep, and if you are called, reply,
'Speak, LORD, for your servant is listening.'"
When Samuel went to sleep in his place,
the LORD came and revealed his presence,
calling out as before, "Samuel, Samuel!"
Samuel answered, "Speak, for your servant is listening."

Samuel grew up, and the LORD was with him,
not permitting any word of his to be without effect.
Thus all Israel from Dan to Beersheba
came to know that Samuel was an accredited prophet of the LORD.

Dear friends, I wonder how many of us have heard His voice in some way. I believe God can speak to us any way he chooses, possibly to see if we are paying attention to Him. He can speak to us through anything in Creation. Maybe it is that gentle tap on the shoulder that directs you to what it is He wants you to consider. The problem is there are countless distractions. May we say 'Speak, LORD, for your servant is listening' if we are blessed to receive His voice or message.

Blessings

God morning, branches,

Today's Reading I
1 John 5:1-9

> Beloved:
> Everyone who believes that Jesus is the Christ is begotten by God,
> and everyone who loves the Father
> loves also the one begotten by him.
> In this way we know that we love the children of God
> when we love God and obey his commandments.
> For the love of God is this,
> that we keep his commandments.
> And his commandments are not burdensome,
> for whoever is begotten by God conquers the world.
> And the victory that conquers the world is our faith.
> Who indeed is the victor over the world
> but the one who believes that Jesus is the Son of God?
>
> This is the one who came through water and blood, Jesus Christ,

not by water alone, but by water and blood.
The Spirit is the one who testifies,
and the Spirit is truth.
So there are three that testify,
the Spirit, the water, and the blood,
and the three are of one accord.
If we accept human testimony,
the testimony of God is surely greater.
Now the testimony of God is this,
that he has testified on behalf of his Son.

Dear friends, may we obey His commandments. Remember, there are ten, not the tens of thousands of man-made laws. Follow His ten and everything else is easy. His commandments are not burdensome.

Did you know that you are the victor over the world?

Blessings

God morning, branches,

Today's Reading 1
1 John 5:5-13

Beloved:
Who indeed is the victor over the world
but the one who believes that Jesus is the Son of God?

This is the one who came through water and Blood, Jesus Christ,
not by water alone, but by water and Blood.
The Spirit is the one who testifies,
and the Spirit is truth.
So there are three that testify,

the Spirit, the water, and the Blood,
and the three are of one accord.
If we accept human testimony,
the testimony of God is surely greater.
Now the testimony of God is this,
that he has testified on behalf of his Son.
Whoever believes in the Son of God
has this testimony within himself.
Whoever does not believe God has made him a liar
by not believing the testimony God has given about his Son.
And this is the testimony:
God gave us eternal life,
and this life is in his Son.
Whoever possesses the Son has life;
whoever does not possess the Son of God does not have life.

I write these things to you so that you may know
that you have eternal life,
you who believe in the name of the Son of God.

Dear friends, when you feel tired or things do not seem to be going well, recall today's Reading and rejoice that you are the victor over the world and have eternal life. Things are looking up, get it?

Blessings

God morning,

Today's Reading I
1 John 3:7-10

    Children, let no one deceive you.

*The person who acts in righteousness is righteous,
just as he is righteous.
Whoever sins belongs to the Devil,
because the Devil has sinned from the beginning.
Indeed, the Son of God was revealed to destroy the works of the Devil.
No one who is begotten by God commits sin,
because God's seed remains in him;
he cannot sin because he is begotten by God.
In this way,
the children of God and the children of the Devil are made plain;
no one who fails to act in righteousness belongs to God,
nor anyone who does not love his brother.*

Dear friends, do not be deceived, we are God's children. We are called to be righteous, but our human condition makes us easy targets for the evil one. May we remember to whom we belong, act righteously and reject sin.

Blessings

God morning, disciples,

*Today's Gospel
Mt 7:21-29*

*Jesus said to his disciples:
"Not everyone who says to me, 'Lord, Lord,'
will enter the Kingdom of heaven,
but only the one who does the will of my Father in heaven.
Many will say to me on that day,
'Lord, Lord, did we not prophesy in your name?*

Did we not drive out demons in your name?
Did we not do mighty deeds in your name?'
Then I will declare to them solemnly,
'I never knew you. Depart from me, you evildoers.'

"Everyone who listens to these words of mine and acts on them
will be like a wise man who built his house on rock.
The rain fell, the floods came,
and the winds blew and buffeted the house.
But it did not collapse; it had been set solidly on rock.
And everyone who listens to these words of mine
but does not act on them
will be like a fool who built his house on sand.
The rain fell, the floods came,
and the winds blew and buffeted the house.
And it collapsed and was completely ruined."

When Jesus finished these words,
the crowds were astonished at his teaching,
for he taught them as one having authority,
and not as their scribes.

Dear friends, may we listen to His words and act on them. If we do, we build our lives on Jesus, who is referred to as a rock. For example, Psalm 18:1-3 - The Lord is the rock, the fortress, the shield, and the place of safety for those who love him. When we read Scripture, may it be as if Jesus, as one having authority, were reading to us.

Blessings

God morning, sisters and brothers,

Today's Reading 2
1 Thes 5:1-6

> Concerning times and seasons, brothers and sisters,
> you have no need for anything to be written to you.
> For you yourselves know very well that the day of the Lord will come
> like a thief at night.
> When people are saying, "Peace and security, "
> then sudden disaster comes upon them,
> like labor pains upon a pregnant woman,
> and they will not escape.
>
> But you, brothers and sisters, are not in darkness,
> for that day to overtake you like a thief.
> For all of you are children of the light
> and children of the day.
> We are not of the night or of darkness.
> Therefore, let us not sleep as the rest do,
> but let us stay alert and sober.

Dear friends, may we stay alert and sober.

Blessings

God morning, branches,

Today's Reading 1
2 Maccabees 6:18-31

> Eleazar, one of the foremost scribes,
> a man of advanced age and noble appearance,

was being forced to open his mouth to eat pork.
But preferring a glorious death to a life of defilement,
he spat out the meat,
and went forward of his own accord to the instrument of torture,
as people ought to do who have the courage to reject the food
which it is unlawful to taste even for love of life.
Those in charge of that unlawful ritual meal took the man aside privately,
because of their long acquaintance with him,
and urged him to bring meat of his own providing,
such as he could legitimately eat,
and to pretend to be eating some of the meat of the sacrifice
prescribed by the king;
in this way he would escape the death penalty,
and be treated kindly because of their old friendship with him.
But Eleazar made up his mind in a noble manner,
worthy of his years, the dignity of his advanced age,
the merited distinction of his gray hair,
and of the admirable life he had lived from childhood;
and so he declared that above all
he would be loyal to the holy laws given by God.

He told them to send him at once
to the abode of the dead, explaining:
"At our age it would be unbecoming to make such a pretense;
many young people would think the ninety-year-old Eleazar
had gone over to an alien religion.
Should I thus pretend for the sake of a brief moment of life,
they would be led astray by me,
while I would bring shame and dishonor on my old age.
Even if, for the time being, I avoid the punishment of men,

I shall never, whether alive or dead,
escape the hands of the Almighty.
Therefore, by manfully giving up my life now,
I will prove myself worthy of my old age,
and I will leave to the young a noble example
of how to die willingly and generously
for the revered and holy laws."

Eleazar spoke thus,
and went immediately to the instrument of torture.
Those who shortly before had been kindly disposed,
now became hostile toward him because what he had said
seemed to them utter madness.
When he was about to die under the blows,
he groaned and said:
"The Lord in his holy knowledge knows full well that,
although I could have escaped death,
I am not only enduring terrible pain in my body from this scourging,
but also suffering it with joy in my soul
because of my devotion to him."
This is how he died,
leaving in his death a model of courage
and an unforgettable example of virtue
not only for the young but for the whole nation.

Dear friends, I would add that Eleazar was also a model of courage and an unforgettable example of virtue for future generations.

Blessings

SCRIPTURE NOTES

God morning, branches,

Today's Gospel
Luke 21:5-11

> While some people were speaking about
> how the temple was adorned with costly stones and votive offerings,
> Jesus said, "All that you see here—
> the days will come when there will not be left
> a stone upon another stone that will not be thrown down."
>
> Then they asked him,
> "Teacher, when will this happen?
> And what sign will there be when all these things are about to happen?"
> He answered,
> "See that you not be deceived,
> for many will come in my name, saying,
> 'I am he,' and 'The time has come.'
> Do not follow them!
> When you hear of wars and insurrections,
> do not be terrified; for such things must happen first,
> but it will not immediately be the end."
> Then he said to them,
> "Nation will rise against nation, and kingdom against kingdom.
> There will be powerful earthquakes, famines, and plagues
> from place to place;
> and awesome sights and mighty signs will come from the sky."

Dear friends, the world has witnessed numerous wars, insurrections, earthquakes, famines and plagues. It has also seen many false prophets who proclaimed the end was near. Jesus tells us to not be deceived. Years ago, I asked an old great friend how will we know when Jesus returns and he is not a false prophet. The reply was something like "Oh, you WILL know." I pray we will be prepared should the Lord appear in our lifetimes.

Blessings

God morning, branches,

Today's Reading I
Amos 7:12-15

> Amaziah, priest of Bethel, said to Amos,
> "Off with you, visionary, flee to the land of Judah!
> There earn your bread by prophesying,
> but never again prophesy in Bethel;
> for it is the king's sanctuary and a royal temple."
> Amos answered Amaziah, "I was no prophet,
> nor have I belonged to a company of prophets;
> I was a shepherd and a dresser of sycamores.
> The LORD took me from following the flock, and said to me,
> Go, prophesy to my people Israel."

Dear friends, Amos heard what the Lord wanted him to do. We all have something to do for the Lord. I have been blessed to hear His calls, this ministry being one of them. How about you? Have you heard His instruction for your life? If not, may you pay closer attention.

Blessings

SCRIPTURE NOTES

God morning, branches,

Today's Gospel
Matthew 15:29-37

At that time:
Jesus walked by the Sea of Galilee,
went up on the mountain, and sat down there.
Great crowds came to him,
having with them the lame, the blind, the deformed, the mute,
and many others.
They placed them at his feet, and he cured them.
The crowds were amazed when they saw the mute speaking,
the deformed made whole,
the lame walking,
and the blind able to see,
and they glorified the God of Israel.

Jesus summoned his disciples and said,
"My heart is moved with pity for the crowd,
for they have been with me now for three days
and have nothing to eat.
I do not want to send them away hungry,
for fear they may collapse on the way."
The disciples said to him,
"Where could we ever get enough bread in this deserted place
to satisfy such a crowd?"
Jesus said to them, "How many loaves do you have?"
"Seven," they replied, "and a few fish."
He ordered the crowd to sit down on the ground.
Then he took the seven loaves and the fish,

gave thanks, broke the loaves,
and gave them to the disciples, who in turn gave them to the crowds.
They all ate and were satisfied.
They picked up the fragments left over-seven baskets full.

Dear friends, great crowds came to Jesus, having with them the lame, the blind, the deformed, the mute, and many others. He cured them all. Then He was moved with pity for the crowd. Today's Gospel is about compassion and the abundance that comes from God. May we have the faith of those who came to Jesus, be compassionate and take joy in what little we may have as unfathomable abundance awaits us.

Blessings

God morning, disciples,

Today's Gospel
Mt 7:21, 24-27

Jesus said to his disciples:
"Not everyone who says to me, 'Lord, Lord,'
will enter the Kingdom of heaven,
but only the one who does the will of my Father in heaven.

"Everyone who listens to these words of mine and acts on them
will be like a wise man who built his house on rock.
The rain fell, the floods came,
and the winds blew and buffeted the house.
But it did not collapse; it had been set solidly on rock.
And everyone who listens to these words of mine
but does not act on them

will be like a fool who built his house on sand.
The rain fell, the floods came,
and the winds blew and buffeted the house.
And it collapsed and was completely ruined.

Dear friends, may you listen to the Lord's words and act on them. May you build a house solidly on rock.

Blessings

God morning, branches,

Today's Second Reading:
2 Peter 3:8-14

> Do not ignore this one fact, beloved,
> that with the Lord one day is like a thousand years
> and a thousand years like one day.
> The Lord does not delay his promise, as some regard "delay,"
> but he is patient with you,
> not wishing that any should perish
> but that all should come to repentance.
> But the day of the Lord will come like a thief,
> and then the heavens will pass away with a mighty roar
> and the elements will be dissolved by fire,
> and the earth and everything done on it will be found out.
> Since everything is to be dissolved in this way,
> what sort of persons ought you to be,
> conducting yourselves in holiness and devotion,
> waiting for and hastening the coming of the day of God,
> because of which the heavens will be dissolved in flames

and the elements melted by fire.
But according to his promise
we await new heavens and a new earth
in which righteousness dwells.
Therefore, beloved, since you await these things,
be eager to be found without spot or blemish before him, at peace.

Dear friends, the Lord is patient with us, therefore we should be patient with Him. Remember, His time is not like our time. Patience is indeed a virtue.

Blessings

God morning, branches,

Today's Gospel
Matthew 11:16-19

> Jesus said to the crowds:
> "To what shall I compare this generation?
> It is like children who sit in marketplaces and call to one another,
> 'We played the flute for you, but you did not dance,
> we sang a dirge but you did not mourn.'
> For John came neither eating nor drinking, and they said,
> 'He is possessed by a demon.'
> The Son of Man came eating and drinking and they said,
> 'Look, he is a glutton and a drunkard,
> a friend of tax collectors and sinners.'
> But wisdom is vindicated by her works."

Dear friends, imagine John the Baptist thought to be possessed by a demon and Jesus being considered a glutton and drunkard. The world has always seen prejudices and preconceived notions and they certainly continue today. John and Jesus were clearly different from the world, but they proved their doubters wrong. Be careful not to be prejudiced. Remember it is not our place to judge.

Blessings

God morning, branches,

Today's Second Reading:
1 THES 5:16-24

> *Rejoice always. Pray without ceasing.*
> *In all circumstances give thanks,*
> *for this is the will of God for you in Christ Jesus.*
> *Do not quench the Spirit.*
> *Do not despise prophetic utterances.*
> *Test everything; retain what is good.*
> *Refrain from every kind of evil.*
> *May the God of peace make you perfectly holy*
> *and may you entirely, spirit, soul, and body,*
> *be preserved blameless for the coming of our Lord Jesus Christ.*
> *The one who calls you is faithful,*
> *and he will also accomplish it.*

Dear friends, the beginning of the reading says: Rejoice always. Pray without ceasing. In all circumstances give thanks.

It is difficult to follow these commands given our lives are so busy and cluttered. Perhaps we can let go of some of the things

that are not as important as we think and make more room for what really matters. In doing so, it is likely our peace will increase.

Blessings

God morning, branches,

Today's Gospel
Matthew 1:18-25

> This is how the birth of Jesus Christ came about.
> When his mother Mary was betrothed to Joseph,
> but before they lived together,
> she was found with child through the Holy Spirit.
> Joseph her husband, since he was a righteous man,
> yet unwilling to expose her to shame,
> decided to divorce her quietly.
> Such was his intention when, behold,
> the angel of the Lord appeared to him in a dream and said,
> "Joseph, son of David,
> do not be afraid to take Mary your wife into your home.
> For it is through the Holy Spirit
> that this child has been conceived in her.
> She will bear a son and you are to name him Jesus,
> because he will save his people from their sins."
> All this took place to fulfill
> what the Lord had said through the prophet:
>
> Behold, the virgin shall be with child and bear a son,
> and they shall name him Emmanuel,
>
> which means "God is with us."

> *When Joseph awoke,*
> *he did as the angel of the Lord had commanded him*
> *and took his wife into his home.*
> *He had no relations with her until she bore a son,*
> *and he named him Jesus.*

Dear friends, we never hear much about Joseph. This righteous man did not want to expose Mary to shame and decided to divorce her quietly. God spoke to him and he decided to follow what he was told. His life was to change into something he could never have imagined. He helped bring into this world the Son of God and raise Him. What an honor! If God called you to do something like this, what would you do? Note that it is through the family lineage that Joseph brings that Jesus will be connected to the line of David. In fact, this is the only time that someone besides Jesus is called "Son of David" in the New Testament.

Blessings

God morning, branches,

Today's Gospel
Luke 1:5-25

> *In the days of Herod, King of Judea,*
> *there was a priest named Zechariah*
> *of the priestly division of Abijah;*
> *his wife was from the daughters of Aaron,*
> *and her name was Elizabeth.*
> *Both were righteous in the eyes of God,*
> *observing all the commandments*
> *and ordinances of the Lord blamelessly.*

SCRIPTURE NOTES

But they had no child, because Elizabeth was barren
and both were advanced in years.

Once when he was serving as priest
in his division's turn before God,
according to the practice of the priestly service,
he was chosen by lot
to enter the sanctuary of the Lord to burn incense.
Then, when the whole assembly of the people was praying outside
at the hour of the incense offering,
the angel of the Lord appeared to him,
standing at the right of the altar of incense.
Zechariah was troubled by what he saw, and fear came upon him.

But the angel said to him, "Do not be afraid, Zechariah,
because your prayer has been heard.
Your wife Elizabeth will bear you a son,
and you shall name him John.
And you will have joy and gladness,
and many will rejoice at his birth,
for he will be great in the sight of the Lord.
He will drink neither wine nor strong drink.
He will be filled with the Holy Spirit even from his mother's womb,
and he will turn many of the children of Israel
to the Lord their God.
He will go before him in the spirit and power of Elijah
to turn the hearts of fathers toward children
and the disobedient to the understanding of the righteous,
to prepare a people fit for the Lord."

Then Zechariah said to the angel,

"How shall I know this?
For I am an old man, and my wife is advanced in years."
And the angel said to him in reply,
"I am Gabriel, who stand before God.
I was sent to speak to you and to announce to you this good news.
But now you will be speechless and unable to talk
until the day these things take place,
because you did not believe my words,
which will be fulfilled at their proper time."
Meanwhile the people were waiting for Zechariah
and were amazed that he stayed so long in the sanctuary.
But when he came out, he was unable to speak to them,
and they realized that he had seen a vision in the sanctuary.
He was gesturing to them but remained mute.

Then, when his days of ministry were completed, he went home.

After this time his wife Elizabeth conceived,
and she went into seclusion for five months, saying,
"So has the Lord done for me at a time when he has seen fit
to take away my disgrace before others."

Dear friends, how often have we thought whether or when God answers our prayers? Today's Gospel shows God does hear our prayers and answers them at the proper time. Keep the faith, my friends.

Blessings

God morning, branches,

> To be grateful is to recognize the Love of God in everything He has given us - and He has given us everything. Every breath we draw is a gift of His love, every moment of existence is a grace, for it brings with it immense graces from Him. Gratitude therefore takes nothing for granted, is never unresponsive, is constantly awakening to new wonder and to praise of the goodness of God. For the grateful person knows that God is good, not by hearsay but by experience. And that is what makes all the difference.
> *Thomas Merton*
>
> In every way and everywhere we accept this with all gratitude. *Acts 24:3*

Dear friends, everything we have is a gift from God. May we always be grateful and never take anything for granted. Time and life are precious. May we constantly awaken to a new wonder and praise God. Take this message from someone who has experienced many blessings and hardships, including being a widower.

Blessings

God morning, branches,

Today's Reading 1
1 John 2:12-17

> I am writing to you, children,
> because your sins have been forgiven for his name's sake.
>
> I am writing to you, fathers,
> because you know him who is from the beginning.
>
> I am writing to you, young men,
> because you have conquered the Evil One.

I write to you, children,
because you know the Father.

I write to you, fathers,
because you know him who is from the beginning.

I write to you, young men,
because you are strong and the word of God remains in you,
and you have conquered the Evil One.

Do not love the world or the things of the world.
If anyone loves the world, the love of the Father is not in him.
For all that is in the world,
sensual lust, enticement for the eyes, and a pretentious life,
is not from the Father but is from the world.
Yet the world and its enticement are passing away.
But whoever does the will of God remains forever.

Dear friends, do not love the world or the things of the world as the world and its enticement are passing away. But whoever does the will of God remains forever.

Blessings

God morning, branches,

Today's Reading 1
Jeremiah 23:1-6

> Woe to the shepherds
> who mislead and scatter the flock of my pasture,
> says the LORD.
> Therefore, thus says the LORD, the God of Israel,

SCRIPTURE NOTES

*against the shepherds who shepherd my people:
You have scattered my sheep and driven them away.
You have not cared for them,
but I will take care to punish your evil deeds.
I myself will gather the remnant of my flock
from all the lands to which I have driven them
and bring them back to their meadow;
there they shall increase and multiply.
I will appoint shepherds for them who will shepherd them
so that they need no longer fear and tremble;
and none shall be missing, says the LORD.
Behold, the days are coming, says the LORD,
when I will raise up a righteous shoot to David;
as king he shall reign and govern wisely,
he shall do what is just and right in the land.
In his days Judah shall be saved,
Israel shall dwell in security.
This is the name they give him:
"The LORD our justice."*

Dear friends, according to recent data, we and our leaders are failing to shepherd God's flock. On any given weekend, about three in 10 U.S. adults attend religious services, down from 42% two decades ago. Church attendance will likely continue to decline in the future, given younger Americans' weaker attachments to religion. This is worrisome given that the vast majority of Americans (90%) believe in some kind of higher power, but only 56% professing faith in God as described in the Bible. Leaders of all kinds have been removing God from all aspects of life. Even the most sacred holidays are increasingly secular. Is it any wonder that the world's problems are increasing? If religion and God are losing, you know who is winning. May we and others be better shepherds and lead others to a deeper, more meaningful, proactive and purposeful faith and life.

Blessings

God morning, branches,

Today's Reading 1
Acts 4:1-12

> After the crippled man had been cured,
> while Peter and John were still speaking to the people,
> the priests, the captain of the temple guard,
> and the Sadducees confronted them,
> disturbed that they were teaching the people
> and proclaiming in Jesus the resurrection of the dead.
> They laid hands on Peter and John
> and put them in custody until the next day,
> since it was already evening.
> But many of those who heard the word came to believe
> and the number of men grew to about five thousand.
>
> On the next day, their leaders, elders, and scribes
> were assembled in Jerusalem, with Annas the high priest,
> Caiaphas, John, Alexander,
> and all who were of the high-priestly class.
> They brought them into their presence and questioned them,
> "By what power or by what name have you done this?"
> Then Peter, filled with the Holy Spirit, answered them,
> "Leaders of the people and elders:

> If we are being examined today
> about a good deed done to a cripple,
> namely, by what means he was saved,
> then all of you and all the people of Israel should know
> that it was in the name of Jesus Christ the Nazorean
> whom you crucified, whom God raised from the dead;
> in his name this man stands before you healed.
> He is the stone rejected by you, the builders,
> which has become the cornerstone.
> There is no salvation through anyone else,
> nor is there any other name under heaven
> given to the human race by which we are to be saved."

Dear friends, there is no salvation through anyone else, nor is there any other name under heaven given to the human race by which we are to be saved.

Is Jesus the cornerstone of your life?

Blessings

God morning, sisters and brothers,

Today's Reading 1
2 Cor 4:7-15

> Brothers and sisters:
> We hold this treasure in earthen vessels,
> that the surpassing power may be of God and not from us.
> We are afflicted in every way, but not constrained;
> perplexed, but not driven to despair;
> persecuted, but not abandoned;

struck down, but not destroyed;
always carrying about in the body the dying of Jesus,
so that the life of Jesus may also be manifested in our body.
For we who live are constantly being given up to death
for the sake of Jesus,
so that the life of Jesus may be manifested in our mortal flesh.

So death is at work in us, but life in you.
Since, then, we have the same spirit of faith,
according to what is written, I believed, therefore I spoke,
we too believe and therefore speak,
knowing that the one who raised the Lord Jesus
will raise us also with Jesus
and place us with you in his presence.
Everything indeed is for you,
so that the grace bestowed in abundance on more and more people
may cause the thanksgiving to overflow for the glory of God.

Dear friends, may the life of Jesus be manifested in our mortal flesh and may we be thankful and glorify God.

Blessings

God morning,

Today's Reading 1
2 Kgs 4:42-44

A man came from Baal-shalishah bringing to Elisha, the man of God,
twenty barley loaves made from the firstfruits,
and fresh grain in the ear.
Elisha said, "Give it to the people to eat."

> But his servant objected,
> "How can I set this before a hundred people?"
> Elisha insisted, "Give it to the people to eat."
> "For thus says the LORD,
> 'They shall eat and there shall be some left over.'"
> And when they had eaten, there was some left over,
> as the LORD had said.

Dear friends, I am sure you are familiar with Sunday's Gospel, John 6:1-15, in which Jesus feeds about five thousand people with five barley loaves and two fish with some bread being left over. The first reading is similar in that God is able to provide for us with plenty to spare. When we trust in God, we are not just getting by in life by the skin of our teeth. His love, mercy and blessings are boundless.

Blessings

God morning, sisters and brothers,

Today's Reading 2
Eph 4:17, 20-24

> Brothers and sisters:
> I declare and testify in the Lord
> that you must no longer live as the Gentiles do,
> in the futility of their minds;
> that is not how you learned Christ,
> assuming that you have heard of him and were taught in him,
> as truth is in Jesus,
> that you should put away the old self of your former way of life,
> corrupted through deceitful desires,

and be renewed in the spirit of your minds,
and put on the new self,
created in God's way in righteousness and holiness of truth.

Dear friends, may we put away the old self of our former ways of life and put on the new self, created in God's way in righteousness and holiness of truth. I imagine we should do this on a regular basis as the world constantly seeks to corrupt us.

Blessings

God morning, sisters and brothers,

Today's Reading 2
Eph 5:15-20

> Brothers and sisters:
> Watch carefully how you live,
> not as foolish persons but as wise,
> making the most of the opportunity,
> because the days are evil.
> Therefore, do not continue in ignorance,
> but try to understand what is the will of the Lord.
> And do not get drunk on wine, in which lies debauchery,
> but be filled with the Spirit,
> addressing one another in psalms and hymns and spiritual songs,
> singing and playing to the Lord in your hearts,
> giving thanks always and for everything
> in the name of our Lord Jesus Christ to God the Father.

Dear friends, may try to understand what is the will of the Lord and give thanks always and for everything in the name of our Lord Jesus Christ to God the Father.

Blessings

God morning, branches,

Today's Reading 1
Ez 34:1-11

> The word of the Lord came to me:
> Son of man, prophesy against the shepherds of Israel,
> in these words prophesy to them to the shepherds:
> Thus says the Lord GOD: Woe to the shepherds of Israel
> who have been pasturing themselves!
> Should not shepherds, rather, pasture sheep?
> You have fed off their milk, worn their wool,
> and slaughtered the fatlings,
> but the sheep you have not pastured.
> You did not strengthen the weak nor heal the sick
> nor bind up the injured.
> You did not bring back the strayed nor seek the lost,
> but you lorded it over them harshly and brutally.
> So they were scattered for the lack of a shepherd,
> and became food for all the wild beasts.
> My sheep were scattered
> and wandered over all the mountains and high hills;
> my sheep were scattered over the whole earth,
> with no one to look after them or to search for them.

Therefore, shepherds, hear the word of the LORD:
As I live, says the Lord GOD,
because my sheep have been given over to pillage,
and because my sheep have become food for every wild beast,
for lack of a shepherd;
because my shepherds did not look after my sheep,
but pastured themselves and did not pasture my sheep;
because of this, shepherds, hear the word of the LORD:
Thus says the Lord GOD:
I swear I am coming against these shepherds.
I will claim my sheep from them
and put a stop to their shepherding my sheep
so that they may no longer pasture themselves.
I will save my sheep,
that they may no longer be food for their mouths.

For thus says the Lord GOD:
I myself will look after and tend my sheep.

Dear friends, two millennia or so and nothing is different. The Lord God will come in His time to look after and tend His sheep. Until then, may we do what we can to be good shepherds.

Blessings

God morning, disciples,

Today's Gospel
Mt 17:22-27

> *As Jesus and his disciples were gathering in Galilee, Jesus said to them,*

"The Son of Man is to be handed over to men,
and they will kill him, and he will be raised on the third day."
And they were overwhelmed with grief.

When they came to Capernaum,
the collectors of the temple tax approached Peter and said,
"Does not your teacher pay the temple tax?"
"Yes," he said.
When he came into the house, before he had time to speak,
Jesus asked him, "What is your opinion, Simon?
From whom do the kings of the earth take tolls or census tax?
From their subjects or from foreigners?"
When he said, "From foreigners," Jesus said to him,
"Then the subjects are exempt.
But that we may not offend them, go to the sea, drop in a hook,
and take the first fish that comes up.
Open its mouth and you will find a coin worth twice the temple tax.
Give that to them for me and for you."

Dear friends, I think we sometimes read things and do not understand what we read or do not wonder about the reading. I thought about several things in today's Gospel. Notice Jesus asks From whom do the kings of the earth take tolls or census tax? Jesus and His Father are the Kings of kings. Foreigners pay the tax, subjects are exempt. We are subjects of His Kingdom and do not and will not pay a tax. Think of all the fish in the sea and the first fish that is caught will have a coin to pay the tax for Jesus and Simon. That is not a coincidence. He has planned and knows everything.

Blessings

God morning, branches,

Today's Reading 1
Acts 17:15, 22–18:1

> After Paul's escorts had taken him to Athens,
> they came away with instructions for Silas and Timothy
> to join him as soon as possible.
>
> Then Paul stood up at the Areopagus and said:
> "You Athenians, I see that in every respect
> you are very religious.
> For as I walked around looking carefully at your shrines,
> I even discovered an altar inscribed, 'To an Unknown God.'
> What therefore you unknowingly worship, I proclaim to you.
> The God who made the world and all that is in it,
> the Lord of heaven and earth,
> does not dwell in sanctuaries made by human hands,
> nor is he served by human hands because he needs anything.
> Rather it is he who gives to everyone life and breath and everything.
> He made from one the whole human race
> to dwell on the entire surface of the earth,
> and he fixed the ordered seasons and the boundaries of their regions,
> so that people might seek God,
> even perhaps grope for him and find him,
> though indeed he is not far from any one of us.
> For 'In him we live and move and have our being,'
> as even some of your poets have said,
> 'For we too are his offspring.'
> Since therefore we are the offspring of God,
> we ought not to think that the divinity is like an image

fashioned from gold, silver, or stone by human art and imagination.
God has overlooked the times of ignorance,
but now he demands that all people everywhere repent
because he has established a day on which he will 'judge the world with justice' through a man he has appointed,
and he has provided confirmation for all
by raising him from the dead."

Dear friends, if you ever have a bad day or doubt yourself, remember you are God's offspring.

Blessings

God morning sisters and brothers,

Today's Reading 2
Ephesians 1:17-23

Brothers and sisters: May the God of our Lord Jesus Christ, the Father of glory, give you a Spirit of wisdom and revelation resulting in knowledge of him. May the eyes of your hearts be enlightened, that you may know what is the hope that belongs to his call, what are the riches of glory in his inheritance among the holy ones, and what is the surpassing greatness of his power for us who believe, in accord with the exercise of his great might, which he worked in Christ, raising him from the dead and seating him at his right hand in the heavens, far above every principality, authority, power, and dominion, and every name that is named not only in this age but also in the one to come. And he put all things beneath his feet and gave him as head over all things to the church, which is his body, the fullness of the one who fills all things in every way.

Dear friends, may God grant you the spirit of wisdom and revelation into a deeper and more intimate knowledge of Him so that you will have a continual revelation of Him and His ways, which will transform your lives. God wants us to know Him intimately, and because His ways are so unfathomable, He has given us the Holy Spirit to enable us to come into that continual revelation, or the communication of the knowledge of God to the soul.

Blessings

God morning, sisters and brothers.

Today's Reading I
James 5:9-12

> Do not complain, brothers and sisters, about one another,
> that you may not be judged.
> Behold, the Judge is standing before the gates.
> Take as an example of hardship and patience, brothers and sisters,
> the prophets who spoke in the name of the Lord.
> Indeed we call blessed those who have persevered.
> You have heard of the perseverance of Job,
> and you have seen the purpose of the Lord,
> because the Lord is compassionate and merciful.
>
> But above all, my brothers and sisters, do not swear,
> either by heaven or by earth or with any other oath,
> but let your "Yes" mean "Yes" and your "No" mean "No,"
> that you may not incur condemnation.

Dear friends, is there any one among us who does not live in a glass house?

Blessings

God morning, branches,

Today's Reading I
1 Peter 1:10-16

> Beloved:
> Concerning the salvation of your souls
> the prophets who prophesied about the grace that was to be yours
> searched and investigated it
> investigating the time and circumstances
> that the Spirit of Christ within them indicated
> when it testified in advance
> to the sufferings destined for Christ
> and the glories to follow them.
> It was revealed to them that they were serving not themselves but you
> with regard to the things that have now been announced to you
> by those who preached the Good News to you
> through the Holy Spirit sent from heaven,
> things into which angels longed to look.
>
> Therefore, gird up the loins of your mind, live soberly,
> and set your hopes completely on the grace to be brought to you
> at the revelation of Jesus Christ.
> Like obedient children,
> do not act in compliance with the desires of your former ignorance
> but, as he who called you is holy,

be holy yourselves in every aspect of your conduct,
for it is written, Be holy because I am holy.

Dear friends, we are called on to imitate the holiness of God himself. The adversary goes to great lengths to keep us from doing so. Be careful of the way you live and the choices you make, for it is written, be holy because I am holy.

Blessings

God morning, branches,

Today's Gospel
Mark 12:18-27

> Some Sadducees, who say there is no resurrection,
> came to Jesus and put this question to him, saying,
> "Teacher, Moses wrote for us,
> If someone's brother dies, leaving a wife but no child,
> his brother must take the wife
> and raise up descendants for his brother.
> Now there were seven brothers.
> The first married a woman and died, leaving no descendants.
> So the second brother married her and died, leaving no descendants,
> and the third likewise.
> And the seven left no descendants.
> Last of all the woman also died.
> At the resurrection when they arise whose wife will she be?
> For all seven had been married to her."
> Jesus said to them, "Are you not misled
> because you do not know the Scriptures or the power of God?

SCRIPTURE NOTES

> When they rise from the dead,
> they neither marry nor are given in marriage,
> but they are like the angels in heaven.
> As for the dead being raised,
> have you not read in the Book of Moses,
> in the passage about the bush, how God told him,
> I am the God of Abraham, the God of Isaac,
> and the God of Jacob?
> He is not God of the dead but of the living.
> You are greatly misled."

Dear friends, I imagine you take time to discuss a sporting event, movie or such. I think it could be good to discuss Scripture once in a while so we might not be misled.

Blessings

God morning, branches,

Today's Reading 1
2 Thes 1:1-5, 11-12

> Paul, Silvanus, and Timothy to the Church of the Thessalonians
> in God our Father and the Lord Jesus Christ:
> grace to you and peace from God our Father
> and the Lord Jesus Christ.
>
> We ought to thank God always for you, brothers and sisters,
> as is fitting, because your faith flourishes ever more,
> and the love of every one of you for one another grows ever greater.
> Accordingly, we ourselves boast of you in the churches of God
> regarding your endurance and faith in all your persecutions

and the afflictions you endure.
This is evidence of the just judgment of God,
so that you may be considered worthy of the Kingdom of God
for which you are suffering.

We always pray for you,
that our God may make you worthy of his calling
and powerfully bring to fulfillment every good purpose
and every effort of faith,
that the name of our Lord Jesus may be glorified in you,
and you in him,
in accord with the grace of our God and Lord Jesus Christ.

Dear friends, may God make us worthy of His calling and powerfully bring to fulfillment every good purpose and every effort of faith, that the name of our Lord Jesus may be glorified in us, and we in Him.

Blessings

God morning, sisters and brothers.

Today's Reading 1
1 Cor 1:17-25

Brothers and sisters:
Christ did not send me to baptize but to preach the Gospel,
and not with the wisdom of human eloquence,
so that the cross of Christ might not be emptied of its meaning.

The message of the cross is foolishness to those who are perishing,
but to us who are being saved it is the power of God.

For it is written:

I will destroy the wisdom of the wise,
and the learning of the learned I will set aside.

Where is the wise one?
Where is the scribe?
Where is the debater of this age?
Has not God made the wisdom of the world foolish?
For since in the wisdom of God
the world did not come to know God through wisdom,
it was the will of God through the foolishness of the proclamation
to save those who have faith.
For Jews demand signs and Greeks look for wisdom,
but we proclaim Christ crucified,
a stumbling block to Jews and foolishness to Gentiles,
but to those who are called, Jews and Greeks alike,
Christ the power of God and the wisdom of God.
For the foolishness of God is wiser than human wisdom,
and the weakness of God is stronger than human strength.

Dear friends, Christ did not send me to baptize but to preach the Gospel, and not with the wisdom of human eloquence. I am a simple and humble man. The plain preaching of a crucified Jesus is more powerful than all the oratory and philosophy of our world. Our hopes and happiness rest on His crucifixion. I do not believe God can be foolish or weak, but if He could, His wisdom and strength would still exceed our understanding.

Blessings

God morning, sisters and brothers,

Today's Reading 2
Jas 1:17-18, 21b-22, 27

> Dearest brothers and sisters:
> All good giving and every perfect gift is from above,
> coming down from the Father of lights,
> with whom there is no alteration or shadow caused by change.
> He willed to give us birth by the word of truth
> that we may be a kind of firstfruits of his creatures.
>
> Humbly welcome the word that has been planted in you
> and is able to save your souls.
>
> Be doers of the word and not hearers only, deluding yourselves.
>
> Religion that is pure and undefiled before God and the Father is this:
> to care for orphans and widows in their affliction
> and to keep oneself unstained by the world.

Dear friends, may we humbly welcome and be doers of the Word and do our best to be unstained by the world, which is controlled by you know who.

Blessings

God morning, disciples,

Today's Gospel
Matthew 7:6, 12-14

> Jesus said to his disciples:
> "Do not give what is holy to dogs, or throw your pearls before swine,

lest they trample them underfoot, and turn and tear you to pieces.

"Do to others whatever you would have them do to you.
This is the Law and the Prophets.

"Enter through the narrow gate;
for the gate is wide and the road broad that leads to destruction,
and those who enter through it are many.
How narrow the gate and constricted the road that leads to life.
And those who find it are few."

Dear friends, I was taught to not follow the crowds. I pray we follow the constricted road to the narrow gate.

By the way, ever heard the expression "pearls before swine"?

Blessings

God morning, disciples,

Today's Gospel
Mt 10:1-7

Jesus summoned his Twelve disciples
and gave them authority over unclean spirits to drive them out
and to cure every disease and every illness.
The names of the Twelve Apostles are these:
first, Simon called Peter, and his brother Andrew;
James, the son of Zebedee, and his brother John;
Philip and Bartholomew,
Thomas and Matthew the tax collector;
James, the son of Alphaeus, and Thaddeus;
Simon the Cananean, and Judas Iscariot

who betrayed Jesus.

Jesus sent out these Twelve after instructing them thus,
"Do not go into pagan territory or enter a Samaritan town.
Go rather to the lost sheep of the house of Israel.
As you go, make this proclamation: 'The Kingdom of heaven is at hand.'"

Dear friends, we are called to be laborers for Jesus. We may not have the authority over unclean spirits or to cure anyone, at least directly. Our work may lead the afflicted to the One who does cure. May we gather some sheep for our Shepherd.

Blessings

God morning, branches,

Today's Gospel
Matthew 10:24-33

Jesus said to his Apostles:
"No disciple is above his teacher,
no slave above his master.
It is enough for the disciple that he become like his teacher,
for the slave that he become like his master.
If they have called the master of the house Beelzebul,
how much more those of his household!
"Therefore do not be afraid of them.
Nothing is concealed that will not be revealed,
nor secret that will not be known.
What I say to you in the darkness, speak in the light;
what you hear whispered, proclaim on the housetops.
And do not be afraid of those who kill the body but cannot kill the soul;

rather, be afraid of the one who can destroy
both soul and body in Gehenna.
Are not two sparrows sold for a small coin?
Yet not one of them falls to the ground without your Father's knowledge.
Even all the hairs of your head are counted.
So do not be afraid; you are worth more than many sparrows.
Everyone who acknowledges me before others
I will acknowledge before my heavenly Father.
But whoever denies me before others,
I will deny before my heavenly Father."

Dear friends, even all the hairs of your head are counted. I often think about that when I travel in a crowded subway. God knows every star in the sky by name. He knows everything because He has created everything. May we never deny Jesus before others or even ourselves.

Blessings

God morning, branches,

Today's Gospel
Mt 13:1-9

On that day, Jesus went out of the house and sat down by the sea.
Such large crowds gathered around him
that he got into a boat and sat down,
and the whole crowd stood along the shore.
And he spoke to them at length in parables, saying:
"A sower went out to sow.
And as he sowed, some seed fell on the path,

and birds came and ate it up.
Some fell on rocky ground, where it had little soil.
It sprang up at once because the soil was not deep,
and when the sun rose it was scorched,
and it withered for lack of roots.
Some seed fell among thorns, and the thorns grew up and choked it.
But some seed fell on rich soil, and produced fruit,
a hundred or sixty or thirtyfold.
Whoever has ears ought to hear."

Dear friends, may we be like rich soil and hear the word and accept it and bear fruit a hundred or sixty or thirtyfold.

Blessings

God morning, branches,

Today's Gospel
Mt 22:1-14

> Jesus again in reply spoke to the chief priests and the elders of the people in parables
> saying, "The Kingdom of heaven may be likened to a king
> who gave a wedding feast for his son.
> He dispatched his servants to summon the invited guests to the feast,
> but they refused to come.
> A second time he sent other servants, saying,
> 'Tell those invited: "Behold, I have prepared my banquet,
> my calves and fattened cattle are killed,
> and everything is ready; come to the feast."'
> Some ignored the invitation and went away,

one to his farm, another to his business.
The rest laid hold of his servants,
mistreated them, and killed them.
The king was enraged and sent his troops,
destroyed those murderers, and burned their city.
Then the king said to his servants, 'The feast is ready,
but those who were invited were not worthy to come.
Go out, therefore, into the main roads
and invite to the feast whomever you find.'
The servants went out into the streets
and gathered all they found, bad and good alike,
and the hall was filled with guests.
But when the king came in to meet the guests
he saw a man there not dressed in a wedding garment.
He said to him, 'My friend, how is it
that you came in here without a wedding garment?'
But he was reduced to silence.
Then the king said to his attendants, 'Bind his hands and feet,
and cast him into the darkness outside,
where there will be wailing and grinding of teeth.'
Many are invited, but few are chosen."

Dear friends, may we be among the few who are chosen.
Blessings

God morning, branches,

If only you would listen to his voice today! Psalm 95:7

One might listen for His voice in the quiet of the morning, before the noisiness of the day's activities takes hold.

Someone has observed that God gave us two ears and one mouth—it stands to reason that we should listen twice as much as we speak!

Blessings

God morning, branches,

> Give something, however small, to the one in need. For it is not small to one who has nothing. Neither is it small to God, if we have given what we could. – *St. Gregory Nazianzen*

Dear friends, I imagine we donate money and things around the holidays and perhaps on other occasions. Imagine the joy you bring to perfect strangers anytime you donate money or something.

True joy lies in the act of giving without an expectation of receiving something in return.

Blessings

God morning, branches,

> "He that is kind is free, though he is a slave; he that is evil is a slave, though he be a king." - *St. Augustine*

Dear friends, if you can be anything, be kind. A kind word, a thoughtful smile, a simple 'thank you' can go a long way. Kindness is known to make people happier and all people involved in acts of kindness

will experience some form of happiness. We don't have to agree on anything to be kind to one another.

Blessings

God morning, branches,

> There is neither Jew nor Greek, there is neither slave nor free, there is no male and female, for you are all one in Christ Jesus. *Galatians 3:28*

Dear friends, rather than uniting people, many in the world seek to divide us as part of their divide and conquer strategy. As Mark 3:25 says, "If a house is divided against itself, that house cannot stand". Our faith is under constant pressure. Do not allow yourselves to be intimidated or influenced by anti-Christian zealots.

Blessings

God morning, disciples,

Today's Gospel
Luke 6:39–42

Jesus told his disciples a parable:

> "Can a blind person guide a blind person? Will not both fall into a pit? No disciple is superior to the teacher; but when fully trained, every disciple will be like his teacher.
> Why do you notice the splinter in your brother's eye, but do not perceive the wooden beam in your own? How can you say to your brother, 'Brother, let me remove that splinter in your eye,'

when you do not even notice the wooden beam in your own eye? You
   hypocrite! Remove the wooden beam from your eye first; then you
   will see clearly
to remove the splinter in your brother's eye."

Dear friends, may we remove the wooden beams from our eyes.
Blessings

God morning, branches,

Today's Alleluia
Acts 16:14b

> Open our hearts, O Lord, to listen to the words of your Son.
> Alleluia, alleluia

Dear friends, may you not just listen to His words, but act on them.
Blessings

God morning, branches,

Today's Verse Before the Gospel
Ezekiel 18:31

> Cast away from you all the crimes you have committed, says the LORD, and make for yourselves a new heart and a new spirit.

Dear friends, repent and open your eyes, and let the clear, convincing light of God's words and will shine upon you.
Blessings

God morning, branches,

> Do not forget the works of the Lord!
>
> *Psalm 78:3-4* What we have heard and know, and what our fathers have declared to us, we will declare to the generation to come. The glorious deeds of the LORD and his strength.

Dear friends, may we declare to younger generations the glorious deeds of the LORD and His strength.

Blessings

God morning, branches,

> But you, man of God, flee from all this, and pursue righteousness, godliness, faith, love, endurance and gentleness. *1 Timothy 6:11*

Dear friends, may you flee from the adversary's distractions and weapons that surround us to pursue righteousness, godliness, faith, love, endurance and gentleness.

Blessings

God morning, branches,

> "When we are overcome by sadness, fear, or suffering; when the pains of loss overwhelm us; when evil seems to have taken power; let us look to the cross and be filled with peace, knowing that Christ has walked this road and walks it now with us and with all our brothers and sisters."
> ~*St Teresa of Avila*

Blessings

God morning, branches,

> The most powerful weapon to conquer the devil is humility.
>
> For, as he does not know at all how to employ it, neither does he know how to defend himself from it. *Saint Vincent de Paul*

Dear friends, the Lord is humble. May you be likewise.

Blessings

God morning, branches,

> Do not trust in princes,
> In mortal man, in whom there is no salvation.
> *Psalm 146:3*

Dear friends, substitute government officials and bureaucrats for princes in our times.

Blessings

God morning, branches,

As each one has received a gift, use it to serve one another as good stewards of God's varied grace.

> Whoever preaches, let it be with the words of God; whoever serves, let it be with the strength that God supplies, so that in all things God may be glorified through Jesus Christ, to whom belong glory and dominion forever and ever. Amen.

May you use well the gifts God gave you.

Blessings

SCRIPTURE NOTES

God morning, branches,

Below is another everyday phrase and its biblical origin.

> I am at my wits' end.
> They reel to and fro, and stagger like a drunken man, and are at their wits' end. *Psalm 107:27*

You have probably quoted part of Psalm 107:27 numerous times and never knew it.

Blessings

God morning, branches,

> And amazement seized them all, and they glorified God and were filled with awe, saying, "We have seen extraordinary things today." *Luke 5:26*

Dear friends, God's creation is replete with extraordinary things. May you be filled with awe and wonder as you view the sunrise, sunset and life.

Blessings

God morning, sisters and brothers,

Today's Reading I
Ephesians 4:1-6

> Brothers and sisters:
> I, a prisoner for the Lord, urge you to live in a manner worthy of the call you have received,
> with all humility and gentleness, with patience, bearing with one another through love,

striving to preserve the unity of the spirit through the bond of peace;
one Body and one Spirit, as you were also called to the one
hope of your call; one Lord, one faith, one baptism;
one God and Father of all, who is over all and through all and in all.

Dear friends, may we live in a manner worthy of the call we have received, with all humility and gentleness, with patience, bearing with one another through love, striving to preserve the unity of the spirit through the bond of peace.

Blessings

God morning, disciples,

Today's Gospel
Matthew 6:19-23

Jesus said to his disciples:

"Do not store up for yourselves treasures on earth,
where moth and decay destroy, and thieves break in and steal. But store up treasures in heaven,
where neither moth nor decay destroys, nor thieves break in and steal. For where your treasure is, there also will your heart be.

"The lamp of the body is the eye.
If your eye is sound, your whole body will be filled with light; but if your eye is bad, your whole body will be in darkness.
And if the light in you is darkness, how great will the darkness be."

Dear friends, I suggest the Way to keep your eyes sound and your body filled with light is to see Jesus wherever you look and in everything you see.

Blessings

God morning, branches,

> If you read history you will find that the Christians who did most for the present world were precisely those who thought most of the next. It is since Christians have largely ceased to think of the other world that they have become so ineffective in this. *C. S. Lewis*

Dear friends, may we think more of the next world to be better in this one.

Blessings

God morning, branches,

Today's Gospel
Luke 15:3-7

> Jesus addressed this parable to the Pharisees and scribes: "What man among you having a hundred sheep and losing one of them would not leave the ninety-nine in the desert and go after the lost one until he finds it? And when he does find it, he sets it on his shoulders with great joy and, upon his arrival home, he calls together his friends and neighbors and says to them, 'Rejoice with me because I have found my lost sheep.' I tell you, in just the same way there will be more joy in heaven over one sinner who repents than over ninety-nine righteous people who have no need of repentance."

Dear friends, I wonder how many of us might be lost sheep. Count me among the lost sheep.

Blessings

God morning, branches,

> Sweet friendships refresh the soul and awaken our hearts with joy, for good friends are like the anointing oil that yields the fragrant incense of God's presence. *Proverbs 27:9*

Dear friends, my blessings increased a couple of nights ago when I made new friends in a widow/widower group. I was already blessed with wonderful friends, some for decades. May you refresh your souls and awaken your hearts with joy and experience the fragrant incense of God's presence.

Blessings

God morning, branches,

Today's Reading 1
Hebrews 10:32-39

> Remember the days past when, after you had been enlightened,
> you endured a great contest of suffering.
> At times you were publicly exposed to abuse and affliction;
> at other times you associated yourselves with those so treated.
> You even joined in the sufferings of those in prison
> and joyfully accepted the confiscation of your property,
> knowing that you had a better and lasting possession.
> Therefore, do not throw away your confidence;

it will have great recompense.
You need endurance to do the will of God and receive what he has promised.
For, after just a brief moment,
he who is to come shall come;
he shall not delay.
But my just one shall live by faith,
and if he draws back I take no pleasure in him.
We are not among those who draw back and perish,
but among those who have faith and will possess life.

Dear friends, may we have endurance to do the will of God and receive what He has promised.

Blessings

God morning, branches,

"Prayer can truly change your life, for it turns your attention away from yourself and directs your mind and your heart towards the Lord. If we look only at ourselves, with our own limitations and sins, we quickly give way to sadness and discouragement. But if we keep our eyes fixed on the Lord, then our hearts are filled with hope, our minds are washed in the light of truth, and we come to know the fullness of the Gospel with all its promise and life." *Pope John Paul II*

Dear friends, I pray that you find time to direct your minds and hearts toward the Lord. I imagine we all would like a little or more peace in our lives. Jesus is our source of peace.

Peace

God morning, branches,

Today's Reading II
John 2:18-21

> Children, it is the last hour;
> and just as you heard that the antichrist was coming, so now many antichrists have appeared.
> Thus we know this is the last hour.
> They went out from us, but they were not really of our number; if they had been, they would have remained with us.
> Their desertion shows that none of them was of our number. But you have the anointing that comes from the Holy One, and you all have knowledge.
> I write to you not because you do not know the truth
> but because you do, and because every lie is alien to the truth.

Dear friends, there certainly are many antichrists (simply anyone against Christ) in the world and among us. As far as John saying it is the last hour, consider yesterday's note with a thousand years and one day.

Blessings

God morning, branches,

> The great danger for family life, in the midst of any society whose idols are pleasure, comfort and independence, lies in the fact that people close their hearts and become selfish. *Pope John Paul II*

Dear friends, may you never close your hearts and become selfish.

Blessings

God morning, branches,

> The Lord is good to those who wait for him,
> to the soul who seeks him.
> It is good that one should wait quietly
> for the salvation of the Lord.
> *Lamentations 3:25-26*

Dear friends, we live in the age of instant gratification where we expect everything to come to us instantly from our deliveries, texts, etc. Well, God is not subject to our time or whims. God's timing is always perfect and it is a good idea to wait quietly for Him.

Blessings

God morning, branches,

> God created man in his own image, in the image of God he created him; male and female he created them" *Genesis 1:27*

Dear friends, one is either male or female as God intended. Nothing anyone says or does can change what God created. Yes, this sounds simple, but the attacks on our faith keep increasing. The enemy knows no boundaries. May you never give in to the nonsense about whether one is male or female.

Blessings

God morning, branches,

Gospel
John 14:21-26

SCRIPTURE NOTES

Jesus said to his disciples:
""Whoever has my commandments and observes them
is the one who loves me.
Whoever loves me will be loved by my Father,
and I will love him and reveal myself to him.""
Judas, not the Iscariot, said to him,
""Master, then what happened that you will reveal yourself to us
and not to the world?""
Jesus answered and said to him,
""Whoever loves me will keep my word,
and my Father will love him,
and we will come to him and make our dwelling with him.
Whoever does not love me does not keep my words;
yet the word you hear is not mine
but that of the Father who sent me.

""I have told you this while I am with you.
The Advocate, the Holy Spirit
whom the Father will send in my name--
he will teach you everything
and remind you of all that I told you.""

Dear friends, may we keep His word and commandments. This sounds easy, but the evil one does all he can to keep us from doing what we are called to do.

Blessings

God morning, branches,

"You have heard that it was said, 'You shall love your neighbor

SCRIPTURE NOTES

and hate your enemy.'
But I say to you, love your enemies, and pray for those who persecute you,
that you may be children of your heavenly Father, for he makes his sun rise on the bad and the good, and causes rain to fall on the just and the unjust.
For if you love those who love you, what recompense will you have? Do not the tax collectors* do the same?
And if you greet your brothers only, what is unusual about that? Do not the pagans do the same?*
So be perfect,* just as your heavenly Father is perfect.
Matthew 5:43–48

Dear friends, we have numerous enemies because of our faith in Christ. Still, He tells us to love our enemies. While you might think that is impossible to do, remember nothing is impossible for Him and we are called to be like Him. While we may not attain perfection in this life, we should strive for it nonetheless. I think it is also a good idea to love those who are neither our enemies nor friends.
Blessings

God morning, branches,

> We brought nothing into the world, and we can take nothing out of it;
> *1 Timothy 6:7*

Dear friends, remember you never see a Brinks truck following a hearse. Life is not about the phrase "He who dies with the most toys wins." There is more to life than our stuff. Perhaps you might consider that we have more material wealth than much of the world and it would not hurt to help someone in need. Perhaps you could share your God-given gift(s) with others. Perhaps you can donate some time to help another. "Time is the most valuable thing a man can spend." (Theophrastus) When you help someone don't you feel good in your heart? Aren't we here to help others and glorify God?

Blessings

God morning, branches,

> Put on then, as God's chosen ones, holy and beloved, heartfelt compassion, kindness, humility, gentleness, and patience,
> bearing with one another and forgiving one another, if one has a grievance against another; as the Lord has forgiven you, so must you also do.
> And over all these put on love, that is, the bond of perfection.
> *Colossians 3:12-14*

Dear friends, love is not limited to one day in the second month. I gave flowers often to my wife, who was called home to Heaven seventeen months ago, for the simple reason of just because I loved her.

Love

God morning, branches,

> Today is Memorial of Saint Maximilian Kolbe, Priest and Martyr.
> The 47-year-old Franciscan Conventual priest volunteered to die in place of a stranger August 14, 1941, at the German Nazi concentration and death camp of Auschwitz in Poland.

> "Let us remember that love lives through sacrifice and is nourished by giving...Without sacrifice there is no love." *St Maximilian*

Dear friends, Saint Maximilian volunteered to die in place of a stranger. Think about that every now and again. What could you do for someone?

Blessings

God morning, branches,

> But Peter and the apostles answered, "We must obey God rather than men. *Acts 5:29*

Dear friends, there is so much insanity in the world. A federal judge ruled recently that a Catholic hospital in Maryland discriminated against a biological female patient who identifies as a transgender man by refusing to provide her with a hysterectomy. The Catholic hospital was obeying God, not man.

Blessings

God morning, branches,

> Oh, how great is the goodness of God, greater than we can understand. There are moments and there are mysteries of the divine mercy over which the heavens are astounded. Let our judgment of souls cease, for God's mercy upon them is extraordinary. *Mary Faustina Kowalska*

Dear friends, imagine even the heavens are astounded by moments and mysteries of the divine mercy!

Blessings

God morning, branches,

> Look carefully then how you walk, not as unwise but as wise, making the best use of the time, because the days are evil. *Ephesians 5:15-16*

Dear friends, "walking" refers to how one lives. The days are evil because the adversary is in control. Be careful.

Blessings

God morning, branches,

Today's Gospel
Luke 8:16-18

> Jesus said to the crowd:
> "No one who lights a lamp conceals it with a vessel
> or sets it under a bed;
> rather, he places it on a lampstand
> so that those who enter may see the light.
> For there is nothing hidden that will not become visible,
> and nothing secret that will not be known and come to light.
> Take care, then, how you hear.
> To anyone who has, more will be given,
> and from the one who has not,
> even what he seems to have will be taken away."

Dear friends, please take care in how we listen to God. The adversary is constantly trying to distract us from God. May we be reflections of His glorious light.

Blessings

God morning, branches,

Be completely humble and gentle; be patient, bearing with one another in love. Ephesians 4:2

According to Scripture, patience is a virtue and a fruit of the Spirit, a sign of someone who trusts in God. According to 1 Samuel "lack of patience can cause you to miss blessings."

Think of how many blessings you may have missed.

You did not miss this one.

Blessings

God morning, branches,

So, as those who have been chosen of God, holy and beloved, put on a heart of compassion, kindness, humility, gentleness and patience. Colossians 3:12

"If you want more kindness in the world put it there."

Blessings

God morning, branches,

All scripture is inspired by God and is useful for teaching, for refutation, for correction, and for training in righteousness, 2Timothy 3:16

Dear friends, as I was doing research for my notes, I came across the following:

Don't say God has been silent when your bible has been closed.

Most of us want to hear from God but we often neglect the words that He has already spoken to us through the Bible. 2 Timothy

3:16-17 tells us that the words in the Bible are the words of God. We cannot say that God isn't speaking to us when we aren't listening to His Word.

This also reminded me of the following:

You may be the only Bible some people read...

You may be the only Jesus some people see...

Blessings

God morning, branches,

"Grace and peace to you from God our Father and the Lord Jesus Christ. Praise be to the God and Father of our Lord Jesus Christ, the Father of compassion and the God of all comfort, who comforts us in all our troubles, so that we can comfort those in any trouble with the comfort we ourselves have received from God" (2 Corinthians 1:2-4).

Dear friends, may we comfort others.

Blessings

God morning, branches,

Human pride and egoism always create divisions, build walls of indifference, hate and violence. The Holy Spirit, on the other hand, makes hearts capable of understanding the languages of all, as he re-establishes the bridge of authentic communication between earth and Heaven.
Pope Benedict XVI

Dear friends, may we seek guidance more often from the Holy Spirit.

Blessings

God morning, branches,

> "Will God ever ask you to do something you are not able to do? The answer is yes--all the time! It must be that way, for God's glory and kingdom. If we function according to our ability alone, we get the glory; if we function according to the power of the Spirit within us, God gets the glory. He wants to reveal Himself to a watching world." *Henry Blackaby*

Dear friends, I imagine many (most?) of us have faced something that seemed impossible with which to deal. I know I have, more than a couple of times. We succeeded with the grace of God. Recall that Jesus said "What is impossible with man is possible with God."

Blessings

God morning, branches,

Ephesians 2:10

> For we are God's handiwork, created in Christ Jesus to do good works, which God prepared in advance for us to do.

Dear friends, each of us is unique and amazing. God prepared what He wanted us to do for Him long ago. Each of us was created by God to serve Him in this world. I wonder if you know your mission in this place and time.

Blessings

God morning, branches,

I imagine you have heard or said the four corners of the earth expression, but probably did not know of its biblical origin. The phrase corners of the earth is used in several places in the Bible as a figurative term for the outermost borders or most distant parts of the earth.

You may have thought it came from Shakespeare, who used the phrase 'the four corners of the earth' in The Merchant of Venice: *Act 2, Scene 7*. The Bard referenced the Bible many times in his plays.

Blessings

God morning, branches,

> "God speaks in the silence of the heart. Listening is the beginning of prayer." *Saint Teresa of Calcutta*

Dear friends, I imagine you know Psalm 46:10, "Be still and know that I am God". I wonder if you know this quote of the French philosopher Blaise Pascal: "All of humanity's problems stem from man's inability to sit quietly in a room alone.' Matthew 6:6 begins with "But when you pray, go into your inner room, shut your door, and pray". There is so much noise in our world (any wonder why?). May you find quiet time with God.

Blessings

God morning, branches,

> We need to give Christ a chance to make use of us, to be His word and His work, to share His food and His clothing in the world today. If we do not radiate the light of Christ around us, the sense of the darkness that prevails in the world will increase. *Mother Teresa*

Dear friends, may we radiate the light of Christ around us.

Blessings

God morning, branches,

My help comes from the LORD, the maker of heaven and earth. Psalm 121:2

Dear friends, God uses us to help others. When we ask Him for help, He provides it, often through others. The definition of godsend is a very helpful or valuable event, person, or thing. Sometimes we might say something or someone was Heaven-sent.

Blessings

God morning, branches,

No trial has come to you but what is human. God is faithful and will not let you be tried beyond your strength; but with the trial He will also provide a way out, so that you may be able to bear it. 1 Corinthians 10:13

Dear friends, temptation is all around us. Depend on God and He will help you. Ignore God at your peril.

Blessings

God morning, branches,

Do not love the world or the things of the world. If anyone loves the world, the love of the Father is not in him. For all that is in the world, sensual lust, enticement for the eyes, and a pretentious life, is not from the Father but is from the world. 1 John 2:15-16

Dear friends, it is easier to read the above passage than to live it. We are constantly bombarded with all kinds of advertisements about the things of this world and how you need them to make yourself better and complete. Remember who rules the world. Remember the world and the things within it cannot solve your problems, are temporary and will pass away. Only God can solve your problems and life in Heaven is wonderful and eternal for those who believe in His Son.

Blessings

God morning, disciples,

> ...but they did not listen to their judges either, for they prostituted themselves by following other gods, bowing down to them. They were quick to stray from the way their ancestors had taken, who obeyed the commandments of the LORD; but these did not. *Judges 2:17*

Dear friends, John Adams, a Founding Father, once said "Our Constitution was made only for a moral and religious people. It is wholly inadequate to the government of any other." Many in our country are following other gods and not obeying the commandments of the Lord. Pray that your actions and words will show others the errors of their ways and lead them to the Lord.

Blessings

God morning, branches,

> For God has not given us a spirit of fear, but of power and of love and of a sound mind. *2 Timothy 1:7*

With all the problems in the world, big and small, real and imagined, God has given us the tools to surmount them. It is as if God says "don't worry, be happy".

Blessings

God morning, branches,

> Do you not know that your body is a temple of the holy Spirit within you, whom you have from God, and that you are not your own? For you have been purchased at a price. Therefore, glorify God in your body. *1 Corinthians 6:19-20*

Dear friends, I wonder how many realize we are not our own.

Blessings

God morning, branches,

> There is one glory of the sun, and another glory of the moon, and another glory of the stars; for star differs from star in glory. *1 Corinthians 15:41*

Dear friends, there is glory in each of us and no two are the same. Shine on and glorify God by your actions.

Blessings

God morning, branches,

> "Pray as though everything depended on God. Work as though everything depended on you." *Saint Augustine*

Dear friends, God is in control and has a plan for everything. In a way, though, God depends on us. He does not force Himself on anyone or into their lives. Our job is to show them The Way, share the Good News and lead others to Him.

Blessings

God morning, branches,

> "Knowing that of the Lord ye shall receive the reward of the inheritance: for ye serve the Lord Christ." *Colossians 3:24*

My Boss is a Jewish carpenter.

Blessings

God morning, branches,

> Great love can change small things into great ones, and it is only love which lends value to our actions. *Saint Faustina*

Dear friends, we are taught that actions speak louder than words. May those actions be done with love.

Blessings

God morning, disciples,

Today's Gospel
Mark 3:20-21

> Jesus came with his disciples into the house. Again the crowd gathered,- making it impossible for them even to eat.

> When his relatives heard of this they set out to seize him, for they said, "He is out of his mind."

Dear friends, I imagine some of us may have been thought of as out of our minds by our families. None of us, though, could have been as misunderstood as was Jesus.

May you have the courage to let yourselves be led more by the spirit of God.

Blessings

God morning, branches,

> I firmly believe that the moment our hearts are emptied of pride and selfishness and ambition and self-seeking and every thing that is contrary to God's law, the Holy Ghost will come and fill every corner of our hearts; but if we are full of pride and conceit and ambition and self-seeking and pleasure and the world, there is no room for the Spirit of God; and I believe many a man is praying to God to fill him when he is full already with something else. *Dwight L. Moody*

Dear friends, may we make room in our hearts for the Holy Spirit.

Blessings

God morning, branches,

Below is another everyday phrase and its biblical origin.

> And I will say to my soul, "Soul, you have many goods laid up for many years to come; take your ease, eat, drink and be merry." *Luke 12:19*

You have probably quoted Luke numerous times and never knew it.

As you eat, drink and are merry this Memorial Day weekend, please say a prayer for those who made the ultimate sacrifice for our freedoms.

Blessings

God morning, branches,

> For I am the LORD your God who takes hold of your right hand and says to you, Do not fear; I will help you *Isaiah 41:13*

Dear friends, let God hold your hand.

> One day you were crossing a bridge with God. You were scared so you asked GOD, "Can I hold your hand so I won't fall into the river?"

> GOD said, "No my child, I should hold your hand..."

> You asked, "What's the difference?"

> GOD replied, "If you hold my hand and something happens, you might let go. If I hold your hand, no matter what happens, I'll never let go...."

Blessings

God morning, sisters and brothers,

Todat's Reading II
Eph 3:2-3a, 5-6

> Brothers and sisters: You have heard of the stewardship of God's grace that was given to me for your benefit, namely, that the mystery was made known to me by revelation. It was not made known to people in

other generations as it has now been revealed to his holy apostles and prophets by the Spirit: that the Gentiles are coheirs, members of the same body, and copartners in the promise in Christ Jesus through the gospel.

Dear friends, may we always rejoice that we are coheirs, members of the same body, and copartners in the promise in Christ Jesus through the gospel.

Blessings

God morning, branches,

In today's mass,
The Baptism of the Lord:

> The heavens were opened and the voice of the Father thundered: This is my beloved Son, listen to him. *Mark 9:7*

Listen to Him, indeed!
Blessings

God morning, branches,

> "If you learn everything except Christ, you learn nothing. If you learn nothing except Christ, you learn everything." *Saint Bonaventure*

Dear friends, may we learn Christ. He is all we need.
Blessings

SCRIPTURE NOTES

God morning, branches,

Today's First Reading

Wisdom 7:7-11

> I prayed, and prudence was given me;
> I pleaded, and the spirit of wisdom came to me. I preferred her to scepter and throne,
> and deemed riches nothing in comparison with her, nor did I liken any priceless gem to her;
> because all gold, in view of her, is a little sand, and before her, silver is to be accounted mire.
> Beyond health and comeliness I loved her, and I chose to have her rather than the light,
> because the splendor of her never yields to sleep.
> Yet all good things together came to me in her company, and countless riches at her hands.

May you have wisdom, my friends.

Blessings

God morning, branches,

> To put it simply: the Holy Spirit bothers us. Because he moves us, he makes us walk, he pushes the Church to go forward. And we are like Peter at the Transfiguration: 'Ah, how wonderful it is to be here like this, all together!' ... But don't bother us. We want the Holy Spirit to doze off ... we want to domesticate the Holy Spirit. And that's no good. because he is God, he is that wind which comes and goes and you don't know where. He is the power of God, he is the one who gives us consolation

and strength to move forward. But: to move forward! And this bothers us. It's so much nicer to be comfortable. *Pope Francis*

Dear friends, remember that we were not made to be comfortable. *Blessings*

God morning, branches,

Today's Reading I

> Thus says the LORD:
> Cursed is the one who trusts in human beings, who seeks his strength
>   in flesh,
> whose heart turns away from the LORD. He is like a barren bush in
>   the desert
> that enjoys no change of season, but stands in a lava waste,
> a salt and empty earth.
> Blessed is the one who trusts in the LORD, whose hope is the LORD.
> He is like a tree planted beside the waters
> that stretches out its roots to the stream: it fears not the heat when
>   it comes;
> its leaves stay green;
> in the year of drought it shows no distress, but still bears fruit.

Dear friends, may you not be like a barren bush in the desert. *Blessings*

God morning, branches,

Today's Gospel
Luke 11:27–28

While Jesus was speaking,
a woman from the crowd called out and said to him, "Blessed is the womb that carried you
and the breasts at which you nursed." He replied,
"Rather, blessed are those
who hear the word of God and observe it."

May you hear the word of God and, more importantly, observe it.

Blessings

God morning, branches,

Today's Reading
1 Lv 19:1-2, 17-1

The LORD said to Moses,
"Speak to the whole Israelite community and tell them:
Be holy, for I, the LORD, your God, am holy.

"You shall not bear hatred for your brother or sister in your heart.
Though you may have to reprove your fellow citizen,
do not incur sin because of him.
Take no revenge and cherish no grudge against any of your people.
You shall love your neighbor as yourself.
I am the LORD."

Dear friends, this sinner has been guilty of hating a brother or sister, holding a grudge and not loving a neighbor as myself. I am sorry.

Blessings

God morning, brothers and sisters,

Today's Reading II
1 Cor 12:12-14, 27

> Brothers and sisters:
> As a body is one though it has many parts,
> and all the parts of the body, though many, are one body,
> so also Christ.
> For in one Spirit we were all baptized into one Body,
> whether Jews or Greeks, slaves or free persons,
> and we were all given to drink of one Spirit.
>
> Now the body is not a single part, but many.
>
> Now you are Christ's Body, and individually parts of it.

Dear friends, you are Christ's body. Say that slowly a few times and just let it sink in. Amazing.

Blessings

God morning, branches,

> "One must see God in everyone." *St. Catherine Laboure*

Dear friends, I imagine this is difficult for us. Remember that Jesus associated with everyone, especially those considered outcasts and sinners. All were created in His image and we are called to follow in the Lord's footsteps. It is never a bad time or too late to show kindness and love to someone other than our family and friends. Try to be as trusting, humble and accepting as a child. We are all His children.

Blessings

God morning, branches,

> "To love means loving the unlovable. To forgive means pardoning the unpardonable. Faith means believing the unbelievable. Hope means hoping when everything seems hopeless." *Gilbert K. Chesterton*

Dear friends, it is easy to love the lovable. As Jesus said "If you love those who love you, what reward will you get?".

Blessings

God morning, sisters and brothers,

Today's Reading II
Romans 8:8-11

> Brothers and sisters:
> Those who are in the flesh cannot please God.
> But you are not in the flesh;
> on the contrary, you are in the spirit,
> if only the Spirit of God dwells in you.
> Whoever does not have the Spirit of Christ does not belong to him.
> But if Christ is in you,
> although the body is dead because of sin,
> the spirit is alive because of righteousness.
> If the Spirit of the one who raised Jesus from the dead dwells in you,
> the one who raised Christ from the dead
> will give life to your mortal bodies also,
> through his Spirit dwelling in you.

Dear friends, may the Spirit of the one who raised Jesus from the dead dwell in you.

Blessings

God morning, branches,

Today's Reading 1
Sir 3:17-18, 20, 28-29

> My child, conduct your affairs with humility, and
> you will be loved more than a giver of gifts.
> Humble yourself the more, the greater you are,
> and you will find favor with God.
> What is too sublime for you, seek not,
> into things beyond your strength search not.
> The mind of a sage appreciates proverbs,
> and an attentive ear is the joy of the wise.
> Water quenches a flaming fire,
> and alms atone for sins.

Dear friends, may you be humble like the Lord. There are dozens of bible verses on being humble.

Blessings

God morning, branches,

Today's Alleluia
Matthew 4:19

> R. Alleluia, alleluia.

Come after me, says the Lord,
and I will make you fishers of men.
R. Alleluia, alleluia.

Dear friends, may your actions make you fishers of men.

Blessings

God morning, branches,

Today's Reading II
Hebrews 2:14–18

> Since the children share in blood and flesh,
> Jesus likewise shared in them,
> that through death he might destroy the one
> who has the power of death, that is, the Devil,
> and free those who through fear of death
> had been subject to slavery all their life.
> Surely he did not help angels
> but rather the descendants of Abraham;
> therefore, he had to become like his brothers and sisters
> in every way,
> that he might be a merciful and faithful high priest before God
> to expiate the sins of the people.
>
> Because he himself was tested through what he suffered,
> he is able to help those who are being tested.

Dear friends, I imagine we are all being tested. Well, you know who can help each of us. Just ask Him.

Blessings

SCRIPTURE NOTES

God morning, branches,

Today's Gospel
Luke 17:20–25

> Asked by the Pharisees when the Kingdom of God would come, Jesus said in reply,
> "The coming of the Kingdom of God cannot be observed, and no one will announce, 'Look, here it is,' or, 'There it is.'
> For behold, the Kingdom of God is among you."
> Then he said to his disciples,
> "The days will come when you will long to see one of the days of the Son of Man, but you will not see it.
> There will be those who will say to you,
> 'Look, there he is,' or 'Look, here he is.'
> Do not go off, do not run in pursuit.
> For just as lightning flashes
> and lights up the sky from one side to the other,
> so will the Son of Man be in his day.
> But first he must suffer greatly and be rejected by this generation."

Dear friends, the Lord has been rejected by many generations. May your actions and words lead others to accept Him.

Blessings

God morning, branches,

> Now the Lord is the Spirit, and where the Spirit of the Lord is, there is liberty. *2 Corinthians 3:17*

We hold these truths to be self-evident, that all men are created equal, that they are endowed by their Creator with certain unalienable Rights, that among these are Life, Liberty and the pursuit of Happiness.

Declaration of Independence

Clearly, the Founders did not exclude God. Some are trying to remove God from our schools, the public square and government. Without the Spirit of the Lord, there is no liberty. Without liberty, can life and the pursuit of happiness remain as we have known them?

Blessings

God morning, branches,

The month of June is dedicated to the Sacred Heart of Jesus, a devotion that began in the 12th century and became more popular after Jesus appeared to St. Margaret Mary Alacoque in the 1670s, revealing to her the image of his Sacred Heart.

Love overcomes, Love delights, those who love the Sacred heart rejoice!
St. Bernadette Sorbirous

Dear friends, may you love the Sacred Heart and rejoice.

Blessings

God morning, branches,

But now faith, hope, love, abide these three; but the greatest of these is love. 1 Corinthians 13:13

We can never have or give enough love.

God is love. *1 John 4:8*

We were created in His Divine Image.

Love

God morning, branches,

> This is the verdict: Light has come into the world, but people loved darkness instead of light because their deeds were evil. Everyone who does evil hates the light, and will not come into the light for fear that their deeds will be exposed. But whoever lives by the truth comes into the light, so that it may be seen plainly that what they have done has been done in the sight of God. *John 3:19-21*

Dear friends, soon we will celebrate the day the Light of the World came to free us from the darkness. There are many who prefer darkness and evil. May your actions show those in the darkness the way to truth and the light.

Blessings

God morning, branches,

> Let all bitterness and wrath and anger and clamor and slander be put away from you, along with all malice. *Ephesians 4:31*

Dear friends, we are called to follow in the Lord's footsteps and He did not have the mentioned characteristics. Unfortunately, we are not perfect and reside in a corrupt world where those characteristics are common.

Blessings

God morning, branches,

God has given each of you a gift from his great variety of spiritual gifts. Use them well to serve one another. Do you have the gift of speaking? Then speak as though God himself were speaking through you. Do you have the gift of helping others? Do it with all the strength and energy that God supplies. Then everything you do will bring glory to God through Jesus Christ. All glory and power to him forever and ever! Amen.

May you use well the gifts God gave you.

Blessings

God morning, branches,

Draw near to God, and he will draw near to you. Cleanse your hands, you sinners, and purify your hearts, you double-minded. *James 4:8*

God does not force Himself on us. It is up to us to get closer to Him (and away from the enemy) and He will then get closer to us. It is that simple. We all think we have busy days and life is hectic at times. I think if we take a little time to seek Him (and cleanse our hands and purify our hearts), we will be better able to deal with our busy and hectic lives. Time is limited and precious. Make time for Him.

Blessings

God morning, disciples,

Today's Gospel
Matthew 5:13-16

SCRIPTURE NOTES

Jesus said to his disciples:
"You are the salt of the earth.
But if salt loses its taste, with what can it be seasoned?
It is no longer good for anything
but to be thrown out and trampled underfoot.
You are the light of the world.
A city set on a mountain cannot be hidden.
Nor do they light a lamp and then put it under a bushel basket;
it is set on a lampstand,
where it gives light to all in the house.
Just so, your light must shine before others,
that they may see your good deeds
and glorify your heavenly Father."

Dear friends, may your light shine before others, that they may see your good deeds and glorify your heavenly Father.

Blessings

God morning, disciples,

Today's Gospel
Matthew 18:12-14

Jesus said to his disciples:
"What is your opinion?
If a man has a hundred sheep and one of them goes astray,
will he not leave the ninety-nine in the hills
and go in search of the stray?
And if he finds it, amen, I say to you, he rejoices more over it
than over the ninety-nine that did not stray.

In just the same way, it is not the will of your heavenly Father that one of these little ones be lost."

May you live your life in such a way that a lost sheep returns to the fold and any thinking of leaving reconsiders the idea.

Blessings

God morning, sisters and brothers,

Today's Reading I
Galatians 5:1-6

> Brothers and sisters:
> For freedom Christ set us free;
> so stand firm and do not submit again to the yoke of slavery.
> It is I, Paul, who am telling you
> that if you have yourselves circumcised,
> Christ will be of no benefit to you.
> Once again I declare to every man who has himself circumcised
> that he is bound to observe the entire law.
> You are separated from Christ,
> you who are trying to be justified by law;
> you have fallen from grace.
> For through the Spirit, by faith, we await the hope of righteousness.
> For in Christ Jesus,
> neither circumcision nor uncircumcision counts for anything,
> but only faith working through love.

Dear friends, many have submitted to debt, a form of slavery. May our faith be shown through love.

Blessings

God morning, brothers and sisters,

A Reading
Phil 4:4-7

> Brothers and sisters:
> Rejoice in the Lord always.
> I shall say it again: rejoice!
> Your kindness should be known to all.
> The Lord is near.
> Have no anxiety at all, but in everything,
> by prayer and petition, with thanksgiving,
> make your requests known to God.
> Then the peace of God that surpasses all understanding
> will guard your hearts and minds in Christ Jesus.

May the peace of God that surpasses all understanding guard your hearts and minds in Christ Jesus.

Peace

God morning, branches,

> Never let the presence of a storm cause you to doubt the presence of God. *Craig Groeschel*

Dear friends, I imagine we have all been through storms and wondered about God.

God's promise that "I will never leave you nor forsake you" is found in multiple books of the Bible, in both the Old and New Testaments. With this promise, we can be assured that He is always with us and encouraged to always be with God in faith and spirit.

Blessings

SCRIPTURE NOTES

God morning, branches,

> *Devote yourselves to prayer, keeping alert in it with an attitude of thanksgiving.* Colossians 4:2

Dear friends, President George Washington signed the first Thanksgiving proclamation, setting aside Thursday, November 26, 1789 as "A Day of Publick[sic] Thanksgiving and Prayer...to be observed by acknowledging with grateful hearts the many and signal favors of Almighty God." Although not the first such observance in American history, this holiday as designated by Washington represents the first official observance by the new United States.
Source: Conservapedia

Blessings

God morning, branches,

Today's Gospel
Mark 3:31–35

> The mother of Jesus and his brothers arrived at the house.
> Standing outside, they sent word to Jesus and called him.
> A crowd seated around him told him,
> "Your mother and your brothers and your sisters
> are outside asking for you."
> But he said to them in reply,
> "Who are my mother and my brothers?"
> And looking around at those seated in the circle he said,
> "Here are my mother and my brothers.
> For whoever does the will of God
> is my brother and sister and mother."

SCRIPTURE NOTES

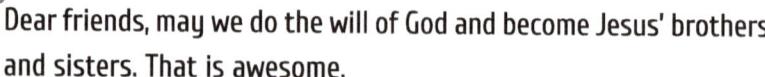

Dear friends, may we do the will of God and become Jesus' brothers and sisters. That is awesome.

Blessings

God morning, branches,

Today's Gospel acclamation:

> Behold, the Lord comes to save his people; blessed are those prepared to meet him.

Dear friends, are you prepared to meet Him?

Blessings

God morning, disciples,

Today's Gospel
Luke 11:1-4

> Jesus was praying in a certain place, and when he had finished, one of his disciples said to him,
> "Lord, teach us to pray just as John taught his disciples."
> He said to them, "When you pray, say:
>
> Father, hallowed be your name,
> your Kingdom come.
> Give us each day our daily bread
> and forgive us our sins
> for we ourselves forgive everyone in debt to us,
> and do not subject us to the final test."

Dear friends, we can never pray too much, especially The Lord's Prayer.

Blessings

God morning, branches,

> So you are no longer aliens or foreign visitors; you are fellow-citizens with the holy people of God and part of God's household. You are built upon the foundations of the apostles and prophets, and Christ Jesus himself is the cornerstone. Every structure knit together in him grows into a holy temple in the Lord; and you too, in him, are being built up into a dwelling-place of God in the Spirit. *Ephesians 2:19-22*

Dear friends, whenever you feel unloved, unimportant or insecure remember to whom you belong! Our Father is the King of Heaven!

Blessings

God morning, branches,

Below is another everyday phrase and its biblical origin.
The writing on the wall.

> Suddenly, opposite the lampstand, the fingers of a human hand appeared, writing on the plaster of the wall in the king's palace. When the king saw the hand that wrote, his face became pale; his thoughts terrified him, his hip joints shook, and his knees knocked. *Daniel 5:5-6*

You have probably quoted Daniel many times and never knew it.

Blessings

God morning, branches,

> But the LORD said to Samuel: Do not judge from his appearance or from his lofty stature, because I have rejected him. God does not see as a mortal, who sees the appearance. The LORD looks into the heart. *1 Samuel 16:7*

We often judge others by their physical appearance, status and possessions. You have heard it said, though, that looks can be deceiving. God looks into a person's heart and can never be deceived. What is in your heart?

Blessings

God morning, branches,

> This world in which we live needs beauty in order not to sink into despair. Beauty, like truth, brings joy to the human heart, and is that precious fruit which resists the erosion of time, which unites generations and enables them to be one in admiration. And all this through the work of your hands . . . Remember that you are the custodians of beauty in the world. *Pope Benedict XVI*

Dear friends, the evil one works tirelessly to destroy beauty and sow despair. Remember that we are the custodians of beauty in the world. May we not shirk our duty to care for God's creation in word or deed.

Blessings

God morning, branches,

The simple believes everything, but the prudent gives thought to his steps. Proverbs 14:15

Think.

I grew up in a time when one was taught how to think. Following generations were told what to think.

The enemy uses any means possible to distract us from thinking. May you discover, or rediscover, the art of thinking.

Blessings

God morning, branches,

If it is displeasing to you to serve the LORD, choose today whom you will serve, the gods your ancestors served beyond the River or the gods of the Amorites in whose country you are dwelling. As for me and my household, we will serve the LORD. Joshua 24:15

Dear friends, there are some who might treat things of the modern world such as money and technology as godlike. May you choose to serve Him in sincerity and in truth, and put away false gods.

Blessings

God morning, branches,

I take no pleasure in the death of the wicked man, says the Lord, but rather in his conversion that he may live. Ezekiel 33:11

Dear friends, it is obvious there is much wickedness in our world. May your words and actions lead to the conversion of a wicked person. Be mindful that you might not even know that person. It is said God works in mysterious ways. Well, to us, not Him.

Blessings

God morning, branches,

> It is not wrong to want to live better; what is wrong is a style of life which is presumed to be better when it is directed towards 'having' rather than 'being,' and which wants to have more, not in order to be more but in order to spend life in enjoyment as an end in itself. Pope John Paul I

Dear friends, we are human beings, not human havings. We often think that having more things will make us happy or better. To get more things we must work more. Our time is finite. May you make time to just be in the present moment. Admire the beauty of His creation. I believe doing so is a form of prayer and can result in living, or being, better.

Blessings

God morning, branches,

> "I plead with you — never, ever give up on hope; never doubt, never tire and never become discouraged. Be not afraid." - St. John Paul II

Dear friends, I imagine we have all experienced times when we felt like there was no hope for something. Remember, Jesus is our hope. Can you ever give up on, doubt, tire of or be discouraged with Jesus?

> "To live without hope is to cease to live." - Aristotle

Blessings

God morning, branches,

> "Will God ever ask you to do something you are not able to do? The answer is yes--all the time! It must be that way, for God's glory and kingdom. If we function according to our ability alone, we get the glory; if we function according to the power of the Spirit within us, God gets the glory. He wants to reveal Himself to a watching world." *Henry Blackaby*

Dear friends, I imagine many (most?) of us have faced something that seemed impossible with which to deal. I know I have, more than a couple of times. We succeeded with the grace of God. Recall that Jesus said "What is impossible with man is possible with God."

Blessings

God morning, branches,

> Imagine yourself as a living house. God comes in to rebuild that house. At first, perhaps, you can understand what He is doing. He is getting the drains right and stopping the leaks in the roof and so on; you knew that those jobs needed doing and so you are not surprised. But presently He starts knocking the house about in a way that hurts abominably and does not seem to make any sense. What on earth is He up to? The explanation is that He is building quite a different house from the one you thought of - throwing out a new wing here, putting on an extra floor there, running up towers, making courtyards. You thought you were being made into a decent little cottage: but He is building a palace. He intends to come and live in it Himself. *C.S. Lewis, Mere Christianity*

Dear friends, each palace is unique. God is a master builder.

Blessings

God morning, branches,

I imagine you have heard or said "a drop in the bucket". Well, it is another expression used in everyday language.
with biblical origin.

> *Behold, the nations are like a drop in a bucket, and are regarded as a speck of dust on a balance. Isaiah 40:15*

Blessings

God morning, branches,

> *"For the time will come when they will not endure sound doctrine, but according to their own desires, because they have itching ears, they will heap up for themselves teachers; and they will turn their ears away from the truth, and be turned aside to fables." 2 Timothy 4:3-4*

Dear friends, does it not seem that this quote from 2 Timothy became a reality in recent times? People have turned away from the truth and our collective morals and values have been under a vicious never-ending attack. May our words and actions show the way back to the truth.

Blessings

God morning, branches,

> *Let no corrupting talk come out of your mouths, but only such as is good for building up, as fits the occasion, that it may give grace to those who hear. Ephesians 4:29*

Dear friends, you know the Bible has many rules to live by. I think many people say there is nothing in the Bible about cursing. The above is one of many examples against foul language. Your mom was right to wash out your mouth with soap.

Blessings

God morning, branches,

Today's Reading 2
Romans 12:1-2

> I urge you, brothers and sisters, by the mercies of God,
> to offer your bodies as a living sacrifice,
> holy and pleasing to God, your spiritual worship.
> Do not conform yourselves to this age
> but be transformed by the renewal of your mind,
> that you may discern what is the will of God,
> what is good and pleasing and perfect.

Dear friends, this is one of my favorite readings; Do not conform yourselves to this age but be transformed by the renewal of your mind.

Blessings

God morning, branches,

Philippians 1:27

> Only conduct yourselves in a manner worthy of the gospel of Christ, so that whether I come and see you or remain absent, I will hear of you

that you are standing firm in one spirit, with one mind striving together for the faith of the gospel;

Dear friends, may we conduct ourselves in a manner worthy of the gospel of Christ and stand firm in one spirit, with one mind striving together for the faith of the gospel.

Blessings

God morning, sisters and brothers,

Today's Reading 2
Romans 14:7-9

> Brothers and sisters:
> None of us lives for oneself, and no one dies for oneself.
> For if we live, we live for the Lord,
> and if we die, we die for the Lord;
> so then, whether we live or die, we are the Lord's.
> For this is why Christ died and came to life,
> that he might be Lord of both the dead and the living.

Dear friends, I imagine there are some who live for themselves. Perhaps that changes when they are in a troubled state. Remember, whether we live or die, we are the Lord's and should act accordingly.

Blessings

God morning, branches,

Today's Gospel
Luke 8:19-21

> The mother of Jesus and his brothers came to him
> but were unable to join him because of the crowd.
> He was told, "Your mother and your brothers are standing outside
> and they wish to see you."
> He said to them in reply, "My mother and my brothers
> are those who hear the word of God and act on it."

Dear friends, many say that blood is thicker than water and family comes first. Well, blood may be thicker than water, but consider Jesus is our living water and God comes first.

Blessings

God morning, branches,

> To be grateful is to recognize the Love of God in everything He has given us - and He has given us everything. Every breath we draw is a gift of His love, every moment of existence is a grace, for it brings with it immense graces from Him. Gratitude therefore takes nothing for granted, is never unresponsive, is constantly awakening to new wonder and to praise of the goodness of God. For the grateful person knows that God is good, not by hearsay but by experience. And that is what makes all the difference.
> *Thomas Merton*

Dear friends, may we always be grateful for everything and constantly awaken to new wonder. Now, I am sure you are grateful, but wonder if you still have the sense of wonder.

Blessings

SCRIPTURE NOTES

God morning, branches,

> At the center of our being is a point of nothingness which is untouched by illusion, a point of pure truth, a point or spark which belongs entirely to God, which is never at our disposal, from which God disposes of our life, which is inaccessable to the fantasies of our own mind or the brutalities of our own will. This little point of nothingness and of absolute poverty is the pure glory of God in us. *Thomas Merton*

Dear friends, I love a song called Let's See Action by Pete Townsend. I especially love the end of the song where he repeats Nothing is Everything. After reading the quote of Merton, my love for the song grew beyond belief. Rejoice my friends as the pure glory of God is in us!

Blessings

God morning, branches,

> The greatest need of our time is to clean out the enormous mass of mental and emotional rubbish that clutters our minds. *Thomas Merton*

Dear friends, the evil one creates a constant barrage of things to distract us from God. If we clean out the enormous mass of mental and emotional rubbish that clutters our minds, we can spend more time communicating with God.

Blessings

God morning, branches,

> "I am worried about America! I am not so much worried about its politics and economics, important though they are. I am worried about its soul

> After all, politics and economics are determined by the sense of values which underlies them."- *Ven. Fulton Sheen*

Dear friends, everything we do is determined by the sense of values we possess and by which we live. May we neither neglect nor sacrifice our values, especially when confronted by those whose values are different from ours or seemingly nonexistent.

Blessings

God morning, branches,

Today's Alleluia
1 Thessalonians 2:13

> Receive the word of God, not as the word of men,
> but as it truly is, the word of God.

Dear friends, God speaks to us in many ways. Men and women have created great works of art in different forms. Think of great art. Now think of a sunrise, sunset or anything in nature. I do not think anything by humans can be compared to anything created by God. There have been numerous great books written by men and women. Can any one of them compare to His written word? May we receive the word of God, not as the word of men, but as it truly is, the word of God.

Alleluia

God morning, branches,

> *From the Byzantine Matins of Great & Holy Saturday:*
> *"Today the one who holds all creation in his hand*

> is himself held in the tomb,
> a rock covers the One who covered the heavens with beauty,
> Life has fallen asleep,
> Hades is seized with fear,
> and Adam is freed from his bonds.
> Glory to your work of salvation;
> through it you have accomplished the eternal Sabbath rest,
> and You grant us the gift of your holy resurrection."

Dear friends, Hades is seized with fear, indeed.

Blessings

God morning, branches,

> "Remember who you are. Don't compromise for anyone, for any reason. You are a child of the Almighty God. Live that truth." – *Lysa Terkeurst*

Dear friends, we often define ourselves by our jobs or what we do. We might say I am a mother or father. Doctor. Lawyer. Indian chief. We might accept our roles so much as to compromise in some way(s). I once answered a query that asked to define myself in three words with child of God. I do not think there is anything better than that. We are here for a reason, but some (many?) struggle with this. In any event, spend more time with God. He has all the answers. Open your heart and mind to His voice. No matter what you say you are or do, you are a child of God.

Blessings

God morning, branches,

> The marvel is not so much that Christians are happy, but that they are not happier. We need to awaken to a new consciousness of our divine origin. Born of God—what a heritage! *Billy Graham*

Dear friends, we profess to be Christians and it is tough to be one. Mr. Graham makes a wonderful statement. Despite the difficulty being a Christian, rejoice that you are one. As Mr. Graham says, Born of God—what a heritage! Also, you know you will one day return to your true home. Until then, smile, God loves you!

Blessings

God morning, branches,

> Scripture repeatedly makes clear that heaven is a realm of unsurpassed joy, unfading glory, undiminished bliss, unlimited delights, and unending pleasures. Nothing about it can possibly be boring or humdrum. It will be a perfect existence. We will have unbroken fellowship with all heaven's inhabitants. Life there will be devoid of any sorrows, cares, tear, fears, or pain.–*John MacArthur*

Dear friends, I do not think we can possibly fathom what Heaven is like. The above quote and all others like it are just words written by humans. To understand Heaven is similar to understanding God, which I think is not possible in our current form. To my mind, imagination is wonderful, but falls short of what Heaven must be like.

Blessings

God morning, brothers and sisters,

Today's Reading II:
1 Jn 3:1-2

> Beloved:
> See what love the Father has bestowed on us
> that we may be called the children of God.
> Yet so we are.
> The reason the world does not know us
> is that it did not know him.
> Beloved, we are God's children now;
> what we shall be has not yet been revealed.
> We do know that when it is revealed we shall be like him,
> for we shall see him as he is.

My dear brothers and sisters, we often describe ourselves in many ways. Have you ever described yourself as a child of God? First and foremost, you are and always will be a child of God. Think about The Lord's Prayer, which begins with Our Father. We are members of a divine family and should treat one another accordingly. If we did, perhaps "Thy will be done on earth as it is in heaven" would become a reality.

Blessings

God morning, branches,

> God has promised to supply all of our needs, but He's never promised to supply all of our greeds. *Billy Graham*

Whoever loves money never has enough; whoever loves wealth is never satisfied with their income. This too is meaningless. Ecclesiastes 5:10

Dear friends, God knows what is essential for our lives. The evil one tempts us with greed. All material things are meaningless. As the expression goes, the Brinks truck does not follow the hearse. I wonder, though, if one can be greedy for love because the more love we give, the more love we get. God is love and love can never be meaningless.

Blessings

God morning, sisters and brothers,

Today's Reading 2
Eph 4:30–5:2

> Brothers and sisters:
> Do not grieve the Holy Spirit of God,
> with which you were sealed for the day of redemption.
> All bitterness, fury, anger, shouting, and reviling
> must be removed from you, along with all malice.
> And be kind to one another, compassionate,
> forgiving one another as God has forgiven you in Christ.
>
> So be imitators of God, as beloved children, and live in love,
> as Christ loved us and handed himself over for us
> as a sacrificial offering to God for a fragrant aroma.

Dear friends, may we be imitators of God, as beloved children, and live in love.

Blessings

SCRIPTURE NOTES

God morning, branches,

Luke 22:19-2

> Then he took the bread, said the blessing, broke it, and gave it to them, saying, "This is my body, which will be given for you; do this in memory of me."
> And likewise the cup after they had eaten, saying, "This cup is the new covenant in my blood, which will be shed for you."

Dear friends, The Passover solemnity was usually concluded with eating a little bread and drinking a cup of wine. Jesus, therefore, when he instituted the Lord's supper, did not appoint any new rite, but appropriated an old one to a new purpose. Hence the propriety of the expression, This do in remembrance of me.

Blessings

God morning, sisters and brothers,

Today's Reading II
Romans 8:31b-34

> Brothers and sisters:
> If God is for us, who can be against us?
> He who did not spare his own Son
> but handed him over for us all,
> how will he not also give us everything else along with him?
>
> Who will bring a charge against God's chosen ones?
> It is God who acquits us, who will condemn?
> Christ Jesus it is who died—or, rather, was raised—
>
> who also is at the right hand of God,

who indeed intercedes for us.

Dear friends, well, you know who is against us. He and his followers will go to any length to try to keep us from God. May we always be on guard of the traps set before us.

Blessings

God morning, branches,

> "If you believe what you like in the Gospel, and reject what you don't like, it is not the Gospel you believe, but yourself." *Saint Augustine*

Dear friends, I imagine a good number of us have rejected Gospels we don't like for whatever reasons. The Gospels are not like a menu where you can pick or choose those to your liking. They are God's instructions for everyone in all situations. May we believe in God's words, not our own words no matter how difficult they might be. His words are for our own good.

Blessings

God morning, branches,

Today's first Reading:
1 Pt 5:1-4

> Beloved:
> I exhort the presbyters among you,
> as a fellow presbyter and witness to the sufferings of Christ
> and one who has a share in the glory to be revealed.
> Tend the flock of God in your midst,
> overseeing not by constraint but willingly,

as God would have it, not for shameful profit but eagerly.
Do not lord it over those assigned to you,
but be examples to the flock.
And when the chief Shepherd is revealed,
you will receive the unfading crown of glory.

Dear friends, we, too, are to be examples of Christ to the world. What an awesome responsibility and privilege.

Blessings

God morning, branches,

Today's Gospel
Mark 1:12-15

The Spirit drove Jesus out into the desert,
and he remained in the desert for forty days,
tempted by Satan.
He was among wild beasts,
and the angels ministered to him.

After John had been arrested,
Jesus came to Galilee proclaiming the gospel of God:
"This is the time of fulfillment.
The kingdom of God is at hand.
Repent, and believe in the gospel."

Dear friends, may our words and actions lead others to repent and believe in the Gospel.

Blessings

God morning, branches,

> Don't let failure or disappointment cut you off from God or make you think that the future is hopeless. When God closes one door, He often opens another door - if we seek it. *Billy Graham*

Dear friends, I am sure we have all heard about the closing and opening of the doors. What is very important here is that we must seek the newly opened door. Think about it, God is always with us, but will never intrude in our affairs; we need to invite (or seek) Him into our lives. When a door closes, we might be mad or frustrated. God is still with us though. We must forget the anger or frustration and seek God. Remember He has plans for each and every one of us, loves us and wants only the best for us, His children. He will lead us to the open door when we are ready.

Blessings

God morning, branches,

> God is unchanging in His love. He loves you. He has a plan for your life. Don't let the newspaper headlines frighten you. God is still sovereign; He's still on the throne. *Billy Graham*

Dear friends, God has a plan for our lives, but I think our egos get in the way as does the evil one. We have free will. I think His plans for us can change depending on we are in our lives. He desires only the best for us, but we need to listen to Him.

Blessings

God morning, branches,

Today's Reading 2
1 Corinthians 7:32-35

> Brothers and sisters: I should like you to be free of anxieties. An unmarried man is anxious about the things of the Lord, how he may please the Lord. But a married man is anxious about the things of the world, how he may please his wife, and he is divided. An unmarried woman or a virgin is anxious about the things of the Lord, so that she may be holy in both body and spirit. A married woman, on the other hand, is anxious about the things of the world, how she may please her husband. I am telling you this for your own benefit, not to impose a restraint upon you, but for the sake of propriety and adherence to the Lord without distraction.

Dear friends, the evil one has created an environment which causes us to be anxious about so many things. The Good Book has many quotes to help us with anxiety such as:

> *1 Peter 5:7* - "Cast all your anxiety on him because he cares for you."

> *John 14:27* - "Peace I leave with you; my peace I give you. I do not give to you as the world gives. Do not let your hearts be troubled and do not be afraid.

May we seek His help to be free of anxieties.
Blessings

God morning, branches.

> If Christianity is valid, why is there so much evil in the world?" To this the famous preacher replied, "With so much soap, why are there so many

dirty people in the world? Christianity, like soap, must be personally applied if it is to make a difference in our lives. *Billy Graham*

Dear friends, I imagine many of us have wondered why there is so much evil in the world. Well, remember who is in control of the world. Then think about the above quote and apply some Christianity.

Blessings

God morning, sisters and brothers,

Today's Reading II
Eph 3:2-3a, 5-6

> Brothers and sisters:
> You have heard of the stewardship of God's grace
> that was given to me for your benefit,
> namely, that the mystery was made known to me by revelation.
> It was not made known to people in other generations
> as it has now been revealed
> to his holy apostles and prophets by the Spirit:
> that the Gentiles are coheirs, members of the same body,
> and copartners in the promise in Christ Jesus through the gospel.

Dear friends, may we always rejoice that we are coheirs, members of the same body, and copartners in the promise in Christ Jesus through the gospel.

Blessings

SCRIPTURE NOTES

God morning, branches,

> "To be grateful is to recognize the Love of God in everything He has given us - and He has given us everything. Every breath we draw is a gift of His love, every moment of existence is a grace, for it brings with it immense graces from Him.
>
> Gratitude therefore takes nothing for granted, is never unresponsive, is constantly awakening to new wonder and to praise of the goodness of God. For the grateful person knows that God is good, not by hearsay but by experience. And that is what makes all the difference."
> –*Thomas Merton*

Dear friends, everything we have is from God. I imagine we give thanks several times a day, if not more. If every breath and moment are gifts, should we not be thankful more often. Recall that 1 Thessalonians 5:17 instructs us to pray without ceasing. That is nearly impossible for most of us considering our many obligations, but if we find more time to be thankful, I believe we will be happier and less stressed.

Blessings

God morning, branches,

> "Solitude is a way to defend the spirit against the murderous din of our materialism." *Thomas Merton*

Dear friends, distractions and noise are everywhere. However, some of it is self-imposed. Can we put away, even for a few minutes, our cell phones. Shut off the tv? Take off the headphones? It is quite quiet in my home as I write this. It is a wonderful way to compose this note. I work in midtown NYC and when I want to experience quiet, I can go to a nearby church when a mass is not being offered. Saint Patrick's is a great place for reflection, but it is busy more often than not. I suggest even a few minutes of quiet refreshes the spirit. You can do it and I hope you do so. You might find yourself seeking silence more than you expected because while God is there in all His glory and majesty, it is just you and Him. Spoken words are not necessary.

Blessings

God morning, branches,

Today's Reading 1
Wis 1:13-15; 2:23-24

> God did not make death,
> nor does he rejoice in the destruction of the living.
> For he fashioned all things that they might have being;
> and the creatures of the world are wholesome,
> and there is not a destructive drug among them
> nor any domain of the netherworld on earth,
> for justice is undying.
> For God formed man to be imperishable;
> the image of his own nature he made him.
> But by the envy of the devil, death entered the world,
> and they who belong to his company experience it.

Dear friends, God can only make good things. I believe it is impossible for Him to do otherwise. Bad things are in the world because of the evil one. God gave us free will. Choose wisely.

Blessings

God morning, branches,

> "And do not forget to do good and to share with others, for with such sacrifices God is pleased." *Hebrews 13:16*

> At the day of judgment we shall not be asked what we have read but what we have done. *Thomas Kempis*

Dear friends, I imagine we were all taught as children to help others and do good. Then we grew up and life got busy and complicated. I also imagine many or most would like to relive our childhoods. Well, put aside your cell phone, step away from whatever gadget and help or share with someone. Don't you feel good when you help someone? That is called "helper's high". The body releases natural feel-good chemicals called endorphins. So, the person you help feels good and so do you. It just might be contagious, too, like a smile. Why not give it a try every now and then and make God smile.

Blessings

God morning, branches,

> Blessed are the simple, for they shall have much peace.
> *Thomas A. Kempis*

Dear friends, Jesus was a simple man. Recall how He came into and left this world. He was not burdened with a cell phone, technology or things. He said he had nowhere to sleep. Certainly, He had peace and said in John 14:27 "Peace I leave with you; my peace I give to you. Not as the world gives do I give to you." I imagine you have heard of the KISS method. May we be simple and have the only true peace, Jesus.

Peace

God morning, branches,

Today's Gospel
Luke 19:45-48

> *Jesus entered the temple area and proceeded to drive out*
> *those who were selling things, saying to them,*
> *"It is written, My house shall be a house of prayer,*
> *but you have made it a den of thieves."*
> *And every day he was teaching in the temple area.*
> *The chief priests, the scribes, and the leaders of the people, meanwhile,*
> *were seeking to put him to death,*
> *but they could find no way to accomplish their purpose*
> *because all the people were hanging on his words.*

Dear friends, our bodies are temples and surely we wish for Jesus to reside in our temples. Unfortunately, He finds the temples cluttered. May we drive out that which clutters our temples so that we may focus on His words.

Blessings

SCRIPTURE NOTES

God morning, branches,

> The rush and pressure of modern life are a form, perhaps the most common form, of contemporary violence. To allow oneself to be carried away by a multitude of conflicting concerns, to surrender to too many demands, to commit oneself to too many projects, to want to help everyone in everything, is to succumb to violence. The frenzy of our activity neutralizes our work for peace. It destroys our own inner capacity for peace. It destroys the fruitfulness of our own work, because it kills the root of inner wisdom which makes work fruitful. *Thomas Merton*

> How much better to get wisdom than gold, to get insight rather than silver! *Proverbs 16:16*

Dear friends, I imagine there are many among us who are victims of the frenzy of our activities. Take a step back and get wisdom, which is better than gold.

Blessings

God morning, branches,

> but whoever drinks of the water that I will give him shall never thirst; but the water that I will give him will become in him a well of water springing up to eternal life. John 4:14

Dear friends, there are a few mentions of living water in The Bible. About 71% of the earth's surface is water. Water accounts for 60-75% of our body weight. A loss of just 4% of total body water leads to dehydration, and a loss of 15% can be fatal. Likewise, a person could survive a month without food but wouldn't survive 3 days without water. This crucial dependence on water broadly governs all life forms. Water is also important for the survival of all living organisms. It supports cell functions and allows chemical reactions to take place, which are necessary for gaining energy, growth, and getting rid of waste. In summary, water is a vital component of life and is necessary for the proper functioning of our bodies and the survival of all living organisms. Clearly, our lives here and in Paradise depend on water.

May we consider Jesus when we see or come into contact with water.

Blessings

God morning, branches,

> Life with God is not immunity from difficulties, but peace in difficulties.
> *C. S. Lewis*

Dear friends, I imagine you know the phrase trials and tribulations. The phrase "trials and tribulations" originates from the Bible, specifically the New Testament, where "trial" signifies the testing of faith and "tribulation" refers to suffering or distress. There are at least two dozen passages in The Bible about trials and tribulations. We were never told we would not have trials and tribulations, but we know God will never abandon us and get us through our difficulties. May we always seek His help.

Blessings

God morning, branches,

> When wealth is lost, nothing is lost; when health is lost, something is lost; when character is lost, all is lost. *Billy Graham*

> Not only so, but we also glory in our sufferings, because we know that suffering produces perseverance; perseverance, character; and character, hope. *Romans 5:3-4*

> And so, Lord, where do I put my hope? My only hope is in you. *Psalm 39:7*

Dear friends, I am sure no one looks forward to suffering, but it cannot and should not be avoided. The good news (pun intended) is that it ultimately leads to hope, which is everything.

Blessings

God morning, branches,

> For a child has been born for us, a son given to us; authority rests upon his shoulders; and he is named Wonderful Counselor, Mighty God, Everlasting Father, Prince of Peace. *Isaiah 9:6*

Dear friends, in a few days, we will celebrate the birth of our Lord & Savior. As you know, He is also called Prince of Peace. I wonder if you know the story of the Christmas Truce, which was a miraculous and otherwise unexplained cessation of combat on or near Christmas Day on the Western Front during World War I, in 1914, among combatants who would otherwise engage in some of the most brutal warfare in world history. It was a spirit that swept the Western Front without authorization and direction, as men came out of their trenches and exchanged gifts and good will to the other side. Some even played games of soccer. You might want to read the story by clicking on The Christmas Truce of 1914 - LewRockwell. When you hear or sing Silent Night, I wonder if you

will recall this story and I encourage you to share it. Indeed, Jesus is truly the Prince of Peace.

Blessings

God morning, branches,

> Always keep a good distance between yourself and lying, quarreling, detracting, insulting and gossip. The person who can do that will some day learn to enjoy the silence. Thomas a Kempis

Dear friends, I wonder how many of us achieve and enjoy silence. I imagine some find silence awkward. Life is full of noise and distractions because that is the plan of the evil one to keep us from hearing and contemplating God and His words. May we achieve silence to hear God as clearly as possible.

Blessings

God morning, branches,

> The farther we get from God, the more the world spirals out of control. Billy Graham

> We know that we are children of God, and that the whole world is under the control of the evil one. 1 John 5:19

Dear friends, what was celebrated in Paris a few days ago speaks to the above quotes.

Blessings

God morning, branches,

Today's Second Reading:
1 Jn 2:1-5a

> My children, I am writing this to you
> so that you may not commit sin.
> But if anyone does sin, we have an Advocate with the Father,
> Jesus Christ the righteous one.
> He is expiation for our sins,
> and not for our sins only but for those of the whole world.
> The way we may be sure that we know him is to keep
> his commandments.
> Those who say, "I know him," but do not keep his commandments
> are liars, and the truth is not in them.
> But whoever keeps his word,
> the love of God is truly perfected in him.

Dear friends, may we always keep His commandments.
Blessings

God morning, branches,

> You can use your time to no better advantage than to pray whenever you have a moment, either alone, or with others, while at work, at rest, or walking down the street! Anywhere!! *Ole Hallesby*

Dear friends, one does need to wait to be in church to pray or at the dining table. There are 86,400 seconds in a day. We all think we are busy, but do we really exhaust each of the 86,400 seconds in a day. We can have a conversation with God anytime and anywhere.

God will meet us wherever we are and whenever we choose to be. It just might be the best few seconds of the day.

Blessings

God morning, branches,

> For pride is spiritual cancer: it eats up the very possibility of love, or contentment, or even common sense *C.S. Lewis*,
>
> When pride comes, then comes dishonor,
> But with the humble is wisdom. *Proverbs 11:2*

Dear friends, may we not be prideful, but humble. As the expression goes, pride goeth before the fall.

Blessings

God morning, branches,

> However great may be the work for which we are responsible, we will always do well if we pause to spend time in sacred praise.
> *Charles Spurgeon*
>
> "Pause a moment, Job, and listen; consider the wonderful things God does." *Job 37:14*

Dear friends, on average, we take about 20,000 breaths in a day. Why not use just a few to pause and spend time in sacred praise, which includes admiring the beauty of His creation? Those breaths taken to pause and reflect may make others easier.

Blessings

God morning, branches,

Today is the Solemnity of the Assumption of the Blessed Virgin Mary.

"O sinner, be not discouraged, but have recourse to Mary in all your necessities. Call her to your assistance, for such is the divine Will that she should help in every kind of necessity." – *Saint Basil the Great*

Dear friends, I think some may take Mary for granted. We do pray to her, though. Think about Hail Mary, which includes Mother of God, pray for us sinners, now and at the hour of our death. She can always pray for us. Maybe we should think about this prayer and her help more often.

Blessings

God morning, disciples,

Today's Gospel
John 15:9-11

Jesus said to his disciples:

"As the Father loves me, so I also love you.
Remain in my love.
If you keep my commandments, you will remain in my love,
just as I have kept my Father's commandments
and remain in his love.
"I have told you this so that
my joy might be in you and
your joy might be complete."

Dear friends, may we keep His commandments, remain in His love and our joy be compete.

Blessings

God morning, branches,

> The spiritual life is first of all a life. It is not merely something to be known and studied, it is to be lived. *Thomas Merton*

Dear friends, I wonder how often we live a spiritual life. Merton wrote "In devouring pleasures and joys, I had found distress and anguish and fear." Despite all the pleasures the world has to offer, he found himself thirsty. May we reflect more often on Jesus Christ, the Living Water and not find ourselves thirsty.

Blessings

God morning, branches,

> I have come to think that care of the soul requires a high degree of resistance to the culture around us, simply because that culture is dedicated to values that have no concern for the soul. *Thomas Merton*

Dear friends, according to Isaiah 26:8, our souls desire the Lord's name and renown. Also, 1 Thessalonians 5:17 says to pray without ceasing. One may ask why the culture around us is dedicated to values that have no concern for the soul. Well, consider who rules this world. Satan tries without ceasing to distract us any way he can. May we take the time to care for our souls.

Blessings

SCRIPTURE NOTES

God morning, disciples,

Today's Gospel
Matthew 5:33-37

Jesus said to his disciples:

> "You have heard that it was said to your ancestors, Do not take a false oath, but make good to the Lord all that you vow. But I say to you, do not swear at all; not by heaven, for it is God's throne; nor by the earth, for it is his footstool; nor by Jerusalem, for it is the city of the great King. Do not swear by your head, for you cannot make a single hair white or black.

Dear friends,
   Let your 'Yes' mean 'Yes,' and your 'No' mean 'No.' Anything more is from the Evil One."
This is as simple as it can be.
Blessings

God morning, branches,

> Our job is to love others without stopping to inquire whether or not they are worthy. That is not our business and, in fact, it is nobody's business. What we are asked to do is to love, and this love itself will render both ourselves and our neighbors worthy. *Thomas Merton*

Dear friends, Jesus tells us to love one another, even our enemies. I imagine we may think our enemies are unworthy of our love, but remember it is not for us to judge. God is love. God works miracles. Therefore, love works miracles.

Love

God morning, branches,

Our world is obsessed with success. But how does God define success? Success in God's eyes is faithfulness to His calling. Billy Graham

Dear friends, many strive for well-paying jobs, big homes, fancy cars, fine clothes, etc. We might do these things to satisfy ego or impress others. God is not impressed with our possessions. He looks into one's heart and how one is serving Him. I wonder how many know their calling. May we spend more time with God to discover our calling if we do not know it.

Blessings

God morning, branches,

Today's Gospel
Matthew 11:28–30

Jesus said: "Come to me, all you who labor and are burdened, and I will give you rest. Take my yoke upon you and learn from me, for I am meek and humble of heart; and you will find rest for yourselves. For my yoke is easy, and my burden light."

Dear friends, may we learn from Jesus, especially about being meek and humble in today's me, me, me world.

Blessings

God morning, branches,

When anger enters the mind, wisdom departs. Thomas a Kempis

Refrain from anger and turn from wrath; do not fret—it leads only to evil.

> For those who are evil will be destroyed, but those who hope in the LORD will inherit the land. *Psalm 37:8-9*

Dear friends, be wise, not angry as anger leads only to evil. May we heed Thomas Jefferson's advice: When angry, count to ten before you speak. If very angry, count to one hundred.

Blessings

God morning, branches,

> The Bible is not an option; it is a necessity. You cannot grow spiritually strong without it. *Billy Graham*

Dear friends, think about some necessities we have. Food. Money. A place to live. To love and be loved. Not sure about a cell phone. We have many options in life, but as the quote says The Bible is not one of them. It is read at Mass and perhaps that is all some read it. We keep many things on our desks or attached to the refrigerator to remind us of something important. Why not place a Bible in plain sight? It is that important, right? Even if it is not read regularly, it will be a constant reminder of God, who wrote the book for us.

Blessings

God morning, branches,

> A wise man will hear and increase in learning,
> And a man of understanding will acquire wise counsel, *Proverbs 1:5*

> Learning softeneth the heart and breedeth gentleness and charity. *Mark Twain*

May you increase in learning.

Blessings

God morning, branches,

> Do not let kindness and truth leave you; Bind them around your neck, Write them on the tablet of your heart. *Proverbs 3:3*

Make someone's day with a random act of kindness. You will both feel good and it could be contagious.

Blessings

God morning, branches,

> Therefore confess your sins to each other and pray for each other so that you may be healed. The prayer of a righteous person is powerful and effective. *James 5:16*

Dear friends, may we pray for one another. There is no limit to prayers.

Blessings

God morning, branches,

> "If God sends you many sufferings it is a sign that He has great plans for you, and certainly wants to make you a saint." *St. Ignatius of Loyola*

Welcome your sufferings, my friends.

Blessings

God morning, branches,

> A wise man will hear and increase in learning,
> And a man of understanding will acquire wise counsel, *Proverbs 1:5*

> Learning softeneth the heart and breedeth gentleness and charity.
> *Mark Twain*

May you increase in learning.

Blessings

God morning, branches,

> Come and see the wonders of God; his acts for humanity are awe-inspiring.
> *Psalm 66:5*

Dear friends, take time to admire the beauty of God's creation. Stop looking down so much at the tops of your shoes, phone or gadget. Look all around to see some miracles.

Blessings

God morning, branches,

Dear friends, I imagine that when you wanted to show someone how much you love them, you stretched out your arms and said "I love you this much".

Blessings

God morning, branches,

> for nothing will be impossible for God. *Luke 1:37*

Dear friends, look at the first two letters of the word "impossible" and consider that "I'm" is the contraction for I am. Then consider I Am is one of God's names. So, all things are possible for I Am.

Blessings

God morning, branches,

> The most powerful weapon to conquer the devil is humility.
> For, as he does not know at all how to employ it, neither does he know how to defend himself from it. *Saint Vincent de Paul*

Dear friends, the Lord is humble. May you be likewise.

Blessings

God morning, branches,

> Do not trust in princes,
> In mortal man, in whom there is no salvation. *Psalm 146:3*

Dear friends, substitute government officials and bureaucrats for princes in our times.

Blessings

God morning, branches,

> The end of a matter is better than its beginning; Patience of spirit is better than haughtiness of spirit. *Ecclesiastes 7:8*

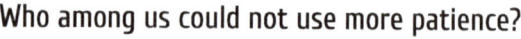

SCRIPTURE NOTES

Who among us could not use more patience?

Blessings

God morning, branches,

> Whoever is slow to anger has great understanding, but he who has a hasty temper exalts folly. *Proverbs 14:29*

May you be slow to anger.

Blessings

God morning, branches,

> Do not be deceived: "Bad company corrupts good morals." *1 Corinthians 15:33*

I am sure you have heard the expression "Show me your friends, I'll tell you who you are."

Blessings

God morning, branches,

> Whoever keeps his mouth and his tongue keeps himself out of trouble. *Proverbs 21:23*

At some time in your life you may have been told to watch your mouth.

Blessings

God morning, branches,

What unites us, is much greater than what divides us. Pope John XXIII

Dear friends, for some time, some have sought to divide us any way possible. When we are in such a situation, please remember the above quote.

Blessings

God morning, branches,

"The world offers you comfort. But you were not made for comfort. You were made for greatness." – *Pope Benedict XVI*

Dear friends, may you not accept being comfortable.

Blessings

God morning, branches,

"And whosoever shall compel thee to go a mile, go with him twain." *Matthew 5:41*

Dear friends, surely you have used or heard the expression "Go the extra mile", but were you aware the expression comes from the greatest book ever written?

Blessings

God morning, branches,

"Every breath we draw is a gift of God's love; every moment of existence is a grace." – *Thomas Merton*

SCRIPTURE NOTES

Dear friends, I realize life is hectic and we might not pray or give thanks as often as we should. Today's quote is a gentle reminder about prayer.

Blessings

God morning, branches,

> The Word gave life to everything that was created, and his life brought light to everyone. The light shines in the darkness, and the darkness can never extinguish it. *John 1:4-5*

Dear friends, in the darkness, one stumbles around. In the light, the path is true and clear.

Blessings

God morning, branches,

> "Glory to God, who is able to do far beyond all that we could ask or imagine by his power at work within us." *Ephesians 3:20*

Dear friends, nothing you ask or imagine is impossible for God. His expectations are higher than ours. Do not place limits on yourselves. His power (the Spirit) is at work within us.

Blessings

God morning, branches,

> In all created things discern the providence and wisdom of God, and in all things give Him thanks. *Saint Teresa of Ávila*

Dear friends, we celebrate Thanksgiving on the fourth Thursday of November. We should be thankful every day.

Blessings

God morning, branches,

> And when you stand praying, if you hold anything against anyone, forgive them, so that your Father in heaven may forgive you your sins. *Mark 11:25-26*

Dear friends, make sure to forgive everyone so that you may be forgiven by God. This is not always easy, but necessary.

Blessings

God morning, branches,

> But grow in the grace and knowledge of our Lord and Savior Jesus Christ. To him be the glory both now and to the day of eternity. *Amen. 2 Peter 3:18*

Dear friends, may you continually realize a deeper and more blessed consciousness of Christ's love and favor as yours.

Blessings

God morning, branches,

> And when you stand praying, if you hold anything against anyone, forgive them, so that your Father in heaven may forgive you your sins. *Mark 11:25-26*

Dear friends, make sure to forgive everyone so that you may be forgiven by God. This is not always easy, but necessary.

Blessings

God morning, branches,

> Beloved, do not believe every spirit, but test the spirits to see whether they are from God, for many false prophets have gone out into the world. *1 John 4:1*

Dear friends, be careful as there are many false prophets in this internet age.

Blessings

God morning, branches,

> I perceived that there is nothing better for them than to be joyful and to do good as long as they live. *Ecclesiastes 3:12*

Dear friends, may you be joyful (happy Friday) and do good.

Blessings

God morning, branches,

> The one who understands a matter finds success, and the one who trusts in the Lord will be happy. *Proverbs 16:20*

May you trust in the Lord.

Blessings

SCRIPTURE NOTES

God morning, branches,

> "Now, we must all fear evil men. But there is another kind of evil which we must fear most, and that is the indifference of good men."
> – *Monsignor, The Boondock Saints*

Dear friends, may we never be indifferent.

Blessings

God morning, branches,

> A tranquil heart gives life to the flesh, but envy makes the bones rot.
> *Proverbs 14:30*

May you not be envious.

Blessings

God morning, branches,

> "God made us for joy. God is joy, and the joy of living reflects the original joy that God felt in creating us."
> *St. Pope John Paul II*

Dear friends, I imagine many of us fall short of being joyful on a regular basis. We only have so much time here, so why be anything less than for what God made us.

Blessings

God morning, branches,

> The Lord is my shepherd. I have all I need. *Psalm 23:1*

Dear friends, there is a big difference between need and want.

Blessings

God morning, branches,

> Commit to the Lord whatever you do, and he will establish your plans. Proverbs 16:3

Dear friends, your plans or His plans? Do you really have to think about this?

Blessings

God morning, branches,

> Let us ask the Holy Spirit for the grace to live daily according to the mind of Jesus and his Gospel. – Pope Francis

Dear friends, may you follow Pope Francis' suggestion.

Blessings

God morning, branches,

> When pride comes, disgrace follows, but with humility comes wisdom. Proverbs 11:2

Dear friends, followers of Jesus should be humble and, therefore, wise. Unfortunately, we might be prideful at times.

Blessings

God morning, branches,

> Everyone comes naked from their mother's womb, and as everyone comes, so they depart.
> They take nothing from their toil that they can carry in their hands. Ecclesiastes 5:15

Dear friends, do not be greedy or materialistic. That is not His way.
Blessings

God morning, branches,

> "Tribulation is a gift from God - one that he especially gives His special friends." St. Thomas More

Dear friends, I wonder if anyone is not a special friend to God.
Blessings

God morning, branches,

> How can you believe, when you receive glory from one another and do not seek the glory that comes from the only God? John 5:44

Dear friends, may you seek the glory that comes from the only God.
Blessings

God morning, branches,

> They promise them freedom, but they themselves are slaves of corruption. For whatever overcomes a person, to that he is enslaved. 2 Peter 2:19

Dear friends, be careful not to be enslaved to anything.

Blessings

God morning, branches,

Today is the Solemnity of the Assumption of the Blessed Virgin Mary.

> "Happy is he who lives and dies under the protection of the Blessed Virgin." *Saint John Vianney*

Dear friends, may you be under the protection of the Blessed Virgin.

Blessings

God morning, branches,

> And he has given us this command: Anyone who loves God must also love their brother and sister. *1 John 4:21*

Notice the word "must".

Blessings

God morning, branches,

> And whatever you ask in prayer, you will receive, if you have faith. *Matthew 21:22*

Dear friends, our Heavenly Father loves to shower us with His gifts. Notice, though, today's verse does not mention time. Remember, everything is done at His time, not ours.

Blessings

God morning, branches,

> Peace comes not from the absence of trouble, but from the presence of God. *Alexander MacLaren*

Dear friends, we all have troubles. May we make more time for God.
Blessings

God morning, branches,

> Hear the word of the LORD, you Israelites, because the LORD has a charge to bring against you who live in the land: "There is no faithfulness, no love, no acknowledgment of God in the land." *Hosea 4:1*

Dear friends, it seems as if this could apply to our time and place.
Blessings

God morning, branches,

> do not merely look out for your own personal interests, but also for the interests of others. Have this attitude in yourselves which was also in Christ Jesus, *Philippians 2:4-5*

This goes along with His command to love one another as He loves us.
Blessings

God morning, branches,

Today the Church celebrates Memorial of The Queenship of the Blessed Virgin Mary.

"Humility is like a pair of scales: the lower one side falls, the higher rises the other. Let us humble ourselves like the Blessed Virgin and we shall be exalted." *Saint John Vianney*

Dear friends, may we humble ourselves like the Blessed Virgin.

Blessings

God morning, branches,

> Your eye is the lamp of your body. When your eye is healthy, your whole body is full of light, but when it is bad, your body is full of darkness. *Luke 11:34*

May your eyes be healthy.

Blessings

God morning, branches,

Below is another everyday phrase and its biblical origin.

> I am at my wits' end.
> They reel to and fro, and stagger like a drunken man, and are at their wits' end. *Psalm 107:27*

You have probably quoted part of Psalm 107:27 numerous times and never knew it.

Blessings

God morning, branches,

> In hard work there is always profit, but too much chattering leads to poverty. The crown of the wise is their wealth, but the stupidity of fools is just that—stupidity! *Proverbs 14:23-24*

May you work hard and be wise.

Blessings

God morning, branches,

> When a man's ways are pleasing to the Lord,
> He makes even his enemies to be at peace with him.
> *Proverbs 16:7*

Apparently there are so many whose ways are not pleasing to the Lord.

> May your enemies be at peace with you.

Blessings

God morning, branches,

> When your dread comes like a storm
> And your calamity comes like a whirlwind,
> When distress and anguish come upon you.
> *Proverbs 1:27*

Dear friends, whenever your life seems to be storm-tossed, know that God is our strength and refuge.

Blessings

God morning, branches,

> "The secret to happiness is to live moment by moment and to thank God for what He is sending us every day in His goodness."
> – St. Gianna Molla

Dear friends, I pray for our happiness. May we live in the moment. After all, that is all we have.

Blessings

God morning, branches,

> From the fullness of His grace we have all received one blessing after another. John 1:16

Dear friends, perhaps you thought it was luck that something happened.

Blessings

God morning, branches,

Do not let your heart envy sinners,

> But live in the fear of the Lord always. Proverbs 23:17

Bear in mind, my friends, we are all sinners.

Blessings

God morning, branches,

> The deeds you do may be the only sermon some persons will hear today.
> St. Francis of Assisi

May you do a good deed today.

Blessings

God morning, branches,

> Everyone talks about how loyal and faithful he is, but just try to find someone who really is! *Proverbs 20:6*

Dear friends, I imagine this Proverb is as true today as it was when it was written. May you be loyal and faithful.

Blessings

God morning, branches,

> There are many who say, "You can trust me!" But can they be trusted? *Proverbs 20:6*

Dear friends, I imagine this Proverb is as true today as it was when it was written.

Blessings

God morning, branches,

> The Lord does not look at the things man looks at ... the Lord looks at the heart. *1 Samuel 16:7*

What is in your heart, my friend?

Blessings

God morning, branches,

> Above all, let your love for one another be intense, because love covers a multitude of sins. *Peter 4:8*

Dear friends, I imagine you have heard the phrase "covers a multitude of ..." in various expressions.

Blessings

God morning, branches,

> For by your words you will be justified, and by your words you will be condemned. *Matthew 12:37*

Words matter, my friends.

Blessings

God morning, branches,

> So God created mankind in his own image, in the image of God he created them; male and female he created them. *Genesis 1:27*

Male. Female. No other. End of story.

Blessings

God morning, branches,

> But if you do not forgive others their trespasses, neither will your Father forgive your trespasses. *Matthew 6:15*

Dear friends, do we not pray "forgive us our trespasses, as we forgive those who trespass against us"? I wonder if we always truly forgive others.

Blessings

God morning, branches,

> Commit your way to the LORD; trust in him and he will act. Psalm 37:5

God has a plan. Who better to trust?

Blessings

God morning, branches,

> For such is the will of God that by doing right you may silence the ignorance of foolish men. 1 Peter 2:15

May you do right often as there is much ignorance.

Blessings

God morning, branches,

> For sin shall no longer be your master, because you are not under the law, but under grace. Romans 6:14

Dear friends, the adversary goes to great lengths to get us to sin so he might become our master. Beware temptation.

Blessings

God morning, branches,

> "The nation doesn't simply need what we have. It needs what we are."
> –St. Teresia Benedicta (Edith Stein)

Dear friends, the government takes much in taxes and despite the "In God We Trust" slogan (and national motto) on its currency appears to have faith only in itself.

Blessings

God morning, branches,

> Being a Christian is more than just an instantaneous conversion - it is a daily process whereby you grow to be more and more like Christ.
> Billy Graham

Dear friends, are you growing to be more like Christ every day?

Blessings

God morning, branches,

> For this is the message you heard from the beginning: We should love one another. *1 John 3:11*

Love

God morning, branches,

> Whoever walks in integrity walks securely, but he who makes his ways crooked will be found out. *Proverbs 10:9*

May you always walk in integrity.

Blessings

God morning, branches,

> They profess to know God, but by their deeds they deny Him, being detestable and disobedient and worthless for any good deed. *Titus 1:16*

May you not deny Him by your deeds.

Blessings

God morning, branches,

> He who walks with wise men will be wise,
> But the companion of fools will suffer harm. *Proverbs 13:20*

Choose your friends and acquaintances wisely.

Blessings

God morning, branches,

> Wise words bring many benefits, and hard work brings rewards. *Proverbs 12:14*

Dear friends, may you work hard and speak wisely.

Blessings

God morning, branches,

"While the world changes, the cross stands firm." *Saint Bruno*

Blessings

God morning, branches,

Dear children, let us not love with words or speech but with actions and in truth. 1 John 3:18

Actions speak louder than words.

Blessings

God morning, branches,

"In the same way, faith by itself, if it is not accompanied by action, is dead. But someone will say, "You have faith; I have deeds." Show me your faith without deeds, and I will show you my faith by what I do." James 2:14-18

May your actions be louder than your words.

Blessings

God morning, branches,

Nothing great is ever achieved without enduring much. St. Catherine of Siena

Dear friends, we must struggle to meet success. Our challenges are many. The reward is heavenly.

Blessings

God morning, branches,

> But I am afraid that, as the serpent deceived Eve by his cunning, your thoughts may be corrupted from a sincere [and pure] commitment to Christ. *2 Corinthians 11:3*

Beware of false teachings, my friends.

Blessings

God morning, branches,

> There are many who say, "You can trust me!" But can they be trusted? *Proverbs 20:6*

Dear friends, I imagine this Proverb is as true today as it was when it was written.

Blessings

God morning, branches,

> For you are a holy people to the Lord your God; the Lord your God has chosen you to be a people for His own possession out of all the peoples who are on the face of the earth. *Deuteronomy 7:6*

Dear friends, you have been chosen by God. May your life guide others to Him.

Alleluia

Good morning, branches,

> Who among you is wise and understanding? Let him show by his good behavior his deeds in the gentleness of wisdom. *James 3:13*

May you be wise and understanding.

Blessings

Good morning, branches,

> Boast not thyself of to morrow; for thou knowest not what a day may bring forth. *Proverbs 27:1*

Dear friends, we can plan and prepare for tomorrow, but only God knows what the future holds.

Blessings

Good morning, branches,

> Live as free people, but do not use your freedom as a cover-up for evil; live as God's slaves. *1 Peter 2:16*

May you live as a slave of God.

Blessings

Good morning, branches,

> To fear the Lord is to hate evil; I hate pride and arrogance, evil behavior and perverse speech. *Proverbs 8:13*

Dear friends, the world is full of pride, arrogance, evil behavior and perverse speech. May we have the strength not to succumb to the ways of the world.

Blessings

God morning, branches,

> A single sunbeam is enough to drive away many shadows.
> *St Francis of Assisi*

May you drive away many shadows.

Blessings

God morning, branches,

> But they did not listen or pay attention; instead, they followed the stubborn inclinations of their evil hearts. They went backward and not forward. *Jeremiah 7:24*

May you listen and pay attention.

Blessings

God morning, branches,

> You will keep in perfect peace those whose minds are steadfast, because they trust in you. *Isaiah 26:3*

May you be in perfect peace.

Blessings

God morning, branches,

> A tranquil heart gives life to the flesh, but envy makes the bones rot. *Proverbs 14:30*

May you not be envious.

Blessings

God morning, branches,

> For whatever is born of God overcomes the world. And this is the victory that has overcome the world— our faith. *1 John 5:4*

Dear friends, may your faith lead you to victory over the world, which is ruled by the evil one.

Blessings

God morning, branches,

> For the Spirit God gave us does not make us timid, but gives us power, love and self-discipline. *2 Timothy 1:7*

God never forces Himself on us. We can choose to be guided by the Spirit. May you choose wisely.

Blessings

God morning, branches,

> A soft answer turns away wrath, but a harsh word stirs up anger. *Proverbs 15:1*

May you never be harsh.

Blessings

God morning, branches,

> Now there are varieties of gifts, but the same Spirit. *1 Corinthians 12:4*

Dear friends, each of us has a gift given to him or her by Spirit. No gift is better than any other. They are to be used for the glory of our Heavenly Father.

Blessings

God morning, branches,

> From a wise mind comes wise speech; the words of the wise are persuasive. Kind words are like honey—sweet to the soul and healthy for the body. *Proverbs 16:23-24*

Words matter.

Blessings

God morning, branches,

> the one who says he abides in Him ought himself to walk in the same manner as He walked. *1 John 2:6*

May we walk as He walked.

Blessings

God morning, branches,

> Prayer is for every moment of our lives, not just for times of suffering or joy. Prayer is really a place, a place where you meet God in genuine conversation. *Billy Graham*

Dear friends, do you have genuine conversations with God?

Blessings

God morning, branches,

> In this world of ours, every believer must be a spark of light, a center of love, a vivifying ferment for the mass; and it will be that all the more as, in the depths of his being, he lives in communion with God. *Pope John XXIII*

Dear friends, may you be a spark of light, a center of love, a vivifying ferment for the mass and live in communion with God.

Blessings

God morning, branches,

> the one who says he abides in Him ought himself to walk in the same manner as He walked. *1 John 2:6*

May you walk as He walked.

Blessings

SCRIPTURE NOTES

God morning, branches,

The Holy Spirit does not speak to a soul that is distracted and garrulous. He speaks by His quiet inspirations to a soul that is recollected, to a soul that knows how to keep silence. Saint Faustina

Psalm 62:5-6 My soul, wait in silence for God only, For my hope is from Him. He only is my rock and my salvation, My stronghold; I shall not be shaken.

Dear friends, silence is golden. Listen, learn and grow.

Blessings

God morning, branches,

The heart of the righteous weighs its answers, but the mouth of the wicked gushes evil. Proverbs 15:28

Dear friends, may you weigh your answers.

Blessings

God morning, branches,

And let us consider how to stir up one another to love and good works, not neglecting to meet together, as is the habit of some, but encouraging one another, and all the more as you see the Day drawing near. Hebrews 10:24-25

Dear friends, may we stir up one another to love and good works.

Blessings

SCRIPTURE NOTES

God morning, branches,

> "To love means loving the unlovable. To forgive means pardoning the unpardonable. Faith means believing the unbelievable. Hope means hoping when everything seems hopeless."
> Gilbert K. Chesterton

Dear friends, it is easy to love the lovable. As Jesus said "If you love those who love you, what reward will you get?".
Steve

God morning, branches,

> False messiahs and false prophets will arise, and they will perform signs and wonders so great as to deceive, if that were possible, even the elect. Matthew 24:24

Dear friends, know that signs and wonders so great should not be confused with miracles. Be careful.
Blessings

God morning, branches,

> For where your treasure is, there your heart will be also. Matthew 6:21

May your treasure be above, not on earth.
Blessings

God morning, branches,

> Let the peace of Christ control your hearts; Let the word of Christ dwell in you richly. Colossians 3:15a,16a

Dear friends, we are called to follow in His footsteps. Peace can be ours when we do so and show others how to do so.

Peace

God morning, branches,

> Why, my soul, are you downcast? Why so disturbed within me? Put your hope in God, for I will yet praise him, my Savior, and my God.
> *Psalm 43:5*

Dear friends, should you ever feel downcast or disturbed, remember God is in control and will help you. Have hope and patience.

Blessings

God morning, branches,

> And not only this, but we also exult in our tribulations, knowing that tribulation brings about perseverance; and perseverance, proven character; and proven character, hope; and hope does not disappoint, because the love of God has been poured out within our hearts through the Holy Spirit who was given to us.
> *Romans 5:3-5*

May you persevere.

Blessings

God morning, branches,

> The Lord looked into the depth of my being with great kindness; I thought I would die for joy under that gaze. *St. Faustina*

Dear friends, I think the joy Saint Faustina felt is beyond our ability to understand.

Blessings

God morning, branches,

> Who among you is wise and understanding? Let him show by his good behavior his deeds in the gentleness of wisdom. *James 3:13*

May you be wise and understanding.

Blessings

God morning, branches,

> If you help the poor, you are lending to the LORD–and he will repay you! *Proverbs 19:17*

May you help the poor.

Blessings

God morning, branches,

> Great is his faithfulness; His mercies begin afresh each morning. *Lamentations 3:23*

An angel woke you because your purpose in life is yet to be fulfilled.

Blessings

God morning, branches,

> A happy heart enlightens the face, but a sad heart reflects a broken spirit. A discerning mind seeks knowledge, but the mouth of fools feeds on stupidity. The entire life of the afflicted seems disastrous, but a good heart feasts continuously.
> *Proverbs 15:13-15*

Dear friends, may our hearts feast continuously.

Blessings

God morning, branches,

> Take care of your body as if you were going to live forever;
> and take care of your soul as if you were going to die tomorrow.
> *Saint Augustine*

Dear friends, I imagine many pay more attention to the body. May you tend to your soul. Remember, tomorrow is not promised to anyone.

Blessings

God morning, branches,

> May the Lord direct your hearts to the love of God and to the steadfastness of Christ. *2 Thessalonians 3:5*

Know that the adversary is relentless as he tries to direct your hearts away from God.

Blessings

God morning, branches,

> "And no wonder, for Satan himself masquerades as an angel of light."
> 2 Corinthians 11:14

Among other names, the evil one is known as the Great Deceiver. When something or someone appears to be too good to be true, you might want to consider if the god of this world is involved.

Blessings

God morning, branches.

> The eye cannot say to the hand, 'I don't need you!' And the head cannot say to the feet, 'I don't need you!' On the contrary, those parts of the body that seem to be weaker are indispensable. 1 Corinthians 12:21-22

Dear friends, you are indispensable to Christ's church. Each of you is different, but of equal importance. I am sure many have questioned their value. Remember, every part is important.

Blessings

God morning, branches,

> There is no fear in love, but perfect love casts out fear. For fear has to do with punishment, and whoever fears has not been perfected in love. 1 John 4:18

Dear friends, may you be perfected in love.

Blessings

God morning, branches,

> And we know that in all things God works for the good of those who love him, who have been called according to his purpose. *Romans 8:28*

May you love God more each day. Many say family is first, but remember what Jesus says is the first and greatest commandment.

Alleluia

God morning, branches,

> Make sure you don't take things for granted and go slack in working for the common good; share what you have with others. God takes particular pleasure in acts of worship - a different kind of "sacrifice" - that take place in kitchen and workplace and on the streets. *Hebrews 13:16*

Dear friends, share with and love one another. Take nothing for granted, not even the rising of the sun.

Blessings

God morning, branches,

> If I have the gift of prophecy, and know all mysteries and all knowledge; and if I have all faith, so as to remove mountains, but do not have love, I am nothing. *1 Corinthians 13:2*

If we do not love, we are nothing. God is love and we were created in His Divine Image. May you not be nothing.

Blessings

God morning, branches,

> A man's pride will bring him low,
> But a humble spirit will obtain honor. *Proverbs 29:23*

May your spirit be humble.

Blessings

God morning, branches,

> Whenever anything disagreeable or displeasing happens to you, remember Christ crucified and be silent. *Saint John of the Cross*

Blessings

God morning, branches,

> The rich rules over the poor,
> And the borrower becomes the lender's slave. *Proverbs 22:7*

This Proverb is so true in our time with so many types of loans and credit cards available to us. I imagine most of us are or were debt slaves. The adversary pushes instant gratification, but it comes with long-term slavery.

Blessings

God morning, branches,

> It is not what goes into the mouth that defiles a person, but what comes out of the mouth; this defiles a person. *Matthew 15:11*

Be mindful of your words and actions. Over time more words and actions, which were once considered vulgar or in bad taste have become commonplace.

Blessings

God morning, branches,

> Jesus gives us the gift of the Holy Spirit, yet when the Spirit comes, He is loaded with packages! He desires to release much more in us and through us than we could ever imagine. These gifts are given for delivery, not for accumulation. We receive them to pass them on to others. *Jack W. Hayford*

Dear friends, may you distribute your gifts.

Blessings

God morning, branches,

> Now hear this, O foolish and senseless people, Who have eyes but do not see;
> Who have ears but do not hear. *Jeremiah 5:21*

Dear friends, may we not be foolish and senseless.

Blessings

God morning, branches,

> Prayer is the raising of the mind to God. We must always remember this. The actual words matter less. *Pope John XXIII*

Dear friends, may we raise our minds to God.

Blessings

God morning, branches,

> *You shall not follow the masses in doing evil, nor shall you testify in a dispute so as to turn aside after a multitude in order to pervert justice;*
> *Exodus 23:2*

Dear friends, the adversary has the masses doing evil every moment of every day around the globe. We must stand firm in our Christian beliefs and avoid joining the masses in doing evil. We are in a constant battle with the evildoers, but our Savior will help us prevail.

Blessings

God morning, branches,

> *But He turned and said to Peter, "Get behind Me, Satan! You are a stumbling block to Me; for*
> *you are not setting your mind on God's interests, but man's."*
> *Matthew 16:23*

Dear friends, is your mind on God's interests or man's? The adversary has numerous ways to distract us from God.

Blessings

God morning, branches,

> He has saved us and called us to a holy life—not because of anything we have done but because of his own purpose and grace. This grace was given us in Christ Jesus before the beginning of time. *2 Timothy 1:9*

Dear friends, may you be thankful for the grace that was given to you and remember your calling when dealing with others.

Blessings

God morning, branches,

> Make sure that no one captivates you with the empty lure of a 'philosophy' of the kind that human beings hand on, based on the principles of this world and not on Christ. *Colossians 2:8*

Dear friends, always remember there is only one Truth.

Blessings

God morning, branches,

> Prayer is powerful beyond limits when we turn to the Immaculata who is queen even of God's heart. *Maximilian Kolbe*

Blessings

God morning, branches,

> Blessed is a man who perseveres under trial; for once he has been approved, he will receive the crown of life which the Lord has promised to those who love Him. *James 1:12*

May you persevere under trial.

Blessings

God morning, branches,

> Pure holy simplicity confounds all the wisdom of this world and the wisdom of the flesh. *St. Francis of Assisi*

Perhaps one way to think of this is to love one another for God is love and we were created in His image.

Blessings

God morning, branches,

> And do not neglect doing good and sharing, for with such sacrifices God is pleased. *Hebrews 13:16*

Dear friends, we are a week from Thanksgiving. There are many who need help and not just at Thanksgiving.

Blessings

God morning, branches,

> In today's Mass, the Responsorial Psalm includes Here am I, Lord; I come to do your will.

Dear friends, that is what Jesus said to His Heavenly Father. As Christians, we are called to do likewise.

Blessings

SCRIPTURE NOTES

God morning, branches,

> Then He said to them, "Beware, and be on your guard against every form of greed; for not even when one has an abundance does his life consist of his possessions." *Luke 12:15*

Do you own your possessions or do they own you? Christ's kingdom is spiritual, and not of this world.

Blessings

God morning, branches,

> Suffering is a great grace; through suffering the soul becomes like the Savior; in suffering love becomes crystallized; the greater the suffering, the purer the love *Saint Faustina*

Dear friends, I wonder if any of us truly welcomes suffering.

Blessings

God morning, branches,

> Please receive instruction from His mouth
> And establish His words in your heart. *Job 22:22*

May you establish His words in your heart.

Blessings

God morning, branches,

> Folly brings joy to one who has no sense, but whoever has understanding keeps a straight course. *Proverbs 15:21*

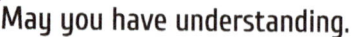

May you have understanding.

Blessings

God morning, branches,

Just going to church doesn't make you a Christian any more than standing in your garage makes you a car. *G.K. Chesterton*

Blessings

God morning, branches,

For those who are according to the flesh set their minds on the things of the flesh, but those who are according to the Spirit, the things of the Spirit. *Romans 8:5*

May your minds be on things of the Spirit.

Blessings

God morning, branches,

He replied, "Isaiah was right when he prophesied about you hypocrites; as it is written: " 'These people honor me with their lips, but their hearts are far from me. *Mark 7:6*

Dear friends, may your hearts be close to the Lord.

Blessings

God morning, branches,

> But, beloved, be not ignorant of this one thing, that one day is with the Lord as a thousand years, and a thousand years as one day. *2 Peter 3:8*

Dear friends, if you think He is not responding to your prayers, be patient.

Blessings

God morning, branches,

> The Lord said to Satan, "From where do you come?" Then Satan answered the Lord and said, "From roaming about on the earth and walking around on it." *Job 1:7*

Dear friends, the adversary is still roaming about on the earth and walking around on it. Our planet abounds with troubles. Be careful.

Blessings

God morning, branches,

> But you, man of God, flee from all this, and pursue righteousness, godliness, faith, love, endurance and gentleness. *1 Timothy 6:11*

Dear friends, may you flee from the adversary's distractions and weapons that surround us to pursue righteousness, godliness, faith, love, endurance and gentleness.

Blessings

God morning, branches,

> The end of a matter is better than its beginning; Patience of spirit is better than haughtiness of spirit. *Ecclesiastes 7:8*

Who among us could not use more patience?

Blessings

God morning, branches,

> Whoever is slow to anger has great understanding, but he who has a hasty temper exalts folly. *Proverbs 14:29*

May you be slow to anger.

Blessings

God morning, branches,

> Do not be deceived: "Bad company corrupts good morals."
> *1 Corinthians 15:33*

I am sure you have heard the expression "Show me your friends, I'll tell you who you are."

Blessings

God morning, branches,

> "When we are overcome by sadness, fear, or suffering; when the pains of loss overwhelm us; when evil seems to have taken power; let us look

to the cross and be filled with peace, knowing that Christ has walked this road and walks it now with us and with all our brothers and sisters."
~St Teresa of Avila

Blessings

God morning, branches,

From a wise mind comes wise speech; the words of the wise are persuasive. Kind words are like honey-sweet to the soul and healthy for the body. Proverbs 16:23-24

Words matter.

Blessings

God morning, branches,

And let the peace of Christ rule in your hearts, to which indeed you were called in one body. And be thankful. Colossians 3:15

Thanksgiving should not be just the fourth Thursday of the eleventh month.

I wish you a happy and blessed Thanksgiving.

Alleluia

God morning, branches,

"Jesus, help me to simplify my life by learning what you want me to be - and becoming that person." St. Thérèse of Lisieux

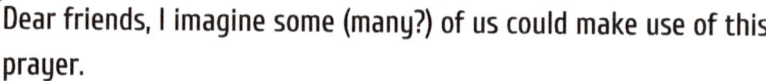

Dear friends, I imagine some (many?) of us could make use of this prayer.

Blessings

God morning, branches,

> Attribute to God every good that you have received. If you take credit for something that does not belong to you, you will be guilty of theft. Anthony of Padua

Dear friends, may we not be thieves.

Blessings

God morning, branches,

> Remember this: Whoever sows sparingly will also reap sparingly, and whoever sows generously will also reap generously. 2 Corinthians 9:6

May you sow generously.

Blessings

God morning, branches,

> You shall not follow the masses in doing evil, nor shall you testify in a dispute so as to turn aside after a multitude in order to pervert justice. Exodus 23:2

Dear friends, always think for yourselves and do not follow the masses without thinking. Too many follow the crowd without serious thought.

Blessings

God morning, branches,

> For even though they knew God, they did not honor Him as God or give thanks, but they became futile in their speculations, and their foolish heart was darkened. *Romans 1:21*

Dear friends, the adversary puts many obstacles in your way to try to keep you from honoring God and giving thanks. Do not let your hearts darken. Take time to pray and give thanks. It is priceless.

Blessings

God morning, branches,

> do not merely look out for your own personal interests, but also for the interests of others. *Philippians 2:4*

Just as we are to love one another.

Blessings

God morning, branches,

> "The devil fears hearts on fire with love of God." *St. Catherine of Siena*

Dear friends, may your hearts be on fire with love of God.

Blessings

God morning, branches,

For anger slays the foolish man, And jealousy kills the simple. Job 5:2

Do not be angry or jealous, my friends.

Blessings

God morning, branches,

Having a seeking heart opens me up to receive more of You. Matthew 7:7

Dear friends, may our hearts seek Christ more often than just in times of trouble or uncertainty.

Blessings

God morning, branches,

Do not say, "Why were the old days better than these?" For it is not wise to ask such questions. Ecclesiastes 7:10

Dear friends, I imagine most (all?) of us have at some point thought the good old days were better than these days. I did not know about this reading.

Blessings

God morning, branches,

Since we have gifts that differ according to the grace given to us, each of us is to exercise them accordingly: if prophecy, according to the proportion of his faith; Romans 12:6

Are you exercising your gifts?

Blessings

God morning, branches,

> Prayer is simply a two-way conversation between you and God.
> *Billy Graham*

Dear friends, praying to God is just like talking with a friend. No special language is required. No fancy words. It can be done at anytime. Why not now? Why not say a prayer for your family members, friends, colleagues, acquaintances, strangers, enemies and yours truly. Prayer is powerful. Thank you.

Blessings

God morning, branches,

> "True friends challenge us and help us to be faithful on our journey."
> *Pope Benedict XVI*

Dear friends, may all your friends be true.

Blessings

God morning, branches,

> Do not be overcome by evil, but overcome evil with good. *Romans 12:21*

Dear friends, the evil ones are wily and persistent, but no match for those who follow Christ.

Blessings

God morning, branches,

> The wise of heart will receive commandments, but a babbling fool will come to ruin. *Proverbs 10:8*

May you be wise of heart.

Blessings

God morning, branches,

> Wait for the Lord; be strong and take heart and wait for the Lord. *Psalm 27:14*

Dear friends, while waiting you may get frustrated, but remember His time is not like ours and His time is always perfect.

Peace

God morning, branches,

> "There is no peace," says my God, "for the wicked." *Isaiah 57:21*

May you never be wicked, my friends, and lead the wicked to the light.

Blessings

God morning, branches,

> You made me; you created me. Now give me the sense to follow your commands. May all who fear you find in me a cause for joy, for I have put my hope in your word. *Psalm 119:73-74*

Dear friends, God created us and gave us free will. We are not programmed or forced to love Him or follow His commands. You can choose to follow His commands or not. The adversary knows this and does all he can to keep us from following God and His commands. Choose wisely.

Blessings

God morning, branches,

> Each of us is the result of a thought of God. Each of us is willed. Each of us is loved. Each of us is necessary. Pope Benedict XVI

Dear friends, many (most or all?) have wondered why we are here. It was through nothing we did that we were created. God created us for a reason. May we pray to learn our calling if it is not yet known. None of us is here by accident.

Blessings

God morning, branches,

> "If the angels were capable of envy, they would envy us for two things: one is the receiving of Holy Communion, and the other is suffering" Saint Faustina

Dear friends, when you think you are suffering, consider the angels are envious of your situation.

Blessings

God morning, branches,

> Take the helmet of salvation and the sword of the Spirit, which is the word of God. *Ephesians 6:17*

Dear friends, following yesterday's note, here is another quote about His sword. The helmet of salvation represents assurance of salvation.

Blessings

God morning, branches,

> Evil plans are an abomination to the Lord, But pleasant words are pure. *Proverbs 15:26*

Dear friends, may your plans never be evil.

Blessings

God morning, branches,

> Above all, keep loving one another earnestly, since love covers a multitude of sins. *1 Peter 4:8*

May you cover a multitude of sins.

Blessings

God morning, branches,

> Words kill, words give life; they're either poison or fruit - you choose. *Proverbs 18:21*

May your words be like fruit.

Blessings

God morning, sisters and brothers,

> My dear brothers and sisters, take note of this: Everyone should be quick to listen, slow to speak and slow to become angry. *James 1:19*

Dear friends, the above is excellent advice. If only everyone were aware of and followed it.

Blessings

God morning, branches,

> Diligent people, in contrast to lazy people, often have more money. *Proverbs 10:4.*

May you be diligent.

Blessings

God morning, branches,

> The night is almost gone; the day of salvation will soon be here. So remove your dark deeds like dirty clothes, and put on the shining armor of right living. *Romans 13:12*

The Light of the World will soon be here.

Blessings

God morning, branches,

> So Jacob served seven years to get Rachel, but they seemed like only a few days to him because of his love for her. *Genesis 29:20*

Dear friends, love is more than a good thing.

Blessings

God morning, branches,

> But thanks be to God, who always leads us as captives in Christ's triumphal procession and uses us to spread the aroma of the knowledge of him everywhere. *Corinthians 2:14*

May your actions spread the aroma of knowledge of Him everywhere.

Blessings

God morning, branches,

> Don't have anything to do with foolish and stupid arguments, because you know they produce quarrels. And the Lord's servant must not be quarrelsome but must be kind to everyone, able to teach, not resentful. *2 Timothy 2:23-24*

May you not quarrel.

Blessings

God morning, branches,

> For the LORD watches over the way of the righteous, but the way of the wicked leads to destruction. *Psalm 1:6*

May the Lord watch over you.

Blessings

God morning, branches,

> In everything you do, put God first, and he will direct you and crown your efforts with success. *Proverbs 3:6*

Dear friends, I wonder how many of us put God first in everything we do.

Blessings

God morning, branches,

> Be angry and do not sin; do not let the sun go down on your anger. *Ephesians 4:26*

Dear friends, I imagine you have heard or said the quote about going to bed angry, but probably did not know its biblical origin.

Blessings

God morning, branches,

> "We should ever be grateful for and love the vocation to which God has called us. This applies to every vocation because, after all, what a privilege it is to serve God, even in the least capacity!" *Solanus Casey*

Dear friends, indeed, it is a privilege to serve God in any way possible. You might serve Him simply by being kind to others. Remember, we were created in His Divine Image. Let others see God in us.

Blessings

God morning, branches,

> One gives freely, yet gains even more; another withholds what is right, only to become poor. *Proverbs 11:24*

May you give freely.

Blessings

God morning, branches,

> "Who except God can give you peace? Has the world ever been able to satisfy the heart? *St. Gerard Majella*

Dear friends, may God's peace be with you.

Blessings

God morning, branches,

> My God will use his wonderful riches in Christ Jesus to give you everything you need. *Philippians 4:19*

Dear friends, we just celebrated Christmas and you probably received gifts you wanted. Needs and wants are not the same thing. God will give you everything you need.

Blessings

God morning, branches,

> "Since love grows within you, so beauty grows. For love is the beauty of the soul." – *Saint Augustine*

May your soul grow in beauty every day.

Blessings

God morning, branches,

> "Now he who supplies seed to the sower and bread for food will also supply and increase your store of seed and will enlarge the harvest of your righteousness." *2 Corinthians 9:10*

Dear friends, we are now into the hustle and bustle of the Christmas season. Please remember the less fortunate. The more you do so, the more you will be rewarded. Not all rewards are tangible.

Blessings

God morning, branches,

> From the world's perspective, there are many places you can go to find comfort. But there is only one place you will find a hand to catch your tears and a heart to listen to your every longing. True peace comes only from God. *Charles Stanley*

Dear friends, may the peace of God be with you.

Blessings

God morning, branches,

> The Lord your God is with you. He is like a powerful soldier. He will save you. He will show how much he loves you and how happy he is with you. He will laugh and be happy about you. *Zephaniah 3:17*

Smile, God loves you.

Blessings

God morning, branches,

> "Most Sacred Heart of Jesus, teach me an entire forgetfulness of myself, since that is the only way one can find entrance into You."
> – *St. Alphonsas*

Dear friends, the world has increasingly become about me, me, me. May we strive for entire forgetfulness of ourselves so as to find entrance into the Lord.

Blessings

God morning, branches,

> We are God's work of art, created in Christ Jesus for the good works which God has already designated to make up our way of life. *Ephesians 2:10*

May you do good works.

Blessings

God morning, branches,

> In all your ways acknowledge Him, and He shall direct your paths.
> *Proverbs 3:6*

Your choice should be easy if you want to be on the right paths.

Blessing

God morning, branches,

> Our society strives to avoid any possibility of offending anyone - except God. *Billy Graham*

Dear friends, I think that is so true. You could probably add God-fearing people.

Blessings

God morning, branches,

> Wisdom is found in the old, and discretion comes with great age.
> *Job 12:12*

Dear friends, unfortunately this passage does not apply to everyone. May it apply to you.

Blessings

God morning, branches,

> But the Spirit explicitly says that in later times some will fall away from the faith, paying attention to deceitful spirits and doctrines of demons,
> *1 Timothy 4:1*

It seems time may be later than we think. Are your affairs in order?

Blessings

God morning, branches,

> Do not merely listen to the word, and so deceive yourselves. Do what it says. *James 1:22*

Dear friends, we are called to act God's word.

Blessings

God morning, branches,

> And who of you by being worried can add a single hour to his life? *Matthew 6:27*

> Cast all your worries on Him, for He cares for you. *1 Peter 5:7*

I imagine most of us worry too much.

Blessings

God morning, branches,

> "From him [Jesus] the whole body, joined and held together by every supporting ligament, grows and builds itself up in love, as each part does its work" (*Ephesians 4:16*).

Dear friends, you are an important part of the body of Christ and have something important to contribute.

Blessings

God morning, branches,

"Nowhere other than looking at himself in the mirror of the Cross can man better understand how much he is worth." *St. Anthony of Padua*

Blessings

God morning, branches,

"Love grows through love."
Pope Benedict XVI

Dear friends, the above quote seems simple, but is so powerful.

Love

God morning, branches,

I will meditate on your precepts and fix my eyes on your ways. I will delight in your statutes; I will not forget your word. *Psalm 119:15-16*

Dear friends, I imagine you have many questions. I know God has all the answers. The above Psalm could help bridge the gap between your questions and His answers.

Blessings

God morning, branches,

The fear of man bringeth a snare, but whoso putteth his trust in the Lord shall be safe. *Proverbs 29:25*

Hmmm, trust man or the Lord? Sounds like an easy one, but I imagine we make the wrong choice more than we would care to admit.

Blessings

God morning, branches,

> They have all turned aside, together they have become corrupt; There is no one who does good, not even one. *Psalm 14:3*

Dear friends, when it seems the world has turned aside and become corrupt, may you do good. Better yet, always do good.

Blessings

God morning, branches,

> You, my brothers and sisters, were called to be free. But do not use your freedom to indulge the flesh; rather, serve one another humbly in love. *Galatians 5:13*

May you serve one another humbly in love.

Blessings

God morning, branches,

> What the wicked fears will come upon him, But the desire of the righteous will be granted. *Proverbs 10:24*

May you be righteous.

Blessings

God morning, branches,

It is not that I want merely to be called a Christian, but to actually be one.
Saint Ignatius

Dear friends, actions speak louder than words.

Blessings

God morning, branches,

Woe to those who call evil good and good evil, who put darkness for light and light for darkness, who put bitter for sweet and sweet for bitter!
Isaiah 5:20

Dear friends, my how our nation has changed. It has a new law that officially voids the Defense of Marriage Act, which defined marriage as between a man and a woman.

Blessings

God morning, branches,

A democracy without values easily turns into open or thinly disguised totalitarianism. Pope John Paul II

Dear friends, these are words of wisdom from someone who experienced totalitarianism.

Blessings

God morning, branches,

> Love never fails. But whether there are prophecies, they will fail; whether there are tongues, they will cease; whether there is knowledge, it will vanish away. *1 Corinthians 13:8*

Love never fails because God is love and God cannot fail. When it is said the world can use more love, it should also be said it could use more God. Unfortunately, much of the world wants less or no God.
Blessings

God morning, branches,

> For it is in giving that we receive. *Francis of Assisi*

Dear friends, we are all blessed in many ways.
May you not just think of St. Francis' message, but act on it.
Blessings

God morning, branches,

> "Love to be real, it must cost—it must hurt—it must empty us of self." *Saint Theresa of Calcutta*

Love

God morning, branches,

> Hatred stirs up conflict, but love covers over all wrongs. *Proverbs 10:12*

Dear friends, I imagine this Proverb sounds familiar, yes?
Blessings

God morning, branches,

> To answer before listening— that is folly and shame. *Proverbs 18:13*

Dear friends, may we listen attentively.

Blessings

God morning, branches,

> "May the Mother of Jesus and our Mother, always smile on your spirit, obtaining for it, from her Most Holy Son, every heavenly blessing."

Dear friends, may we help someone today.

Blessings

God morning, branches,

> And God saw that the wickedness of man was great in the earth, and that every imagination of the thoughts of his heart was only evil continually. *Genesis 6:5*

Dear friends, we are called to resist the ways of this world and lead others to the right path. This is difficult until you realize who stands with you.

Blessings

God morning, branches,

> "This is my command—be strong and courageous! Do not be afraid or discouraged. For the Lord your God is with you wherever you go." *Joshua 1:9*

Dear friends, the evil one is relentless in placing obstacles and distractions wherever we are in our lives. Fear not as the Lord is our protector.

Blessings

God morning, branches,

> "For since death came through a man, the resurrection of the dead comes also through a man." *1 Corinthians 15:21*

Blessings

God morning, branches,

> An intelligent heart acquires knowledge, and the ear of the wise seeks knowledge. *Proverbs 18:15*

May you seek and acquire knowledge.

Blessings

God morning, branches,

> Don't do anything from selfish ambition or from a cheap desire to boast, but be humble toward one another, always considering others better than yourselves. *Philippians 2:3*

May you always consider others better than yourselves.

Blessings

God morning, branches,

> A kind man benefits himself, but a cruel person brings ruin on himself. *Proverbs 11:17*

May you perform a random act of kindness.

Blessings

God morning, branches,

> Every good and perfect gift is from above, coming down from the Father of the heavenly lights, who does not change like shifting shadows. *James 1:17*

Dear friends, with joy we await the perfect gift.

Peace

God morning, branches,

> Keep your lives free from the love of money and be content with what you have, because God has said, "Never will I leave you; never will I forsake you." *Hebrews 13:5*

I imagine a good number of us have not followed this Proverb at one time or another.

Blessings

God morning, branches,

> And there were in the same country shepherds abiding in the field, keeping watch over their flock by night. *Luke 2:8*

Isn't it interesting that the Light of the World was born in darkness?
Blessings

God morning, branches,

> Make sure that your character is free from the love of money, being content with what you have; for He Himself has said, "I will never desert you, nor will I ever forsake you," *Hebrews 13:5*

May you be content with what you have.
Blessings

God morning, branches,

> You will be enriched in every way so that you can be generous on every occasion, and through us your generosity will result in thanksgiving to God. *2 Corinthians 9:11*

Dear friends, may we be generous, especially to the less fortunate.
Blessings

God morning, branches,

> The great danger for family life, in the midst of any society whose idols are pleasure, comfort and independence, lies in the fact that people close their hearts and become selfish. *Pope John Paul II*

Dear friends, may you never close your hearts and become selfish.
Blessings

SCRIPTURE NOTES

God morning, branches,

> If knowledge is lacking, your destruction is inevitable. *Hosea 4:6*

Dear friends, never stop learning about God, His laws and providences (sovereign, divine superintendence of all things).

Blessings

God morning, branches,

> Is anyone among you suffering? Then he must pray. Is anyone cheerful? He is to sing praises. *James 5:13*

Keep your mind on God. Always.

Alleluia

God morning, branches,

> The power of evil men lives on the cowardice of the good. *John Bosco*

Dear friends, may you not be a coward. For starters, ignore the conventional wisdom that says do not talk about religion.

Blessings

God morning, branches,

> But if we walk in the light, as he is in the light, we have fellowship with one another, and the blood of Jesus his Son cleanses us from all sin. *1 John 1:7*

May you always walk in the light.

Blessings

God morning, branches,

> And just as they did not see fit to acknowledge God any longer, God gave them over to a depraved mind, to do those things which are not proper. Romans 1:28

Dear friends, the evil one welcomes those who ignore God. It seems there are many around the world who have ignored God. We are called to show the way back to the light.

Blessings

God morning, branches,

> There is no sin nor wrong that gives man such a foretaste of Hell in this life as anger and impatience. St. Catherine Of Siena

Dear friends, I imagine many (most?) of us have been angry and impatient. May we be neither angry nor impatient.

Blessings

God morning, branches,

> But the Lord said to Samuel, "Do not consider his appearance or his height, for I have rejected him. The Lord does not look at the things people look at. People look at the outward appearance, but the Lord looks at the heart." 1 Samuel 16:7

Dear friends, the Lord does not care about what you look like or own. What is in your heart?

Blessings

God morning, branches,

> Examine me, O Lord, and try me;
> Test my mind and my heart. *Psalm 26:2*

Dear friends, how would you fare in the examination and test?

Blessings

God morning, branches,

> Depart from evil, and do good; seek peace, and pursue it. *Psalm 34:14*

Dear friends, evil is all around us; remember who rules the world. May you have the strength to avoid it, do good and seek and pursue peace.

Blessings

God morning, branches,

> How precious are your thoughts about me, O God. . .
> And when I wake up, you are still with me! *Psalm 139: 17, 18*

You were given another day. How will you glorify God today?

Blessings

God morning, branches,

> It is better to say one Our Father fervently and devoutly than a thousand with no devotion and full of distraction. *St. Edmund*

Dear friends, this world makes it easy to say a prayer with no devotion and full of distraction. May we find the quiet room in our mind whenever we pray.

"Be still and know that I am God," the first half of Psalms 46:10

Inhale slowly and deeply
Pray as you exhale slowly and deeply
Blessings

God morning, branches,

The most deadly poison of our time is indifference.
Saint Maximilian Kolbe

Dear friends, In yesterday's note you saw that Saint Maximilian Kolbe was certainly not indifferent. May we not partake of this deadly poison, indifference, which is a tool of the evil one.
Blessings

God morning, branches,

Now may the Lord of peace Himself give you peace at all times and in every way. The Lord be with all of you. 2 Thessalonians 3:16

Dear friends, I imagine we all could use more peace each day. It could be as easy as taking a slow and deep breath and saying "Thank you". This can be done anywhere and anytime.
Peace

God morning, branches,

>Abstain from every form of evil. *1 Thessalonians 5:22*

Dear friends, the above is much easier said than done, but we are to make every effort to do so.

Blessings

God morning, branches,

>Turn to Me and be saved, all the ends of the earth;
>For I am God, and there is no other. *Isaiah 45:22*

Dear friends, you are unusual in today's world as I imagine you do not need to turn to God. It seems that much of the world has turned away from God.

Blessings

God morning, branches,

>"Miracles are not contrary to nature but only contrary to what we know about nature." *St. Augustine*

Dear friends, may we notice the miracles all around us and give thanks.

Blessings

God morning, branches,

>"A single act of pure love pleases me more than a thousand imperfect prayers." *Jesus (According to St. Faustina)*

Dear friends, may we try to please Jesus with acts of pure love. We may even influence, strengthen and convert others. Everyone wins!
Blessings

God morning, branches,

> How much better to get wisdom than gold! To get understanding is to be chosen rather than silver. *Proverbs 16:16*

Dear friends, may we not fall into the trap of material things.
Blessings

God morning, branches,

> We can be certain that God will give us the strength and resources we need to live through any situation in life that he ordains. The will of God will never take us where the grace of God cannot sustain us.
> *Billy Graham*

Dear friends, I imagine many (most) of us have said "God, give me strength." Keep in mind, the quote says God will get us through any situation He ordains. Remember, we have free will. Choose wisely.
Blessings

God morning, branches,

> "Mount Calvary is the academy of love." – *St. Francis de Sales*

Dear friends, I am sure we have all said I love you this much while extending our arms outwards to our sides. Well, that is what our Saviour did on the Cross.

Blessings

God morning, branches,

> "Why did you suffer for me, dear Jesus? For love! The nails...the crown... the cross...all for the love of me!" –*St. Gemma Galgani*

Dear friends, His love for us surpasses knowledge (Ephesians 3:19).

Blessings

God morning, branches,

> "The tragedy of the passion brings to fulfilment our own life and the whole of human history. We can't let Holy Week be just a kind of commemoration. It means contemplating the mystery of Jesus Christ as something which continues to work in our souls."
> –*Saint Josemaria Escriva*

Dear friends, may we contemplate the mystery of Jesus Christ as something which continues to work in our souls.

Blessings

God morning, branches,

> The Christian Gospel is that I am so flawed that Jesus had to die for me, yet I am so loved and valued that Jesus was glad to die for me. This leads to deep humility and deep confidence at the same time. It undermines

both swaggering and sniveling. I cannot feel superior to anyone, and yet I have nothing to prove to anyone. I do not think more of myself nor less of myself. Instead, I think of myself less.
Timothy Keller

Dear friends, may we think of ourselves less.
Blessing

God morning, branches,

I imagine we all pray, but did you ever pray in silence?
    Consider *Psalm 46:10:* Be still and know that I am God.
    Thomas Merton said "In Silence God ceases to be an object and becomes an experience."
    Maybe you wanted to pray, but words got in the way or you were at a loss for words. Understand our prayer life does not require words. May God become an experience.
Blessings

God morning, branches,

    Life without God is like an unsharpened pencil - it has no point.
    Billy Graham

Dear friends, may our pencils always be extra sharp. We need erasers, God does not.
Blessings

SCRIPTURE NOTES

God morning, branches,

> "The sky is my prayer, the birds are my prayer, the wind in the trees is my prayer, for God is all in all." *Thomas Merton*

Dear friends, I imagine most of us are preoccupied with our cell phones even when out in public. Why not take time to admire part(s) of God's creation and engage in prayer or conversation with Him?

Blessings

God morning, branches,

> Therefore, if anyone is in Christ, he is a new creation. The old has passed away; behold, the new has come. *2 Corinthians 5:17*

I wish you and your loved ones a happy and blessed new year.

Blessings

God morning, branches,

> For you were called to freedom, brothers. Only do not use your freedom as an opportunity for the flesh, but through love serve one another. *Galatians 5:13*

Dear friends, our nation's founding documents were influenced by the Christian views of the Founding Fathers. May our nation return to God and receive His mighty and many blessings.

Blessings

God morning, branches,

Today's Gospel
Luke 21:1-4

> When Jesus looked up he saw some wealthy people putting their offerings into the treasury and he noticed a poor widow putting in two small coins. He said, "I tell you truly, this poor widow put in more than all the rest; for those others have all made offerings from their surplus wealth, but she, from her poverty, has offered her whole livelihood."

Dear friends, may we follow the poor widow's example.

Blessings

God morning, branches,

> God has given us two hands, one to receive with and the other to give with. Billy Graham

Dear friends, may we give to those in need. Giving is not just about money.

Blessings

God morning, branches,

> Every time I read the Bible, any part of the Bible—I don't care where I open up—it speaks to me. It's a living book. Billy Graham

Dear friends, some have called the Bible an ancient relic. I wonder if you believe it is a living book that speaks to you.

Blessings

God morning, branches,

> "God can't give us peace and happiness apart from Himself because there is no such thing." – C.S. Lewis

Dear friends, it really is that simple. When things seem to go wrong or we are unhappy, do we not turn to Him for help? I suggest if we put Him first, such things would not happen.

Blessings

God morning, branches,

> There are three of you. There is the person you think you are. There is the person others think you are. There is the person God knows you are and can be through Christ. Billy Graham

Dear friends, I wonder if there are any among us who think they are the person as God knows them.

Blessings

God morning, branches,

> How many observe Christ's birthday! How few, His precepts!
> Benjamin Franklin

Dear friends, may we observe His precepts.

Blessings

God morning, branches,

> Let no pleasure tempt thee, no profit allure thee, no persuasion move thee, to do anything which thou knowest to be evil; so shalt thou always live jollity; for a good conscience is a continual Christmas.
> Benjamin Franklin

Dear friends, my we always have a good conscience.
Blessings

God morning, branches,

> The light shines in the darkness, and the darkness has not overcome it.
> John 1:5

Dear friends, we are on the eve of celebrating the birth of Jesus Christ, our Lord and Saviour and the Light of the world. Each day the world grows darker, and I am not talking about the long winter nights. May we be lights and lead others to the light in an increasingly dark world.
Blessings

God morning, branches,

> I proclaim to you good news of great joy:
> today a Savior is born for us,
> Christ the Lord.
> Luke 2:10-11

Merry & Blessed Christmas to you and your loved ones.
Blessings

God morning, branches,

> Before them the earth shakes, the heavens tremble, the sun and moon are darkened, and the stars no longer shine. *Joel 2:10*

Dear friends, a few days ago NYC experienced an earthquake. Yesterday, there was an eclipse. I wonder how many people thought about Bible verses about an eclipse. There are dozens. I have often commented about admiring His beauty throughout creation. I believe it is a form of prayer.

Blessings

God morning, branches,

> "For you were once darkness, but now you are light in the Lord. Walk as children of light." *Ephesians 5:8*

Dear friends, do not let the spirit of Christmas dissipate. May we always walk as children of light.

Blessings

Dearest Anna

08/03/20

Dearest Anna,

I used to tell Anna I love you more than you'll ever know, which is the title of a great song by Al Kooper on an album by the original Blood, Sweat and Tears. I would add that you will know how much I love you when you get to Heaven. Well, now you know.

* * *

08/05/20

Dearest Anna,

God called you home a month ago today.

It is strange you are not physically here, but everywhere I turn there you are.

I miss you so much.

I understand God has plans for me here.

I am looking forward to the time He calls me home and we can spend eternity together.

* * *

08/09/20

Dearest Anna,

Our marriage vows included till death do us part. Now what? Anna always said I spent way too much time thinking. Well, Cheeks (one of many affectionate nicknames), I have been thinking a lot. You were my everything. You always will be. I planted a yellow rosebush out back. I can see it and your picture at the same time. I miss you so much. I cannot say more than you'll ever know because you are in Heaven and you know. I know God will guide me until I see you again. I love you.

* * *

08/17/20

Dearest Anna,

We met forty-six years ago today, but it seems like yesterday. It was a beautiful Saturday. I spent the day with friends at the beach. My best friend called me in the evening and reminded me about a party that night. I did not feel up to it, but he talked me into going.

You and I met. We spoke for a while. I drove you home when you wanted to leave the party. I walked you to your door. Never tried a move. You later said you were impressed that I was such a gentleman. That is something I will miss now that you are in Heaven. I loved bringing you flowers all those years for no special reason other than just because I love you. I loved how you lovingly accepted them, cut them and arranged them beautifully in a vase and placed them on a table. You never made any demands. It was never about you. My life was always about you. Well, Doll (another of many affectionate nicknames), I am looking forward to when God calls me home so you and I can spend eternity together. As Deacon Hank and I used to greet each other at Mass, another day closer. I am lost without you. To say I miss you does not even come close to how I feel. I love you.

* * *

09/06/20

Dearest Anna,

We were wed forty years ago today. God called you home two months ago. I miss everything about you. My confidant, guide, anchor, lover, soulmate, better half, everything, best friend, life and wife. Happy anniversary. I love you. I am looking forward to when we get to spend eternity together.

All my love, forever.

* * *

09/20/20

Dearest Anna,

A very tough day today. My birthday and Anna is not here with me. Family took me to dinner. It was very good and I made it feel like it was all okay. I could not wait to get home. Everything is so different now without Anna.

* * *

10/05/20

Dearest Anna,

You were called home three months ago today. I miss you so much, Cheeks. I love you so much, Q.

I take comfort in knowing you are at peace in Heaven.

Another day closer.

All my love, yesterday, today and forever.

* * *

11/05/20

Dearest Anna,

God called you home four months ago today.

Amazingly, there is one yellow rose still hanging on the rose-bush I planted after you left.

I love you so much, Cheeks.

I miss you so much, Doll.

One day closer.

Love, yesterday, today and forever.

* * *

01/05/21

Dearest Anna,

God called you home six months ago.

I miss you more than words can say.

I love you, Cheeks.

I am looking forward to you welcoming me home when God calls for me.

All my love yesterday, today and forever.

* * *

03/05/21

Dearest Anna,

God called you home eight months ago.

It is said absence makes the heart grow fonder.

Well, Cheeks, this is absence at its most extreme.

Just as I loved you more each day, Doll, I miss you more each day.

I thank God often for the gift of you and I am looking forward to being with you in Paradise for eternity.

One day closer.

All my love, always and forever

* * *

05/17/21

Dearest Anna,

I went to the beach yesterday. While looking at the vastness of the ocean, I felt insignificant. I never felt that way before you were called home.

Yes, I shook out the sand before going inside, but I am sure you would find I missed a grain!

I miss you, Cheeks.

* * *

06/06/21

Dearest Anna,

The past couple of days were spent getting furniture and things moved to storage in preparation for the next chapter of my life. I spent forty-six wonderful years with Anna in our home. So many memories. A family raised. A lifetime with my confidant, lover, best friend, angel and wife.

I know I must keep going, but. Well, you know. Every once in a while, I would tell friends or colleagues that I was going on a date.

They were surprised and then I said with my wife. Every day was special and no two were the same.

I said good-bye to neighbors and friends. Also to all the trees, bushes, plants and roses I planted.

An extremely difficult time. Part of me will be missing until I am called home, God willing.

* * *

06/08/21

Dearest Anna,

Only the widowed will understand I cannot stop thinking of Anna, the life we had and how everything changed. Triggers and reminders are everywhere. Sometimes I smile and laugh, but not as much as the opposite. Yes, I am thankful. Yes, I know God will not let me down. Yes, I love spreading the Good News and helping others. Over eleven months now and it is tougher, not easier.

* * *

06/23/21

Dearest Anna,

It is said the deeper the love, the deeper the grief. You went home almost eleven months ago. My love for you keeps growing. So, my grief will keep growing.

Recently, I wrote how I felt insignificant as I gazed at the vastness of the ocean. While you were here, there was nothing I could not do, if I wanted. Your presence was everything. Words were not necessary. I miss you more than words can say, Cheeks.

All my love yesterday, today, forever.

07/02/21

Dearest Anna,

My wife passed away last year on July 5. It has been an extremely difficult year. I take comfort knowing that Anna is in Heaven. Sometimes I feel as if I have lost my mind. I like my job and thought it was a distraction from my pain, but I have realized I have not been doing it as I did before Anna was called home. Today, I decided I need to seek help, which was tough to think about because I have always been the one who helps others. The lockdown, combined with my grief, has taken a toll. Somehow, I have to think this is part of His plan. Thank you for reading my note. May God bless and comfort you.

* * *

09/06/21

Dearest Anna,

Forty-one years ago today we became one flesh. Fourteen months ago yesterday you were called home. I miss you more than words can say. We did not need words and I imagine you know how devastated I feel, Cheeks. I experience incredibly intense sadness for me and happiness for you simultaneously. You are constantly in my thoughts, Q. I still have a hard time believing how lucky I was to be married to you. I am trying to carry out whatever plan God has for me. I am looking forward to being with you again in Paradise for eternity.

All my love yesterday, today and forever.

* * *

10/15/21

Dearest Anna,

Happy birthday in Heaven.
I love and miss you more each day, Cheeks.
Love yesterday, today and forever.

* * *

12/14/21

Dearest Anna,

 You know how difficult my life is without you. I miss everything about you. I often look at pictures of you and thank God that He put us together for decades. I am always drawn to your eyes and smile. Heck, your very presence was a wonderful gift. If we had a chance to get married again, I would ask that our wedding song be "Let It Rain" by Clapton. Tears roll down my cheeks now and whenever I think of you, which is often. I imagine my tears are like the rain and your soft touches and presence lovingly caressing me. During the exquisite solo near the end of the song, I imagine our souls wrapping around each other in the most beautiful heavenly way.

 I love and miss you more every day, Doll.
 One day closer, Cheeks.
 All my love yesterday, today and forever.

* * *

01/25/22

Dearest Anna,

Practically everywhere I am there is something that reminds me of you. It does not take much for tears to well up in my eyes (at least my eyes will never be dry). Each time I reach for my cellphone, there you are. Sometimes when I look at you I laugh because it looks like your smile is lovingly teasing me saying, "Ha, ha, I beat you here" (to Heaven). Sometimes it looks like you are saying how wonderful Heaven is and you are looking forward to when we are together again. I always say you deserve to be there, Cheeks.

Well, another day closer, Doll.

All my love yesterday, today and forever.

* * *

02/10/22

Dearest Anna,

Since you were called home, I have felt and said, nothing matters anymore. I am so grateful to God that you were not only part of my life, you were my life and made me who I am. You were an angel sent from the Almighty to make me "Me." Well, I know He is not finished with me and I still have a purpose here. Please pray for me Cheeks. May you guide me on the rest of my journey here. I just listened to the song "Nothing Else Matters." The lyrics:

So close, no matter how far
Couldn't be much more from the heart
Forever trusting who we are
And nothing else matters

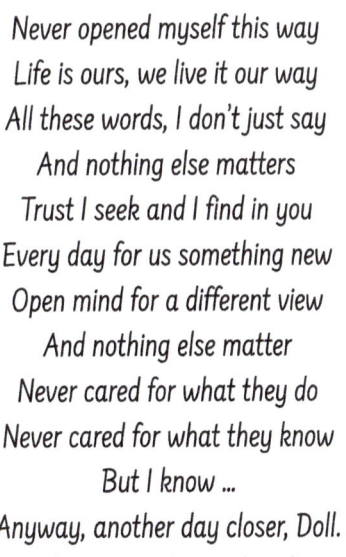

Never opened myself this way
Life is ours, we live it our way
All these words, I don't just say
And nothing else matters
Trust I seek and I find in you
Every day for us something new
Open mind for a different view
And nothing else matter
Never cared for what they do
Never cared for what they know
But I know ...
Anyway, another day closer, Doll.
All my love yesterday, today, forever.

* * *

02/19/22

Dearest Anna,

You are often in my thoughts. There is a song I have heard often recently and part of the lyrics describe how I feel: My heart has gone. I've gone cold.

It is so unbelievably difficult without you here. You were my everything, Cheeks. You are still my everything, Doll.

I will coach the kids in a football game later. I love that, but then I will come back to an empty home.

Another day closer, Q.

All my love yesterday, today, forever.

* * *

02/27/22

Dearest Anna,

I think of you quite a lot. You were called home eighteen months ago and my love for you still grows. I just listened to the magnificent song "Still, You Turn Me On" by Emerson, Lake & Palmer. You are now what the first line of the song is: "Do you wanna be an angel?"

You were an angel here, too, Cheeks.

I miss you more than words will ever say, Doll. The note I sent to friends and family this morning was about Psalm 43: Why, my soul, are you downcast? Why so disturbed within me? Put your hope in God, for I will yet praise him, my Savior, and my God.

Pray for me, Q, as I struggle without you.

All my love yesterday, today, forever.

03/26/22

Dearest Anna,

I heard this line in a song: how wonderful life is while you're in the world.

Well, you get my point, Cheeks.

Another day closer, Doll.

All my love yesterday, today and forever.

* * *

07/04/22

Dearest Anna,

Two years ago you were called home. That is 730 days, 17,520 hours, 1,051,200 minutes, 63,072,200 seconds. The time you have been in Heaven can be counted in my life. What cannot be counted are the tears I cried or the heartaches. As I was there with you, I often wonder what you saw when you left. I try to imagine your last moment with me and then you seeing God.

Cheeks, you know I love music. Recently, I saw a picture of a woman appearing to be asleep on her side. The song's title is "I Feel Eternal," which part of me feels since you went home. I enjoyed watching you sleep.

There is a song that includes the lyrics:

*Can there be more in this world than
the joy of just watching you sleep?*

The song begins:

*You should have been an angel
It would of suited you
My gold-leafed, triptych angel
She knows just what to do;
In the half light of morning,
in our world between the sheets
I swear I saw her angel wing
My vision was complete*

I was watching a guitarist in the subway and a song made me think of the wonderful life I had with you. Then I took the escalator down to the train platform and my heart sank as the escalator moved lower as it seemed I was going in the opposite direction of you.

Another song, "Sway" by Mick Taylor and Carla Olson, is absolutely exquisite. It is about that demon's life. I laugh and cry because I affectionately called you devil woman, which you often wrote. You teased me with your devil horns and tail. Remember how I would draw a heart anywhere, put your name in it and somewhere I placed two horns and a tail. I cannot wait to soar with you around the universe to this magnificent tune.

There are so many songs that bring extreme moods that completely flip in less than a heartbeat. Heck, it isn't just songs that do that to me. Almost anything can be an emotional trigger and roller coaster as we spent almost every day together for over forty years. Pretty much everything reminds me of you and the tears flow. What am I supposed to do? I pray for an answer and help. I can't avoid life. You still have me wrapped around your finger and I would not want it any other way. Your hold on my heart has grown stronger since you went home.

I often want to scream your name at the sky and let it go forever through the universe. When I think of doing so, you whisper in my heart that you are right here with me. Then you lovingly caress me through my tears. You kept me sane in this insane world. Whatever troubles I had disappeared with a word or smile from you.

Our hearts seemed to beat together; our breathing, likewise. I hate being alone. I miss everything. Just your presence was indescribable. I feel incomplete now. I lived for you. It is a struggle now. Please pray for me, Doll.

There is an expression that goes the deeper the love, the deeper the grief. As my love for you, Q, is boundless, so is my grief.

This expression is so true: "Don't marry the person you think you can live with, but the one you can't live without."

I know I have work to do for the Lord, for which I am thankful. That you are not here as you were is a terrible feeling.

Another day closer, Cheeks. All my love yesterday, today and forever.

* * *

08/05/22

Dearest Anna,

You know I get a daily devotion from Jesus Calling via email. A few days ago this was the reading:

> *Therefore you now have sorrow;*
> *but I will see you again and*
> *your heart will rejoice,*
> *and your joy no one will take from you.*
> *~ John 16:22*

I know it is about Jesus, but how could I not think it was from you?

The pain of not having you here increases every day, Cheeks. When anyone asks how I am, I say alright. I am like the song by EC called "Pretending."

Another day closer, Doll.

All my love yesterday, today and forever.

* * *

08/17/22

Dearest Anna,

Forty-eight years ago today, God introduced me to one of His angels. By His Divine intervention, we were brought together at a party neither one of us wanted to attend. Neither of us was looking for anyone or anything, but you found me. I am so thankful for His plan.

Strange that now that you are in Heaven, Cheeks, I could do pretty much anything, but don't want to do anything. It is like the song I wrote of, months ago, "Nothing Else Matters."

I am so lonely without you. I feel like I have a lot of love to give another woman, but perhaps that is not part of His plan now. I will keep on writing my morning notes about His words.

Another day closer, Doll.

All my love yesterday, today and forever

* * *

09/06/22

Dearest Anna,

Forty-two years ago today, we were married. The vows included the standard "To have and to hold, from this day forward, for better, for worse, for richer, for poorer, in sickness and in health, until death do us part."

You always laughed, Cheeks, when I said the priest looked at you when he said better and me when he said worse.

Well, Doll, I have been thinking (you always said I did too much thinking) about the until death do us part. Your physical presence has left, but your spirit remains. I may not have you to hold in my arms, but you are always with me, especially in my mind, heart and soul.

As for music, there is a band called Clutch, which has a song called "Gone Cold." The chorus goes:

My heart is gone, I've gone cold.

This song, like many others, starts the tears. I can be happy (or think I am or try to be) when out of nowhere I become overwhelmed with grief, which has a mind of its own.

I cannot wait to be with you, Cheeks, but as a band called Dorothy sings "Ain't Our Time to Die." I will try to live, not just survive, as I am sure you will tell me. Your hold on me, though, gets stronger every moment. I will keep exploring and sharing God's Word. How I miss our discussions about His Word.

Another day closer, Brook.

All my love yesterday, today and forever.

* * *

12/22/22

Dearest Anna,

It is said that life grows and grief stays the same. Well, life goes on, but my grief does not stay the same. My love for you continues to grow and so does my grief. Love is said to be infinite and I think the same about grief. Each moment, I seem to fall deeper into the abyss of grief and missing you. My heart was broken into infinite pieces when you were called home. Tears seem to be infinite, too. I know I still have work to be done here, but am looking forward to when I hear the bells of Heaven and I am home with you, Brook.

Christmas was always special and it became even more special when we became engaged to be married on Christmas day. The gift of you was and continues to be heavenly.

It is strange, Doll, how I feel you in my tears, so I shed them often. It is also strange how I feel I am not here at times, but not in Heaven when I think of you, which is often. Sometimes I feel like I am chasing after you somewhere. It's like we are playing a child's game through space. I seem to get closer, but then …

I often look at the beauty of God's creation and wonder what you experience.

As for music, I love a band called Radio Moscow (I know you always laughed at and wondered how I found things). I love their song called "250 Miles," which includes, "I miss you little girl, I hope you miss me just the same."

The first album of Blood, Sweat & Tears, called Child is Father to the Man, which could be considered one of the best ever made, contains a song called "My Days are Numbered." The lyrics:

> *I woke up and found*
> *No one beside me*
> *No hand to hold onto*
> *and no lips to guide me*
> *what a hard world to face*
> *in the light of an angry sun*
> *ain't it hard to get on,*
> *if you ain't got that someone*
> *And it seems that my days are numbered*
> *down to a precious few*
> *People I know that*
> *My days are numbered*

'cause I can't get it back together
without you.
I see the heaven moonlight
see it drippin' down my window
flowing like a river
through the tears that I have cried
I gotta find myself, hey
a reason to go on living
but you can't breathe life into somethin'
that's already died
And it seems that my days are numbered
down to a precious few
People I know that
My days are numbered
'cause I can't get it back together
without you.
And it seems that my days are numbered
down to a precious few
People I know that
My days are numbered
'cause I can't get it back together
without you.
Hey Hey
I got ta tell you right now
Every morning

I know we talked about another song on the album. I used to say the title, "I Love You More Than You'll Ever Know," and then you will know when you get to Heaven. You also know there are other songs on this album that fit us, too.

In my mind, I want to write these notes. Catharsis? You already know. It's the only way I have to release my feelings. Somehow this makes me happy.

Another day closer, Cheeks.

All my love yesterday, today and forever

* * *

06/27/23

Dearest Anna,

Soon it will be three years since God called you home. While my grief is deep and painful, this might sound strange, but I celebrate that for you. Three years seems like now. Forty years of marriage and being with you nearly every day for forty-six years seems like now. Everything we did seems like now. We met at a party neither of us wanted to attend and met (divine intervention, indeed!). We dated, married, and raised a family. It all seems like now. I was blessed and beyond ecstatic to have and be with you. Just knowing you were around made everything meaningful and wonderful.

Recently, the last surviving member of Lynyrd Skynyrd passed away. You can guess my next lines. The lyrics start:

If I leave here tomorrow
Would you still remember me?
For I must be traveling on now

Of course you are still here as you are part of my heart (what is left of it), mind and soul. However, it has been extremely difficult getting on without you and I long to be with you in Paradise forever.

> *When two souls have finally found
> each other, there is established between
> them a union which begins on earth
> and continues forever in heaven.*
> ~ *Victor Hugo*

    I recently had meniscus surgery and know you laughed at me because you had both knees done and breezed through it.

    Following up with my new family doctor, the young nurse doing an examination loved hearing my stories about you and us. She said she felt as if she knew you and said it sounds like a movie. While I was waiting in the doctor's office, "Dream On" by Aerosmith came on. When the part "Maybe tomorrow, the good Lord will take you away," played you can imagine my tears and hopes for tomorrow, even now as I write this love letter.

    I recently took a refresher course in CPR as required by Little League. You were front and center there as I used CPR on you. I saw you take your last breath and wonder how you will watch mine.

    Sometimes I watch the clock tick and dust settle and think so what?

    I am trying to decorate our home, which is difficult because it was always about you. When I tell the kids my ideas, they laugh and say Mom would not like that. How many times did I offer an idea to you? You listened with a smile and said good for your idea, but no.

    Listening to the Yes album. Beautiful introduction to classical music, I was a very young teenager, the future was bright...Divine intervention in a few short years... untold happiness...tears...future is past.

    It is said the best is yet to come and God has only our happiness...

Then there is Cream and "Can't Find My Way Home." You were (and still are) my home and now you are in our true home.

Your picture on my iPhone seems to say you are at peace. It also seems to tell me my work here is not over and going well. Remember the brother of one of my best friends from my childhood? Well, one morning, he apparently missed my morning note. He contacted me to see if I was alright. He said he has a string of people who look forward to the Word every morning.

Come for me (another song I love), Q.

> *If you love deeply, you're going to get hurt badly.*
> *But it's still worth it.*
> *~ C.S. Lewis*

My will is to be with you, Doll, but I know it is God's will I must follow. Love is eternal and my grief will end with my last breath and I meet you in Heaven.

Another day closer, Cheeks.

All my love yesterday, today and forever.

* * *

08/17/23

Dearest Anna,

My Cheeks, how it seems strange that God put us together forty-nine years ago (very lucky for me, Doll!) and it feels like yesterday (cue the song). Only through His grace have I been able to survive without you. Yes, survive because life unalterably changed when you went to Heaven.

When I see you on my phone, I smile beyond belief inside and outside. I know it sounds crazy, but I want to hug my phone. Then I realize you can't hug me, at least physically, and I want to throw the phone at a wall. I know you will give me that look. I know you are present in spirit. I feel it, but can't touch you. Your presence is still a great present and I have to accept it until I join you in Paradise.

I have seen so many coleus plants lately and I laugh as I remember how you said that name with a laugh.

Well, Q, you know that I finally contacted a publisher to put my Scripture-based notes, my love letters to you in Heaven and the morning love notes in a book. The publisher is Red Penguin Books. When I received a letter of acceptance, it came from the head of the company and she is known as the head penguin. Steven laughed and said you had a hand in it. I said to him, "Did you know Mom wanted to be a nun? Not just any nun, but the head penguin."

He laughed and said "Oh, I know."

The head penguin laughed, too, when I told her this. The working title of the book is *Thoughts From & To Heaven*. The & will be a Cross with a dove. I loved how we talked about what I might write for the Scripture-based notes and why with you. After all those years we continued to grow in each other and God.

I am glad that you are always in my mind. No matter what happens, there you are. How could you not be?

You know I love the band Steppenwolf. I know you did, too, but I doubt you knew the song called "Corina, Corina," which was written by Bob Dylan. When I listen to it on the live album with the big wolf face on the cover, I change it to Anna, Anna. Tears of joy and sadness flow together.

> Corrina, Corrina
> Girl, where you been so long?
> Corrina, Corrina
> Girl, where you been so long?
> I been worrying about you, baby
> Baby, please come home
>
> I got a bird that whistles
> I got a bird that sings
> I got a bird that whistles
> I got a bird that sings
> But I ain't got Corrina
> Life don't mean a thing
>
> Corrina, Corrina
> Girl, you're on my mind
> Corrina, Corrina
> Girl, you're on my mind
> I'm a-sittin down thinkin' of you
> I just can't keep from crying

There is another Clapton tune that always gets to me. It is called "She's Gone."

> In the middle of the night, in the middle of the day
> She can make me feel alright and make it all okay
> She can make me feel so good by looking in my eye
> She can take me to the edge, take me to the sky
>
> She's gone, she's gone, she's gone
> I'm telling you she's gone

She put her hands in my hair, put her kiss on my face
She puts my heart in my mouth, my soul in its place
Who could love me like she does?
Who could even start to try?
She can love me more than you, I never wonder why

She's gone, she's gone, she's gone
I'm telling you she's gone

She's gone, she's gone, she's gone
I'm telling you she's gone

Like a shadow in the dark, like a ripple on a stream
I see her float across my mind like a picture in a dream
And the more that I know, seems the more that I care
Give the world and all I own
Just to know that she's still there
Like a shadow in the dark, like a ripple in a stream
But you're floating on my mind

She's gone, she's gone, she's gone
I'm telling you she's gone

She's gone, she's gone, she's gone
I'm telling you she's gone

Being a widower is not the same as being single. You see, when I was single I was younger, and the young always think they know everything. When I met you and grew with you, you showed me what really mattered. As I like to say, I was me because of you. My math was simple; $1 + 1 = 1$. Now, it is $1 - 1 = 0$. I will not be me until I am with you in Paradise.

Words are not needed here as our hearts understand the language of love by instinct the moment our souls recognize each other. (Sensual Musing of Jen)

I get great satisfaction writing these love letters. It reminds me of when I wrote them years ago and delivered them to your door. I am also happy knowing I help others put a smile on their face and/or heart.

Dear Brook, please pray for me and guide me.

Another day closer, Cheeks.

All my love yesterday, today and forever.

* * *

11/24/23

Dearest Anna,

This was my fourth Thanksgiving without you. Things do not get easier! The pain is always there and it never diminishes. How many times have I told the story of our first Thanksgiving together. You made lasagna to bring to my parents' home. Everyone loved it. I sat next to my Dad. He leaned over and said, "Don't lose this one." Well, I did not lose you for forty-six years.

We widowers learn that grief comes in waves and are informed to learn how to swim. How can one swim when the waves keep coming without warning? If it is not the waves, then it is the tears. They often flow freely, but sometimes I wonder if I will drown in them as there seems to be no end to them inside of me.

I know I am supposed to be thankful in all situations. I am so thankful for the forty-six years. I am also thankful that you are in Paradise, Cheeks. I know God comes first, but this is so difficult.

Re-inventing myself sucks. I loved being part of us. Recently, Steven and Robin had a commitment ceremony, which was new to me. I now have a new extended family and it sucks that you are not here to be part of it. I think of how we would discuss this, Q. Yesterday, I imagined how we would come home after Thanksgiving with the kids and I would unfasten your necklace, Doll.

These lyrics from "One" by Three Dog Night express my feelings:

> *One is the loneliest number, whoa-oh, worse than two*
> *It's just no good anymore since you went away*
> *Now, I spend my time just making rhymes of yesterday*

Oh, how I long to hear your voice and feel your touch.
One day closer, Cheeks.
All my love yesterday, today and forever.

* * *

12/22/23

Dearest Anna,

This is my fourth Christmas without Anna, with whom I celebrated forty-six. After three lonely years, God granted my wishes and gave me what I wanted and, more importantly, needed in one wonderful woman. She has rescued me. I am so incredibly blessed by all God has done for me in my life. I still would do anything to have Anna again. It is incredibly strange how I can be incredibly happy with Kristina while at the same time heartbroken over Anna. Two exactly opposite feelings sharing the same spot in my mind, heart and soul.

* * *

07/06/24

Dearest Anna,

You were called home four years ago. How can that be? It seems like now. It seems like a long time ago. It seems like a dream.

This may sound strange, but while I grieve, I celebrate your being home in Heaven. It seems I write these love letters to you in Heaven like I did after meeting you. I wish I could have become part of you while passing. We were part of each other in most everything. You still have a great impact on me and my life. How could it not be so? A Native American saying about death: You live in my heart, mind and spirit.

I like a band called Speck Mountain. They have a song called "I Feel Eternal." When I hear or think of it, you come to mind. Well actually, you never left it, the thought is more vivid. Her voice, the words, and music paint pictures of you in my mind. The lyrics:

Whoa...shake it off and lay down your sin
The tides will rise, and they will fall again.
Invisible signs I have seen for days.
Close your eyes and let your dreams pass my way.
And oh...gotta hand up on the soul
And I...I feel eternal
Oh my fall...lay down your head
Love and loss, don't come again
Stars at night and the sun's cruel rays
The abler soul will always know their way
And oh...gotta hand up on the soul
And I...I feel eternal

I came across the following quote, which, I think goes well with the song:

> *For death is no more than a turning of us over*
> *from time to eternity.*
> *~ William Penn*

You are more eternal now, Cheeks.

I recently had a few pictures of you made on glass frames. They are beautiful and a blessing. I smile and talk with you either verbally or in my soul. Often I cry.

Recently, there was a graduation near work. I saw many graduates and thought of how I went to college at night four nights a week for four years. You had French toast ready for me late at night. You never really liked cooking, but when you did cook it was great. Besides the French toast, there is nothing like your chicken cutlets, lasagna, sauce or meatballs. Actually, food just does not taste the same since you were called home. Nothing is the same. Speaking of food, I am thinking of getting a new kitchen table. I never really liked this one, but I shared meals here with you. I am troubled thinking about getting rid of the table and chairs as you sat in them.

I love the poem "Do Not Stand At My Grave and Weep."

Do not stand at my grave and weep;
I am not there. I do not sleep.
I am a thousand winds that blow.
I am the diamond glints on snow.
I am the sunlight on ripened grain.
I am the gentle autumn rain.
When you awaken in the morning's hush

I am the swift uplifting rush
Of quiet birds in circled flight.
I am the soft stars that shine at night.
Do not stand at my grave and cry;
I am not there.
I did not die.

Other things say you are right beside me. Oh, how I wish I could see, hear and hold you if just for a moment.

I look for you everywhere, doll.

No matter where I find myself or what I am doing, it always comes back to you.

I read where a widow wrote "I just want to feel normal again." I thought that will never happen. I dislike the expression "new normal" as now it means pain, sadness and everything else that goes along with you not being here with me. Oh, I know you are still here in spirit, but ...

I usually find a way to speak about you no matter the situation.

Another day closer, Q.

All my love yesterday, today and forever.

* * *

Love Notes

LOVE NOTES

God morning,
A life lived in love will never be dull.
~ *Leo Buscaglia*
Steve
* * *

God morning,
It would not be true love if there were not any problems and people standing in your way. It is true love when you realize that these problems and people don't really matter.
~ *Unknown*
Steve
* * *

God morning,
No man, or woman, is worth your tears, but once you find one that is, he, or she, won't make you cry.
~ *Unknown*
Unless the tears are of happiness.
Steve
* * *

God morning,
Love is walking in the rain together.
~ *Unknown*
Steve
* * *

God morning,
I would be nothing without your unconditional and undying love.
~ *Unknown*

Steve
* * *

God morning,
It has been said that we need just three things in life: Something to do, something to look forward to and someone to love.
~ Unknown
Steve
* * *

God morning,
Life is short, live it.
Love is rare, grab it.
Anger is bad, dump it.
Fear is awful, face it.
Memories are sweet. Cherish them.
~ Unknown
Steve
* * *

God morning,
This wide world holds;
O Love,
My world is you.
~ Unknown
Steve
* * *

God morning,
Where we love is home – home that our feet may leave, but not our hearts.

~ *Oliver Wendell Holmes, Sr.*
Steve
* * *

Good morning,
The sound of a kiss is not so loud as that of a cannon,
but its echo lasts a great deal longer.
~ *Oliver Wendell Holmes, Sr.*
Steve
* * *

Good morning,
The giving of love and understanding is an education in itself.
~ *Eleanor Roosevelt*
Steve
* * *

Good morning,
All you need is love.
~ *John Lennon*
Steve
* * *

Good morning,
Love makes everything that is heavy light.
~ *Thomas A. Kempis*
Steve
* * *

Good morning,
It is love, not reason, that is stronger than death.
~ *Thomas Mann*

Steve

***

Good morning,
True love is usually the most inconvenient kind.
~ *Kiera Cass*
Steve

***

Good morning,
So, fall asleep love, loved by me... for I know love, I am loved by thee.
~ *Robert Browning*
Steve

***

Good morning,
To love means to open ourselves to the negative as well as the positive – to grief, sorrow, and disappointment as well as to joy, fulfillment, and an intensity of consciousness we did not know was possible before
~ *Rollo May*
Steve

***

Good morning,
Only love expands intelligence. To live in love is to accept the other and the conditions of his existence as a source of richness, not as opposition, restriction or limitation.
~ *Humberto Maturana*

Steve

* * *

God morning,

The arms of love encompass you with your present, your past, your future, the arms of love gather you together.
~ *Antoine de Saint-Exupéry*
Steve

* * *

God morning,

Love is the only freedom in the world because it so elevates the spirit that the laws of humanity and the phenomena of nature do not alter its course.
~ *Khalil Gibran*
Steve

* * *

God morning,

It seems everyone's so worried about getting hurt that they forget about letting love happen.
~ *Carlos Salinas*
Steve

* * *

God morning,

They do not love that do not show their love. The course of true love never did run smooth. Love is familiar. Love is a devil. There is no evil angel but Love.
~ *William Shakespeare*

Steve
* * *

God morning,
Take love when love is given.
~ *Sara Teasdale*
Steve
* * *

God morning,
Wherever you find real love, you will also find humility. Remember something: humility is not a weak and timid quality. Too often we feel that humility is a sign of weakness. This is not so. It is the sign of strength and security.
~ *Kathryn Kuhlman*
Steve
* * *

God morning,
But love is always new. Regardless of whether we love once, twice, or a dozen times in our life, we always face a brand-new situation. Love can consign us to hell or to paradise, but it always takes us somewhere. We simply have to accept it, because it is what nourishes our existence. We have to take love where we find it, even if that means hours, days, weeks of disappointment and sadness.
~ *Paulo Coelho*
Steve
* * *

LOVE NOTES

God morning,
Love is, above all, the gift of oneself.
~ *Jean Anouilh*
Steve
* * *

God morning,
That love is reverence, and worship, and glory, and the upward glance. Not a bandage for dirty sores. But they don't know it. Those who speak of love most promiscuously are the ones who've never felt it. They make some sort of feeble stew out of sympathy, compassion, contempt, and general indifference, and they call it love. Once you've felt what it means to love as you and I know it – the total passion for the total height – you're incapable of anything less.
~ *Ayn Rand*
Steve
* * *

God morning,
Things didn't work between the two of them, because they loved the same person. He loved her and she loved herself.
~ *Ravinder Singh*
Steve
* * *

God morning,
In the end, the love you take is equal to the love you make.
~ *Paul McCartney*

Steve

* * *

Good morning,
Who is wise in love, love most, say least.
~ *Alfred Lord Tennyson*
Steve

* * *

Good morning,
We choose those we like; with those we love, we have no say in the matter.
~ *Mignon McLaughlin*
Steve

* * *

Good morning,
Respect was invented to cover the empty place where love should be.
~ *Leo Tolstoy*
Steve

* * *

Good morning,
Love takes up where knowledge leaves off.
~ *Thomas Aquinas*
Steve

* * *

Good morning,
Trust your heart if the seas catch fire, live by love though the stars walk backward.

~ e.e. cummings
Steve
* * *

Good morning,
To love for the sake of being loved is human, but to love for the sake of loving is angelic.
~ Alphonse de Lamartine
Steve
* * *

Good morning,
There is the same difference in a person before and after he is in love, as there is in an unlighted lamp and one that is burning.
~ Vincent van Gogh
Steve
* * *

Good morning,
When you love there is no "I," so you cannot say "I love you," only love is.
~ Ivan Rados
Steve
* * *

Good morning,
There is no instinct like that of the heart.
~ Lord Byron
Steve
* * *

LOVE NOTES

Good morning,
You know, when it works, love is pretty amazing. It's not over-rated. There's a reason for all those songs.
~ Sarah Dessen
Steve
* * *

Good morning,
Never close your lips to those whom you have already opened your heart.
~ Charles Dickens
Steve
* * *

Good morning,
When your happiness is someone else's happiness, that is love.
~ Lana Del Rey
Steve
* * *

Good morning,
Whatever you choose for yourself, give to another. If you choose to be happy, cause another to be happy. If you choose to be prosperous, cause another to prosper. If you choose more love in your life, cause another to have more love in theirs.
~ Neale Donald Walsch
Steve
* * *

God morning,
The best things in life are free. And it is important never to lose sight of that. So look around you. Wherever you see friendship, loyalty, laughter, and love...there is your treasure.
~ *Neale Donald Walsch*
Steve
* * *

God morning,
Death is but a transition from this life to another existence where there is no more pain and anguish. All the bitterness and disagreements will vanish, and the only thing that lives forever is love.
~ *Elisabeth Kubler-Ross*
Steve
* * *

God morning,
If I were to meet the slave-traders who kidnapped me and even those who tortured me, I would kneel and kiss their hands, for if that did not happen, I would not be a Christian and Religious today... The Lord has loved me so much: we must love everyone... we must be compassionate!
~ *Josephine Bakhita*
Steve
* * *

God morning,
What the heart loves, the will chooses, and the mind justifies.
~ *Thomas Cranmer*

Steve

* * *

God morning,
Just as the sun shares itself for all of us to exist, you are here to shine bright with your love.

~ *Harold W. Becker*

Steve

* * *

God morning,
Know that success and inner peace are your birthright, that you are a child of God and as such that you're entitled to a life filled with joy, love and happiness.

~ *Wayne Dyer*

Steve

* * *

God morning,
Send out love and harmony, put your mind and body in a peaceful place, and then allow the universe to work in the perfect way that it knows how.

~ *Wayne Dyer*

Steve

* * *

God morning,
Joy comes not through possession or ownership but through a wise and loving heart.

~ *Gautama Buddha*

Steve
* * *

God morning,

The worst disease in the world is hate. And the cure for hate is love.

~ *India.Arie*

Steve
* * *

God morning,

Be ready for love when it does come. Prepare the field and be ready to nourish love. Be loving, and you will be lovable. Be open and receptive to love.

~ *Louise Hay*

Steve
* * *

God morning,

The universe is wired with the electricity of God, & each of us is a lamp. It doesn't matter the size or shape of the lamp; it only matters that the lamp is plugged in. With every prayer, every thought of forgiveness, every meditation, every act of love, we plug in. The more of us who plug in, the more the darkness of the world will be cast from our midst. Today, let's all increase love's wattage!

~ *Marianne Williamson*

Steve
* * *

God morning,
We have before us the glorious opportunity to inject a new dimension of love into the veins of our civilization.
~ *Martin Luther King, Jr.*
Steve
* * *

God morning,
Loving people is the highest level of spiritual warfare that we could ever do.
~ *Joyce Meyer*
Steve
* * *

God morning,
Love is contagious. When I share love, it comes back to me multiplied. Love opens every door.
~ *Louise Hay*
Steve
* * *

God morning,
Some people consider the practice of love and compassion is only related to religious practice and if they are not interested in religion they neglect these inner values. But love and compassion are qualities that human beings require just to live together.
~ *Dalai Lama*
Steve
* * *

God morning,
If you find it in your heart to care for somebody else, you will have succeeded.
~ *Maya Angelou*
Steve
* * *

God morning,
Love looks around to see who is in need.
~ *T. B. Joshua*
Steve
* * *

God morning,
Too many young folk have an addiction to superficial things and not enough conviction for substantial things like justice, truth and love.
~ *Cornel West*
Steve
* * *

God morning,
Love is what we are; we don't get it from somebody, we can't give it to anybody, we can't fall in it or fall out of it. Love is our true Being.
~ *Krishna Das*
Steve
* * *

God morning,
There is no such thing as a faithless person; we either have faith in the power of love, or faith in the power of fear. For faith is an aspect of consciousness. Have faith in love, and fear will lose its power over you. Have faith in forgiveness, and your self-hatred will fall away. Have faith in miracles, and they will come to you.

~ *Marianne Williamson*
Steve
* * *

God morning,
Love, compassion and concern for others are real sources of happiness. If you have these in abundance, you will not be disturbed even by the most uncomfortable circumstances. If you nurse hatred, however, you will not be happy even in the lap of luxury. Thus, if we really want happiness, we must widen the sphere of love. This is both religious thinking and basic common sense.

~ *Dalai Lama*
Steve
* * *

God morning,
The world can be better if there's love, tolerance and humility.

~ *Irena Sendler*
Steve
* * *

God morning,
While people are often content to criticize and blame others for what goes wrong, surely we should at least attempt to put

forward constructive ideas. One thing is for certain: given human beings' love of truth, justice, peace, and freedom, creating a better, more compassionate world is a genuine possibility. The potential is there.

~ *Dalai Lama*
Steve

* * *

God morning,

God designed it this way; He intended that His great power, wisdom, and love should become visible in very ordinary and otherwise inconsequential people.

~ *Ray Stedman*
Steve

* * *

God morning,

I guarantee that the seed you plant in love, no matter how small, will grow into a mighty tree of refuge. We all want a future for ourselves and we must now care enough to create, nurture and secure a future for our children.

~ *Afeni Shakur*
Steve

* * *

God morning,

Love is heaven and fear is hell. Where you place your attention is where you live.

~ *Alan Cohen*
Steve

* * *

Good morning,
If someone thinks that love and peace is a cliche that must have been left behind in the Sixties, that's his problem. Love and peace are eternal.
~ *John Lennon*
Steve
* * *

Good morning,
We are all born for love. It is the principle of existence, and its only end.
~ *Benjamin Disraeli*
Steve
* * *

Good morning,
At the evening of life, we shall be judged on our love.
~ *John of the Cross*
Steve
* * *

Good morning,
All the beautiful sentiments in the world weigh less than a single lovely action.
~ *James Russell Lowell*
Steve
* * *

Good morning,
There is a land of the living and a land of the dead and the bridge is love, the only survival, the only meaning.

~ *Thornton Wilder*
Steve
* * *

God morning,
I think... if it is true that there are as many minds as there are heads, then there are as many kinds of love as there are hearts.
~ *Leo Tolstoy*
Steve
* * *

God morning,
Love is how you stay alive, even after you are gone.
~ *Mitch Albom*
Steve
* * *

God morning,
The salvation of man is through love and in love.
~ *Viktor E. Frankl*
Steve
* * *

God morning,
In order to create there must be a dynamic force, and what force is more potent than love?
~ *Igor Stravinsky*
Steve
* * *

Good morning,
No, this trick won't work... How on earth are you ever going to explain in terms of chemistry and physics so important a biological phenomenon as first love?
~ Albert Einstein
Steve
* * *

Good morning,
We love life, not because we are used to living but because we are used to loving.
~ Friedrich Nietzsche
Steve
* * *

Good morning,
Eternity is in love with the productions of time.
~ William Blake
Steve
* * *

Good morning,
Love is the most powerful force in the world.
~ Dallin H. Oaks
Steve
* * *

Good morning,
Anyone who falls in love is searching for the missing pieces of themselves.
~ Haruki Murakami

Steve
* * *

Good morning,
Art is not necessary at all. All that is necessary to make this world a better place to live in is to love – to love as Christ loved, as Buddha loved.
~ *Isadora Duncan*
Steve
* * *

Good morning,
If equal affection cannot be, let the more loving be me.
~ *W. H. Auden*
Steve
* * *

Good morning,
To try to write love is to confront the muck of language: that region of hysteria where language is both too much and too little, excessive and impoverished.
~ *Roland Barthes*
Steve
* * *

Good morning,
Love is my religion – I could die for it.
~ *John Keats*
Steve
* * *

God morning,
Love conquers all things except poverty and toothache.
~ Mae West
Steve
* * *

God morning,
Be everything with so much love in your heart that you would never want to do it any other way.
~ Amrit Desai
Steve
* * *

God morning,
Love and you shall be loved. All love is mathematically just, as much as two sides of an algebraic equation.
~ Ralph Waldo Emerson
Steve
* * *

God morning,
What was love, really? Flowers, chocolate, and poetry? Or was it something else? Was it being able to finish someone's jokes? Was it having absolute faith that someone was there at your back? Was it knowing someone so well that they instantly understood why you did the things you did—and shared those same beliefs?
~ Richelle Mead
Steve
* * *

God morning,
Oh, how a quiet love can drown out every fear.
~ *Jessica Katoff*
Steve

* * *

God morning,
Everything but "I LOVE YOU" is small talk.
~ *Andrea Gibson*
Steve

* * *

God morning,
Love knows not distance; it hath no continent; its eyes are for the stars.
~ *Gilbert Parker*
Steve

* * *

God morning,
Love is a force more formidable than any other. It is invisible – it cannot be seen or measured, yet it is powerful enough to transform you in a moment, and offer you more joy than any material possession could.
~ *Barbara De Angelis*
Steve

* * *

God morning,
A very small degree of hope is sufficient to cause the birth of love.

LOVE NOTES

~ Stendhal
Steve

* * *

God morning,
Nirvana or lasting enlightenment or true spiritual growth can be achieved only through persistent exercise of real love.

~ M. Scott Peck
Steve

* * *

God morning,
In love, no question is ever preposterous.

~ André Brink
Steve

* * *

God morning,
We can give without loving, but we can't love without giving. In fact, love is nothing unless we give it to someone.

~ John Wooden
Steve

* * *

God morning,
There is nothing holier in this life of ours than the first consciousness of love, the first fluttering of its silken wings.

~ Henry Wadsworth Longfellow
Steve

* * *

Good morning,
Love cannot endure indifference. It needs to be wanted. Like a lamp, it needs to be fed out of the oil of another's heart, or its flame burns low.
~ *Henry Ward Beecher*
Steve

* * *

Good morning,
Lord, grant that I might not so much seek to be loved as to love.
~ *Francis of Assisi*
Steve

* * *

Good morning,
I have often wondered how it is that every man loves himself more than all the rest of men, but yet sets less value on his own opinions of himself than on the opinions of others.
~ *Marcus Aurelius*
Steve

* * *

Good morning,
Love is life. And if you miss love, you miss life.
~ *Leo Buscaglia*
Steve

* * *

Good morning,
Love is the only gold.
~ *Alfred Lord Tennyson*

Steve

* * *

Good morning,
Love is the ultimate expression of the will to live.
~ *Tom Wolfe*
Steve

* * *

Good morning,
Love will draw an elephant through a key-hole.
~ *Samuel Richardson*
Steve

* * *

Good morning,
The more you are motivated by Love, The more Fearless & Free your action will be.
~ *Dalai Lama*
Steve

* * *

Good morning,
Love, the poet said, is woman's whole existence.
~ *Virginia Woolf*
Steve

* * *

Good morning,
Love is what carries you, for it is always there, even in the dark, or most in the dark, but shining out at times like gold stitches in a piece of embroidery.

~ Wendell Berry
Steve
* * *

God morning,
The best things in life aren't things.
~ Art Buchwald
Steve
* * *

God morning,
Relish love in your old age! Aged love is like aged wine; it becomes more satisfying, more refreshing, more valuable, more appreciated and more intoxicating!
~ Leo Buscaglia
Steve
* * *

God morning,
Could we but think with the intensity we love with, we might do great things.
~ Philip James Bailey
Steve
* * *

God morning,
'Tis said of love that it sometimes goes, sometimes flies; runs with one, walks gravely with another; turns a third into ice, and sets a fourth in a flame: it wounds one, another it kills: like lightning it begins and ends in the same moment: it makes that fort

yield at night which it besieged but in the morning; for there is no force able to resist it.

~ Miguel de Cervantes

Steve

* * *

God morning,
Love is the magician, the enchanter, that changes worthless things to joy, and makes right royal kings and queens of common clay. It is the perfume of that wondrous flower, the heart, and without that sacred passion, that divine swoon, we are less than beasts; but with it, earth is heaven, and we are gods.

~ Robert Green Ingersoll

Steve

* * *

God morning,
Love is the wild card of existence.

~ Rita Mae Brown

Steve

* * *

God morning,
Were it not for love, Poor life would be a ship not worth launching.

~ Edwin Arlington Robinson

Steve

* * *

Good morning,
I know of no better definition of love than the one given by Proust – Love is space and time measured by the heart.
~ Gian Carlo Menotti
Steve

* * *

Good morning,
It is good to love many things, for therein lies the true strength, and whosoever loves much performs much, and can accomplish much, and what is done in love is well done.
~ Vincent van Gogh
Steve

* * *

Good morning,
Use the power of your word in the direction of truth and love.
~ Miguel Angel Ruiz
Steve

* * *

Good morning,
Love goes toward love as schoolboys from their books, But love from love, toward school with heavy looks.
~ William Shakespeare
Steve

* * *

Good morning,
Love is primarily giving. It's an action that leads to a feeling, not a feeling first.

~ Timothy Keller
Steve
* * *

Good morning,
Mysterious love, uncertain treasure, hast thou more of pain or pleasure! Endless torments dwell about thee: Yet who would live, and live without thee!
~ Joseph Addison
Steve
* * *

Good morning,
Let no one who loves be unhappy, even love unreturned has its rainbow.
~ James M. Barrie
Steve
* * *

Good morning,
We love because it's the only true adventure.
~ Nikki Giovanni
Steve
* * *

Good morning,
Give all to love; Obey thy heart.
~ Ralph Waldo Emerson
Steve
* * *

God morning,
Divine love always has met and always will meet every human need.
~ Mary Baker Eddy
Steve
* * *

God morning,
But one of the attributes of love, like art, is to bring harmony and order out of chaos, to introduce meaning and affect where before there was none, to give rhythmic variations, highs and lows to a landscape that was previously flat.
~ Molly Haskell
Steve
* * *

God morning,
Love is the ultimate truth at the heart of the universe and transcends all boundaries.
~ Deepak Chopra
Steve
* * *

God morning,
Hear my soul speak. Of the very instant that I saw you, Did my heart fly at your service.
~ William Shakespeare
Steve
* * *

God morning,
Where love and wisdom drink out of the same cup, in this every-day world, it is the exception.
~ *Suzanne Curchod*
Steve
* * *

God morning,
If love does not know how to give and take without restrictions, it is not love, but a transaction that never fails to lay stress on a plus and a minus.
~ *Emma Goldman*
Steve
* * *

God morning,
Love is seeing without eyes, hearing without ears; hatred is nothing.
~ *Douglas Horton*
Steve
* * *

God morning,
No love is entirely without worth, even when the frivolous calls to the frivolous and the base to the base.
~ *Iris Murdoch*
Steve
* * *

God morning,
He stepped down, trying not to look long at her, as if she were the sun, yet he saw her, like the sun, even without looking.
~ Leo Tolstoy
Steve
* * *

God morning,
You've gotta dance like there's nobody watching, Love like you'll never be hurt.
~ William Watson Purkey
Steve
* * *

God morning,
Eventually, you will come to understand that love heals everything, and love is all there is.
~ Gary Zukav
Steve
* * *

God morning,
Love is most nearly itself when here and now cease to matter.
~ T. S. Eliot
Steve
* * *

God morning,
There is no surprise more magical than the surprise of being loved: It is God's finger on man's shoulder.
~ Charles Morgan

Steve

* * *

God morning,
Riches take wings, comforts vanish, hope withers away, but love stays with us. Love is God.
~ *Lew Wallace*
Steve

* * *

God morning,
Harmony is pure love, for love is a concerto.
~ *Lope de Vega*
Steve

* * *

God morning,
We are most alive when we're in love.
~ *John Updike*
Steve

* * *

God morning,
Love is perfect kindness.
~ *Joseph Campbell*
Steve

* * *

God morning,
Love is a state of mind which has nothing to do with the mind.
~ *Bob Phillips*

Steve
* * *

God morning,

You know love is everything you say A whisper, a word Promises you give You feel it in the heartbeat of the day You know this is the way love is.

~ Enya

Steve
* * *

God morning,

Love is forgiving and Love is for giving.

~ Wayne Dyer

Steve
* * *

God morning,

Goodness is stronger than evil.
Love is stronger than hate.
Light is stronger than darkness.
Life is stronger than death.
Victory is ours through Him who loved us.

~ Desmond Tutu

Steve
* * *

God morning,

Love can never possess. Love is giving freedom to the other. Love is an unconditional gift, it is not a bargain.

~ Rajneesh

Steve

* * *

Good morning,
Some say that true love is a mirage; seek it anyway, for all else is surely desert.

~ *Robert Breault*

Steve

* * *

Good morning,
Love is to the heart what the summer is to the farmer's year. It brings to harvest all the loveliest flowers of the soul.

~ *Billy Graham*

Steve

* * *

Good morning,
Never self-possessed, or prudent, love is all abandonment.

~ *Ralph Waldo Emerson*

Steve

* * *

Good morning,
Love is energy of life.

~ *Robert Browning*

Steve

* * *

Good morning,
He who gives love, receives love.

~ *Omar Torrijos*

Steve
* * *

Good morning,
Being deeply loved by someone gives you strength, while loving someone deeply gives you courage.
~ Laozi
Steve
* * *

Good morning,
Passionate love is a quenchless thirst.
~ Khalil Gibran
Steve
* * *

Good morning,
Love comes unseen; we only see it go.
~ Henry Austin Dobson
Steve
* * *

Good morning,
Love is a spirit all compact of fire.
~ William Shakespeare
Steve
* * *

Good morning,
I can make no apologies for following my heart.
~ Gavin Rossdale

Steve
* * *

Good morning,
It is love, not reason, that is stronger than death.
~ Thomas Mann
Steve
* * *

Good morning,
To fall in love is awfully simple, but to fall out of love is simply awful.
~ Bess Myerson
Steve
* * *

Good morning,
The only reward for love is the experience of loving.
~ John le Carre
Steve
* * *

Good morning,
True love is like ghosts, which everyone talks about and few have seen.
~ Francois de La Rochefoucauld
Steve
* * *

Good morning,
To be brave is to love unconditionally without expecting anything in return.

~ *Madonna Ciccone*
Steve
* * *

Good morning,
He is not a lover who does not love forever.
~ *Euripides*
Steve
* * *

Good morning,
Love is a thing that is full of cares and fears.
~ *Ovid*
Steve
* * *

Good morning,
Love and a red rose can't be hid.
~ *Thomas Holcroft*
Steve
* * *

Good morning,
Love is not a volunteer thing.
~ *Samuel Richardson*
Steve
* * *

Good morning,
In dreams and in love there are no impossibilities.
~ *Janos Arany*

Steve
* * *

God morning,
Love forbids you not to love.
~ *Umberto Giordano*
Steve
* * *

God morning,
Is not a kiss the very autograph of love?
~ *Henry Theophilus Finck*
Steve
* * *

God morning,
In love, we have to dare everything if we really love.
~ *Alain Delon*
Steve
* * *

God morning,
Love is nothing more than a word, and our actions are the only way to truly know it exists.
~ *Sarra Cannon*
Steve
* * *

God morning,
The way to love anything is to realize that it may be lost.
~ *Gilbert K. Chesterton*

Steve
* * *

God morning,
For one human being to love another; that is perhaps the most difficult of all our tasks, the ultimate, the last test and proof, the work for which all other work is but preparation.
~ *Rainer Maria Rilke*
Steve
* * *

God morning,
Love makes your soul crawl out from its hiding place.
~ *Zora Neale Hurston*
Steve
* * *

God morning,
Oh, love will make a dog howl in rhyme.
~ *Francis Beaumont*
Steve
* * *

God morning,
I believe it's so important to love life, enjoy it for its small moments and live without regrets – life is so unpredictable.
~ *Mahesh Manjrekar*
Steve
* * *

God morning,
Love is an energy which exists of itself. It is its own value.

~ Thornton Wilder
Steve
* * *

Good morning,
Speak low, if you speak love.
~ William Shakespeare
Steve
* * *

Good morning,
A loving heart is the truest wisdom.
~ Charles Dickens
Steve
* * *

Good morning,
Love is a two-way street constantly under construction.
~ Carroll Bryant
Steve
* * *

Good morning,
Fear is where there is no love.
Love is where there is no fear.
~ Axl Rose
Steve
* * *

Good morning,
In every living thing there is the desire for love.
~ D. H. Lawrence

Steve
* * *

God morning,
Where there is great love, there are always miracles.
~ Willa Cather
Steve
* * *

God morning,
Love is the only way to grasp another human being in the innermost core of his personality. No one can become fully aware of the very essence of another human being unless he loves him. By his love he is enabled to see the essential traits and features in the beloved person; and even more, he sees that which is potential in him, which is not yet actualized but yet ought to be actualized. Furthermore, by his love, the loving person enables the beloved person to actualize these potentialities. By making him aware of what he can be and of what he should become, he makes these potentialities come true.
~ Viktor E. Frankl
Steve
* * *

God morning,
Love, whether newly born or aroused from a deathlike slumber, must always create sunshine, filling the heart so full of radiance, that it overflows upon the outward world.
~ Nathaniel Hawthorne
Steve
* * *

God morning,
The one thing we can never get enough of is love. And the one thing we never give enough is love.
~ *Henry Miller*
Steve
* * *

God morning,
Love is the emblem of eternity; it confounds all notion of time; effaces all memory of a beginning, all fear of an end.
~ *Madame De Stael*
Steve
* * *

God morning,
A light rain touches my cheek like an angel's butterfly kisses.
~ *Amanda Mosher*
Steve
* * *

God morning,
I have so much of you in my heart.
~ *John Keats*
Steve
* * *

God morning,
Love's greatest gift is its ability to make everything it touches sacred.
~ *Barbara De Angelis*

Steve
* * *

God morning,
Real love is always chaotic. You lose control; you lose perspective. You lose the ability to protect yourself. The greater the love, the greater the chaos. It's a given and that's the secret.
~ *Jonathan Carroll*
Steve
* * *

God morning,
I believe in the immeasurable power of love; that true love can endure any circumstance and reach across any distance.
~ *Steve Maraboli*
Steve
* * *

God morning,
There is the heat of Love, the pulsing rush of Longing, the lover's whisper, irresistible – magic to make the sanest man go mad.
~ *Homer, "The Iliad"*
Steve
* * *

God morning,
A hundred hearts would be too few to carry all my love for you.
~ *Henry Wadsworth*
Steve
* * *

God morning,
Love is the poetry of the senses.
~ Honore de Balzac
Steve
* * *

God morning,
Love is shown more in deeds than in words.
~ St. Ignatius
Steve
* * *

God morning,
It is better to love wisely, no doubt: but to love foolishly is better than not to be able to love at all.
~ William Makepeace Thackeray
Steve
* * *

God morning,
Life is a paradise for those who love many things with a passion.
~ Leo Buscaglia
Steve
* * *

God morning,
Love is never wrong.
~ Melissa Etheridge
Steve
* * *

God morning,
The best love is the kind that awakens the soul and makes us reach for more.
~ *Nicholas Sparks*
Steve
* * *

God morning,
The minute I heard my first love story, I started looking for you.
~ *Rumi*
Steve
* * *

God morning,
Love sneaks up on you like a shadow and shines like a star.
~ *Claire Cross*
Steve
* * *

God morning,
I loved her against reason, against promise, against peace, against hope, against happiness, against all discouragement that could be.
~ *Charles Dickens*
Steve
* * *

God morning,
You gave me a forever within the numbered days, and I'm grateful.
~ *John Green*

Steve
* * *

God morning,
Love unexpectedly leaps from the shadows of the mundane, casting a brilliant light on the ordinary.
~ John Mark Green
Steve
* * *

God morning,
When love arrives, it's a stranger to our hearts, yet it knows the way better than we do.
~ Nikki Giovanni
Steve
* * *

God morning,
I have found the paradox, that if you love until it hurts, there can be no more hurt, only more love.
~ Mother Teresa
Steve
* * *

God morning,
Lost love is still love. It takes a different form, that's all. You can't see their smile or bring them food or tousle their hair or move them around a dance floor. But when those senses weaken another heightens. Memory. Memory becomes your partner. You nurture it. You hold it. You dance with it.
~ Mitch Albom

Steve
* * *

God morning,
Miracles occur naturally as expressions of love. The real miracle is the love that inspires them. In this sense everything that comes from love is a miracle.
~ Marianne Williamson
Steve
* * *

God morning,
The quarrels of lovers are the renewal of love.
~ Jean Racine
Steve
* * *

God morning,
Love is that micro-moment of warmth and connection that you share with another living being.
~ Barbara Fredrickson
Steve
* * *

God morning,
There is love enough in this world for everybody, if people will just look.
~ Kurt Vonnegut
Steve
* * *

God morning,
This was love: a string of coincidences that gathered significance and became miracles.
~ Chimamanda Ngozi Adichie
Steve
* * *

God morning,
The hours I spend with you I look upon as sort of a perfumed garden, a dim twilight, and a fountain singing to it. You and you alone make me feel that I am alive. Other men it is said have seen angels, but I have seen thee and thou art enough.
~ George Edward Moore
Steve
* * *

God morning,
You know what I am going to say. I love you. What other men may mean when they use that expression, I cannot tell; what I mean is, that I am under the influence of some tremendous attraction which I have resisted in vain, and which overmasters me.
~ Charles Dickens
Steve
* * *

God morning,
Love is a second life.
~ Joseph Addison

Steve

* * *

God morning,

Love is our only reason for living and the only purpose of life. We live for the sake of love, and we live seeking love... It is not surprising that we keep looking for love. All of us are nothing but vibrations of love. We are sustained by love, and in the end we merge back into love.

~ Swami Muktananda

Steve

* * *

God morning,

On the last analysis, then, love is life. Love never faileth and life never faileth so long as there is love.

~ Henry Drummond

Steve

* * *

God morning,

Love built on beauty, soon as beauty, dies.

~ John Donne

Steve

* * *

God morning,

I Cannot Exist Without You. I Am Forgetful Of Everything But Seeing You Again.

~ John Keats

Steve
* * *

God morning,
True love blooms when we care more about another person than we care about ourselves. That is Christ's great atoning example for us, and it ought to be more evident in the kindness we show, the respect we give, and the selflessness and courtesy we employ in our personal relationships.
~ *Jeffrey R. Holland*
Steve
* * *

God morning,
No one can love you until you love yourself, and you cannot love anyone else, until you love yourself.
~ *Raymond Charles Barker*
Steve
* * *

God morning,
Paradise is always where love dwells.
~ *Jean Paul*
Steve
* * *

God morning,
You are the sunshine of my life! Thanks for brightening my world with the warmth of your Love.
~ *Jennie Garth*

Steve
* * *

God morning,

I get that you're scared and that you've been hurt. But doing what is easy and safe is no way to live, and a life without passion and love is so far beneath what you deserve.

~ Kiersten White

Steve
* * *

God morning,

If there's a thing I've learned in my life it's to not be afraid of the responsibility that comes with caring for other people. What we do for love: those things endure. Even if the people you do them for don't.

~ Cassandra Clare

Steve
* * *

God morning,

It is sad not to love, but it is much sadder not to be able to love.

~ Miguel de Unamuno

Steve
* * *

God morning,

Love brings to life whatever is dead around us.

~ Franz Rosenzweig

Steve
* * *

God morning,
Gamble everything for love, if you're a true human being.
~ *Rumi*
Steve
* * *

God morning,
Love is an act of endless forgiveness, a tender look which becomes a habit.
~ *Peter Ustinov*
Steve
* * *

God morning,
Love is fed by the imagination, by which we become wiser than we know, better than we feel, nobler than we are: by which we can see life as a whole, by which and by which alone we can understand others in their real and their ideal relation. Only what is fine, and finely conceived can feed love. But anything will feed hate.
~ *Oscar Wilde*
Steve
* * *

God morning,
Love is not in our choice but in our fate.
~ *John Dryden*
Steve
* * *

LOVE NOTES

God morning,
Beauty kindles love, and only the one who remains captivated by it, only the one who is intoxicated by it, only the one who remains a lover while he is investigating its essence, can hope to penetrate its essence.

~ *Dietrich von Hildebrand*
Steve

* * *

God morning,
When we honestly ask ourselves which person in our lives means the most to us, we often find that it is those who, instead of giving much advice, solutions, or cures, have chosen rather to share our pain and touch our wounds with a gentle and tender hand.

~ *Henri Nouwen*
Steve

* * *

God morning,
Love costs all we are
and will ever be.
Yet it is only love
which sets us free.
A Brave and Startling Truth.

~ *Maya Angelou*
Steve

* * *

Good morning,
A purpose of human life, no matter who is controlling it, is to love whoever is around to be loved.

~ *Kurt Vonnegut*

Steve

* * *

Good morning,
Love is not the absence of logic but logic examined and recalculated heated and curved to fit inside the contours of the heart.

~ *Tammara Webber*

Steve

* * *

Good morning,
To find someone who will love you for no reason, and to shower that person with reasons, that is the ultimate happiness.

~ *Robert Breault*

Steve

* * *

Good morning,
Without love living is easy; but it's meaningless.

~ *Leo Tolstoy*

Steve

* * *

Good morning,
There is only one kind of love, but there are a thousand imitations.

~ *Francois de La Rochefoucauld*

Steve

* * *

God morning,
It is a rare and beautiful thing when we choose to offer love in situations when most people would choose to scorn or ignore.

~ Lysa TerKeurst
Steve

* * *

God morning,
Let love flow so that it cleanses the world. Then man can live in peace, instead of the state of turmoil he has created through his past ways of life, with all those material interests and earthly ambitions.

~ Sai Baba
Steve

* * *

God morning,
We are shaped and fashioned by what we love

~ Johann Wolfgang von Goethe
Steve

* * *

God morning,
Darkness cannot drive out darkness; only light can do that. Hate cannot drive out hate; only love can do that.

~ Martin Luther King, Jr.
Steve

* * *

God morning,
Not where I breathe, but where I love, I live.
~ *Robert Southwell*
Steve
* * *

God morning,
Ask not of me, love, what is love?
Ask what is good of God above;
Ask of the great sun what is light;
Ask what is darkness of the night;
Ask sin of what may be forgiven;
Ask what is happiness of heaven;
Ask what is folly of the crowd;
Ask what is fashion of the shroud;
Ask what is sweetness of thy kiss;
Ask of thyself what beauty is.
~ *Philip James Bailey*
Steve
* * *

God morning,
There is no difficulty that enough love will not conquer: no disease that love will not heal: no door that enough love will not open...It makes no difference how deep set the trouble: how hopeless the outlook: how muddled the tangle: how great the mistake. A sufficient realization of love will dissolve it all. If only you could love enough you would be the happiest and most powerful being in the world.
~ *Emmet Fox*

Steve
* * *

God morning,
Until then, mio dolce amor, a thousand kisses; but give me none in return, for they set my blood on fire.
~ Napoleon Bonaparte
Steve
* * *

God morning,
Gestures, in love, are incomparably more attractive, effective and valuable than words.
~ Francois Rabelais
Steve
* * *

God morning,
Passion makes the world go round. Love just makes it a safer place.
~ Ice T
Steve
* * *

God morning,
Neither a lofty degree of intelligence nor imagination nor both together go to the making of genius. Love, love, love, that is the soul of genius.
~ Wolfgang Amadeus Mozart
Steve
* * *

God morning,
The sweetest joy, the wildest woe is love.
~ Pearl Bailey
Steve
* * *

God morning,
When two people relate to each other authentically and humanly, God is the electricity that surges between them.
~ Martin Buber
Steve
* * *

God morning,
The loving personality seeks not to control, but to nurture, not to dominate, but to empower.
~ Gary Zukav
Steve
* * *

God morning,
Young love is a flame; very pretty, often very hot and fierce, but still only light and flickering. The love of the older and disciplined heart is as coals, deep-burning, unquenchable.
~ Henry Ward Beecher
Steve
* * *

God morning,
Life is pain and the enjoyment of love is an anesthetic.
~ Cesare Pavese

Steve

* * *

God morning,
Whether life is worth living depends on whether there is love in life.
~ R. D. Laing
Steve

* * *

God morning,
Love is the expression of one's values, the greatest reward you can earn for the moral qualities you have achieved in your character and person, the emotional price paid by one man for the joy he receives from the virtues of another.
~ Ayn Rand
Steve

* * *

God morning,
I like not only to be loved, but also to be told I am loved.
~ George Eliot
Steve

* * *

God morning,
Never pretend to a love which you do not actually feel, for love is not ours to command.
~ Alan Watts
Steve

* * *

God morning,
The most precious possession that ever comes to a man in this world is a woman's heart.
~ *J. G. Holland*
Steve
* * *

God morning,
If a person loves only one other person and is indifferent to all others, his love is not love but a symbiotic attachment, or an enlarged egotism.
~ *Erich Fromm*
Steve
* * *

God morning,
Only love can be divided endlessly and still not diminish.
~ *Anne Morrow Lindbergh*
Steve
* * *

God morning,
The most important thing in life is to learn how to give out love, and to let it come in.
~ *Morrie Schwartz*
Steve
* * *

God morning,
True love cannot be found where it does not exist, nor can it be denied where it does.

~ *Torquato Tasso*
Steve
* * *

God morning,
Love is but the discovery of ourselves in others, and the delight in the recognition.
~ *Alexander Smith*
Steve
* * *

God morning,
Love is like quicksilver in the hand. Leave the fingers open and it stays. Clutch it and it darts away.
~ *Dorothy Parker*
Steve
* * *

God morning,
Love the animals, love the plants, love everything. If you love everything, you will perceive the divine mystery in things. Once you perceive it, you will begin to comprehend it better every day. And you will come at last to love the whole world with an all-embracing love.
~ *Fyodor Dostoevsky*
Steve
* * *

God morning,
Love is the triumph of imagination over intelligence.
~ *H. L. Mencken*

Steve
* * *

Good morning,

Pray for the love which allows you to see the good in your companion. Pray for the love that makes weaknesses and mistakes seem small. Pray for the love to make your companion's joy your own. Pray for the love to want to lessen the load and soften the sorrows of your companion.

~ Henry B. Eyring

Steve
* * *

Good morning,

A kiss makes the heart young again and wipes out the years.

~ Rupert Brooke

Steve
* * *

Good morning,

Love has no conditions. When we put conditions, when we put barriers and boundaries, then we lose love. Love is condition-less. Love is barrier-less. Look at the moon, sun, stars, trees. . . they are just on for everyone. When our love also flows for everyone, you become very natural.

~ Chidanand Saraswati

Steve
* * *

LOVE NOTES

God morning,
The mind has a thousand eyes, and the heart has one: yet the light of a whole life dies when love is done.
~ *Daniel Handler*
Steve
* * *

God morning,
Everybody can be great...because anybody can serve. You don't have to have a college degree to serve. You don't have to make your subject and verb agree to serve. You only need a heart full of grace. A soul generated by love.
~ *Martin Luther King, Jr.*
Steve
* * *

God morning,
Love is the force, the energy that animates creativity and peace in each one of us.
~ *Salle Merrill Redfield*
Steve
* * *

God morning,
Where love is concerned, too much is not even enough.
~ *Pierre Beaumarchais*
Steve
* * *

God morning,

Perhaps the feelings that we experience when we are in love represent a normal state. Being in love shows a person who he should be.

~ Anton Chekhov

Steve

* * *

God morning,

The thought manifests as the word. The word manifests as the deed. The deed develops into habit. And the habit hardens into character. So watch the thought and its ways with care. And let it spring from love, born out of concern for all beings.

~ Gautama Buddha

Steve

* * *

God morning,

Body is purified by water. Ego by tears. Intellect is purified by knowledge. And soul is purified with love.

~ Ali ibn Abi Talib

Steve

* * *

God morning,

Love is never afraid of fear.
Fear is always afraid of love.

~ Sri Chinmoy

Steve

* * *

God morning,
Love is not a business. It's not a transaction. It's not an exchange or something you get for doing something. It's not a trade. It's a gift!
~ *Tony Robbins*
Steve
* * *

God morning,
Love seeks no cause beyond itself and no fruit; it is its own fruit, its own enjoyment. I love because I love; I love in order that I may love.
~ *Bernard of Clairvaux*
Steve
* * *

God morning,
Love is anterior to life, posterior to death, initial of creation, and the exponent of breath.
~ *Emily Dickinson*
Steve
* * *

God morning,
If my love were an ocean,
there would be no more land.
If my love were a desert,
you would see only sand.
If my love were a star–
late at night, only light.

And if my love could grow wings,
I'd be soaring in flight.

~ Jay Asher

Steve

* * *

God morning,

If you want a love message to be heard, it has got to be sent out. To keep a lamp burning, we have to keep putting oil in it.

~ Mother Teresa

Steve

* * *

God morning,

Two minds with but a single thought, two hearts that beat as one.

~ Jasper Fforde

Steve

* * *

God morning,

Love is God, and to die means that I, a particle of love, shall return to the general and eternal source.

~ Leo Tolstoy

Steve

* * *

God morning,

We picture love as heart-shaped because we do not know the shape of the soul.

~ Robert Breault

Steve
* * *

God morning,
Love is the expression of the one who loves, not of the one who is loved. Those who think they can love only the people they prefer do not love at all. Love discovers truths about individuals that others cannot see
~ *Soren Kierkegaard*
Steve
* * *

God morning,
We look forward to the time when the Power of Love will replace the Love of Power. Then will our world know the blessings of peace.
~ *William E. Gladstone*
Steve
* * *

God morning,
If you loved someone, you loved him, and when you had nothing else to give, you still gave him love.
~ *George Orwell*
Steve
* * *

God morning,
The greatest weakness of most humans is their hesitancy to tell others how much they love them while they're alive.
~ *Orlando Aloysius Battista*

Steve

* * *

Good morning,

Those who have never known the deep intimacy and the intense companionship of happy mutual love have missed the best thing that life has to give.

~ *Bertrand Russell*

Steve

* * *

Good morning,

There is love of course. And then there's life, its enemy.

~ *Jean Anouilh*

Steve

* * *

Good morning,

None of us has the power to make someone else love us. But we all have the power to give away love, to love other people. And if we do so, we change the kind of world we live in.

~ *Harold S. Kushner*

Steve

* * *

Good morning,

We are each of us angels with only one wing, and we can only fly by embracing one another.

~ *Luciano De Crescenzo*

Steve

* * *

God morning,
Love is when you don't have to be with another person to touch their heart!
~ *Torquato Tasso*
Steve
***

God morning,
A moment of anger can destroy a lifetime of work, whereas a moment of love can break barriers that took a lifetime to build.
~ *Leon Brown*
Steve
***

God morning,
But true love is a durable fire, In the mind ever burning, Never sick, never old, never dead, From itself never turning.
~ *Walter Raleigh*
Steve
***

God morning,
What does love look like? It has the hands to help others. It has the feet to hasten to the poor and needy. It has eyes to see misery and want. It has the ears to hear the sighs and sorrows of men. That is what love looks like.
~ *St. Augustine*
Steve
***

God morning,
Love gives itself; it is not bought.
~ Henry Wadsworth Longfellow
Steve
* * *

God morning,
Love is no assignment for cowards.
~ Ovid
Steve
* * *

God morning,
If you keep in mind that love and love alone is the reason for living, it will calm your heart and free you from your worries.
~ Harold Klemp
Steve
* * *

God morning,
Love is all we have, the only way that each can help the other.
~ Euripides
Steve
* * *

God morning,
For above all, love is a sharing. Love is a power. Love is a change that takes place in our own heart. Sometimes it may change others, but always it changes us.
~ James Dillet Freeman

Steve
* * *

God morning,
Nobody has ever measured, not even poets, how much the heart can hold.
~ Zelda Fitzgerald
Steve
* * *

God morning,
The greatest pleasure of life is love.
~ Euripides
Steve
* * *

God morning,
The only measure of your worth and your deeds will be the love you leave behind when you're gone.
~ Fred Small
Steve
* * *

God morning,
To love another person is to see the face of God.
~ Victor Hugo
Steve
* * *

God morning,
Love is life. All, everything that I understand, I understand only because I love. Everything is, everything exists, only because

I love. Everything is united by it alone. Love is God, and to die means that I, a particle of love, shall return to the general and eternal source.

~ *Leo Tolstoy*
Steve

* * *

God morning,
Whoso loves, believes in the impossible.

~ *Elizabeth Barrett Browning*
Steve

* * *

God morning,
Love is an attempt to change a piece of a dream world into reality.

~ *Theodor Reik*
Steve

* * *

God morning,
Love is the river of life in this world.

~ *Henry Ward Beecher*
Steve

* * *

God morning,
Love is eternal, the aspect may change, but not the essence.

~ *Vincent van Gogh*
Steve

* * *

LOVE NOTES

God morning,
Reason is powerless in the expression of Love.
~ *Rumi*
Steve
* * *

God morning,
Love is a portion of the soul itself, and it is of the same nature as the celestial breathing of the atmosphere of paradise.
~ *Victor Hugo*
Steve
* * *

God morning,
One makes mistakes; that is life. But it is never a mistake to have loved.
~ *Romain Rolland*
Steve
* * *

God morning,
Love is the symbol of eternity.
~ *Madame de Stael*
Steve
* * *

God morning,
All is love... All is love. With love comes understanding. With understanding comes patience. And then time stops. And everything is now.
~ *Brian Weiss*

Steve

* * *

God morning,
We are born to love, we live to love, and we will die to love still more.
~ *St. Joseph*
Steve

* * *

God morning,
When we feel love and kindness toward others, it not only makes others feel loved and cared for, but it helps us also to develop inner happiness and peace.
~ *Dalai Lama*
Steve

* * *

God morning,
Let us always meet each other with a smile, for the smile is the beginning of love.
~ *Mother Teresa*
Steve

* * *

God morning,
If you judge people, you have no time to love them.
~ *Mother Teresa*
Steve

* * *

God morning,
When we feel love and kindness toward others, it not only makes others feel loved and cared for, but it helps us also to develop inner happiness and peace.
~ *Dalai Lama*
Steve
* * *

God morning,
Perhaps love is like a resting place, a shelter from the storm. It exists to give you comfort, it is there to keep you warm, and in those times of trouble when you are most alone, the memory of love will bring you home.
~ *John Denver*
Steve
* * *

God morning,
I almost wish we were butterflies and liv'd but three summer days - three such days with you I could fill with more delight than fifty common years could ever contain.
~ *John Keats*
Steve
* * *

God morning,
Love is energy of life.
~ *Robert Browning*
Steve
* * *

Good morning,
Love is not a because, it's a no matter what.
~ Jodi Picoult
Steve
* * *

Good morning,
In the arithmetic of love, one plus one equals everything, and two minus one equals nothing.
~ Mignon McLaughlin
Steve
* * *

Good morning,
Love means to commit oneself without guarantee, to give oneself completely in the hope that our love will produce love in the loved person. Love is an act of faith, and whoever is of little faith is also of little love.
~ Erich Fromm
Steve
* * *

Good morning,
Love should be a tree whose roots are deep in the earth, but whose branches extend into heaven.
~ Bertrand Russell
Steve
* * *

Good morning,
Love is the master key that opens the gates of happiness.

~ Oliver Wendell Holmes, Sr.
Steve
* * *

God morning,
Love is the only flower that grows and blossoms without the aid of the seasons.
~ Khalil Gibran
Steve
* * *

God morning,
I want you any way I can get you. Not because you're beautiful or clever or kind or adorable, although devil knows you're all those things. I want you because there's no one else like you, and I don't ever want to start a day without seeing you.
~ Lisa Kleypas
Steve
* * *

God morning,
Don't waste your love on somebody who doesn't value it.
~ William Shakespeare
Steve
* * *

God morning,
True love begins when nothing is looked for in return.
~ Antoine de Saint-Exupéry
Steve
* * *

God morning,
Just don't give up trying to do what you really want to do. Where there is love and inspiration, I don't think you can go wrong.
~ Ella Fitzgerald
Steve
* * *

God morning,
To the whole world you might be just one person, but to one person you might just be the whole world.
~ Pablo Casals
Steve
* * *

God morning,
For every beauty there is an eye somewhere to see it.
For every truth there is an ear somewhere to hear it.
For every love there is a heart somewhere to receive it.
~ Ivan Panin
Steve
* * *

God morning,
Understand that you own nothing. Everything that surrounds you is temporary. Only the love in your heart will last forever.
~ Leon Brown
Steve
* * *

God morning,
Give me a kiss, and to that kiss a score;
Then to that twenty, add a hundred more:
A thousand to that hundred: so kiss on,
To make that thousand up a million.
Treble that million, and when that is done,
Let's kiss afresh, as when we first begun.
~ Robert Herrick
Steve
* * *

God morning,
Before you kissed me only winds of heaven
Had kissed me, and the tenderness of rain—
Now you have come, how can I care for kisses
Like theirs again?
~ Sara Teasdale
Steve
* * *

God morning,
I think of love, and you, and my heart grows full and warm, and my breath stands still... I can feel a sunshine stealing into my soul and making it all summer, and every thorn, a rose.
~ Emily Dickinson
Steve
* * *

God morning,
I argue thee that love is life.

And life hath immortality.
~ Emily Dickinson
Steve

* * *

God morning,
You yourself, as much as anybody in the entire universe, deserve your love and affection.
~ Buddha
Steve

* * *

God morning,
So, here I am, all by myself, thinking of you – no one else. There's a feeling inside and as hard as I try, it just won't go away.
~ Angel Hema
Steve

* * *

God morning,
Age does not protect you from love. But love, to some extent, protects you from age.
~ Jeanna Moreau
Steve

* * *

God morning,
You have no idea how hard it is to force myself to stop thinking about you sometimes.
~ Johnneil Bertrand

Steve

* * *

God morning,
Where there is love there is life.
~ *Mahatma Gandhi*
Steve

* * *

God morning,
The regret of my life is that I have not said "I love you" often enough.
~ *Yoko Ono*
Steve

* * *

God morning,
I love you not because of who you are, but because of who I am when I am with you.
~ *Roy Croft*
Steve

* * *

God morning,
All you need is love.
~ *The Beatles*
Steve

* * *

God morning,
I love you, and that's the beginning and end of everything.
~ *F. Scott Fitzgerald*

Steve
* * *

God morning,
Love is in fact an intensification of life, a completeness, a fullness, a wholeness of life.
~ *Thomas Merton*
Steve
* * *

God morning,
Love is undefinable. you can't put to words what love is, it's too powerful, too magical. You can only feel love and love others. Now that is true love.
~ *Unknown*
Steve
* * *

God morning,
If you find someone you love in your life, then hang on to that love.
~ *Princess Diana*
Steve
* * *

God morning,
You are my sun, my moon, and all my stars.
~ *e.e. cummings*
Steve
* * *

God morning,
And yet I wish but for the thing I have;
My bounty is as boundless as the sea,
My love as deep; the more I give to thee,
The more I have, for both are infinite.
~ William Shakespeare
Steve
* * *

God morning,
All the beautiful sentiments in the world weigh less than a single lovely action.
~ James Russell Lowell
Steve
* * *

God morning,
When you're lucky enough to meet your one person, then life takes a turn for the best. It can't get better than that.
~ John Krasinski
Steve
* * *

God morning,
A simple "I love you" means more than money.
~ Frank Sinatra
Steve
* * *

God morning,
Love is a game that two can play and both win.

~ *Eva Gabor*
Steve
* * *

God morning,
Love is a friendship set to music.
~ *E. Joseph Cossman*
Steve
* * *

God morning,
Love is a promise; love is a souvenir, once given, never forgotten, never let it disappear.
~ *John Lennon*
Steve
* * *

God morning,
Life is a flower of which love is the honey.
~ *Victor Hugo*
Steve
* * *

God morning,
We're all a little weird, and life's a little weird. And when we find someone whose weirdness is compatible with ours, we join up with them and fall in mutual weirdness and call it love.
~ *Dr. Seuss*
Steve
* * *

God morning,
Love is the voice under all silences, the hope which has no opposite in fear; the strength so strong mere force is feebleness: the truth more first than sun, more last than star.

~ *e.e. cummings*
Steve

* * *

God morning,
Love consists of this: two solitudes that meet, protect and greet each other.

~ *Rainer Maria Rilke*
Steve

* * *

God morning,
Love
bears all things,
believes all things,
hopes all things,
endures all things...
Love Never Fails

~ *1 Corinthians 13:7*
Steve

* * *

God morning,
Love is undefinable. you can't put to words what love is, it's too powerful, too magical. You can only feel love and love others. Now that is true love.

~ Unknown
Steve
* * *

God morning,
Love is the absence of judgment.
~ Bob Marley
Steve
* * *

God morning,
Love is the answer to everything. It's the only reason to do anything.
~ Ray Bradbury
Steve
* * *

God morning,
The best love is the kind that awakens the soul and makes us reach for more, that plants a fire in our hearts and brings peace to our minds.
~ Nicholas Sparks
Steve
* * *

God morning,
Of all forms of caution, caution in love is perhaps the most fatal to true happiness.
~ Bertrand Russell
Steve
* * *

God morning,
Never sacrifice what you want most for what you want in the moment.
~ *Unknown*
Steve
* * *

God morning,
Love doesn't need to be perfect. It just needs to be true.
~ *Unknown*
Steve
* * *

God morning,
True love never dies, it only gets stronger with time.
~ *Unknown*
Steve
* * *

God morning,
Love is a two-way street constantly under construction.
~ *Carroll Bryant*
Steve
* * *

God morning,
True love is a durable fire in the mind ever burning; Never sick, never old, never dead; From itself never turning.
~ *Unknown*

Steve
* * *

Good morning,
Love is our true destiny. We do not find the meaning of life by ourselves alone – we find it with another.
~ *Thomas Merton*
Steve
* * *

Good morning,
Sitting next to you doing absolutely nothing means absolutely everything to me.
~ *Unknown*
Steve
* * *

Good morning,
Live with no excuses, love with no regrets.
~ *Unknown*
Steve
* * *

Good morning,
True love doesn't have a happy ending because true love doesn't end.
~ *Unknown*
Steve
* * *

Good morning,
Love is like the Moon, when it does not increase, it decreases.

LOVE NOTES

~ *Unknown*
Steve
* * *

God morning,
Love is not something that just happens to you: it is a certain special way of being alive.
~ *Thomas Merton*
Steve
* * *

God morning,
Love has no desire but to fulfill itself.
To melt and be like a running brook
that sings its melody to the night.
To wake at dawn with a winged
heart and give thanks for another day of loving.
~ *Khalil Gibran*
Steve
* * *

God morning,
To love is to receive a glimpse of Heaven.
~ *Karen Sunde*
Steve
* * *

God morning,
The most sincere feelings are the hardest to be expressed by words.
~ *Luvreels*

Steve

* * *

God morning,

Love is a fabric which never fades, no matter how often it is washed in the water of adversity and grief.

~ Unknown

Steve

* * *

God morning,

Love is the solution to everything. Realize how powerful Love is.

~ Unknown

Steve

* * *

God morning,

Love is just love, it can never be explained.

~ Unknown

Steve

* * *

God morning,

Every time I look at the keyboard, I see that u and i are always together.

~ Unknown

Steve

* * *

God morning,

Love comforteth like sunshine after rain.

~ Unknown

Steve
* * *

God morning,
In a sea of hate be a ripple of love.
~ Unknown
Steve
* * *

God morning,
And suddenly all the love songs were about you.
~ Unknown
Steve
* * *

God morning,
A beautiful feeling, when someone tells you I wish I knew you earlier.
~ Unknown
Steve
* * *

God morning,
The most beautiful view is the one I share with you.
~ Unknown
Steve
* * *

God morning,
Tears are more special than smiles. Smiles can be for anyone, but tears are only for those who you really love.
~ Unknown

Steve
* * *

Good morning,
Love is a symbol of eternity. It wipes out all sense of time, destroying all memory of a beginning and all fear of an end.

~ Unknown
Steve
* * *

Good morning,
Love is the only weapon we need.

~ Unknown
Steve
* * *

Good morning,
You know that you are in love when the hardest thing to do is say good-bye!

~ Unknown
Steve
* * *

Good morning,
If you want to know where your heart is, look to where your mind goes when it wanders.

~ Unknown
Steve
* * *

God morning,
Love is when you look into someone's eyes and see everything you need.
~ Unknown
Steve
* * *

God morning,
In a sea of people, my eyes will always search for you.
~ Unknown
Steve
* * *

God morning,
A wise physician said, "The best medicine for humans is love."
Someone asked, "If that doesn't work?"
He smiled and answered, "Increase the dose."
~ Unknown
Steve
* * *

God morning,
True unconditional love starts from you to you. Stop waiting on others to give it to you.
~ Edmond Mbiaka
Steve
* * *

God morning,
The most wonderful thing I decided to do was share my life and heart with you.

~ *Unknown*
Steve
* * *

God morning,
No words are necessary between two loving hearts.
~ *Unknown*
Steve
* * *

God morning,
A woman's beautiful face attracts a flirter.
A woman's beautiful heart attracts a lover.
A woman's beautiful character attracts a man.
~ *Unknown*
Steve
* * *

God morning,
This wide world holds;
O Love,
My world is you.
~ *Unknown*
Steve
* * *

God morning,
Life is short, live it.
Love is rare, grab it.
Anger is bad, dump it.
Fear is awful, face it.

Memories are sweet. Cherish them.
~ *Unknown*
Steve
* * *

God morning,
It has been said that we need just three things in life: Something to do, something to look forward to and someone to love.
~ *Unknown*
Steve
* * *

God morning,
I would be nothing without your unconditional and undying love.
~ *Unknown*
Steve
* * *

God morning,
If one day you have to choose between the world and love, remember this: If you choose the world, you'll be left without love, but if you choose love, with it you will conquer the world.
~ *Albert Einstein*
Steve
* * *

God morning,
The greatest happiness in life is the conviction that we are loved.
~ *Albert Einstein*
Steve
* * *

God morning,
Love is walking in the rain together.
~ *Unknown*
Steve
* * *

God morning,
I've fallen in love many times...always with you.
~ *Unknown*
Steve
* * *

God morning,
Love is giving someone the power to destroy you, but trusting them not to.
~ *Unknown*
Steve
* * *

God morning,
A real man never stops trying to show a woman how much she means to him, even after he's got her.
~ *Unknown*
Steve
* * *

God morning,
Love is the essence of human experience and emotion. It is at the root of all and everything we, as humans, do. Without love, what do we have to live for?
~ *Unknown*

Steve

* * *

God morning,
Where there is love, there is no sin.
~ Unknown

Steve

* * *

God morning,
Before you fall in love, make sure there is someone there to catch you.
~ Unknown

Steve

* * *

God morning,
Live for love.
Without love,
you don't live.
~ Unknown

Steve

* * *

God morning,
Love is the most powerful and still most unknown energy in the world.
~ Pierre Teilhard de Chardin

Steve

* * *

God morning,
Love is the expression of simplicity in emotion, the unattainable longing that comes so unexpectedly, with great subtlety and bliss.
~ *Unknown*
Steve
* * *

God morning,
The one thing we can never
get enough of is love.
And the one thing we never
give enough is love.
~ *Henry Miller*
Steve
* * *

God morning,
Love is not a simple thing...It's hard to understand...It's not an action or a word...But something much more grand...
~ *Heather McKinney*
Steve
* * *

God morning,
If you have love in your life it can make up for a great many things you lack. If you don't have it, no matter what else there is, it's not enough.
~ *Ann Landers*

Steve

✶ ✶ ✶

God morning,
Love knows no limit to its endurance, no end to its trust, no fading of its hope: it can outlast anything. Love still stands when all else has fallen.

~ Unknown

Steve

✶ ✶ ✶

God morning,
It would not be true love if there were not any problems and people standing in your way. It is true love when you realize that these problems and people don't really matter.

~ Unknown

Steve

✶ ✶ ✶

God morning,
Anyone can love a rose, but it takes a lot to love a leaf. It's ordinary to love the beautiful, but it's beautiful to love the ordinary.

~ Unknown

Steve

✶ ✶ ✶

God morning,
Love is not a force between a mind and a body, but a force between two hearts. Your mind and eyes will never tell you when you feel true love, for only the heart can receive the true love that another heart sends directly to it.

~ Unknown
Steve
* * *

God morning,
It is impossible to fall out of love. Love is such a powerful emotion, that once it envelops you it does not depart. True love is eternal. If you think that you were once in love, but fell out of it, then it wasn't love you were in. There are no exit signs in love, there is only an on ramp.
~ Unknown
Steve
* * *

God morning,
How wise are they that are but fools in love.
~ Unknown
Steve
* * *

God morning,
Love is the energizing elixir of the universe, the cause and effect of all harmonies.
~ Unknown
Steve
* * *

God morning,
All love that has not friendship for its base is like a mansion built upon the sand.
~ Ella Wheeler Wilcox

Steve
* * *

God morning,

The heart becomes warmer when the mild heat of love is coming from two persons. one is in eternal cold and desolation without feeling the friction of love.

~ *Michael Bassey Johnson*

Steve
* * *

God morning,

The heart that loves is always young.

~ *Unknown*

Steve
* * *

God morning,

Love is not a temporary feeling or emotion. Emotions and feelings change, sometimes, daily, but true unconditional love is everlasting.

~ *Anonymous*

Steve
* * *

God morning,

If there is anything better than to be loved, it is loving.

~ *Anonymous*

Steve
* * *

Good morning,
For the first time in my life, I've felt whole, alive, free. You were the missing piece of my soul, the breath in my lungs, and the blood in my veins.
~ *J. A. Redmerski*
Steve
* * *

Good morning,
If I can stop time, I would stop it the moment I finally noticed my feelings for you.
~ *Unknown*
Steve
* * *

Good morning,
I know you love me, because there's no way I can be this much in love with you, and not have you feel the same way. It's not possible.
~ *Samantha Young*
Steve
* * *

Good morning,
All love is sweet,
Given or returned.
Common as light is love,
And its familiar voice wearies not ever.
~ *Percy Bysshe Shelley*

Steve
* * *

God morning,
Take away love and our earth is a tomb.
~ Robert Browning
Steve
* * *

God morning,
He stepped down, trying not to look long at her, as if she were the sun, yet he saw her, like the sun, even without looking.
~ Leo Tolstoy
Steve
* * *

God morning,
True love is rare, and it's the only thing that gives life real meaning.
~ Nicholas Sparks
Steve
* * *

God morning,
When I am with you, we stay up all night. When you're not here, I can't go to sleep. Praise God for those two insomnias! And the difference between them.
~ Rumi
Steve
* * *

Good morning,
You are my heart, my life, my one and only thought.
~ Arthur Conan Doyle, "The White Company"
Steve

* * *

Good morning,
It is impossible to manufacture or imitate love.
~ J. K. Rowling
Steve

* * *

Good morning,
Love is born into every human being; it calls back the halves of our original nature together; it tries to make one out of two and heal the wound of human nature.
~ Plato
Steve

* * *

Good morning,
Falling in love is very real, but I used to shake my head when people talked about soul mates, poor deluded individuals grasping at some supernatural ideal not intended for mortals but sounded pretty in a poetry book. Then, we met, and everything changed, the cynic has become the converted, the skeptic, an ardent zealot.
~ E. A. Bucchianeri
Steve

* * *

God morning,
Love is a ripe plum growing on a purple tree. Taste it once and the spell of its enchantment will never let you be.
~ *Langston Hughes*
Steve
* * *

God morning,
Love is the most powerful motivator in the world. It spurs mortals to greatness. Their noblest, bravest acts are done for love.
~ *Rick Riordan*
Steve
* * *

God morning,
You will never be able to escape from your heart. So it's better to listen to what it has to say.
~ *Paulo Coelho*
Steve
* * *

God morning,
Love is a force unto itself. For love, people consider the unthinkable and often achieve the impossible.
~ *Renee Ahdieh*
Steve
* * *

God morning,
The surest way to hurt yourself is to give up on love, just because it didn't work out the first time.
~ Amanda Howells
Steve
* * *

God morning,
Who would give a law to lovers? Love is unto itself a higher law.
~ Boethius
Steve
* * *

God morning,
One day spent with someone you love can change everything.
~ Mitch Albom
Steve
* * *

God morning,
Do I love you because you're beautiful, or are you beautiful because I love you?
~ Richard Rodgers
Steve
* * *

God morning,
To some, you are just a face in the crowd. To the one, you are the star of the show.
~ Giovannie Sadeleer

Steve
***

Good morning,

Every heart sings a song, incomplete, until another heart whispers back. Those who wish to sing always find a song. At the touch of a lover, everyone becomes a poet.

~ Plato

Steve
***

Good morning,

The most painful thing is losing yourself in the process of loving someone too much, and forgetting that you are special too.

~ Ernest Hemingway

Steve
***

Good morning,

Goodbyes are only for those who love with their eyes. Because for those who love with heart and soul there is no such thing as separation.

~ Rumi

Steve
***

Good morning,

Without love we all like birds with broken wings.

~ Mitch Albom

Steve
***

LOVE NOTES

God morning,
If you love deeply, you're going to get hurt badly. But it's still worth it.
~ *C. S. Lewis*
Steve
* * *

God morning,
The best use of life is love. The best expression of love is time. The best time to love is now.
~ *Rick Warren*
Steve
* * *

God morning,
Love withers under constraints: its very essence is liberty: it is compatible neither with obedience, jealousy, nor fear.
~ *Percy Bysshe Shelley*
Steve
* * *

God morning,
The measure of love is to love without measure.
~ *Francis de Sales*
Steve
* * *

God morning,
Love touches the soul and awakens a desire so powerful that even the most vigilant heart is lured by its radiance.
~ *Jamie Lynn Morris*

Steve

* * *

God morning,
Loving someone is giving them the power to break your heart, but trusting them not to.
~ Julianne Moore
Steve

* * *

God morning,
Sometimes our light goes out, but is blown again into instant flame by an encounter with another human being.
~ Albert Schweitzer
Steve

* * *

God morning,
I look at you and I know love. I look away and I know nothing.
~ Christopher Poindexter
Steve

* * *

God morning,
Being with you and not being with you is the only way I have to measure time.
~ Jorge Borges
Steve

* * *

Good morning,
Love is an endless mystery, because there is no reasonable cause that could explain it.
~ Rabindranath Tagore
Steve
* * *

Good morning,
When someone loves you, it's like having a blanket all round your heart.
~ Helen Fielding
Steve
* * *

Good morning,
Sometimes you can't explain what you see in a person. It's just the way they take you to a place where no one else can.
~ Unknown
Steve
* * *

Good morning,
Love can neither be bought nor sold – its only price is love.
~ Jacob Cats
Steve
* * *

Good morning,
Love is when someone gives you a piece of your soul that you never knew was missing.
~ Torquato Tasso

Steve

* * *

God morning,
When two souls recognize each other, everything else ceases to matter.
~ *Unknown*
Steve

* * *

God morning,
When you love someone, you say their name different. Like it's safe inside your mouth.
~ *Jodi Picoult*
Steve

* * *

God morning,
That's when you know you love someone...when you can't experience anything without wishing the other person was there to see it, too.
~ *Kaui Hemmings*
Steve

* * *

God morning,
Love is the way back into Eden. It is the way back to life.
~ *Francine Rivers*
Steve

* * *

Good morning,
The heart has its own language. The heart knows a hundred thousand ways to speak.
~ *Rumi*
Steve
* * *

Good morning,
Don't ever think I fell for you, or fell over you. I didn't fall in love, I rose in it.
~ *Toni Morrison*
Steve
* * *

Good morning,
Love has nothing to do with what you are expecting to get, only with what you are expecting to give, which is everything.
~ *Katharine Hepburn*
Steve
* * *

Good morning,
Love is not the opposite of power. Love is power. Love is the strongest power there is.
~ *Vironika Tugaleva*
Steve
* * *

Good morning,
My heart beats faster as you take my hand, my love grows stronger as you touch my soul.

~ A. C. Van Cherub
Steve

* * *

God morning,

To love or have loved, that is enough. Ask nothing further. There is no other pearl to be found in the dark folds of life.

~ Victor Hugo
Steve

* * *

God morning,

Who, being loved, is poor?

~ Oscar Wilde
Steve

* * *

God morning,

Thinking of you keeps me awake. Dreaming of you keeps me asleep. Being with you keeps me alive.

~ Inconnu
Steve

* * *

God morning,

People always say that, when you love someone, nothing in the world matters. But the truth is that when you love someone, everything in the world matters a little bit more.

~ Jodi Picoult
Steve

* * *

God morning,
Love rests on no foundation. It is an endless ocean, with no beginning or end.

~ *Rumi*
Steve
* * *

God morning,
When the mind falls in love, it's temporary. When the heart falls in love, it lasts a lifetime. When the soul falls in love, its eternal.

~ *Unknown*
Steve
* * *

God morning,
Sometimes, someone comes into your life, so unexpectedly, takes your heart by surprise, and changes your life forever.

~ *Unknown*
Steve
* * *

God morning,
They say we fall in love with the unexpected, but the truth is that it's expected in the heart but not the mind.

~ *Unknown*
Steve
* * *

God morning,
Love is finding someone you can talk to late into the night.

~ *James Patterson*

Steve
* * *

God morning,
When two souls have finally found each other, there is established between them a union which begins on earth and continues forever in heaven.
~ Victor Hugo
Steve
* * *

God morning,
We need not think alike to love alike.
~ Francis David
Steve
* * *

God morning,
True love stories never have endings.
~ Richard Bach
Steve
* * *

God morning,
To love someone is nothing, to be loved by someone is something, to love someone who loves you is everything.
~ Bill Russell
Steve
* * *

Good morning,
Life is short. Kiss slowly, laugh insanely, love truly and forgive quickly.
~ Paulo Coelho
Steve
* * *

Good morning,
This fire that we call Loving is too strong for human minds. But just right for human souls.
~ Aberjhani
Steve
* * *

Good morning,
Love is the bond of perfection.
~ John Winthrop
Steve
* * *

Good morning,
Love is all we have, the only way that each can help the other.
~ Euripides
Steve
* * *

Good morning,
I know of only one duty, and that is to love.
~ Albert Camus
Steve
* * *

God morning,
For true love is inexhaustible; the more you give, the more you have. And if you go to draw at the true fountainhead, the more water you draw, the more abundant is its flow.
~ *Antoine de Saint-Exupéry*
Steve
* * *

God morning,
Anyone can catch your eye but it takes someone special to catch your heart.
~ *Anonymous*
Steve
* * *

God morning,
Don't find love, let love find you. That's why it's called falling in love because you don't force yourself to fall, you just fall.
~ *Anonymous*
Steve
* * *

God morning,
Love is no individual's experience; and though we are imperfect mediums, it does not partake of our imperfection; though we are finite, it is infinite and eternal.
~ *Henry David Thoreau*
Steve
* * *

Good morning,
Love is when you sit beside someone doing nothing, yet you feel perfectly happy.

~ *Anonymous*

Steve

* * *

Good morning,
Love is not consolation. It is light.

~ *Friedrich Nietzsche*

Steve

* * *

Good morning,
Love is not a matter of counting the years, But making the years count.

~ *Michelle Amand*

Steve

* * *

Good morning,
Love is the pursuit of the whole.

~ *Plato*

Steve

* * *

Good morning,
Love is the ultimate truth at the heart of the universe and transcends all boundaries.

~ *Deepak Chopra*

Steve
* * *

Good morning,
Love is in all things a most wonderful teacher.
~ *Charles Dickens*
Steve
* * *

Good morning,
The words "I will forgive you, but I'll never forget what you've done" never explain the real nature of forgiveness.
~ *Martin Luther King, Jr.*
Steve
* * *

Good morning,
Love yourself, accept yourself, forgive yourself, and be good to yourself, because without you the rest of us are without a source of many wonderful things.
~ *Leo Buscaglia*
Steve
* * *

Good morning,
Only a life lived for others is a life worthwhile.
~ *Albert Einstein*
Steve
* * *

God morning,
Spread love everywhere you go. Let no one ever come to you without leaving happier.
~ *Mother Teresa*
Steve
* * *

God morning,
You never lose by loving. You always lose by holding back.
~ *Barbara De Angelis*
Steve
* * *

God morning,
Do not forget that true love sets no conditions; it does not calculate or complain but simply loves.
~ *Pope John Paul II*
Steve
* * *

God morning,
Always remember: You are beautiful. You are worthy. You are important. You are special. You are unique. You are talented and you are irreplaceable.
~ *Anonymous*
Steve
* * *

God morning,
He felt now that he was not simply close to her, but that he did not know where he ended and she began.

~ *Leo Tolstoy*
Steve
* * *

God morning,
Where we love is home – home that our feet may leave, but not our hearts.
~ *Oliver Wendell Holmes, Sr.*
Steve
* * *

God morning,
Love is a sacred reserve of energy; it is like the blood of spiritual evolution.
~ *Pierre Teilhard de Chardin*
Steve
* * *

God morning,
Love is like Pi: natural, irrational, and very important.
~ *Anonymous*
Steve
* * *

God morning,
When you trip over love, it is easy to get up. But when you fall in love, it is impossible to stand again.
~ *Anonymous*
Steve
* * *

God morning,
We are most alive when we're in love.
~ John Updike
Steve
* * *

God morning,
The best and most beautiful things in this world cannot be seen or even heard, but must be felt with the heart.
~ Helen Keller
Steve
* * *

God morning,
Till I loved I never lived.
~ Emily Dickinson
Steve
* * *

God morning,
To get the full value of a joy, you must have somebody to divide it with.
~ Mark Twain
Steve
* * *

God morning,
Love is our true destiny. We do not find meaning of life by ourselves alone – we find it with another.
~ Thomas Merton

Steve

* * *

God morning,
We were together even when we were apart.
~ *Shannon A. Thompson*
Steve

* * *

God morning,
To be fully seen by somebody, then, and be loved anyhow—this is a human offering that can border on miraculous.
~ *Elizabeth Gilbert*
Steve

* * *

God morning,
Keep love in your heart. A life without it is like a sunless garden when the flowers are dead.
~ *Oscar Wilde*
Steve

* * *

God morning,
The greatest happiness of life is the conviction that we are loved; loved for ourselves, or rather, loved in spite of ourselves.
~ *Victor Hugo*
Steve

* * *

God morning,
All you need is love. But a little chocolate now and then doesn't hurt.
~ Charles Schulz
Steve

* * *

God morning,
All, everything that I understand, I understand only because I love.
~ Leo Tolstoy
Steve

* * *

God morning,
When we are in love we seem to ourselves quite different from what we were before.
~ Blaise Pascal
Steve

* * *

God morning,
Only in the eyes of love you can find infinity.
~ Sorin Cerin
Steve

* * *

God morning,
And now here is my secret, a very simple secret: It is only with the heart that one can see rightly; what is essential is invisible to the eye.

~ *Antoine de Saint-Exupéry*
Steve
* * *

Good morning,
The best things ever my hands have ever held are yours.
~ *Unknown*
Steve
* * *

Good morning,
The spaces between our fingers were created so that another person's fingers could fill them in.
~ *Anonymous*
Steve
* * *

Good morning,
Sometimes the heart sees what is invisible to the eye.
~ *H. Jackson Brown, Jr.*
Steve
* * *

Good morning,
Love is just a word until someone comes along and gives it meaning.
~ *Paulo Coelho*
Steve
* * *

God morning,
When you love someone, you love them as the person they are, and not as you'd like them to be.
~ *Leo Tolstoy*
Steve
* * *

God morning,
Love recognizes no barriers. It jumps hurdles, leaps fences, penetrates walls to arrive at its destination full of hope.
~ *Maya Angelou*
Steve
* * *

God morning,
A life without love, without the presence of the beloved, is nothing but a mere magic-lantern show. We draw out slide after slide, swiftly tiring of each, and pushing it back to make haste for the next.
~ *Johann Wolfgang von Goethe*
Steve
* * *

God morning,
You don't love someone for their looks, or their clothes or for their fancy car, but because they sing a song only you can hear.
~ *Oscar Wilde*
Steve
* * *

God morning,
Love does not dominate; it cultivates.
~ Johann Wolfgang von Goethe
Steve
* * *

God morning,
Say "I love you" out loud and often.
~ Mary Davis
Steve
* * *

God morning,
The greatest thing you'll ever learn is just to love and be loved in return.
~ Eden Ahbez
Steve
* * *

God morning,
To fail to love is not to exist at all.
~ Mark Van Doren
Steve
* * *

God morning,
Love is of all passions the strongest, for it attacks simultaneously the head, the heart and the senses.
~ Lao Tzu
Steve
* * *

God morning,
If I know what love is, it is because of you.
~ *Hermann Hesse*
Steve
* * *

God morning,
It is love that makes the impossible possible.
~ *Indian proverb*
Steve
* * *

God morning,
It is love that asks, that seeks, that knocks, that finds, and that is faithful to what it finds.
~ *St. Augustine*
Steve
* * *

God morning,
Being in love with you makes every day an interesting one.
~ *Unknown*
Steve
* * *

God morning,
If you want to be loved, be lovable.
~ *Ovid*
Steve
* * *

God morning,
You come to love not by finding the perfect person, but by seeing an imperfect person perfectly.
~ Sam Keen
Steve
* * *

God morning,
Love has three kinds of origin, namely: suffering, friendship and love. A human love has a corporal and intellectual origin.
~ Boethius
Steve
* * *

God morning,
Kindness in words creates confidence, Kindness in thinking creates profoundness, Kindness in giving creates love.
~ Lao Tzu
Steve
* * *

God morning,
Fortune and love favor the brave.
~ Ovid
Steve
* * *

God morning,
Two souls with but a single thought, two hearts that beat as one.
~ John Keats

Steve
* * *

Good morning,
In true love it is the soul that envelops the body.
~ *Friedrich Nietzsche*
Steve
* * *

Good morning,
Love must be as much a light as it is a flame.
~ *Henry David Thoreau*
Steve
* * *

Good morning,
They say nothing lasts forever, we'll have to prove them wrong.
~ *Unknown*
Steve
* * *

Good morning,
We're all a little weird. And life is a little weird. And when we find someone whose weirdness is compatible with ours, we join up with them and fall into mutually satisfying weirdness – and call it love – true love.
~ *Robert Fulghum*
Steve
* * *

Good morning,
You will forever be my always.

~ Unknown
Steve
* * *

God morning,
Love is the expansion of two natures in such fashion that each include the other, each is enriched by the other.
~ Felix Adler
Steve
* * *

God morning,
Love's gift cannot be given, it waits to be accepted.
~ Rabindranath Tagore
Steve
* * *

God morning,
What force is more potent than love?
~ Igor Stravinsky
Steve
* * *

God morning,
Eternity is in love with the productions of time.
~ William Blake
Steve
* * *

God morning,
Genuine love involves not only passion, but also commitment and wisdom.

~ Unknown
Steve
* * *

God morning,
What is love? It is the morning and the evening star.
~ Sinclair Lewis
Steve
* * *

God morning,
Unable are the loved to die, for love is immortality.
~ Emily Dickinson
Steve
* * *

God morning,
Love comforteth like sunshine after rain.
~ William Shakespeare
Steve
* * *

God morning,
One is loved because one is loved. No reason is needed for loving.
~ Paulo Coelho
Steve
* * *

God morning,
If music be the food of love, play on.
~ William Shakespeare

Steve

* * *

Good morning,
It was love at first sight, at last sight, at ever and ever sight.
~ *Vladimir Nabokov*
Steve

* * *

Good morning,
A life lived in love will never be dull.
~ *Leo Buscaglia*
Steve

* * *

Good morning,
When we love, we always strive to become better than we are. When we strive to become better than we are, everything around us becomes better too.
~ *Paulo Coelho*
Steve

* * *

Good morning,
Love does not consist in gazing at each other, but in looking outward together in the same direction.
~ *Antoine de Saint-Exupéry*
Steve

* * *

Good morning,
Love looks not with the eyes, but with the mind,

And therefore is winged Cupid painted blind.
~ *William Shakespeare*
Steve

* * *

God morning,
Love all, trust a few, do wrong to none.
~ *William Shakespeare*
Steve

* * *

God morning,
A life without love, no matter how many other things we have, is an empty, meaningless one.
~ *Leo Buscaglia*
Steve

* * *

God morning,
Love is the only sane and satisfactory answer to the problem of human existence.
~ *Erich Fromm*
Steve

* * *

God morning,
Love has no errors, for all errors are the want for love.
~ *William Law*
Steve

* * *

God morning,
The cure for all the ills and wrongs, the cares, the sorrows, and the crimes of humanity, all lie in the one word "love." It is the divine vitality that everywhere produces and restores life.
~ Lydia M. Child
Steve
* * *

God morning,
Be mindful. Be grateful. Be positive. Be true. Be kind.
~ Roy T. Bennett
Steve
* * *

God morning,
The truth is that there is only one terminal dignity – love. And the story of a love is not important – what is important is that one is capable of love. It is perhaps the only glimpse we are permitted of eternity.
~ Helen Hayes
Steve
* * *

God morning,
The way to know life is to love many things.
~ Vincent Van Gogh
Steve
* * *

God morning,
Love is that splendid triggering of human vitality the supreme activity which nature affords anyone for going out of himself toward someone else.
~ *Jose Ortega y Gasset*
Steve

* * *

God morning,
Looking back, I have this to regret, that too often when I loved, I did not say so.
~ *Ray Stannard Baker*
Steve

* * *

God morning,
Familiar acts are beautiful through love.
~ *Percy Bysshe Shelley*
Steve

* * *

God morning,
Ultimately love is everything.
~ *M. Scott Peck*
Steve

* * *

God morning,
We may give without loving, but we cannot love without giving.
~ *Bernard Meltzer*

Steve
* * *

Good morning,

For above all things Love means sweetness, and truth, and measure; yea, loyalty to the loved one and to your word. And because of this I dare not meddle with so high a matter.

~ Marie de France

Steve
* * *

Good morning,

Love is a springtime plant that perfumes everything with its hope, even the ruins to which it clings.

~ Gustave Flaubert

Steve
* * *

Good morning,

He who loves, flies, runs, and rejoices; he is free and nothing holds him back.

~ Henri Matisse

Steve
* * *

Good morning,

Love is what you've been through with somebody.

~ James Thurber

Steve
* * *

God morning,
There are never enough I Love You's.
~ Lenny Bruce
Steve
* * *

God morning,
In a full heart there is room for everything, and in an empty heart there is room for nothing.
~ Antonio Porchia
Steve
* * *

God morning,
Love is the greatest gift that God has given us. It's free.
~ Taraji P. Henson
Steve
* * *

God morning,
Love is supreme and unconditional; like is nice but limited.
~ Duke Ellington
Steve
* * *

God morning,
Great thoughts come from the heart.
~ Luc de Clapiers
Steve
* * *

God morning,
The eyes those silent tongues of love.
~ *Miguel de Cervantes*
Steve

* * *

God morning,
I believe in the compelling power of love. I do not understand it. I believe it to be the most fragrant blossom of all this thorny existence.
~ *Theodore Dreiser*
Steve

* * *

God morning,
Love is blind.
~ *Geoffrey Chaucer*
Steve

* * *

God morning,
To love is to admire with the heart; to admire is to love with the mind.
~ *Theophile Gautier*
Steve

* * *

God morning,
The degree of loving is measured by the degree of giving.
~ *Edwin Louis Cole*

Steve

* * *

Good morning,
Pains of love be sweeter far than all other pleasures are.
~ *John Dryden*
Steve

* * *

Good morning,
Love is a great beautifier.
~ *Louisa May Alcott*
Steve

* * *

Good morning,
Love is a smoke made with the fume of sighs.
~ *William Shakespeare*
Steve

* * *

Good morning,
There is always something left to love. And if you ain't learned that, you ain't learned nothing.
~ *Lorraine Hansberry*
Steve

* * *

Good morning,
Suffering passes, while love is eternal. That's a gift that you have received from God. Don't waste it.
~ *Laura Ingalls Wilder*

Steve

* * *

God morning,
It is difficult to know at what moment love begins; it is less difficult to know that it has begun.
~ Henry Wadsworth Longfellow
Steve

* * *

God morning,
You will find as you look back upon your life that the moments when you have truly lived are the moments when you have done things in the spirit of love.
~ Henry Drummond
Steve

* * *

God morning,
Follow love and it will flee, flee love and it will follow thee.
~ John Gay
Steve

God morning,
Come live in my heart, and pay no rent.
~ Samuel Lover
Steve

* * *

Good morning,
The truth is that love smashes into your life like an ice floe, and even if your heart is built like the Titanic you go down.
~ Jeanette Winterson
Steve
* * *

Good morning,
There isn't any formula or method. You learn to love by loving – by paying attention and doing what one thereby discovers has to be done.
~ Aldous Huxley
Steve
* * *

Good morning,
We are all born for love. It is the principle of existence, and its only end.
~ Benjamin Disraeli
Steve
* * *

Good morning,
Love is the great miracle cure. Loving ourselves works miracles in our lives.
~ Louise L. Hay
Steve
* * *

Good morning,
A loving heart is the beginning of all knowledge.

~ Thomas Carlyle
Steve
* * *

God morning,
I can live without money, but I cannot live without love.
~ Judy Garland
Steve
* * *

God morning,
The way to love anything is to realize that it may be lost.
~ Gilbert K. Chesterton
Steve
* * *

God morning,
When love is not madness, it is not love.
~ Pedro Calderon de la Barca
Steve
* * *

God morning,
A part of kindness consists in loving people more than they deserve.
~ Joseph Joubert
Steve
* * *

God morning,
Love is not only something you feel, it is something you do.
~ David Wilkerson

Steve
* * *

God morning,
Love you will find only where you may show yourself weak without provoking strength.
~ Theodor W. Adorno
Steve
* * *

God morning,
There is no surprise more magical than the surprise of being loved: It is God's finger on man's shoulder.
~ Charles Morgan
Steve
* * *

God morning,
Absence sharpens love, presence strengthens it.
~ Thomas Fuller
Steve
* * *

God morning,
Love him and let him love you. Do you think anything else under heaven really matters?
~ James Baldwin
Steve
* * *

God morning,
Love is the difficult realization that something other than oneself is real.
~ *Iris Murdoch*
Steve
* * *

God morning,
Blessed is the influence of one true, loving human soul on another.
~ *George Eliot*
Steve
* * *

God morning,
Love is the crowning grace of humanity, the holiest right of the soul, the golden link which binds us to duty and truth, the redeeming principle that chiefly reconciles the heart to life, and is prophetic of eternal good.
~ *Petrarch*
Steve
* * *

God morning,
Love feels no burden, thinks nothing of trouble, attempts what is above its strength, pleads no excuse of impossibility; for it thinks all things lawful for itself, and all things possible.
~ *Thomas A Kempis*
Steve
* * *

God morning,
He loves but little who can say and count in words, how much he loves.
~ Dante Alighieri
Steve
* * *

God morning,
Love is the greatest refreshment in life.
~ Pablo Picasso
Steve
* * *

God morning,
Age does not protect you from love. But love, to some extent, protects you from age.
~ Anais Nin
Steve
* * *

God morning,
One word
Frees us of all the weight and pain of life:
That word is love.
~ Sophocles
Steve
* * *

God morning,
There is always some madness in love. But there is also always some reason in madness.

~ *Friedrich Nietzsche*
Steve
* * *

God morning,
Be of love a little more careful than of anything.
~ *e. e. cummings*
Steve
* * *

God morning,
Love in its essence is spiritual fire.
~ *Lucius Annaeus Seneca*
Steve
* * *

God morning,
I believe that imagination is stronger than knowledge.
That myth is more potent than history.
That dreams are more powerful than facts.
That hope always triumphs over experience.
That laughter is the only cure for grief.
And I believe that love is stronger than death.
~ *Robert Fulghum*
Steve
* * *

God morning,
Each moment of a happy lover's hour is worth an age of dull and common life.
~ *Aphra Behn*

Steve

* * *

Good morning,
We can only learn to love by loving.
~ *Iris Murdoch*
Steve

* * *

Good morning,
You can give without loving, but you can never love without giving.
~ *Robert Louis Stevenson*
Steve

* * *

Good morning,
Love is like an hourglass, with the heart filling up as the brain empties.
~ *Jules Renard*
Steve

* * *

Good morning,
Love is always bestowed as a gift – freely, willingly and without expectation. We don't love to be loved; we love to love.
~ *Leo Buscaglia*
Steve

* * *

God morning,
A flower cannot blossom without sunshine, and man cannot live without love.
~ *Max Muller*
Steve
* * *

God morning,
Faith makes all things possible... love makes all things easy.
~ *Dwight L. Moody*
Steve
* * *

God morning,
Love has no age, no limit; and no death.
~ *John Galsworthy*
Steve
* * *

God morning,
Love is the only reality and it is not a mere sentiment. It is the ultimate truth that lies at the heart of creation.
~ *Rabindranath Tagore*
Steve
* * *

God morning,
We may be just a drop in the ocean, but even the ocean envies the depth of our love.
~ *Maria Elena*

Steve
* * *

God morning,
He belongs to me, and I to him, without each other, we are merely two lost pieces, empty, without purpose.
~ Chelsea Radojcic
Steve
* * *

God morning,
The heart has its reasons, of which reason knows nothing.
~ Blaise Pascal
Steve
* * *

God morning,
There is more pleasure in loving than in being beloved.
~ Thomas Fuller
Steve
* * *

God morning,
Love is the flower you've got to let grow.
~ John Lennon
Steve
* * *

God morning,
I have looked into your eyes with my eyes. I have put my heart near your heart.
~ Pope John XXIII

Steve

* * *

God morning,
For small creatures such as we, the vastness is bearable only through love.
~ *Carl Sagan*
Steve

* * *

God morning,
Love isn't something you find. Love is something that finds you.
~ *Loretta Young*
Steve

* * *

God morning,
Love is a mutual self-giving which ends in self-recovery.
~ *Fulton J. Sheen*
Steve

* * *

God morning,
To love and be loved is to feel the sun from both sides.
~ *David Viscott*
Steve

* * *

God morning,
Love and compassion are necessities, not luxuries. Without them humanity cannot survive.
~ *Dalai Lama*

Steve
* * *

Good morning,
Love cures people – both the ones who give it and the ones who receive it.
~ Karl A. Menninger
Steve
* * *

Good morning,
What we have once enjoyed we can never lose. All that we love deeply becomes a part of us.
~ Helen Keller
Steve
* * *

Good morning,
Time is too slow for those who wait, too swift for those who fear, too long for those who grieve, too short for those who rejoice, but for those who love, time is eternity.
~ Henry Van Dyke
Steve
* * *

Good morning,
Life without love is like a tree without blossoms or fruit.
~ Khalil Gibran
Steve
* * *

God morning,
To the world, you may be one person, but to one person you are the world.
~ Bill Wilson
Steve
* * *

God morning,
True Love never dies, it only gets stronger with time.
~ Anonymous
Steve
* * *

God morning,
They say that you can fall in love only once; I do not believe it to be true, because every time I see you I fall in love with you all over again.
~ Unknown
Steve
* * *

God morning,
Love is the immortal flow of energy that nourishes, extends and preserves. Its eternal goal is life.
~ Smiley Blanton
Steve
* * *

God morning,
If I had to choose between breathing and loving you I would use my last breath to tell you I love you.

~ DeAnna Anderson
Steve
* * *

Good morning,
In my dreams you're mine, in my life you're my dream.
~ Unknown
Steve
* * *

Good morning,
My love for you is a journey starting at forever and ending at never.
~ Unknown
Steve
* * *

Good morning,
Just in case you ever foolishly forget; I'm never not thinking of you.
~ Virginia Woolf
Steve
* * *

Good morning,
If anyone wants to know what love is, I will just show them a picture of you.
~ Unknown
Steve
* * *

LOVE NOTES

Good morning,
When you trip over love, it is easy to get up. But when you fall in love, it is impossible to stand again.
~ *Albert Einstein*
Steve
* * *

Good morning,
One day you will ask me which is more important? My life or yours? I will say mine and you will walk away not knowing that you are my life.
~ *Khalil Gibran*
Steve
* * *

Good morning,
Whatever our souls are made of, his and mine are the same.
~ *Emily Bronte*
Steve
* * *

Good morning,
We may have started as individuals, but now we are as one.
~ *Bryon Pulsifer*
Steve
* * *

Good morning,
There is no remedy for love but to love more.
~ *Henry David Thoreau*

Steve

* * *

God morning,
Do not seek a love that you desire. True love finds you on its own!
~ Avijeet Das
Steve

* * *

God morning,
I am my beloved's and my beloved is mine.
~ Song of Solomon 6:3
Steve

* * *

God morning,
The best thing to hold onto in life is each other.
~ Audrey Hepburn
Steve

* * *

God morning,
If things on earth may be to Heaven resembled, it must be love, pure, constant, undissembled.
~ Aphra Behn
Steve

* * *

God morning,
We loved with a love that was more than love.
~ Edgar Allen Poe

Steve
* * *

God morning,
Love is a friendship set to music.
~ Joseph Campbell
Steve
* * *

God morning,
The moment you have in your heart this extraordinary thing called love and feel the depth, the delight, the ecstasy of it, you will discover that for you the world is transformed.
~ Jiddu
Steve
* * *

God morning,
The consciousness of loving and being loved brings a warmth and richness to life that nothing else can bring.
~ Oscar Wilde
Steve
* * *

God morning,
Love is the beauty of the soul.
~ St. Augustine
Steve
* * *

LOVE NOTES

Good morning,
Do I love you? My God, if your love were a grain of sand, mine would be a universe of beaches.
~ *William Goldman*
Steve

* * *

Good morning,
Two souls with but a single thought; two hearts that beat as one.
~ *Friedrich Halm*
Steve

* * *

Good morning,
For it was not into my ear you whispered, but into my heart. It was not my lips you kissed, but my soul.
~ *Judy Garland*
Steve

* * *

Good morning,
Falling in love consists merely in uncorking the imagination and bottling the common-sense.
~ *Helen Rowland*
Steve

* * *

Good morning,
Love won't be tampered with, love won't go away. Push it to one side and it creeps to the other.
~ *Louise Erdrich*

Steve

* * *

God morning,
In this world of extremes, we can only love too little.
~ Richard Cannarella
Steve

* * *

God morning,
Love is like an eternal flame — once it is lit, it will continue to burn for all time.
~ Kamila
Steve

* * *

God morning,
I have decided to stick with love. Hate is too great a burden to bear.
~ Martin Luther King, Jr.
Steve

* * *

God morning,
Love comes with hunger.
~ Diogenes
Steve

* * *

God morning,
Love is a beautiful journey where every step is a destination & every moment eternity.

~ *Apoore Dubey*
Steve
* * *

God morning,
Time is very slow for those who wait. Very fast for those who are scared. Very long for those who lament. Very short for those who celebrate. But for those who love, time is eternal.
~ *William Shakespeare*
Steve
* * *

God morning,
The more I think about it, the more I realize there is nothing more artistic than to love others.
~ *Vincent Van Gogh*
Steve
* * *

God morning,
True love is eternal, infinite, and always like itself. It is equal and pure, without violent demonstrations: it is seen with white hairs and is always young in the heart.
~ *Honoré de Balzac*
Steve
* * *

God morning,
We love truly only when we love without reason.
~ *Anatole France*

Steve
* * *

God morning,
Love is that condition in which the happiness of another person is essential to your own.
~ Robert A. Heinlein
Steve
* * *

God morning,
Love sought is good, but given unsought is better.
~ Wiliam Shakespeare
Steve
* * *

God morning,
Love doesn't make the world go round, Love is what makes the ride worthwhile.
~ Elizabeth Barrett Browning
Steve
* * *

God morning,
What do you want? You want the moon? Just say the word and I'll throw a lasso around it and pull it down.
~ It's a Wonderful Life
Steve
* * *

God morning,
Life is based on love. It holds marriages together, makes a woman complete, and it is the prime ingredient of a fine spaghetti sauce.
~ *Sophia Loren*
Steve

* * *

God morning,
Drink to me only with thine eyes,
And I will pledge with mine;
Or leave a kiss but in the cup,
And I'll not look for wine.
~ *Ben Jonson*
Steve

* * *

God morning,
Love conquers all things; let us too surrender to Love.
~ *Virgil*
Steve
[The phrase "love conquers all" became popular in the 14th century, with a character from Chaucer's Canterbury Tales wearing a brooch with the phrase in Latin (Amor vincit omnia).]

* * *

God morning,
Nothing in the world is single;
All things by a law divine
In one another's being mingle:

Why not I with thine?
~ Percy Bysshe Shelley
Steve
* * *

Good morning,
Love is an irresistible desire to be irresistibly desired.
~ Robert Frost
Steve
* * *

Good morning,
There is only one happiness in this life, to love and be loved.
~ George Sand
Steve
* * *

Good morning,
Love is rewarded with love.
~ Unknown
Steve
* * *

Good morning,
You may hold my hand for a while, but you hold my heart forever.
~ Unknown
Steve
* * *

Good morning,
People who are sensible about love are incapable of it.

~ Douglas Yates
Steve
* * *

God morning,

Once upon a time there was a boy who loved a girl, and her laughter was a question he wanted to spend his whole life answering.

~ Nicole Krauss
Steve
* * *

God morning,

A kiss is a lovely trick designed by nature to stop speech when words become superfluous.

~ Ingrid Bergman
Steve
* * *

God morning,

And the trouble is, if you don't risk anything, you risk even more.

~ Erica Jong
Steve
* * *

God morning,

Lovers don't finally meet somewhere. They're in each other all along.

~ Rumi
Steve
* * *

God morning,
Love is composed of a single soul inhabiting two bodies.
~ Aristotle
Steve
* * *

God morning,
For the two of us, home isn't a place. It is a person. And we are finally home.
~ Stephanie Perkins
Steve
* * *

God morning,
Two people in love, alone, isolated from the world, that's beautiful.
~ Milan Kundera
Steve
* * *

God morning,
Love is so short, forgetting is so long.
~ Pablo Neruda
Steve
* * *

God morning,
Time doesn't matter, love is forever.
~ Unknown
Steve
* * *

God morning,
Loving you never was an option – it was a necessity.
~ Unknown
Steve
* * *

God morning,
Never love anyone who treats you like you're ordinary.
~ Oscar Wilde
Steve
* * *

God morning,
Tis better to have loved and lost
Than never to have loved at all.
~ Alfred Lord Tennyson
Steve
* * *

God morning,
If I had a flower for every time I thought of you...I could walk through my garden forever.
~ Alfred Tennyson
Steve
* * *

God morning,
You don't love someone because they're perfect, you love them in spite of the fact that they're not.
~ Jodi Picoult

Steve
* * *

God morning,
I love you without knowing how, or when, or from where. I love you simply, without problems or pride: I love you in this way because I do not know any other way of loving but this, in which there is no I or you, so intimate that your hand upon my chest is my hand, so intimate that when I fall asleep your eyes close.
~ *Pablo Neruda*
Steve
* * *

God morning,
We accept the love we think we deserve.
~ *Stephen Chbosky*
Steve
* * *

God morning,
You know you're in love when you can't fall asleep because reality is finally better than your dreams.
~ *Dr. Seuss*
Steve
* * *

God morning,
It is not a lack of love, but a lack of friendship that makes unhappy marriages.
~ *Friedrich Nietzsche*

Steve
* * *

God morning,

There is never a time or place for true love. It happens accidentally, in a heartbeat, in a single flashing, throbbing moment.

~ Sarah Dessen

Steve
* * *

God morning,

Being deeply loved by someone gives you strength, while loving someone deeply gives you courage.

~ Lao Tzu

Steve
* * *

God morning,

How do I love thee? Let me count the ways. I love thee to the depth and breadth and height My soul can reach.

~ Elizabeth Barrett Browning

Steve
* * *

God morning,

Gravitation is not responsible for people falling in love.

~ Albert Einstein

Steve
* * *

God morning,
It is not love that makes a relationship complicated; it's the people in it who do.
~ *Unknown*
Steve
* * *

God morning,
Love is something sent from heaven to worry the hell out of you.
~ *Dolly Parton*
Steve
* * *

God morning, branches,
Kindness in words creates confidence. Kindness in thinking creates profundity. Kindness in giving creates love.
~ *Lao Tzu*
Steve
* * *

God morning,
When I look at you I see a lot of things; my best friend, my soul mate, my secret holder, my tear stopper, my future.
~ *Anonymous*
Steve
* * *

God morning,
It is only with the heart that one can see rightly; what is essential is invisible to the eye.
~ *Antoine de Saint-Exupéry*

Steve

* * *

God morning,
Women are meant to be loved, not to be understood.

~ Oscar Wilde

Steve

* * *

God morning,
I need you like a heart needs a beat.

~ Unknown

Steve

* * *

God morning,
I saw that you were perfect, and so I loved you. Then I saw that you were not perfect and I loved you even more.

~ Angelita Lim

Steve

* * *

God morning,
Falling in love with someone unexpectedly is one of the most beautiful things, you don't have to force anything because there is already a strong connection.

~ Unknown

Steve

* * *

God morning,
What greater thing is there for two human souls than to feel that they are joined to strengthen each other and to be at one with each other in silent unspeakable memories.

~ *George Eliot*
Steve

* * *

God morning,
Life takes you to unexpected places. Love brings you home.

~ *Unknown*
Steve

* * *

God morning,
The best kind of relationships are unexpected when you get the astonished feeling and everything happens so suddenly. "That's why you don't look for love," it comes to you just at the right time; the time you never thought it would have.

~ *Unknown*
Steve

* * *

God morning,
There is no fear in love, but perfect love casts out fear. For fear has to do with punishment, and whoever fears has not been perfected in love.

~ *1 John 4:18*
Steve

* * *

God morning,

Maybe if you can't get somebody out of your head, they're supposed to be there.

~ *Anonymous*

Steve

* * *

God morning,

The best part of beauty is that which no picture can express.

~ *Francis Bacon*

Steve

* * *

God morning,

All the little things you do warm my heart. You are a constant source of joy in my life.

~ *Anonymous*

Steve

* * *

God morning,

To love without condition, to talk without intention, to give without reason, to care without expectation; That's the spirit of true love. We love truly only when we love without reason. True love begins when nothing is looked for in return. Real love begins where nothing is expected in return.

~ *Anonymous*

Steve

* * *

LOVE NOTES

Good morning,
Doubt thou the stars are fire, Doubt that the sun doth move.
Doubt the truth to be a liar, But never doubt I love.
~ William Shakespeare
Steve
* * *

Good morning,
Why do we close our eyes when we pray, cry, kiss or dream?
Because the most beautiful things in life are not seen but felt by the heart.
~ Unknown
Steve
* * *

Good morning,
Beauty is the illumination of your soul.
~ John O'Donohue
Steve
* * *

Good morning,
Beauty is not in the face; beauty is a light in the heart.
~ Khalil Gibran
Steve
* * *

Good morning,
God gave us eyes to see the beauty in nature and hearts to see the beauty in each other.
~ Anonymous

Steve
* * *

God morning,

Every time you look at me and see me smiling, just know that I am thinking of you.

~ Anonymous

Steve
* * *

God morning,

Be a hand that reaches out.
Be a smile for those who have no reason to smile.
Be a light for those who live in darkness.
Show them what it means to truly love.

~ Unknown

Steve
* * *

God morning,

Wind is to fire like distance is to love; it extinguishes the small and enflames the great.

~ Anonymous

Steve
* * *

God morning,

You have found true love when you realize that you want to wake up beside your love every morning even when you have your differences.

~ Unknown

Steve
* * *

God morning,

I may not be your first date, kiss or love...but I want to be your last everything.

~ Anonymous
Steve
* * *

God morning,

God is so good. He knows where a person will be happy, where they can love and be loved, where heaven on earth is. Now I know why he put me near you.

~ Anonymous
Steve
* * *

God morning,

Always tell someone how you feel because opportunities are lost in the blink of an eye but regret can last for a lifetime.

~ Anonymous
Steve
* * *

God morning,

The rule of unconditional love; it is in the giving that you make the other person realize.

~ Unknown
Steve
* * *

God morning,
The person who does not decide to love forever will find it very difficult to really love for even one day.
~ *St. John Paul II*
Steve
* * *

God morning,
You don't marry someone you can live with – you marry the person whom you cannot live without.
~ *Anonymous*
Steve
* * *

God morning,
Love is like playing the piano. First you must learn to play by the rules, and then you must forget the rules and play from your heart.
~ *Michel de Montaigne*
Steve
* * *

God morning,
What most people need to learn in life is how to love people and use things instead of using people and loving things.
~ *Unknown*
Steve
* * *

God morning,
Be completely humble and gentle; be patient, bearing with one another in love.
~ *Ephesians 4:2*
Steve
* * *

God morning,
God loves each of us as if there were only one of us.
~ *St. Augustine*
Steve
* * *

God morning,
Love to be real, it must cost—it must hurt—it must empty us of self.
~ *St. Theresa of Calcutta*
Steve
* * *

God morning,
If I speak in the tongues of men or of angels, but do not have love, I am only a resounding gong or a clanging cymbal.
~ *1 Corinthians 13:1*
Steve
* * *

God morning,
It is not so essential to think much as to love much.
~ *St. Teresa of Jesus, OCD*

Steve

* * *

God morning,
Mercy, peace and love be yours in abundance.

~ Jude 1:2

Steve

* * *

God morning,
Hatred stirs up conflict, but love covers over all wrongs.

~ Proverbs 10:12

Steve

* * *

God morning,
No one has ever seen God; but if we love one another, God lives in us and his love is made complete in us.

~ 1 John 4:12

Steve

* * *

God morning,
We love because He first loved us.

~ 1 John 4:19

Steve

* * *

God morning,
Everything comes from love, all is ordained for the salvation of man, God does nothing without this goal in mind.

~ St. Catherine of Siena

Steve

* * *

God morning,
Let us love, since that is what our hearts were made for.
~ St. Therese of Lisieux
Steve

* * *

God morning,
A single act of pure love pleases me more than a thousand imperfect prayers.
~ Jesus (According to St. Faustina)
Steve

* * *

God morning,
Be devoted to one another in love. Honor one another above yourselves.
~ Romans 12:10
Steve

* * *

God morning,
My command is this: Love each other as I have loved you.
~ John 15:12
Steve

* * *

God morning,
Love must be sincere. Hate what is evil; cling to what is good.
~ Romans 12:9

Steve

* * *

God morning,
Anyone who does not love does not know God, because God is love.
~ 1 John 4:8
Steve

* * *

God morning,
Let all that you do be done in love.
~ 1 Corinthians 16:14
Steve

* * *

About the Author

Steve Digilio was born, raised, and continues to reside in Queens, New York. He shared forty beautiful years of marriage with his wife, with whom he spent a total of forty-six years. Together, they raised two sons, one of whom is now in Heaven.

A product of the New York public school system, Steve graduated from Pace University with a Bachelor of Business Administration. As a dedicated and hardworking student, he started as a full-time freshman but later balanced his education with work, attending evening, early morning, and weekend classes to fund his studies. Since his first year of college, Steve has built a successful career in the financial industry.

In his late teens, Steve discovered his passion for coaching youth football. Over the decades, he has coached countless young athletes, even becoming a "grandcoach" when he had the privilege of coaching the son of one of his former players. His love for mentorship extended to other sports, as he also coached Little League baseball, CYO basketball, hockey, and soccer.

Several years ago, after the loss of a dear friend, Steve began writing and sharing Scripture-based notes. What started as a small gesture to three individuals has grown into a heartfelt ministry reaching over a hundred recipients. Many of these notes have been shared further, offering inspiration to an ever-widening circle.

Following the passing of his beloved wife in 2020, Steve began writing *Dearest Anna*, a series of deeply personal letters to her in Heaven. These love letters, shared with family, friends, and widow support groups, have brought comfort to many, eloquently expressing the universal feelings of love and loss. Inspired by the response, Steve expanded his efforts, creating and sharing "love notes"—quotations and reflections on love—through emails and online platforms.

Steve begins each Scripture and love note with "God morning," a heartfelt reminder that God is love and that both are meant to be shared. His book, *Thoughts From & To Heaven*, is a collection of Scripture-based reflections, *Dearest Anna* letters, and love notes. Encouraged by the suggestions of many recipients, this compilation serves as a testament to the enduring power of love and faith.

www.ingramcontent.com/pod-product-compliance
Lightning Source LLC
Chambersburg PA
CBHW072139070526
44585CB00015B/975